FOUNDATION
of the FORCE

Air Force Enlisted Personnel Policy
1907–1956

Mark R. Grandstaff

AIR
FORCE
History
and
Museums
PROGRAM

1997

Library of Congress Cataloging-in-Publication Data

Grandstaff, Mark R.
     Foundation of the Force: Air Force enlisted personnel policy,
1907–1956 / Mark R. Grandstaff.
          p. cm.
     Includes bibliographical references and index.
     1. United States. Air Force—Non-commissioned officers—History.
2. United States. Air Force—Personnel management—History. I. Title.
UG823.G75 1996   96–33468
358.4'1338'0973—DC20   CIP

For sale by the U.S. Government Printing Office
Superintendent of Documents, Mail Stop: SSOP, Washington, DC 20402-9328
ISBN 0-16-049041-3

Foreword

THE UNITED STATES AIR FORCE is a diverse military organization, composed of officers, enlisted members, and civilians. One characteristic defining it is that of professionalism in all three of its personnel components. Though professionalism has been recognized as an important part of military culture and organization over the centuries, it has become critically important in the twentieth century, the century of flight. For the Air Force, the weapons systems that the service employs are maintained, supported, and operated by members of the enlisted force. Inheritors of a proud tradition of service dating to the earliest days of American military aviation, enlisted members have fought—and too often died—in hostile skies around the world, in every conflict in which American aviators have participated.

Organizing and training Air Force enlisted personnel have been among the greatest challenges to the service's leadership, as well as among its greatest accomplishments. Young men and women from varied social, cultural, and educational backgrounds enter the service; are introduced to its culture, heritage, and traditions; are trained to fulfill myriad tasks; and then already imbued with a sense of service before self, go forth to their first assignments. Ongoing career training and professionalization continue throughout their careers. That the Air Force has met the challenge of training its enlisted force well is evidenced by its members' record of accomplishments in America's wars and other times of national emergencies.

This work traces how the service built its enlisted cadre in the key, early years of the service when the Air Force was itself a new and unsettled organization. The lessons offered in this book present valuable perspective to decision-makers today as they grapple with force drawdown and maintaining appropriate standards of training and professionalism even as America's Air Force is called upon to serve in new and increasingly more demanding roles.

RICHARD P. HALLION
Air Force Historian

Preface

THE IMPETUS FOR THIS STUDY evolved from the early days of my youth. My great-grandfather, grandfather, and father served in the ranks during the three major American wars of the nineteenth and twentieth centuries, and I heard stories of Gettysburg and the Meuse-Argonne and of fighting at the Bulge. Moreover, motion pictures and television shows of the 1950s and 1960s focused on war themes with, as I recall, movies and TV series about marines, sailors, soldiers, but with little about airmen.

As an eighteen-year-old, fresh from high school, I, like thousands of youths growing up during the Vietnam War, pondered my future. Recognizing the possibility of being drafted and becoming cannon fodder, as my former-soldier relatives called it, I opted to join the Navy. As an enlisted person I was subjected to all kinds of hell. Six years after my enlistment, however, I obtained a bachelor's degree and, at the prompting of my wife, left the Navy. It was off to graduate school (thanks to the GI Bill) and an eventual commission in the Air Force through ROTC. With a master's degree in hand and a gold bar on my shoulder, my first assignment was as a missile officer at Malmstrom AFB, Montana, an assignment that brought about my first exposure to enlisted airmen.

There were similarities between what I experienced as a sailor and what I perceived as the enlisted culture in the Air Force, but there were differences too—less formality, a professionalism I had not experienced in my Navy career, and a confidence that comes from knowing that your branch of service "takes care of its own." When I was selected by the Air Force Historian's office to attend the University of Wisconsin at Madison to obtain a doctoral degree, Dr. Richard H. Kohn, the then Air Force historian, specifically asked me to write a one-volume history of the Air Force enlisted corps. I was simultaneously delighted and intimidated. I was delighted because I knew that little had been written on the subject but intimidated to know that my work would be the first foray into what I perceived to be a significant segment of working-class America.

Consequently, this book is not simply a study of military policy or a class of military personnel. In its largest context it is about the growth of the United States and its movement to a what some might call an organizational society during the first five decades of the twentieth century. The assumptions and beliefs that permeated those who shaped the Air Force's enlisted personnel policy reflect those of civilians who did the same for large businesses and corporations. The Air Force's claim to be free from military traditions, its dependence on technology, and its dreams of separation from the army provided the impetus from which it adapted the thinking and practices of big business governing its personnel. Thus, in another context, this is also a study of an American institution's birth and coming of age as seen through the prism of enlisted personnel policy. Most important, it is the study of Air Force enlisted personnel, who over the years helped define not only what the larger institution of the Air Force would become, but also fostered the professionalization of Air Force noncommissioned officers (NCOs) in the 1950s. By 1955, the results of this professionalization would set the Air Force NCO apart from his contemporaries in the other services in terms of culture and image.

The saying that when the right moment arrives, a teacher will emerge seems particularly appropriate to my relationship with Edward (Mac) Coffman. Coffman is my idea of the quintessential scholar—well-read, brilliant, liberal minded, and dedicated to the study of history—and most of all, humble and helpful. His social history of the Old Army is superb and certainly a significant guide to my own thinking. He remains a good friend, a mentor, and most important, an inspiration. Others who helped shape my thinking (for good or for ill) on these issues include John Sharpless and David Zonderman of the University of Wisconsin; Herman Wolk, Bernard Nalty, and David Tretler at the Center for Air Force History; and David Segal at the University of Maryland, College Park. I am also indebted to William Mahoney at the National Archives and a score of other librarians at the Truman and the Eisenhower Libraries, the Military History Institute at Carlisle Barracks, the Library of Congress, the Pentagon Library, and the Air University Library, and to numerous Air Force field historians across the globe who answered my inquiries and gathered hundreds of Enlisted Experience questionnaires. I am also thankful to the Air Force Historian's office for funding the project and to Brigham Young University for providing me with a grant so that I might revise and complete the final draft.

Finally, I extend my most sincere appreciation to my best friend and spouse, Tamara, and to my children, Jared, Ferrin, Camber, and Brittia who were inspirational. My father, Raymond, and mother, Dolores, both passed away during the writing of this book. I dedicate this work to them.

MARK R. GRANDSTAFF

Contents

Chapters

Contents

Chart

Tables

Contents

Illustrations

Contents

Introduction

DURING MARCH AND APRIL 1946 in the old Labor Department building in Washington, D.C., a six-member board headed by former Army Air Forces Lt. Gen. James H. Doolittle met with forty-two officers and enlisted personnel to discuss the relationship between the two groups during the war just ended. World War II had brought thousands of young men and women into uniform, thereby reducing the military's isolation from the civilian world and opening the institution to criticism of its procedures and culture. Many civilian-soldiers found military life distasteful, degrading, abusive, and a throwback to the "Prussian" military. In short, life in the military was akin more to totalitarianism than to its parent democratic society.

It seemed clear to people such as Army Chief of Staff Dwight D. Eisenhower that when testifying before the Secretary of War's Officer and Enlisted Man's Relationship Board (otherwise known as the Doolittle Board), if the military were to be made less abusive and an expanded defense establishment were to be maintained in the postwar period, new peacetime forces would necessarily need to reflect the democratic nature of American society as a whole. Leaders understood that future recruitment and retention as well as civilian acceptance of a standing military depended on how well the armed forces perceived and implemented social reform, and how service in the armed forces was marketed as an acceptable option for youth.

In this work, I examine specific legislation, policy, and historical events that garnered public support for the growth and maintenance of a large peacetime military, changed a long tradition of distrust for standing armies, and, in turn, reflected a trend away from the "mass army" model that typified the American way of waging war since the American Revolution.[1] In what some scholars have deemed to be the dominant model of military organization in western society through World War II, the mass army model consisted of a small professional cadre augmented by reserves, conscription, and cycles of mobilization and demobilization.

A product of the American and French Revolutions, the mass army reflected the needs of a growing democratic society in war—civilian resistance to large military expenditures, a distrust of standing armies, a redefinition of military service as a right and responsibility of citizenship, and a willingness to mobilize fully society's resources in order to wage total war. In the aftermath of World War II and with the rise of the Cold War and nuclear technology, public support waned for the mass army in favor of a standing army that was highly specialized and geared toward a new military mission—deterring war, not waging it.[2] In this case, the military of today is moving toward a post–Cold War model—one described as internally segmented and pluralistic as well as externally convergent with civilian institutions.

The notion of convergence, as articulated by sociologist Charles Moskos in his seminal 1977 article, "From Institution to Occupation: Trends in the Military Organization," is also examined.[3] Moskos suggests that the military was moving away from an institutional format based on duty and service to an occupational model that implied self-interest and marketplace economics. He further argues that the erosion of the institutional model was recent (the advent of the all-volunteer force occurred in 1973) and would severely undercut a soldier's organizational commitment and performance as well as undermine institutional values. "A military based on marketplace principles," one of his students wrote, "can lead to the worst of two worlds: a military isolated from civilian society and a lack of cohesion within the military."[4] In short, a fairly recent phenomena in the military caused it to diverge from its parent society and institutional format.

Contrary to Moskos, this study agrees with Morris Janowitz, who found that the military was actually civilianizing, that is, converging with the larger American society. The military bureaucratic structure and its procedures were changing to meet society's economic, organizational, and social structures.[5] Much of my work delineates reasons for this convergence and argues that the occupational model was established, not in 1973 with the genesis of the all-volunteer force (AVF) as Moskos and Janowitz have argued, but in the first decade after World War II, and in the case of the Air Force (Air Corps), as early as the 1920s.

Almost from its inception, the Air Force was a precursor to the type of force that Moskos and other sociologists saw developing in the early 1970s. Awarding more pay to personnel with technical skills, emphasizing scientific management principles in recruiting and classification, encouraging a large amount of technical specialization, and placing technical skills above military performance—these were present in the Air Force almost since its origin as an aeronautical division of the U.S. Army Signal Corps in 1907. More than the Army or the Navy, the Air Force, a product of twentieth-century technology, is an example of a military service whose cultural and organizational roots were steeped in the bureaucratic rationalism and technological form that punctuated the growing organizational society of the late nineteenth and twentieth centuries.

Regarding the military's convergence, this study shows that to make a large standing military acceptable in a democratic society in the Cold War era, external and internal changes were required to make the military appear more American. These changes, which Moskos sees as divergent and threatening to the military as an institution, were necessary to assimilate the armed forces into society's ideology and daily life. Central to this assimilation was the military's willingness to assume the role of "Americanizer"—an institution from which youth could learn middle-class and democratic values and prepare themselves for a place in America's technically driven and corporate future. Also important to this assimilation process were changes in legislation regarding retirement, housing, marriage, dependents, and fraternization which greatly facilitated the concept that the military offered more than employment to marginal personnel; it could be a job and a respected career (in the middle-class sense of a calling or a life devoted to good works). In the case of the Air Force, nuclear weapons, the communist threat, technological specialization, and the high cost of training personnel, combined with acute retention problems, forced the Air Force to introduce a policy that de-emphasized the pre–World War II image of an institution offering skills and an opportunity to reenter the civilian job market. The Air Force became a place where enlisted personnel were assured a career and "a great way of life." This is the first study to explore the ways that these events fostered a collective view in society and among airmen that a career in the Air Force (and later, in the armed forces in general) was similar to service in a middle-class profession.[6]

Another important theme found in this work is the professionalization of the Air Force noncommissioned officer. In this work professions are considered as "somewhat exclusive groups of individuals applying somewhat abstract knowledge to particular cases."[7] A subordinate profession is what Robert H. Weibe called "a profession within a profession,"[8] and, according to Andrew Abbott, is "generally a public and legal settlement" that arises when one profession does not wish to share its jurisdiction. In this case, a subordinate profession forms to accomplish tasks and formulate abstract knowledge in areas in which the dominant profession sees as necessary, but not a part of their knowledge, jurisdiction, or division of work.[9] The term *professionalization* thus denotes a process whereby an occupation moves toward becoming a profession.[10] A career enlisted force is created when airmen are deemed as career-bound (second enlistment and beyond), serve as noncommissioned officers, and obtain a high degree of technical and military expertise.

In many ways, the professionalization of noncommissioned officers was part of a much longer trend in American society toward a new middle class and corporatism. At least since the 1870s, lawyers, doctors, financiers, businessmen, personnel managers, scholars, and scientists formed national networks and established entry standards into their specialties.[11] Army and Naval officers took steps as early as the 1830s and 1840s to establish new promotion regulations, professional journals, elaborate systems of military education, and national organizations.[12]

Foundation of the Force

Between 1950 and 1956, NCOs began to professionalize as they hammered out a professional definition, established academies for professional military education, formulated promotion and NCO certification criteria, obtained more jurisdictional authority from the military profession (officers), and formed a professional association (which occurred in 1961). Significantly aiding the professionalization movement were congressional legislation, presidential committees, and Department of Defense and Air Force policies that attempted to build and sustain a career force and thus indirectly foster the professionalization process.*

Although much of the secondary literature† assumes that the military is a profession for only those who manage violence (commissioned officers), it may be argued that the 1950s' professionalization movement produced Air Force NCOs who today form a subordinate profession whose primary function is to manage and apply military resources that meet and sustain the Air Force mission.[13]

While this work stresses enlisted personnel and concentrates on policies that led to a large standing military, creation of a career enlisted force, and professionalization of noncommissioned officers, it also examines extensively the evolution of Air Force personnel policies and the rise of Air Force organizations designed to formulate and enact those policies. In 1954, for instance, Air Force recruiters who formerly worked in a joint Army–Air Force recruiting command separated and formed an autonomous Air Force recruiting group. The study also analyzes why the group formed and how it marketed the concept of a large standing air force. Additionally, this study traces the inner workings of the personnel department of the Air Force, analyzes the air planners' worldview, and shows how Air Force personnel policymakers adopted and used the personnel management techniques and practices of large industrial firms.

The work ends in 1956 because the confluence of congressional legislation, internal reform, and increased reenlistment rates suggests that the Air Force had successfully created an enlisted career program that attracted, trained, promoted, and retained the type of person that the air service desired. In fact, the course of enlisted personnel policy was firmly in place by 1956, so that even today, airmen are the clear-cut beneficiaries of a system that has been in place for nearly forty years. Thus, in a sense, this is a study of a significant segment of the American labor force.

It is important to note that this is not a study of aviation cadets, enlisted pilots, commissioning programs, or the Air Force Reserve. Each of these topics is noteworthy and deserves separate treatment. Neither does it extensively cover policies regarding women and minorities. Only when minority policies

---

* These are discussed in Chapter 5.
† For citations, see Chapter 6 and the Bibliographic Note.

differed from those aimed at creating a career force do I make a distinction. For the most part, however, career polices in the 1940s and 1950s pertained to all Air Force enlisted personnel regardless of race, gender, or ethnicity. Pragmatic and socially conservative planners created policies based upon the needs of the Air Force, the social context of the times, and their own personal and professional biases. Finally, airman culture, either in the barracks or in the workplace is not examined. This remains an important area awaiting further work.

In addition to difficulties with primary and secondary sources enumerated in the Bibliographic Note, three additional difficulties arise when studying personnel policy and are worth listing here. Frederick Harrod, in his *Manning the New Navy*, suggests that one of the problems has to do with continuity and change in policymaking.[14] Change is rarely sudden and complete, and some policies were considered for a long time before air planners implemented them. Few policies were watersheds in the sense that old ways immediately stopped and new approaches were automatically embraced. This study may contrast the difference between the new Air Force and the old Army Air Corps, but the delineation is only clear on paper. Vestiges of pre–World War II enlisted culture remained well into the 1960s. Accordingly, this work could reveal only trends, not absolutes, and specific policies are merely guidelines, not watersheds.

Another problem has to do with the flow of policy and the determination of who was responsible for its creation. Part of the problem lies in the sources themselves. Because much of the documentation comes from official and semiofficial sources such as departmental reports, operational histories, and action proposals, seldom does one gain an understanding of why officials introduced or modified a given policy. Generally, however, it seems that the Adjutant General's office during the interwar period—the G–1 (A–1) during World War II and the Deputy Chief of Staff, Personnel Office (DCS/P) after 1947—served as the centralized focus of personnel policymaking.

Although these departments created and issued policy, they left it up to the commands to supervise the policy's implementation; and the commanding generals exercised broad discretion in implementing policies of their own. Especially in the postwar period, the DCS/P saw itself as a coordinating body that set its general policy by legitimizing past practices and then by communicating to the commands how these policies and techniques were to be used in other Air Force settings.[15] Standardization of general personnel policy increased during the late 1950s and 1960s as reporting procedures and computer technology became more available.

A final problem deals with formulating generalizations about enlisted airmen, given the size of the enlisted force. Indeed, *airman* is not one person, but many. The term includes raw recruits and noncommissioned officers who have served for many years. Additionally, each airman has experienced life in

Foundation of the Force

the Air Force differently, and, as a result, absolute generalization is defied because contradictions abound in every case. This does not stop us, however, from observing and documenting the changes and trends taking place in the enlisted force.

✦1✦

The Foundation of
Air Force Enlisted Personnel Policies
1907–1945

ON SEPTEMBER 18, 1947, the United States Air Force was established as an independent entity, coequal with the Departments of the Army and the Navy. In short, it was given a life of its own—a life separated from the Army hierarchy, budget, and traditions. Indeed, the new service found itself, especially with regard to enlisted personnel policy, as much an autonomous entity capable of innovation as a product of its Army heritage.

Undoubtedly, the fledgling Air Force owed much of its enlisted personnel philosophy to technology. After all, throughout most of this century, the Air Force and its predecessors wanted persons, primarily men, to fly, repair, and maintain its aviation wonders. Just as aviation technology changed throughout the twentieth century from biplane to jet, so did enlisted policy grow to meet those demands.

To overlook the Army aviation's experiences gained as a small section of the Signal Corps, its later transformations into the Air Service during World War I, the Army Air Corps in 1926, and the Army Air Forces (AAF) before World War I, along with the experiences of two wars and the consistent struggle for autonomy, would miss the impact that tradition, war, and societal influences had on the creation and evolution of policy. Indeed, the forty years from the AAF's inception to its separation from the Army in 1947 proved to be a period of trying, testing, and modifying Army and industrial personnel policies and practices to meet the enlisted manpower demands of the new aviation service.

Beginnings

From its inception as an Aeronautical Division within the Army Signal Corps in 1907, aviators had to deal with establishing, recruiting, and training a cadre

Foundation of the Force

A Wright Model A airplane is seen at Fort Myer, Virginia, in 1908 (*top left*). At the *top right*, Grover C. Loening is seen flying the Wright airboat. *Beneath* is a view of Fort Myer with a Wright aircraft seen in flight on July 20, 1909. *Top left*, facing page, is seen a French Caudron hydroplane. At the *top right* is Hugh Willoughby's Pelican hydroplane, photographed on November 10, 1910. The *center* of the page depicts the French Farman hydroplane, and the Wright-Martin K–3 Scout is seen at the *bottom*.

of enlisted men to care for their twentieth-century technological marvel—the airplane. On July 18, 1914, Congress, convinced of the need to bolster military aviation as a result of the impending war in Europe, passed an important legislative bill, An Act to Increase the Efficiency of the Aviation Service of the Army, and for Other Purposes (HR 5304). Important from an enlisted personnel

policy perspective, this act established a new Aviation Section within the Army Signal Corps and authorized for it 101 enlisted men.[1] Of these men, only a maximum of forty could train as Aviation Mechanicians, while another twelve could receive flight training. The remaining forty-nine went directly to the squadrons where they served in a second tier of occupational specialties, including fireman, fuel-truck operator, and cook.[2]

One of the problems the fledgling Aviation Section first faced was recruiting its initial complement of men. Eschewing untrained men fresh from the recruiting depot, the new Aviation Section requested Army volunteers who had already undergone basic military training and could immediately begin technical training. Enlisted men who desired duty in aviation applied through their commanding officers to the Chief of the Signal Corps. If the Army approved their requests, they could move to their new station, often at their own cost, and assume the rank of private under the Aviation Section's Table of Organization.[3] For noncommissioned officers (NCOs), this meant a reduction in pay grade, prestige, and responsibility.[4]

It must be said that in the Old Army, this was simply a fact of life. The Adjutant General formulated organizational personnel rosters and designated the correct number of men in each pay grade to efficiently man each post. Those who chose to leave a company or change branches of the Army (such as the Infantry, Cavalry, Quartermaster Corps) did so at the sake of their hard-earned stripes. Yet to some, the Aviation Section as a new part of the Signal Corps seemed worth the risk as promotion opportunity looked promising.[5]

On December 5, 1914, forty-four men transferred to the new Aviation Section—twenty-four from Fort Leavenworth, Kansas, and the remainder from Army posts in New York, Colorado, California, Texas, and Hawaii.[6] Following their transfer, some attended the Technical Instruction School at San Diego, California, and received systematic instruction in the operation, care, and repair of aeronautical engines and planes.

In the years before World War I, aviation mechanical training was neither elaborate nor well organized in America or the Aviation Section. It took time for civilian and military aviation instructors to design a course, set requirements, devise testing methodology, and establish the hours required for its completion. Most early training was hands-on with little in the way of formal lectures. Additionally, the course developers emphasized a specialized curriculum aimed at teaching the students only enough to make minor repairs. Not desiring to produce finished machinists, aviation instructors were concerned about balancing time, money, and the amount of skilled training provided each individual.[7] For the Air Force, as with the commercial aviation industry, specialization would become increasingly important in the years ahead, but its roots went back to 1914.

Although the first thirty-seven of the enlisted mechanics earned their specialty rating through on-the-job training and the passing of a standardized

The landing field at the Marine Barracks located in San Diego, California, is shown above.

test prepared by aviation instructors, completion of a formal course usually meant certification in the Aviation Mechanician specialty. To receive this specialty, an enlisted man was required to apply to the Adjutant General (personnel officer) for an examination. A board consisting of three pilot-officers would then convene to test the candidate's theoretical and practical knowledge.[8]

By July 1915, however, aviation instructors at the Technical Instruction School at San Diego, California, had designed a comprehensive test consisting of two parts. Trainees needed to demonstrate proficiency in airframe maintenance and repair as well as in engine construction and maintenance. After achieving a passing grade of 75 on both the practical and theoretical parts of the test and successfully completing a physical exam, graduates received certifications of competency. As a powerful incentive, enlisted men receiving a mechanician's certificate (for technical proficiency) or a pilot's rating (for flying) received a 50 percent pay raise.[9] The Air Mechanician specialty would continue until the Air Corps Act of 1926 replaced the archaic designation with two grades of specialized air mechanics.

On the eve of World War I, and within the first few years of their existence, enlisted "airmen" had an identifiable image consisting of a technically driven and skilled cadre of experts who by sheer novelty of their

11

technology differentiated themselves from other Army branches. This image persisted throughout all of the air arm's recruiting and training policies until well beyond the 1950s.

World War I

In April 1917, after a series of U-boat sinkings and pressure from the Allied powers, President Woodrow Wilson asked Congress for a declaration of war. With the grandiose objective of "making the world safe for democracy," Wilson committed the United States to a massive buildup of machines, weapons, and men. Not the least of his objectives was to increase vastly the production of aircraft and to send an American expeditionary force overseas.[10]

At the time of America's intervention in Europe, military leaders found the Aviation Section of the Signal Corps in sad shape. Compared with European standards in aviation technology and tactical training, America lagged far behind. With only 65 officers, 1,120 enlisted men, and 200 obsolete planes, both the Army and industry faced a monumental task as the Allied powers requested in April 1917 a minimum of 2,000 planes per month and the requisite number of officers and airmen to fly and repair them.[11]

By late May, the Allies reconsidered the request and decided the figures were too low. On May 23, French Premier Alexander Ribot requested 5,000 pilots, 50,000 mechanics, and 45,000 planes. This request not only changed the scope of American aviation planning, it became the basis of America's future air contribution during the war. By midsummer 1917, Congress appropriated funds to meet these requirements, and the Air Service, now separated from the Signal Corps and part of the AEF, was busy working with the Aircraft Production Board to fulfill the demands of the Allies.

The Allies helped by furnishing plans for America's major technical contribution to the war—mass production of the observation and day-bombing plane, the British DeHaviland (DH–4). In addition, the French and the British would also train and logistically supply the bulk of the American aviators and enlisted mechanics.[12]

World War I proved critical to the development of the American Air Service. The call for large numbers of men and planes greatly expanded the Service's roles and mission. No longer viewed as an extension of balloon reconnaissance, the plane acquired added dimensions; it could be used in aerial combat pursuit, reconnaissance, and tactical maneuvers as well as strategic bombardment. The implication of these new roles was quickly grasped by the more progressive thinkers among American aviators like Col. William "Billy" Mitchell, the American Expeditionary Forces (AEF) air officer on General John J. Pershing's staff.[13] Mitchell became American air power's most outspoken advocate after the war.

General William Mitchell is shown in the cockpit (*above*) during the Dayton Races held in 1922 at Selfridge Field, Michigan, and with his staff (*below*) at Coblenz, Germany, on January 15, 1919.

Foundation of the Force

For Mitchell and many American aviators like him, military aviation would change the course of future wars. Homelands were no longer geographically isolated from strikes, nor were troops and supply lines safe from air attack. For the next thirty years, air advocates pushed for an autonomous air force, a coherent strategic bombardment doctrine, and a technologically superior heavy bomber from which to apply this doctrine.[14] The origins of this ideological campaign, however, can be traced to England and France during the period 1914 to 1918.

If World War I served as a catalyst for expansion, technological growth, and the formation of an aviation ideology, it also furthered the development of enlisted personnel policies and traditions. Personnel policy, especially in the areas of recruiting, training, and promoting, reflected the demands of the expansion and the new technology upon the army personnel system. Originally, the Aviation Section (pre–World War I) recruited only experienced enlisted personnel from within the Army Signal Corps. With the expansion due to the war and the growth in technology, however, this selection process was no longer acceptable.

The wartime need for recruits to repair expensive aircraft, man and repair air-to-ground radio stations, repair and fuze armaments, pack parachutes, and prepare technical directives and memos created new recruitment and quality problems. To meet these needs, the new Air Service began to recruit actively from the Army's total existing labor pool. The expanded requirements resulted in a personnel imbalance within the Army that demanded new thinking about total mobilization for war. Air planners wanted to know how to distribute manpower equitably. What service or branch of service would get which men?

Early in the war, military aviation drew from the civilian labor pool a large number of highly intelligent and skilled men who chose to enlist rather than to face the draft. The other branches of the Army seemed to get the dregs. This inequity eventually led to a ban upon enlistments and a call for a more efficient means of classifying and distributing manpower within the Army and across the services.

World War I accelerated aviation's need for intelligent labor and encouraged the efficient use of manpower and training funds. For one thing, the war changed how the American military would obtain its men. The entry of America into the war and the passage of the Selective Service Act of 1917 demonstrated the confluence of two impulses—"to make the world safe for an 'American' brand of democracy" and to do so efficiently. American volunteer-ism was simply inefficient and wasteful. "Our objective," President Wilson wrote, "is a mobilization of all the productive and active forces of the nation, and their development to the highest point of cooperation and efficiency. . . . The volunteer system does not do this. . . . When men choose for themselves, they sometimes choose without due regard to their other responsibilities."[15]

One way to use military personnel efficiently was through classification,

14

finding the right man for the right job. Personnel classification had its origins at the turn of the century in the work of Frederick W. Taylor, the father of the scientific management movement, who believed that every man was suitable to a particular job.[16] Accordingly, each job with its requirements had to be identified and measurably quantified. Efficiency experts then constructed a test to measure the correct degree of aptitude to learn and become proficient at such skills.[17]

The Regular Army, however, did not have such a classification system in 1917, and no one in the military knew how to establish one. This led Secretary of War Newton D. Baker, at the suggestion of the President of the American Psychological Association and Reserve Army Major Robert M. Yerkes, to establish a classification committee under the auspices of the War Department. Formed in August 1917 and directed by two prominent industrial psychologists temporarily in uniform, Col. Walter D. Scott and Major Yerkes, this group formulated a set of guiding principles that called for defining the job, establishing a set of criteria for its measurement, and then finding the right man to fulfill the requirements.[18]

This pioneering venture eventually led to the construction of eighty-three trade tests and the formulation of tables of occupational needs for various military units. These new Tables of Organization and Equipment, based upon mission requirements, became the foundation for manning units after the war. Trade tests established who could fulfil the jobs listed in these manning tables. Additionally, the committee published the trade specifications and occupational indices used by both selective service and military personnel specialists from which to cross-rate civilian trades to military jobs.[19]

Within a year, the Army directed the implementation of the new classification system. Each soldier filled out 5" x 8" qualification card upon which he recorded background information, education, occupational experience, and desires. Officers then forwarded such information up to group and division levels for a centralized placement of needed specialists. Besides these classification cards, the committee also produced a series of general classification tests known as the Alpha and Beta examinations. This testing not only proved a breakthrough for matching men to occupations, it also provided social scientists with information about the general intellectual quality of American males.[20] This use of the social sciences continued in World War II and culminated in Samuel Stouffer's massive four-volume study on the American soldier.[21]

Not satisfied with examinations testing only general mechanical aptitude, the Air Service in 1918 convinced the Classification Committee to design special tests in order to select only those mechanically inclined for jobs in military aviation. That same year, the committee constructed a new examination to test mechanical aptitude for aviation specialties and then validated it against proficient Air Service mechanics. As an additional supplement to the

15

general Alpha and Beta tests, the new exam ensured that the Air Service would continue to siphon off the "more trainable" inductees.[22]

The growth in aviation technology also pushed for further specialization of mechanic duties. The prewar Aviation Section of the Army's Signal Corps used only the generalized specialty of Air Mechanician. The World War I mobilization, however, demanded that the specialty be broken into at least five subspecialties consisting of airplane engine expert, airplane cloth worker, general airplane mechanic, air-propeller maker, and air-propeller tester and inspector. Additionally, the planners created new specialties in armament, communications, engineering, photography, and weather to meet the changing roles of the Air Service.[23]

Though several of these specialties could be filled under the selected service system, many, such as the aircraft mechanic and armorer specialties, could not. At the outbreak of the war few recruits were trained airplane mechanics. As a result, the Air Service established schools stateside and overseas to train men who had little in the way of mechanical experience. The Mechanics School, created at Kelly Field, Texas, by the Air Service in 1917, offered courses in airplane and engine mechanics along with shorter courses in aircraft armament, parachute rigging, flight instruments, and welding.[24]

Especially important were the French and British contributions toward training aircraft mechanics, as even those who had some mechanical background were ignorant of European technology (the majority of airplanes used during the war were European). Thus, in September 1917, 500 American enlisted men arrived in Southampton, England, and then went on to British and French factories. Later, in December, the Air Service and the Allies agreed that a pool of 15,000 men be kept in England to work and train in British schools and factories. Unfortunately, the Army had too few troop ships to transport the men from the United States and could supply only a fraction of the 15,000.[25]

Maj. Gen. Mason M. Patrick, Chief of Air Service (AEF), in his final report to the Commander in Chief (AEF), wrote candidly of his problems regarding the European experiment in training enlisted men:

> The supply of enlisted personnel was from the first mainly a physical problem for the American Expeditionary prewar Forces, the procurement of a sufficient tonnage to transport the needed troops. Several factors, however, combined to raise this to a point of supreme importance second to none in its relation to Air Service development. Facing the Air Service was the newness of the aviation forces in the United States, the practical nonexistence there of mechanical training centers, the variety of the types of foreign airplanes, and the tools with which our mechanics would have to deal, and the great amount of construction necessary in the American Expeditionary Forces.[26]

The men enjoy a sack race at Kelly Field (*top*). General Peyton C. March, Army Chief of Staff, is shown at Kelly Field in March 1919 (*bottom*).

French Nieuport 21s are seen at the top. Second from the top is a Roland D-I *Haifisch* (Shark). Next seen is a wreck of a Curtiss JN–4D at Letot, Texas, on October 11, 1918. At the bottom is the first flight of a U.S. Liberty aircraft in France at Romerantin on May 18, 1918.

A German Fokker D–VII is seen at the top. A British Royal Aircraft Factory B.E. 2C is featured second from the top. Third from the top is a French Hanriot Dupont two-seater pursuit plane. An early Russian Sikorsky bomber is shown at the bottom.

Nevertheless, the training received in Europe was an important learning experience for the many enlisted men who attended school there. The technical knowledge imparted by the British and French aided the Air Service in building a cadre of aircraft experts who would find jobs in civilian and military aviation following the war. For the Air Service, however, those who chose to remain in the Army would continue to lay the foundation of personnel policies and enlisted traditions during the interwar years.

World War I: Demobilization and the Air Service

Following the victory in Europe, the Army began to reduce and revert to its smaller peacetime size. After the war, however, there was much debate over the need for Universal Military Training (UMT) and a large peacetime standing army.[27] Eventually, Congress chose to expand the size of the postwar Army by authorizing approximately 300,000 men (appropriations, however, never allowed for more than 160,000), but it refused to consider anything resembling a peacetime draft. Congressional thinking evolved into the National Defense Act of 1920, which codified several ideas, including a single promotion list for officers and a branch chief for the infantry and cavalry, and it reorganized logistical measures under the Assistant Secretary of War. Most important for airpower supporters, the law made the Air Service permanent and it retained the wartime office of Chief of the Air Service.[28]

Like its Army parent, the Air Service had also expanded during the war and now faced a large-scale reduction. Still, it would remain much larger than its prewar strength. By the end of 1920, the AEF was home, with the Army down to fewer than 185,000 enlisted men and the Air Service under 10,000.[29] In retrospect, given manpower numbers and geographical distances, the demobilization was quick (in comparison with World War II), ill-planned, and at best, haphazard.[30]

Although little has been written about the effect of demobilization on the Air Service's regular enlisted cadre, even a cursory approach proves enlightening. For one thing, little was done about retaining enlisted specialists and air mechanicians. Since many soldiers had at least a year remaining on their enlisted contracts, some planners believed plenty of time was available to address this problem.[31]

Yet, quotas and appropriations made by Congress in 1920 aggravated the situation. The Army had to scale back by more than 90 percent, which for many meant early release from their enlistment contracts. Furthermore, to meet congressional demands for manpower and financial economy, military planners prohibited further recruiting for most of 1921 and cut soldiers' pay.[32] The confluence of these two factors, with an upturn in economic expectations in 1922, sent many soldiers racing from the service with the hope of using their

20

newfound skills.[33] The need for critical technical skills would force the Air Service to make recruiting, training, and pay top priorities in the interwar decades.

Another problem affecting the Air Service's enlisted men after the war was promotions. Like the Army in general, wartime expansion called for many regulars to be promoted into NCO slots. This promoted many into higher NCO grades, so that following the war and a reduction in strength, many regulars remained in the Army, thereby restricting the flow of future promotions. Although World War I statistics are sketchy, it follows that during the war and the expansion of the Air Service, many enlisted men were promoted to master sergeants and remained there in the 1920s and 1930s. Similar grade humps would occur after World War II and Korea.

Some have argued that Air Service promotions also suffered from the Army's desire to give its other branches a larger share of the NCO positions designated by Congress. For instance, one historian contended that the Air Corps may have received the troops authorized by Congress during the interwar period, but it failed to obtain "ample upper-level grades to support them." Thus, he wrote, "With fewer intermediate and senior noncommissioned officer slots in proportion to the size of force, advancement slowed to a trickle."[34]

Another historian argued similarly and added that other Army branches simply could not furnish the grades and ratings needed by the Air Corps. Thus, the scholar concluded, the Air Corps was lacking in both higher grades and higher specialty ratings.[35]

A careful analysis of Table 1 shows this was simply not the case. The Air Service and its successors were consistently more top-heavy than was the rest of the Army. A comparison of the median for the Air Corps' (4.2 percent) and the Army's (3.1 percent) top three grades shows the disparity. When all NCO grades are combined, the Air Corps' median percent of all NCOs (27.2 percent) is substantially greater than the median percent of the Army in general (25.1) and of the Infantry (21.8), Cavalry (23.0), and Quartermaster Corps (24.9).

Table 1
Distribution of Ranks
By Selected Years
1920–1940
(In Percent)

Year	Branch	NCO1*	NCO2**	NCO (Total)	PFC/PVT
1926	AC	4.6	23.0	27.5	71.5
	Army	3.1	22.7	25.9	74.1
	Inf	1.7	20.8	22.5	77.5

Table 1—cont'd

Year	Branch	NCO1*	NCO2**	NCO (Total)	PFC/PVT
	Cav	2.0	22.9	24.9	76.1
	QM	5.4	19.9	25.3	74.7
1931	AC	4.3	24.4	28.7	68.1
	Army	3.1	22.0	25.1	74.6
	Inf	1.8	19.6	21.4	78.6
	Cav	2.2	23.0	25.1	74.9
	QM	5.4	19.1	24.6	75.4
1935	AC	4.2	23.4	27.6	69.8
	Army	3.1	22.0	25.1	74.6
	Inf	1.8	20.2	22.1	77.9
	Cav	2.1	23.5	25.7	74.3
	QM	5.2	19.1	24.3	75.7
1939	AC	3.6	21.2	24.9	72.1
	Army	2.5	20.2	22.7	76.9
	Inf	1.4	20.4	21.8	78.2
	Cav	1.7	19.5	21.2	78.8
	QM	4.2	15.0	19.2	80.8
1940	AC	4.2	23.3	27.5	68.5

Medians

1920–1940	Army	AC	Infantry	Cavalry	Q'Master
NCO1	3.1	4.2	1.7	1.8	5.2
All NCOs	25.1	27.2	21.8	23.0	24.9

SOURCE: *War Department Annual Reports*, 1920–1940, Adjutant General Files.
   *NCO1=Master Sergeant, First Sergeant, and Technical Sergeant.
   **NCO2=Staff Sergeant, Sergeant, Corporal.

These historians failed to consider that promotion in the Army was generally slow. The post–World War I grade hump, the grade ceilings placed by Congress, and the requirement that NCO grades be tied to vacancies in the Tables of Organization of units significantly reduced the chances for promotion throughout the Army. Victor Vogel, an enlisted member of 2d Infantry Division at Fort Sam Houston, Texas, recalled the promotion process during the 1920s and 1930s:

The men of an infantry company gathered about the bulletin board to read the order promoting a private to private first class. "What is this man's army coming to?" one soldier complained in disgust. "Hogan is promoted to private first class and he only has six years' service. I'm going to transfer to a good outfit."[36]

Moreover, Vogel remembered that one survey showed the average length of service for privates as three years; that for privates first class as five years; for corporals, twelve years; and for sergeants, eighteen years. "Sergeants of the first three grades, the elite of the noncommissioned officers corps," Vogel added, "averaged twenty-four years [of] service."[37] In comparison with Vogel's impression, Air Corps noncommissioned officers had less time in service when promoted. According to one 1935 promotion list, the average years of those promoted to technical sergeant was 17.7, and to master sergeant, it was 16.2.[38] Opportunity for promotion was better in the Air Corps.

Though promotion opportunity was better in the Air Corps, air planners continued to make changes in promotion policy. In 1933, for example, planners solved part of the problem of slow promotions to technical and master sergeants. Before this, the Air Corps based all first- and second-grade promotions upon squadron commanders' letters of recommendations, specialty examinations, and quotas determined by Air Corps headquarters. Thus, all staff and technical sergeants were immediately promotable to the next higher rank based upon vacancies and test performance. In 1933, the Air Corps adopted a five-year, time-in-grade limitation as a basis for promotion eligibility to the first two grades. Once meeting this requirement, eligible promotees were ranked by total years of service in the Army. According to the 1934 Annual Report, this change in the seniority system to include a time-in-grade requirement resulted in "a more uniform and equitable system of promotion."[39]

Although promotion policies changed, the Air Corps promotion philosophy remained rigid, a reward for technical skill. From its inception, the Air Corps placed an overwhelming premium on the upper grades. Promotions were a reenlistment incentive largely due to three factors relating to the technical nature of the service: a token of respect for the years in service, acknowledgment of the skills developed, and the confidence of the Air Corps in men who repaired the essence of their technological existence, the airplanes.

By World War II, these concepts eventually evolved into a caste system that placed airmen into the highest NCO ranks on the basis of their proximity to the flying mission: aircrewmen (radioman, mechanic, gunner) were at the pinnacle, ground crews were in the next echelon, and support personnel were at the bottom. Noncommissioned officer grade ceilings, however, would not increase drastically until the pre–World War II expansion in the late 1930s. This caused one disgruntled Air Corps private to growl, "Prior to the expansion of the service [World War II], no one expected a promotion and they were rarely disappointed."[40]

Foundation of the Force

Early Manpower Legislation

Though problems remained with the demobilization, the Air Service soon had the short-lived benefit of legislation expanding its size and capabilities. For instance, the National Defense Act of 1920 authorized an enlisted force of 16,000 and stimulated a massive recruiting drive by the Air Service for mechanically gifted men. Chief of the Air Service Maj. Gen. Charles T. Menoher stressed as a selling point the idea that the Air Service was a great opportunity, a chance for a man to become a skilled worker. It was "the opportunity of a lifetime."[41] The official Air Service recruiting motto became "EARN AND LEARN."[42]

With a need to fill 7,000 vacancies under the new act, Army and Air Service recruiters quickly encountered several problems. High employment, illiteracy (especially in the South), and congressional economic measures all hampered effective recruitment. By early 1921, enlisted strength rose to 12,280; it then halted as Congress lowered the Army's enlisted ceiling from 280,000 to 175,000.[43] In turn, the Air Service's size shrank from the authorized 16,000 to 11,500, a 28 percent decrease.[44] In June, the expiration of enlisted contracts and other attrition sent Air Service manpower below 11,000. More cuts that year meant discharging men early to meet the new limit of 10,300.[45]

When recruiting resumed in late 1921, the Air Service continued to experience problems maintaining even a 9,500-man force. Not only were 3,000 men at the end of their enlistment contracts, but because of the Army policy that allowed men to purchase a discharge, some took that avenue; some deserted as civilian employment in skilled trades increased. By June 1922, Congress again cut the Army to 125,000, allocating only 8,500 slots to the Air Service.[46] With the new cuts, the Air Service remained at full strength, but the size and scope of air operations were severely hampered. The Air Service was far from being operationally ready, a continual cause for concern in both its supporters and the War Department.

If the National Defense Act of 1920 and the subsequent economic measures defined early congressional and military attitudes toward the new peacetime Air Service, then the Army Air Corps Act of 1926 went a long way to legitimize air power in the eyes of the Army. This act not only granted the airmen corps status, but it forced the Army to reduce the size and promotion quotas of other of its branches in order to increase these in the Air Corps. The act also gave the corps representation in each General Staff division and an Assistant Secretary of War for Air, thus increasing its prestige and influence in the War and Executive Departments. Most important from a manpower standpoint, however, was the five-year expansion program.[47]

Over a period of five years the Air Corps increased to 1,800 planes, 1,650 officers, and 15,000 enlisted men. With an expansion rate of approximately 1,250 men added to the Corps each year, Congress initially augmented the

125,000 army limit by 6,240 men. Then, in what undoubtedly seemed to some as a recurring nightmare, Congress increased the overall appropriations in fiscal year 1927 to meet Air Corps aircraft procurement, but it decreased the amount authorized to pay all soldiers. This forced the Army (the Air Corps was excluded) to reduce NCO and specialist strength and to freeze promotions until losses in personnel allowed it to meet these new grade limits.[48]

For the Army, the Air Corps expansion was problematic and fueled a growing rift between airmen and the other combat branches. Though Congress authorized a larger Air Corps, both the executive and legislative branches between 1926 and 1935 opposed any increase in the size of the standing army. Consequently, the Air Corps could only grow at the expense of other Army organizations. By the early 1930s, Air Corps enlisted strength increased more than 45 percent (from 9,079 to 13,190) at the expense of five infantry battalions and a regiment of field artillery.[49]

In addition, the Air Corps' advanced technology demanded more specialists than any of the other branches (Table 2). Because specialties, like promotions, operated under a fixed ceiling based on total strength, Air Corps needs could only be met at the expense of the entire Army. As Tables 2 and 3 show, not only did the Air Corps have the largest percentage of its manpower in the higher grades of specialties, but it increasingly shared a larger proportion (20.8 percent) in the late 1930s of all Army specialty grades.

Table 2
Distribution of Specialties
By Selected Years
1920–1940
(In Percent)

		*Category**				
Year	*Branch*	*1*	*2*	*Total (1&2)*	*3&4*	*5&6*
1925	AC	5.8	11.8	17.6	17.4	65.0
	Army	2.6	5.0	7.6	23.7	68.6
	Inf	.5	2.5	3.0	25.5	70.0
	Cav	.4	3.8	4.2	30.7	65.1
	QM	4.6	4.4	9.0	20.7	70.3
1930	AC	5.4	10.7	16.1	19.2	64.7
	Army	2.7	4.0	6.7	23.7	69.6
	Inf	.5	.7	1.2	25.7	73.1
	Cav	.7	.9	1.6	31.7	66.7
	QM	4.6	4.2	8.8	19.9	71.3

Table 2—con't

		Category*				
Year	Branch	1	2	Total (1&2)	3&4	5&6
1935	AC	4.5	15.2	19.7	19.4	60.9
	Army	2.5	4.7	7.2	23.6	69.2
	Inf	.4	.3	.7	24.6	74.7
	Cav	.2	.2	0.4	30.4	69.2
	QM	4.3	4.1	8.4	19.6	72.0
1939	AC	4.6	12.4	17.0	22.5	60.5
	Army	2.4	4.1	6.5	24.2	69.3
1940	AC	4.0	12.0	16.0	23.4	60.6
	Army	2.3	4.7	7.0	24.1	68.9
	Inf	.2	.4	.6	26.2	73.2
	Cav	.2	.7	.9	32.8	66.3
	QM	4.0	3.9	7.9	21.6	70.5

SOURCE: *War Department Annual Reports*, 1920–1940, Adjutant General Files.

*Categories are broken down by specialty pay. Category 1 includes servicemen receiving the most pay and thus represents those most skilled; category 6 includes those lowest paid, and presumably those least skilled.

Table 3
Air Corps Specialization
As a Percent of Total Army Specialization
1924–1940
(In Percent)

Year	Air Corps/Army Specialization*
1924	10.0
1926	10.1
1928	13.2
1930	16.6
1932	20.3
1934	20.7

Table 3—cont'd

Year	Air Corps/Army Specialization*
1936	20.8
1938	20.8
1940	30.5

SOURCE: *War Department Annual Reports*, 1920–1940, Adjutant General Files.

*This percentage is derived by dividing total Air Corps specialists by total Army specialists. Thus by 1940, Air Corps specialists accounted for over 30 percent of all Army specialists while constituting only 19 percent of the Army's total enlisted strength.

In 1930, the Secretary of War reported to Congress that the later reductions in various army grades and personnel due to the Air Corps expansion seriously imperiled the Army's ability to perform its primary mission. In 1930, however, in the midst of a depression that sent Wall Street and business to their knees, Congress had more pressing matters to address.

Recruitment, 1920–1940

During the decade of the twenties, Army personnel planners developed procurement policies designed to recruit and retain enough men to meet losses. While some military planners believed the Army could attract ambitious young men by offering them a chance to learn a trade or vocation, others thought the extensive Army recreation program which included athletics, libraries, movies, and servicemen's clubs would spur enlistments. Still others encouraged patriotic appeals to recruit the necessary numbers.[50] Initially, Army recruiters met with some success, but increasing cost-cutting measures, including a suspension of recruiting for part of the 1921 fiscal year, forced the Army to reduce pay and eliminate the educational and vocational training incentives.[51] Moreover, the Army put an end to centralized recruiting; it authorized posts, camps, and stations to recruit directly.[52] Further handicapping the effort was the requirement that recruits not only had to provide transportation to and from military bases, they also had to pay for their meals until they were formally inducted and sworn in.[53]

These factors, in tandem with slow promotion opportunities and an upturn in the economy after 1922, persuaded few to either join or reenlist. In 1920, for

Foundation of the Force

instance, one recruiting survey reported that "the industrial centers of the population present[ed] too strong an attraction to young men . . . for the Army to compete with."[54] Even the highest paid army specialists made less than the lowest paid skilled laborer in either the manufacturing or building trades (70 percent and 200 percent less, respectively).[55] It became evident that few would enter a peacetime volunteer army simply for patriotic reasons. The combination of pay, training, and benefits served as the biggest attraction.[56]

Although the Air Service relied on the Army to do much of its recruiting, it had its own recruiting stations and recruiters located at various airfields. Air Service recruiters targeted people with interests in manned flight and obtaining a skilled trade. Paralleling its parent organization, the Air Service began recruiting in the spring of 1919 to replace demobilization losses. Its main recruiting message emphasized the novelty of flight, the demands for skilled "aviationists," and that life in the Air Service was a good job. One news release read:

> Men Wanted for Air Service: Have you a good job today? If not, what can you find better than the Air Service? . . . There will always be a large demand for skilled aeroplane pilots and mechanics. Now is the time to learn at government expense.[57]

By 1922, perhaps the biggest selling point was training, hence, to learn a trade. Because aviation technology was new, few civilian institutions could offer courses in this area. The Air Corps could not expect to attract experienced journeymen in the essential mechanical trades, nor, because of its lack of skilled journeymen, could it easily adapt the Army's apprentice program (on-the-job training) to the new technology. It became imperative that the Air Corps establish a formalized school to teach critical skills while also basing its recruiting campaigns on the acquisition of skills useful in civilian life.[58]

For some, such as SMSgt. Elmer J. Howell, who enlisted in the 1930s, the future of commercial aviation looked bright. He thought it a good idea to join the Air Corps to benefit from the Air Mechanics schools at Chanute, Illinois, because he wanted to "finish the three-year enlistment and obtain work at the United Air Lines overhaul facility in Cheyenne, Wyoming."[59] He ended up staying in the Air Corps/Air Force for more than twenty years. When TSgt. August Linkey was asked why he enlisted, he matter of factly responded, "To try for the free $15,000 mechanical course that was used in enlisted advertising."[60]

In the 1930s, base pay, uniform throughout the Army's branches, approximated civilian wages for aviation mechanics and specialists. The army Tables of Organization, which determined unit structure and personnel composition, allocated soldiers by grade, reflecting seven levels of rank from private to master sergeant, and by rating for private and private first class as one of six specialty divisions. Though promotions were often slow, specialists

28

Chanute Field, Rantoul, Illinois, during maneuvers in 1936

received additional pay for skills to offset the promotion pace and provide a retention incentive.

For example, a private with the lowest specialty class (6) received an additional $3.00 per month in addition to his base pay of $21.00. When rated as a specialist first class, the same private's pay went to $51.00 per month. In the early 1920s, the Air Corps authorized the two grades of Air Mechanics to receive incentive pay. A first-class mechanic, regardless of army rank, made the equivalent pay of a technical sergeant ($84.00 per month), and second-class mechanics received the pay of a staff sergeant ($72.00).[61] Enlisted men liked this pay because it helped offset slow promotion by paying them more for skill proficiency while not charging them with additional military responsibility.

An air mechanic or specialist of the first three classes also received pay common to all soldiers, which also compensated for the civilian income differential and aided retention. A second-class air mechanic, besides his $864.00 yearly base pay, received room and board ($480), a clothing allowance ($170), and retirement ($500) for a total of $2,014.00 per year.[62] Add to this the benefits of free medical care, athletics and amusements, opportunity for travel, and a thirty-year retirement at three-fourths pay, and a private had a tidy pay and compensation package that compared nicely to the $885 yearly average received by twenty- to twenty-five-year-old civilian laborers and the $1,695 that skilled workers took home in the late 1920s and the 1930s.[63] Undoubtedly, enlisted men of the other Army branches as well as civilian laborers were envious of the air mechanic's higher pay.

Primarily as a vehicle for self advancement, the Air Corps also attracted many ex-servicemen. One magazine advertisement proclaimed:

> A bright energetic young man with initiative, should not remain a private long. The enlisted man with a high school education who applied himself, had a good knowledge of planes and motors, and could pass the physical exams could learn to fly. He would then have a good opportunity for a commission. Here was the opportunity of a lifetime.[64]

CWO Alfred Saxon, a thirty-year man who enlisted in 1937, recalled the opportunities in the new aviation branch during the 1930s:

> I voluntarily gave up my Army grade of sergeant to return to the U.S. and reenlist in the Air Corps because I felt that there were greater opportunities there for me. As it turned out that was exactly what happened. Because I had three years [of] prior experience and because of the rapid build up of the Air Corps [during the mid- to late 1930s] I advanced through every enlisted grade and was appointed warrant officer.[65]

MSgt. Vincent Strauss, another career airman, enlisted in the Air Corps in 1934 "because it offered a better chance for advancement than the infantry. I also wanted from early childhood to become an airplane mechanic."[66] Some also joined because they thought it easier to gain entrance into West Point from inside the Army rather than to wait for a congressional appointment.

Still others were attracted by the glamour of aviation and patriotic sentiment. "As a teenager," Lt. Col. Robert E. Thomas recorded, "I developed a keen interest in aviation from books and 'up close' at county fairs that included some 'barnstormer' airplanes." As college was "out of the question" for him at the time, Thomas enlisted "to attend Tech school in aircraft and engine mechanics," and later gained a commission.[67] On one occasion the heady atmosphere of an Armistice Day parade in downtown Oklahoma City was enough to persuade CMSgt. Steven Davis to enlist. "The sound of the music," Davis wrote, "the drum beat, the American flag, the trim young officer administering the oath, all combined to make it [enlisting] a memorable one."[68] When Charles Lindbergh soloed across the Atlantic to France in May 1927, Air Corps recruiters were quick to point out that he was "trained at Army Flying Schools."[69] Thus, recruiters reinforced the image of the Air Corps as an institution where heroism, the spirit of frontiersmen, advanced technical training, and glamour flourished. By the end of the 1920s and well into the 1930s, the Air Corps rarely needed selling.

While glamour, patriotism, the desire for aviation training, or just plain army life attracted youth, more than anything else, the economic depression of the period helped to fill quotas, retain men, and form a cadre of dedicated professional airmen ready to take their place as senior NCOs in World War II. Tables 4 and 5 show the partial effects of the depression upon the Army and Air Corps. It apparently encouraged men to stay in the service. In 1932 and 1933, for instance, almost four persons reenlisted for every first-termer recruited (Table 4). Compared with the previous decade, this meant that more reenlisted and fewer deserted (Table 5), netting an increase in the number of Air Corps enlisted personnel with a least three years' experience. The higher the experience level, the greater the benefit to the service.

Table 4
*Ratio of Reenlistment to First Enlistment:**
Building an Experienced Force
1924–1940

Year	Army	Air Corps
1924	.38	.18
1926	.45	.49
1928	.47	.68
1930	.79	.94
1931	1.24	1.69
1932	2.99	3.35
1933	2.17	3.72
1934	.94	1.38
1935	1.15	2.21
1936	.56	1.61
1937	.58	.97
1938	.75	1.21
1939	1.11	1.90
1940	.42	.48

SOURCE: *War Department Annual Reports*, 1920–1940, Adjutant General Files.

*Figures are derived by dividing the number of first enlistments by the number of reenlistments. Until 1931, the number of first-time enlistments exceeded reenlistments; during the depression, the converse was true.

Table 5
Desertion and Unemployment Rates
1922–1940
(Per Thousand Men)

Desertions

Year	Air Corps	Army	Unemployment
1922	3.26	3.27	7.6
1925	5.28	7.39	4.0
1926	5.81	7.26	1.9
1930	2.40	4.78	8.7
1932	1.00	1.83	23.6
1934	1.05	2.33	21.7
1936	0.60	1.81	16.9
1938	0.92	2.52	19.0
1940	0.39	1.73	14.6

SOURCES: *War Department Annual Reports*, 1922–1940; *Historical Statistics of the United States: Colonial Times to 1957* (Washington, D.C.: GPO, 1961), D 46–47.

Planners, once concerned with maintaining and training an adequate force, now concentrated their efforts on advanced training, quality of life issues, and insuring that only premium soldiers could reenlist. As unemployment and hard economic times are periods of manpower abundance both in the military and in industry, enlistment becomes countercyclical to economic features.[70] Table 5 shows that desertions were significantly lower in the Air Corps compared with those in the Army. Further analysis demonstrates that desertion rates were at least partially correlated to the unemployment rate.*

Although the depression helped solidify a body of skilled aviation experts, legislation during the period did little to provide a career path for such people. Men entered the service and stayed in, not just for the skills they could acquire, the legislated benefits, or patriotism; rather, they needed employment. The turnover ratio (Table 6) shows that manpower gains during the interwar period and especially during the depression exceeded losses due to discharge. Ideally, planners wanted to maintain a gain-to-loss ratio of 1.00, unless purposefully expanding or contracting the force.

---

* Spearman's P correlation coefficients are Army, –.86; Air Corps, –.88; and Navy, –.82.

Table 6
Turnover Ratio*
1920–1940

Year	Army	Air Corps
1920	.21	.25
1924	1.02	1.22
1926	.91	.90
1928	.97	1.05
1930	.95	1.09
1932	.80	.90
1934	1.00	1.07
1936	1.56	1.10
1938	1.07	1.18
1940	1.90	2.68

SOURCE: *War Department Annual Reports*, 1920–1940, AG Files.

*The ratio is a simple division of all manpower gains to all losses. With the exception of 1920, 1926, and 1932, the Air Corps either maintained or exceeded its actual size. In 1932, planners consciously reduced the size of the force.

Additionally, enlistment statistics for the 1920s and 1930s (Table 7) demonstrate that during the 1920s, the Army and Air Corps recruited most enlisted men from first-time enlistments. By 1930, this had changed, and prior-service enlistments and reenlistments far exceeded first-time enlistments. In fact, through 1935, Army personnel planners restricted first enlistments since their quotas were easily filled through reenlistments.[71]

Table 7
Total Enlistments*
1920–1940
(In Percent)

	Prior Service		Reenlistments		First-Time Enlistments	
Year	Army	AC	Army	AC	Army	AC
1920	54.4	41.2	NA	NA	NA	58.8
1922	55.6	40.7	NA	NA	NA	59.3
1924	18.6	15.0	22.5	12.9	58.8	72.1

Table 7—cont'd

	Prior Service		Reenlistments		First-Time Enlistments	
Year	Army	AC	Army	AC	Army	AC
1926	13.0	12.0	27.0	29.1	59.9	58.9
1928	13.0	13.1	27.8	35.1	59.2	51.9
1930	10.7	11.1	48.4	55.0	50.0	45.9
1932	7.8	6.4	69.0	72.1	23.1	21.5
1934	6.1	6.4	45.3	54.2	48.4	39.4
1936	5.5	6.8	3.96	57.5	60.6	35.7
1938	6.4	7.3	40.1	50.8	42.0	53.5
1940	3.6	3.5	28.4	31.1	68.0	65.3

SOURCE: *War Department Annual Reports*, 1920–1940, AG Files.

*While during the 1920s first-term enlistments exceeded reenlistments, statistics for the 1930s demonstrated the opposite.

With a high retention rate, the Air Corps could concentrate on retaining a top-quality enlisted force. World War I–type mechanical aptitude tests were reinstituted, and minimum intelligence scores were raised. The Air Corps required letters of recommendation from local officials. Planners also barred married men who were not NCOs from enlistment or reenlistment.[72]

With more experienced enlisted men remaining in the Air Corps, combined with the emphasis on personnel and cost economies and a devastating fire at the major training facilities at Chanute Field, Illinois, in 1934, technical training was constricted. From 1934 through 1937, courses were shortened, and much of the training took place at the unit level on an apprentice basis.[73] Course length and class size were back to normal by mid-1938, when the Air Corps opened a branch of the Technical School at Lowry Field, near Denver, Colorado.[74]

When Victor Vogel reenlisted in the cavalry during the depression, he noted that "the reenlistment rate was high, though there [were] no bonuses, no promises of promotion, and no additional incentives."[75] Furthermore, in 1933, federal employees took a pay cut of 15 percent, decreasing a private's monthly pay from $21.00 to $17.85.[76] As the Army and Air Corps continued special pay for mechanics and specialists, few chose to leave; many military personnel felt fortunate to have jobs. By the late 1930s, Congress permitted the Army to expand gradually and again accept first-timers. Getting into the service did not become easy. "Recruiting was not intense," Sergeant Howell said of his enlistment in 1937, "too many needed jobs!" He added:

I contacted the recruiting station (only one in the state), was given a date to report for exams and did so. I took an aptitude exam and a few knowledge exams for the Air Corps. Besides the physical, only four of over two-hundred qualified for the Air Corps. Two went to March Field, California and two to Selfridge Field, Michigan.[77]

For some enterprising hopefuls, it meant directly importuning the commander of the training center for entrance. For instance, in September of 1932, the commandant of the training center at Chanute wrote to the personnel division at the Office of the Chief of the Air Corps requesting special authorization to enlist two hundred qualified applicants. The commandant pointed out that he had "a waiting list of applicants now numbering 850. . . . They are all high school graduates, many with some additional technical education and all exceptionally qualified as to character, intelligence, and general fitness."[78]

Sgt. Marion E. Waldorf and Sgt. Edward R. Halverson were part of a group that later applied directly to the Chanute commandant. Waldorf recollected:

Shortly after graduating from high school, I got a job with one of the factories where most of the jobs were located and where most of the breadwinners were employed. . . . After several months I was laid off. I was interested in the Army Air Corps and proceeded to try to enlist. Now I say tried because at that time a person had to submit an application and three letters of recommendation before being accepted. My three letters were from the mayor, the high school principal, and the number one man at the factory. . . . I [then] journeyed to Chanute Field, Illinois and enlisted with the intention of becoming the best airplane mechanic in the Army Air Corps.[79]

Similarly, Halverson discussed how he enlisted:

I knew little about the Army Air Corps before enlisting. I had never seen or talked to anyone who was or who had been in this branch of the service. . . . Somehow I did get the address of the Commandant, Army Air Corps Technical School, at Chanute Field, Illinois. I simply asked them if I could join up [May 1939]. Return mail invited me to see if I could qualify. Not having any money, I hit the road one morning and hitched a ride down there [from Gilbert, Minnesota].[80]

Recruiting standards were tough because so many people were unemployed and the Air Corps desired a certain type of individual. Aviation technology demanded intelligent, mechanically gifted young men to work as technicians and advisors to pilot-officers. Even as early as 1920, the chief of the Air Service had an image of an enlisted man:

The work of these [enlisted] men is judged mainly by their ability to care for intricate mechanisms, and the relation of the members of a squadron

35

to the officers who pilot the machines is to a great extent that of advisors and guardians to men whose lives depend on the advice and care given.[81]

In their roles as technicians, advisors, and guardians, enlisted men had to have the "right stuff," which according to air planners included good character, intelligence, and a high school diploma. "It is intended to limit original enlistments," the Air Service's official newsletter said, "to men who have a high school education or to those men whose mentality is sufficiently developed to warrant training in the highly specialized trades required for Air Service work."[82]

Air planners in the 1920s concentrated on building up the force, whereas during the depression they focused on quality by increasing the established entrance requirements. As the U.S. entry into World War II neared, the Air Corps continued to seek only top-quality men. On June 1, 1939, for instance, the Air Corps was authorized an increase of 23,644 men to be recruited within one year. Of these, more than 17,000 needed specialized technical training. Rather than select men on a first-come, first-served basis, however, air planners established stringent requirements for recruits—to pass tests, complete basic training, attend civilian technical training, and be willing to enlist for three years. Most planners believed that it was a small price to pay for the skills received, and they were often self-congratulatory about their abilities to attract high-quality youth. Most recruits, according to one report, were high school graduates and came from "fine American families."[83]

Training and Specialization, 1920–1945

One 1920 article in the *Air Service News Letter* boasted of Army aviation's uncanny draw on young men:

> Red-blooded young men naturally feel the call of the air. It is so new, so measurably different from any other profession or sport, that it draws men as honey does bees. It presents a wonderful opportunity to a man. . . . If a man be a real man, the call of an outdoor life and a profession such as the air game is, is infinitely more attractive than clerking behind a counter or keeping books. It is possible for such a man to become an expert in a new and well paid line, by enlisting in the Air Service of the United States and attending the Air Service's Mechanics School.[84]

It was aviation technology, as differentiated by Air Corp specialties, that drove the recruiting requirements for Air Corps enlisted men of the interwar years. The technology demanded high costs in time, training funds, and manpower from the general labor pool. Costs were necessary, however, as the Air Corps embarked on finding and training men in skills that few possessed. Because many of the new specialties could only be taught in a formalized setting, and not on the job, the Air Corps began to establish centralized training centers. The Mechanics School, which moved from Kelly Field to Chanute, Illinois, in 1921, offered formal courses for many Air Corps specialties, including airplane mechanics, motor mechanics, propeller and fabric workers, magneto and instrument repairmen, radio electricians, welders, carpenters, and photographers.[85]

Premised on practical knowledge, instructors taught specialty courses on the principle that "doing a thing is the best way to learn how." "It was an easy matter," one instructor wrote, "to turn out theoretical experts who could not put in a cotter pin or intelligently fill a ship with gas." It was clear that the Air Corps geared training toward producing engineers and mechanics, not intellectuals.[86] As demonstrated in the 1920 twelve-week airplane mechanic course curriculum, practical training far outweighed theoretical instruction:

> three weeks—theoretical and practical work on aircraft riggings. Lectures included why rigging is necessary and then transitions into building torn down ships into flyable ones.

> three weeks—engine fundamentals—Information was designed to train men in removing and replacing motors, adjusting propellers and carburetors, and testing the completed product. There was no attempt to repair the engine—that was a different specialty.

> six weeks—wire-making, building loops, adjustment of control wires, the inspection of wires, struts, turnbuckles and wing and fuselage connections.[87]

After graduation, new mechanics went to the Flying Department to work for three weeks on actual flying aircraft. According to this philosophy,

> The student has his first ride—and it is a very chastening and stimulating thing for a man on his first ride to look down three thousand feet and realize that soon he will be responsible for keeping the ship in the air. He leaves the school with the same idea he was given when he entered—that his is a great trust, and that he was considered available as a student because his superiors thought him worthy.[88]

The amount of training given one man was a matter of debate. Early course work aimed at generalized training, but technological improvements, smaller training appropriations, and retention caused fluctuations between generalized and specialized training. During World War I, for instance, the great need for mechanics, combined with a short training time, limited funds, and a large manpower pool, pushed air trainers into advocating very specialized instruction.

With these constraints alleviated after the war, air planners took a more generalized approach. By 1930, the Air Corps Technical School at Chanute reported that they had totally revised their curriculum based upon the idea that they could now train mechanics on a broader scale. As a result, trainers revised courses so that an airplane mechanic was

> now trained in all the subjects relative to the maintenance of both airplane and engine. The use of metals in airplanes [elaborated] the course for welders; the machinists' course was broadened and perfected, and in general the courses have been improved, modernized, and expanded.[89]

By 1939, with the prewar expansion in high gear, the availability of more funds, and the coming on-line of more technologically sophisticated aircraft like the B–17 and B–24, the Technical School again opted for specialized course work. Besides general classes in airplane mechanics, there were specialist courses in carburetors; electrical, instrument, and propeller repair; five different types of armorers (based on aircraft type); four specialties in photography; one in bombsight maintenance; and a final course for Air Corps Supply and Technical clerks.[90]

As World War I had accelerated the need for specialized training in aviation, the scope and pace of World War II significantly accelerated the technological sophistication of aircraft and aviation equipment, thereby requiring either highly trained generalists or a host of specialists. Time, money, and manpower dictated the latter. Other factors including the time element and a rapid deployment to Europe and the Far East increased the demand for larger training quotas and tighter class schedules. To these ends, trainers designed courses to be plane-specific, and then taught only parts of the B–17 and B–24 aviation systems to the new airmen.[91] Men who once could be trained in all aspects of an aircraft now specialized in a specific aircraft and specific electrical/mechanical systems.

Providing technical training to all recruits posed a difficult challenge. Air planners had hoped that all new recruits could be sent directly to mechanics' school for testing and training. Unfortunately, during the interwar years, not technology, manpower, nor funds were available to establish a lengthy training pipeline.[92] Though a more centralized pipeline had developed during World War II, the 1920s and 1930s saw the technical schools establish their own training quotas and then send out recruiting parties to enlist potential trainees. Until a centralized process developed, the Air Corps gradually relied on an extensive apprentice program which saw a nucleus of formally schooled air mechanics train new men in their squadrons.[93]

Eventually, planners assigned some squadrons semiannual quotas from the technical schools, but because of operational demands, unit commanders released few to attend. Thus many, such as TSgt. Gerald Driscoll, initially received training on the job and later went to school. He remembered:

> I was assigned to the 3d bombardment Squadron, 6th bombardment group. There was informal training in Airplane Mechanics, wing wiping (fabric cleaning and doping) etc. I finally was placed in the communications

section for training as a radio operator at squadron level. I finally went to school, at Group Level, for Radio Mechanics and Radio Operators. This was my primary assignment for three months. . . . I completed the course, was returned to the squadron and assigned to a B–18 Combat Crew as a Radio Operator-Gunner. As a result of the schools I was qualified to take the exam for Air Mechanic-Radio Operator. . . . I passed the exam and qualified.[94]

Another problem facing the Air Corps was the amount and type of basic training given to enlisted men. Its technological nature significantly differentiated the Air Corps from other branches of the army and increasingly emphasized technical over military training. "Recruit training was very basic," one old Air Corps sergeant said; "it had nothing to do with our job, as our job was to learn to be an airplane mechanic!"[95]

The ongoing need for technical specialists and the nature of aviation equipment eventually eclipsed the need for extensive basic military training. During World War I, basic training for the Air Service was almost nonexistent; the interwar years sparked a debate between Air Corps and War Department planners on the amount of military training needed before attending technical schools. For the most part, however, the Air Corps followed the War Department's General Order 7 (1927), which called for unit recruit training.[96]

Since the Army offered little in the way of standardized military training, the squadron commander and the first sergeant usually dictated the amount and type of training. CMSgt. Jesse Davidson recalled:

At the time of my enlistment (1937) there was no formal recruit training. Each outfit was responsible for indoctrinating all personnel assigned to it. My training was given by a corporal assigned to the task by the first sergeant. The corporal had twenty-six years of service and also was the company barber. The training was highly personalized. It consisted of military history and customs, military courtesy and respect, Army regulations and procedures, and military justice. There was no technical training.[97]

Those who were recruited directly by Chanute Field for technical training had more rigorous basic military training. Sergeant Dayton believed that his recruit training was tough and "highly disciplined. . . . We were awakened at 0600, attended roll call, marched to breakfast (plenty to eat), marched to the drill field, practiced close-order drill till noon, then to the mess hall, and attended classes during the afternoon on military courtesy, small arms, customs of service, etc. By 1700 [5 PM], we were free to go to the mess, gym, movies, or study for examinations."[98]

The thrust of the massive prewar buildup beginning in 1938, combined with a lack of precedent and training directives, resulted in training inconsistencies. The debate over the amount of military training given to airmen was rekindled. With the war escalating, the need for aircraft technicians and training

Aircrew radio operator training, Kansas City, Missouri (*top*). Radio operations on a bomber (*bottom left*). Aircrew radio operator training at Scott Field, Illinois (*bottom right*).

Aircrew gunnery training, Selfridge Field, Mt. Clemens, Michigan, 1930 (*top*). Photo interpretation training at intelligence school, Harrisburg, Pennsylvania (*bottom*).

programs opted for developing technical skills over basic military training.[99]

Problems quickly erupted when an infantry officer was placed in charge of the Air Corps' first replacement center at Jefferson Barracks, Missouri. He insisted on teaching new airmen "soldierly skills" and allotted 127 hours for physical training, drill, marches, and marksmanship; 60 more hours than the War Department had prescribed for its infantry units. Within four months, the officer was transferred, and the school-of-the-soldier part of the curriculum was reduced by a third, reflecting three fewer hours than the War Department standard.[100]

During the first two years of the war, basic military training was secondary to technical schooling. By 1943, however, the decreased need for technicians allowed the Air Force to focus on the type, scope, and duration of recruit training. Trainers extended and changed basic training to reflect the needs of theater commanders who desired more practical training in camouflage, chemical warfare, and first aid. Trainers reduced drill and ceremonies but spent more time on marksmanship. As air fields advanced into enemy territories, trainers taught more about air base defense. Thus, in late 1943 and 1944, recruits in basic training could not graduate without completing a course on using the Springfield 30.06 or the M–1 rifles and the Colt .45-caliber pistol.[101]

After the initial rush to train technicians and air crews, the AAF established a training pipeline in which a consistent flow of manpower emerged with both the military and technical education needed for their newfound duties as airmen. In a tradition extending back to the interwar decades and then reconfirmed during World War II, soldiers of the AAF were clearly technicians first, and soldiers, a distant second. Changes in enlisted policies during World War II only reinforced these beliefs.

Effects of World War II on Enlisted Personnel Policy

The confluence of several factors forced the AAF to create, modify, and adopt new enlisted personnel policies. One key factor was the massive increase in enlisted personnel, from 20,824 in 1939 to 1,900,805 in 1945, due to the pre-1943 selective recruiting campaigns and the draft. Another factor was the rapid acceleration of aircraft technological advances during the 1920s and 1930s, which called for new specialized training programs. Innovations in industrial and military personnel classification and training systems also caused air planners to revise their personnel policies and programs.[102]

As a result of the need to train thousands of young men during World War II, both recruit (military) and technical training had become centralized, standardized, and divorced from the unit, and the two types of training occurred independently of each other. Basic training evolved from learning about military protocol on the job to a system of centralized recruit reception centers, enlisted replacement centers, and unit training centers. Reception centers indoctrinated, classified, and tested recruits and then sent them to replacement and unit training centers (aircraft crews) based upon classification results. These centers conducted both initial and advanced technical training (based on aircraft type).[103] This centralization and division of training was peculiar to all services and continued into the Cold War era.

The need to classify thousands of recruits and train them in the latest technology compelled planners to look to industry and the Navy for a different classification system. Even before World War I, the Navy had developed a classification system based on craft lines that included career paths, in-service training, and a means to classify and consolidate ranks with specialties, something neither the Army nor the Air Corps had developed.[104] To standardize personnel management, the Army and the Air Corps extrapolated the Navy's and industry's classification systems, categorizing all personnel by occupational specialty. By 1945, the Navy had expanded from 36 specialty ratings to 174 separate job classifications; the Army, including the AAF, had devised 532 military occupational specialties (MOSs); and the Marines had moved from simple rank titles (private, corporal, etc.) to 21 broad occupational groupings with 369 specialties.[105]

Once the Army defined its occupational specialties, it devised an information system to report manpower strengths servicewide. As the Army had no integrated manpower planning system before the war to match needs to resources, the development of this classification and reporting system was crucial to personnel planners.[106] For the Air Corps, this meant a centralized system for ascertaining and meeting the various commands' needs. Planners could set quotas for specialists based on the needs of various commands and the size and timing of technical school classes.

Although the new classification system simplified categorizing and assigning enlisted personnel across a spectrum of jobs and units, technological sophistication and the need to train new airmen in a variety of skills increased the number of occupational specialties required.[107] A close look at Air Force classification regulations during the war shows how personnel planners subdivided, or shredded-out, MOSs. For example, in the 1930s, aviation mechanics were craftsmen trained to work on an entire aircraft, from wings to engine to hydraulic system. By 1943, the classification scheme divided mechanics into eight functional groups, of which there were forty-seven subclassifications of mechanics. The Airplane Engine Specialist Group included the following nineteen subgroups:

Airplane Carburetor Specialist Group	Airplane Fabric and Dope Worker
Airplane Crew Chief	Airplane Cable Mechanic
Airplane Engine Mechanic	Airplane Hydraulic Specialist
Airplane Powerplant Specialist	Airplane Line Chief

Airplane Engine Overhaul Shop Chief	Automatic Pilot Specialist
	Depot Engineering Chief
Airplane Supercharger Specialist	Fuel Tank Repairman
Airplane Target Motor Mechanic	Glider Mechanic
Engine Test Operator	Mobile Repair Unit Chief
Airplane and Engine Mechanic	Procurement Inspector[108]

These specializations were then stratified by specific aircraft model and by the echelon of maintenance performed (on the flight line or the various stages of depot maintenance), which geometrically increased the number of specialties. For example, in April 1944 a delineation was made among the technician, mechanic, and repairman categories:

Technician—High-grade man in a technical field, but not in maintenance (i.e. electronics, radar, fire-control, etc.)

Mechanic—Maintenance person who works on the flight-line or can repair equipment with a minimum of parts and tools

Repairman—Maintenance person at intermediate and depot levels of repair. At these levels or echelons, engines are overhauled, radios reworked, and radar equipment diagnosed and repaired.[109]

Besides increased specialization in traditional aircraft areas, innovations in electronics, radar, personnel, and medicine also increased the needs for new specialties and training.[110] During the war, the Air Forces required four technical specialists for every pilot, while the ratio of ground to flight personnel approached seven to one. When all noncombat assignments were compared with flying assignments, the ratio more than doubled to sixteen to one.[111] Table 8 shows that all services became more specialized and required fewer combat specialties. For the Air Forces, more than 50 percent of its enlisted jobs were in mechanical, repair, administrative, and technical specialties.

Table 8
Distribution of Enlisted Positions
By Occupational Area and Service,
End of World War II
(In Percent)

Occupational Area	War Dept Total	Army*	AAF	Navy	Marines
Ground Combat	24.1	39.3	—	—	33.6
Electronics	5.8	3.8	8.1	9.5	8.1
Other Technical	7.2	6.6	7.6	9.1	3.9
Administrative/Clerical	15.3	15.1	19.9	11.1	15.0
Mechanics & Repairmen	20.0	8.9	35.9	37.6	21.8

Table 8—cont'd

Occupational Area	War Dept Total	Army*	AAF	Navy	Marines
Craftsmen	9.2	7.1	4.7	21.9	2.6
Services	16.6	19.2	14.5	10.9	14.9
Miscellaneous (including aerial)	1.9	—	9.5	—	—
Total	100				

SOURCE: Wool, *Military Specialist*, p. 21.
*Excludes AAF manpower statistics.

The advance of technology and the crisis of war, however, led to further specialization, and the age of the all-around craftsman–type of airplane mechanic was over as the Air Force subdivided expertise into small functional areas. In other words, no one mechanic could repair all aspects of an aircraft's powerplant; nor could an electrician be responsible for repairing all radar, navigation, and communication equipment.

The intricacies of technology also demanded educated and intelligent personnel to man new electronic and advanced technical systems. As a Selective Service System report observed, "The military weapons and equipment of World War II reflected the technological advance of civilization." New weapons and appurtenances required better educated and more skilled people to master them.[112]

From the beginning of the war, the AAF demanded men who scored among the top 36 percent of all those tested. The requirement for skilled technicians, the recognition that few were entering via the draft, and the realizations that thousands would need training at schools in condensed and accelerated courses caused air planners to push for a change in War Department manpower procurement policy.

Procurement policy would fluctuate largely because the Army resented policies that assigned them less educated and lower-scoring personnel. Nevertheless, throughout the war the AAF obtained the largest share of the high-scoring manpower pool from the Army General Classification Test and the Mechanical Aptitude tests.[113] The Air Forces' publicized high mental standards, along with its perceived connection to aviation technology, caused some to see assignment in the Air Forces as a prospect for elite status. Slang terms, like GIs, gobs, and grunts, described the other services, yet nothing derogatory developed for the Air Forces.[114] This caused one scholar to speculate that "the creation of the Army Air Forces in 1941 probably marks the true beginning of the modern-age of military specialization and advanced technol-

Aircraft mechanics service a B–18 engine and propeller (*top*) and other men check propellers (*right*).

ogy, as well as the onset of a change in society's less-exalted view of military life."[115] Although the dating of the modern-age of military specialization is debatable, the point about the elite technological nature of the Air Force (versus the elite status of a military elite like the Marines) and the lack of a derogatory stereotype is well taken.

Besides increased technological specializations centering on aircraft, enlisted personnel concerns began to encompass a new grouping of support personnel that the War Department and Adjutant General previously handled. The integration of Arms and Services with the Army Air Forces (ASWAAF) began during 1943 at the consistent prodding of General Henry H. "Hap" Arnold, and it culminated in all support functions, such as medical, quartermaster, and finance, being transferred to Air Force control.[116] Integration of these support forces and the reorganization of the Air Forces under a General Headquarters Air Force in 1935 were significant steps toward ensuring the AAF's future autonomy.[117] Yet in World War II, it seemed a logical outgrowth of the AAF's desire to control all aspects of the operation.

One problem which air personnel planners immediately faced was assimilating this large body of support personnel into the airman ranks. For one thing, it meant changing the way the air arm manned its units. While the Air Corps was a branch of the Army, its table of organization focused on the aircraft and specialties that maintained them. With the addition of combat support personnel, air planners' views necessarily broadened. Staff officers began to prepare exact manning tables for an entire base rather than narrowly focused tables of organization. Maj. Gen. Hubert Harmon, whose work on development of the exact manning table began in mid-1942, expressed his enthusiasm for this manning procedure borrowed from industry and the Navy:

> I'm sold on the exact manning table idea. I don't believe any industry would or could operate on a Table of Organization system such as we are using now. . . . Pretty nearly every civilian employer knows exactly what the people in his establishment are doing. In the Navy, they have no table of organization for a battleship or cruiser. They put on it the number of men that are needed to man the type of engine on it, to mount the guns, cooks, and KPs to feed that number of men, etc.[118]

Besides developing new manning procedures, air planners needed to reconstruct the image of airmen to include these new categories. This image no longer emphasized the airplane mechanic as the preeminent advisor and guardian of pilot-officers, who were, according to General Arnold's philosophy, only part of a team. Whether mechanic, clerk, aerial gunner, or pilot, men (officers and enlisted) had to work together to ensure the destruction of the Axis menace. In a letter of November 6, 1943, addressed to all AAF personnel regarding the integration of the Arms and Service branches, Arnold reinforced the notion of teamwork. Noting that the AAF would no longer have internal branch distinctions, the general emphasized the importance of building an "efficiently functioning, hard hitting team":

> You are all members of this team whether you pilot the planes, repair the guns, build the airfields, maintain the radios, drive the trucks, handle the supplies, or care for the sick and wounded. Your teamwork in the past has been the basic reason for our outstanding success against the enemy. Your efforts toward greater teamwork in the future will hasten the enemy's defeat and "unconditional surrender."[119]

Air Force public relations officers made sure that articles, advertisements, and even wartime comic books reflected the teamwork theme. When, for example, one paper wanted to run a comic strip showing fighters piloted by a solo pilot, public relations suggested that illustrating bombers would be more appropriate; it would emphasize teamwork.[120]

As the war progressed (post-1943), two consequences of the teamwork concept became evident. First, planners ultimately directed the team image at air crews, and second, this emphasis enhanced air crew morale at the expense of officer-enlisted discipline and overall enlisted morale.[121] Personnel planners were very sensitive to the fact that the loss of a B–17 or B–24 often meant the lives of at least three officers and eight enlisted men. By stressing the analogy of a team, enlisted men were coequals to their officer comrades; they were not factory workers dying at the request of their capitalist superiors. Furthermore, working and fighting as a team was quintessentially American—one did it for America, hometown, family, or the girl left behind. It was like suiting up for the Friday night homecoming game; the entire town came out to support and cheer the team on to victory. The team, while down in the third quarter, would find the stamina and grit to come back and win. It was the power engendered by this image that the Air Force hoped would keep the men flying despite huge losses.[122]

During World War II, air crews replaced ground repair crews as the elite group of enlisted men. Samuel Stouffer, in his work on the American soldier, identified the factors that kept morale high among air crews. Their members were well-educated, young volunteers with high ratings and high intelligence scores. Although the entire enlisted cadre of the Air Forces was conscious of the recognition given the Air Corps, those who were part of an air crew "enjoyed the highest degree of status and prestige."[123] This status and prestige was enhanced by Air Force promotion policy. Foremost was the rapid acceleration of promotions during the expansion and buildup of the Air Forces.[124] "Promotions were so fast before and during World War II," one NCO recorded, "that you had to look at the bulletin board to see what rank you were each month. . . . In my first two years I went from private to master sergeant."[125]

Many benefited from increased promotions, but it was the air crews that rceived the fastest promotions. The Air Force often rewarded them with the highest grades not on the basis of seniority, but rather for performance of technical functions.[126] As one airman explained,

> In aviation units it seemed that more NCOs were in place even though performing duties usually performed by privates. For instance, all career gunners were in the grade of buck sergeant. Once in the combat areas, the engineer and radio men were advanced to staff sergeant. This was true among the officers assigned to the crew, the pilots were advanced from second to first lieutenants.[127]

Fast promotions were not without drawbacks, however. Stouffer found that rapid promotions produced feelings of relative deprivation (this was the origin of that term) because each airman knew of someone else who was being promoted faster than he. In 1943, a change in the Air Forces' enlisted rank structure which enhanced the status of air crews at the expense of other enlisted specialties also increased the growing top-heaviness of the enlisted corps.

Although during the 1920s and 1930s the Air Corps followed the Army's rank structure of seven grades and specialties, the war brought about a change. The AAF amalgamated its mechanic specialties into one seven-grade rating system broken down into occupational categories and subspecialties. This new structure eliminated specialist ratings, provided the basis for occupational groupings and job descriptions, and suggested a career plan for vertical promotions within several occupational classes. Though the Navy had been experimenting with this plan for some time, career planning for enlisted members was new to the Army and the Air Forces.

In 1942, the Army abolished specialist ratings in favor of technician grades. Instead of air mechanics receiving specialty pay, the Air Force now designated such sergeants as aircraft mechanics. This eliminated private first class air mechanics from receiving the pay of a staff or technical sergeants. The Army now distributed pay in seven categories, not in the fifteen possible prior to the change.[128]

This change encouraged a streamlined promotion system. In a step toward centralizing promotions, the amalgamation of rank and specialty allowed a command to delegate promotions based upon a bulk allotment quota rather than on a specific opening on a unit's table of organization.[129]

Finally, perhaps most importantly, the change blurred the distinction between NCO and specialist as the technician grades dissolved the barrier between the identities of a noncommissioned officer who supervised and the technician who worked at his specialty.[130] In a rebuttal to War Department planners who were determined to preserve the distinction between technicians and NCOs, air personnel planners argued that

> it is not believed that such a distinction is necessary since in the majority of organizations in the Army, command functions are clearly defined, are not overlapping, and require no differentiation in command authority as

between equivalent grades of non-commissioned officers assigned to the same type of duty. It has been the experience of the Army Air Forces that it is desirable for the most skilled technicians to exercise the command functions, particularly in the sections of units engaged in servicing and maintenance and in which technicians predominate.[131]

The AAF now expected technicians to progress through the ranks and become shop supervisors, and progressively less technically oriented. The new ranking system was much like the Army's old system without the specialty and mechanic's pay, and it created problems for many technicians who believed that craftsmen should not be burdened with supervisory chores. Many, such as Sergeant Howell, who had come in before the change were angry.

My experience as an NCO was miserable from the start when I was reduced in pay from $84.00 per month as an Air Mechanic 1st to $72.00 when I made staff sergeant! I gained no privileges except I could get married and live off base (with CO permission). I was now subject to a whole raft of NCO type details, always in charge of something (like barracks chief)![132]

The elimination of the specialty pay grades did not ensure the ascendance of quality NCOs. Moreover, the amalgamation seemed to exaggerate the difference between technicians who were technical experts and those who were good NCOs. In a service that depended upon technical skills, some frowned upon NCO duties largely because they found supervisory work taking time away from their areas of expertise. "We ended up with way too many chiefs," Sergeant Howell recalled, "mostly incapable and way too few good technicians because the T.O.E. required NCOs to be assigned NCO duties *as well as Technical Duties*. The NCO duties were always relegated to the 'few' that could handle them."[133]

The merging of skill with supervisor status is subject to several interpretations. First, it could be viewed as an attempt by management to instill the company view within its work force. Second, internal promotion policies could discourage a working-class consciousness from developing, as it could segregate a growing proletariat via specialization and encourage competition for standing in the company. Promotion along job ladders (by skill) not only would differentiate workers by job specialties (thus, making them less likely to support each others causes), but it would increase competition among workers (from the same job specialty) for promotion.[134]

None of these interpretations fits the air planner's view of why the Army system of specialties and grades was amalgamated into a seven-grade rating system. Planners based their decision on two factors—reduced administrative problems (mainly in pay and classification) and the concept that an airman was a technician first and always. As the March 29, 1946, Grade Structure Plan stipulated,

> Enlisted Personnel will not normally be charged with any command responsibility. These personnel will form the body of specially trained and qualified individuals required for actual performance of the many duties incident to the operation of the Air Forces. The principle of increased stature for and monetary compensation commensurate with technical skill and proficiency is here recognized.[135]

The Air Forces based promotion and rank upon technical skills. Promotion was thus a reward for technical expertise and a means to retain qualified personnel.

The results of this new rank/specialty system were twofold. On the one hand, by merging specialty and rank together, the technical aspects of the job took precedence over traditional NCO-command functions, and military authority was diffused. On the other hand, this melding caused a homogenization of diverse skills under an umbrella of traditional military rankings. In the prewar period, for instance, enlisted men were stratified by skill, the work's proximity to the aircraft, and a sharp division between lower enlisted and NCO ranks. During World War II and afterward, enlisted men were stratified by technical function, that is, soft or hard technical skills and, to a lesser extent, by rank. The fusion of an industrial classification and promotion system with the technical requirements of the AAF caused the new ranking system to promote occupational expertise, not military values.

A similar problem existed in the Navy as World War II technology forced an emphasis on occupational skills over traditional military structure. Like the Air Corps, the Navy also stressed rate (or rank) rather than a combination of rate and rating (rank and specialty). This made it difficult to determine who was in charge, except in technical work centers. In short, authority was diffused throughout the enlisted force, perhaps beyond the military's need for authority positions.[136] In other words, as Sergeant Howell pointed out, both the Navy and the Air Corps had too many chiefs and not enough Indians. The diffusion of authority in the Air Forces' rank structure, frozen promotions, dichotomy between supervisor and technician, loss of NCO prestige, and need to design a system to compensate technical skills in the postwar period—all were directly related to these changes in rank and promotion policy.

Arnold's emphasis on teamwork and the new rank and promotion structure favored aircrew morale at the expense of other Air Force enlisted men. It also defined new boundaries between officers and enlisted men. Little communication between officer and enlisted man characterized the interwar Air Corps. The unit's first sergeant mediated most squadron problems.[137] Thus, when General Arnold and Chief of Staff General George C. Marshall toured various air bases in 1943, they were appalled at the lack of discipline. "There is a general lack of proper military courtesy," Arnold furiously complained, "and a . . . lack of good discipline." He also asserted that problems in war-fighting capability were directly related to ground discipline and that junior officers were to blame for the current conditions. They were lax in saluting, uniform regulations, and

General George C. Marshall and Rep. I. Buell Snyder, Chairman of the House Military Appropriations Committee at Camp Beauregard, Louisiana, on April 11, 1941 (*top*). General Junius Jones conferring with a younger officer at Fort Worth, Texas (*center*). Movie actress Bebe Daniels and Lt. Col. Henry H. Arnold at Long Beach, California in October 1932 (*bottom*).

military courtesy. "In many instances," Arnold fumed, "they have been seen associating with enlisted men in bar rooms and other places."[138]

In the midst of formulating fraternization policy, air policymakers received a letter addressed to the Secretary of War from Senator W. Lee O'Daniel, which forced them to reconsider their restrictive thinking.[139] The Senator was furious that the Air Corps promoted a caste system in a civilian army! The Senator wrote:

> It may be well advised that in this time of crisis [that] enlisted personnel are constituted very largely of individuals who are peers of any persons any where, whether those standards be social, moral, intellectual, or commercial. I . . . cannot but resent this attempt to inculcate snobbery by a military elite. . . . If there is a *custom of the service* which confines association between officers and enlisted personnel, to official business, it is bad, not good.[140]

Compounding this problem was the fraternization occurring between male officers and females in the Women's Army Auxiliary Corps.[141] Beginning in early 1942, a combination of political pressure and manpower shortages forced planners to rethink the role of women in the Army. By 1944, more than 120,000 women were in uniform serving in a variety of military jobs including parachute riggers, gunner instructors, aero-photographers, and administration so that men might be free for combat duties.[142] The introduction of women into the military so quickly sent planners scrambling for answers on how to handle relationships between the sexes in a military organization.

Air personnel planners eventually agreed that fraternization policy was complicated by a citizen army, the novelty of women in the Army, and the war.[143] Some planners advocated a new stance on fraternization. "It is suggested," Air Inspector General Maj. Gen. Junius Jones wrote, "that a letter be sent to the major commanders in the United States indicating the difficulty of adhering to the hard and fast rules of peacetime association between enlisted and commissioned officers . . . great care should be exercised to avoid the association between enlisted and commissioned personnel, both male and female, when they are in the same direct chain of command."[144] Though no action was taken to define fraternization policy, the door to enlisted–officer relations outside the workplace and in the direct chain of command was opened. In 1946, the Doolittle Board would again study this issue, producing a bitter and intense debate.[145]

In a letter to the Air Provost Marshal in response to Arnold's inquiry to the Air Forces Training Command at Fort Worth, Texas, in April 1944 regarding military discipline, one old Air Corps pilot-officer aptly described the new Air Force culture emanating from the war. He wrote:

> I feel very strongly that the present situation [poor discipline] has been brought on by the Air Forces themselves. During the period of the Great

Expansion [1936–1943] the idea that an Air Force soldier, or officer, must also be trained as a soldier was not only considered but was disparaged. The publicity given the Air Forces didn't help either. The boys began to believe that the result of the whole conflict was in their hands. I have heard many a young officer quickly raised to responsible rank and position actually express the opinion that the Air Force was a technical branch and above the discipline as known in the "old-fashioned Army." Bomber crews are encouraged to mix; Sunday morning in towns like El Paso will show drunken officers assisted by enlisted men and drunken enlisted men carrying drunken officers. Inquiry proves them members of the same crew given passes together "to build a close-knit organization."[146]

If the mixing of officers and enlistees, and of males and females was troublesome for air planners, so was the introduction of blacks into the AAF. Only in the expansion year of 1939 were blacks admitted into the Air Corps. Before that, there were simply none in the ranks, as the Air Corps required "men of technical and mechanical ability." Influenced by cultural stereotypes, military planners, like most of white America, did not believe blacks capable of retaining technical training.[147] While the AAF accepted some blacks for flight training at the segregated Tuskegee Institute in Alabama, most blacks (never more than 6.1 percent in the AAF), regardless of mental aptitude, found themselves in segregated labor battalions.[148]

Thus, during World War II, the changes in promotion policies, the

Women's Airforce Service Pilots (WASPs) with North American AT–6 trainers at Avenger Field, Sweetwater, Texas, March 9, 1944.

54

emphasis on teamwork at the cost of military discipline, the introduction of minorities, the continued reliance on technological advances, and specialization molded the Air Forces into a more democratic structure. Technological specialization furthered the idea that a person was just one piece in a giant machine. All parts had to work in unison to produce the desired results— victory over Japan and Germany. Promotion policy, while favoring the air crew, affected the entire enlisted corps simultaneously. The results were a preeminence of technicians in traditional authoritarian positions and, ultimately, a subjugation of rank to occupational skill. Add to this the introduction and gradual integration of women and blacks into the Air Forces and a new worldview was constructed from which postwar enlisted policy would be formed.

Is it any wonder why some of the old Army Air Corps could not help reflecting upon the interwar years as a Golden Age of Army aviation? After the war, the institution was never the same. No longer small, isolated, and limited in scope, the postwar Air Force would evolve into a modernized corporate institution complete with a global mission and a vast army of personnel managers developing policy based on a bedrock of assumptions and values instilled during World War I, the interwar period, and World War II. It would remain for postwar society to provide its own set of assumptions and values from which the military would hammer out future enlisted policy—a constellation of values and assumptions that would take into account a reliance on technology and industrial theory.

✦2✦

The Military American:
Personnel Policymaking
1945–1955

WITH THE PASSAGE OF the National Security Act in July 1947, the Army Air Forces dream of independence became a reality. Its separation from the Army that September meant, among other things, that it had to form and codify its own personnel policy. Although some in the Air Force believed policy could be created unfettered by the "barnacled procedures" of the Army, that simply was not the case. The basis for Air Force personnel policy was wedded to its experience as a branch of the Army, membership in the new National Defense Establishment (later, the Department of Defense), and evolving civilian personnel theory and practices of the 1940s and 1950s.[1]

This background of Army experience and the adoption of industrial personnel theory and practices, however, were not the only sources on which personnel planners developed an enlisted personnel policy. A societal context existed as well. Woven deeply into the fabric of American culture was a profound dislike for a large standing peacetime military establishment. From the Revolution through World War II, American society opted for a small military during peacetime and a large mass army raised from the civilian population at the breakout of war.

After World War II, Americans, for the first time in their history, accepted a large, peacetime defense establishment. This change was occasioned when U.S. political leaders asserted that, with the rise of a global communism, the threat of nuclear war, and the development of long-range bombers, the United States would no longer have the luxury of an extended time to mobilize. Rather, the next war would be fast and nuclear and would involve strikes on the American homeland.

Although concerns over the spread of communism and a nuclear war helped solidify support for a large peacetime military, reforms within the military convinced U.S. citizens that a peacetime military establishment was needed to ensure American security. By 1956, changes in the Department of

Defense (DOD) and various service personnel policies and programs made it apparent that the military could serve many purposes. It could teach youth democratic values and discipline as well as serve the public in a business sense—as a place where youth could train for a good job, obtain fair pay and good benefits, and find a career. The Air Force found itself creating and implementing enlisted policy in an era that embraced a new approach toward military manpower— creating policy dedicated to making the military more democratic, more progressive, and more corporate.

Changing Attitudes: Advertising, Standing Armies, and Military Careers

During the war, the Selective Service Act of 1940 was the instrument used to supply the services with sufficient manpower. Congress extended the system in 1945 and 1946, but terminated it in April 1947.[2] Top military officials, such as General Dwight D. Eisenhower, predicted that with the end of the draft, American society entered a "critical juncture" in the development of its military establishment. No precedent existed for manning and governing a large peacetime military. There were "no sign-posts to go by, no experience on which to base sure forecasts," he told his commanding generals in March 1947. What we need, he said, were, "public understanding, public support, and public action." "Americans must understand," he added, "that the Army offers able Americans not only three things every man wants—good pay, a real career, a chance for advancement—but also the honor and dignity which is associated with National service in time of need." What Eisenhower wanted was 30,000 recruits per month, "of high-quality and every one must be a volunteer."[3]

The military, however, found it initially difficult to recruit high-quality volunteers, and eventually petitioned Congress to reinstate the draft in July 1948.[4] Even the Air Force, which attracted more of the middle class into its ranks than the Army did, still was forced to accept many slow learners and unruly recruits. An initial public opinion survey, conducted by a national advertising firm in 1947 at the request of the Army, showed many of the "problems" enlisted in urban areas to escape potential family or community conflicts, while the higher socioeconomic levels joined with a desire to learn, prepare for civilian life, or to make the military a career.[5] The pollsters warned the armed forces that "too large a proportion of such unambitious youth means that there will be an inadequate supply of men who want to make the most of every opportunity and who are eager for positions of responsibility and leadership." Associating moral qualities with socioeconomic levels, the pollsters concluded that lower classes required "considerable supervision," intimating that these classes were lazy and morally inferior.[6]

The survey contended that the biggest problem for the Air Force, and to a lesser extent the Navy, was the inability of the American public to understand what the military did in peacetime, a failing that could cause civilians to frown upon the idea of a large standing peacetime military establishment. Neither did the public look favorably upon the military as a possible lifetime career, as "military positions, whether technician, noncom or officer, do not receive the same status accorded civilian occupations." Middle-class parents, especially those in business and professions, viewed a military career as suitable only for those who could not succeed in civilian life. They were also afraid, the survey report contended, of what "loose morals and evil companions" would do to their sons. Furthermore, these parents believed that service personnel could not have a normal home and family life. "In the face of these attitudes," the public opinion report pessimistically concluded, "it will be difficult to attract able, ambitious boys, especially from the middle class" into the ranks of the military and retain them.[7]

Because the military wanted public support for a standing armed force, it sought advice from adverting agencies to project an image that would attract volunteers and sustain public approval. These commercial advertising specialists proposed a solution to the military's need—create an image of a standing force composed of good, dependable, democratic citizens (the middle class), not the dregs of society (the lower classes). It was reasoned that the public would sustain a standing military if, first, there was a credible threat and if, second, the standing military posed no threat to American society.[8]

At first, the firm of N.W. Ayer and Sons directed an advertising campaign aimed at convincing war-weary veterans that the postwar army and air force "would be greatly unlike their wartime prototype and had genuine benefits and opportunities to offer volunteers."[9] The Ayer firm believed that the attitude of veterans created an antimilitary bias in prospective recruits who needed a new and different outlook on understanding the postwar armed services. In 1947 the Army and the Air Force, after determining that many veterans supported the military, jointly hired Gardner Advertising to shift advertising emphasis from veterans to middle-class parents and youth in order to increase "the prestige of military jobs and careers," and change the attitudes of middle-class parents toward military life.[10]

From 1946 through 1955, the major theme underlying all Army and Air Force public relations and advertising campaigns was that a standing military was necessary and that military service was an "appropriate career."[11] The use of the word *career* seemed to stress the idea that the American military was not an institution to fear; rather it, like other businesses, offered youth a job and a chance for upward mobility. The meaning of *career* has changed over time, but in the 1940s it was coming to denote an accepted occupation rewarded with education, promotion opportunity, good pay, benefits, and a retirement.[12]

Advertising consultants formed a campaign with two distinct phases. From 1946 through 1948 they concentrated their advertising and public relations efforts at the national level and involved all forms of media and institutions. Ayer advisors convinced the four major radio networks to donate time for recruiting programs.[13] The Advertising Council (formerly the War Advertising Council) also volunteered to help by eliciting aid from the National Association of Magazine Publishers and the American Newspaper Publisher's Association. These groups urged their members throughout the country to promote and build the prestige of the Army and the Air Force. Magazines, like *Colliers*, *The Saturday Evening Post*, and *Life*, printed free, full-page advertisements on such topics as "Be an Air Force Specialist" and "Picture a Man Starting His Higher Education [in the Army and Air Force]."[14] By the late 1940s, the Army and Air Force were spending millions of dollars on radio, television, and magazine advertising.

By the middle of 1947 and through the 1950s, some of the largest national organizations, such as the Knights of Columbus, the Veterans of Foreign Wars, and the Sons and Daughters of the American Revolution, actively promoted military service. Many of these groups aided the advertising efforts from a sense of patriotism, fear of another world war, and a desire to support our armed forces during the Cold War.

The American Legion even went as far as developing a mobilization effort and a recruiting plan that called for each Legion post to help actually recruit. With more than eight million members in chapters, lodges, and posts across the country, these organizations gave military recruiting a large national network through their membership and publications. Some organizations extended themselves further not only when they conducted direct mail campaigns, but also when, at the community level, they established permanent recruiting committees to aid Army and Air Force recruiters locally.[15] Although no records detail how successful these amateur recruiters were, they undoubtedly helped foster positive attitudes toward the military by publicizing the need for a large standing force and the benefits youth received from military training.

Once advertisers began to saturate the national market, they concentrated on the second phase of their campaign—local community participation. By September 1947, the Army and Air Force Recruiting Service was avidly encouraging recruiters to become public relations experts, as in "Community Relations Pay Off!" "All recruiters should take an active interest in civic organizations," wrote an editor of the *Recruiting Service Letter*, "by cooperating and assisting these groups you will earn their gratitude and . . . will reward the Army and Air Force Recruiting Service many times over."[16]

Recruiters added training in community relations to their school curriculum.* By December, the Recruiting Service adopted a new public relations program that established a civilian Military Manpower Committee to "marshal, unify and coordinate community support" in each community with a recruiting

---

* For a discussion of the recruiter school curriculum, see Chapter 3.

station.[17] The American Legion, the Eagles, Elks, Kiwanis, and Lions clubs, and the United States Junior Chamber of Commerce all agreed to establish committees and serve as spokesmen for the military in their communities.

Central to this plan was the Community Relations Kit designed by the Recruiting Service and Ayer advertising. In these kits, sent to all recruiting stations and local chapters of consenting national organizations, recruiters enclosed how-to books for setting up committees and preparing speeches and newspaper releases, and a directive from the chief of the Military Personnel Procurement Service to add official sanction.

One guidebook found in the kit directed recruiters to select an important member of the community to head a recruiting committee and train committee members to use the enclosed advertising to publicize America's need for a strong Army and Air Force. Other advertising topics included emphasizing the high-quality opportunities and benefits open to volunteers, achievements of local men in the services, and the benefits of the Army and Air Force to the community itself.[18] The recruiter's message to the local community was clear: National security needs strong armed forces; the military offers pay and benefits, just like a civilian job; and the military is really part of the community because not only does it bolster the local economy, its service personnel are neighbors as well as the community's sons and daughters.

Making the Military American: The Doolittle Board and the Framework for Postwar Reform

Although advertisers, recruiters, and community associations attempted to convince the public that working in the modern military was similar to employment in a middle-class career and that it could benefit youth, reforms within the military also helped Americans see the armed forces in a new light. By 1955, the armed forces began to resemble an institution patterned after society's democratic heritage.

Much of the impetus for these reforms came when veterans, immediately after returning from the war in 1945 and 1946, complained that the military was far from being an American (democratic) institution. They argued that a caste system of enlisted men whose personal liberty was controlled by a small group of officer-elites resembled more a totalitarian institution than one governed by a democracy.

On March 27, 1946, The Officer and Enlisted Man's Relationship Board met in the International Brotherhood of Electrical Worker's Building in Washington, D.C., at the request of Secretary of War Robert P. Patterson to address veterans' complaints.[19] The board, nicknamed the Doolittle Board after its chairman, former AAF Lt. Gen. James H. Doolittle, sought "a way to make the Army more compatible with a democratic nation."[20] "During this postwar phase [of an interim Army]," the board's report read:

> Note must be taken of changing concepts, social unrest, a transitional
> period in which thinking is directed toward the perfection of democratic
> processes, with greater emphasis on human relations, security, the dignity
> of the individual—all the result of the great war years and many of the
> factors, i.e., greater education of the masses, greater world-wide dissemi-
> nation of information, increased speed of transportation, geographical
> dislocation of peoples, etc.[21]

The board, which consisted of three ex-officers and three ex-enlisted men,
met for two months, interviewed forty-two servicemen, and read more than a
thousand letters from officers and enlisted personnel.[22] Discussions surrounded
promotion, quarters, pay, segregation, enlisted men's rights, fraternization,
custom and courtesies, venereal disease, wives' clubs, dating, and chaplains.[23]
The final report, signed by Secretary Patterson, condemned the undemocratic
"Prussian" holdovers of social distinction in the American Army and demanded
changes.[24]

Besides condemning the caste system, the report also sketched the
framework for postwar military reform. On a practical level, these suggested
reforms connected pay scales in industry to military pay; reinforced the concept
that promotion should be based on merit, not seniority; specified the need for
a codified set of grievance procedures and a manual of enlisted men's rights;

Lt. James H. Doolittle stands on the pontoon of his Curtiss Racer after winning the
Schneider Cup Race in Baltimore, Maryland, in October 1925.

and advocated that all off-duty military personnel be free to "pursue normal social patterns comparable to our democratic ways of life."[25]

Furthermore, the board encouraged military personnel to live "in civilian communities, rather than on Army posts" so as not to "divorce military personnel from [a] civilian outlook."[26] On an ideological level, some of the recommended reforms were aimed at justice, social leveling, racial and gender integration, and morality. The committee suggested an overhaul of the military justice system including giving enlisted men the right to sit on court-martial boards. The board also criticized the segregation of blacks and urged an acceleration of the Gillem Board's recommendations.[27]

Finally, the Doolittle Board recommended that service in the military should improve "character, knowledge, and the competency of those serving."[28] Though the board had no legislative power, within the next five years most of its recommendations were acted upon. By 1950, a new Uniform Code of Military Justice replaced the old Articles of War.[29] The new code standardized penalties imposed by commanders and court-martial boards, placed enlisted men on courts, and introduced the Bad Conduct Discharge in lieu of the Dishonorable Discharge for some offenses.[30] Other committees reviewed racial and gender discrimination and called for the "highest standards of democracy [through ensuring] equality of treatment and opportunity" in the Armed Forces.[31] In 1948, Executive Order 9981, which in effect ordered the military to desegregate, put the military on the path toward ending segregation, while Congress established the legal basis for women in the military.[32] Neither action ended discrimination, but the executive order and legislation were the beginning of controlled change.

The Hook Committee studied pay and allowances in 1947 and 1948.[33] Named after the President of American Rolling Mills, Charles R. Hook, the DOD joint military-civilian group reviewed life insurance, retirement, survivor benefits, tax exemptions, post exchanges, and various forms of pay. The Career Compensation Act of 1949 (PL 81-351, 63 Stat. 802) incorporated many of the committee's recommendations. The act provided an 18.8 percent total pay raise and revamped an outdated compensation system.[34] Pay and allowances were factored to reflect industrial wages and were then tied to a service person's pay grade and length of service.[35] Special pays, such as flight pay, hazardous duty pay, and foreign duty pay, were then added to the basic pay, as were the two most important nontaxable allowances, those for quarters and subsistence (food). Other financial remunerations established by the act included changes in hazardous duty pay, survivor benefits, retirement, and reenlistment bonuses.

Several committees continued to scrutinize pay and benefits in the 1950s. The Womble Committee in 1952* and the Cordiner Committee in 1957 followed along the lines established by the Doolittle Board, the Hook

---

* See Chapter 5 for more discussion.

Committee, and the 1949 legislation.[36] The Womble and Cordiner Committees, like the Hook Committee, suggested legislation that would make a career in the military more attractive, namely, with increased retirement benefits, medical care for dependents, various reenlistment and proficiency pay incentives, and promotion based on merit.[37]

The Military as Employer and Labor Force: An Analogy For Reform

Changes in the military compensation structure pointed up some of the growing similarities between enlisted personnel in the Armed Forces and the civilian labor force.[38] What made the military's compensation system germane to workers in the period 1946–1950 was that in many industries, such as steel, auto, meat-packing, rubber, and electronics, a series of collective bargaining rounds hammered out wage patterns and social welfare programs.

Many employers adopted the results of these bargaining sessions by adding new pensions, health benefits, and supplemental unemployment payment packages to their company's personnel policies. Thus, union leaders and workers would be very familiar with the contents of various compensation packages and could look at the military as a progressive employer offering its employees good benefits. Moreover, civilian workers could read about the military compensation system and compare it with their own situations.[39] The military apparently compensated its personnel for the hardships caused by service life with fair wages and good benefits which included a twenty-year retirement.[40]

The military twenty-year retirement provision paid better than many companies' retirement plans.[41] In 1945, Congress authorized voluntary retirement to Army enlisted personnel after twenty years of active service and, within three years after World War II, all military branches adopted the twenty-year retirement as legislated in the Army and Air Force Vitalization and Retirement Equalization Act of 1948 (Title 62, U.S. Statute 1081, 1948). Pension plans became a major factor in labor relations after World War II when their tax status was clarified and wages were stabilized via regulations. Heated negotiations by the steel, coal, and auto industries during this time influenced all the major features of pension plans—financing, benefit formulas, eligibility requirements, retirement policies, and vesting policies.

Although it is debatable whether military pensions paid more than industrial pensions, soldiers did not directly contribute to a retirement fund. According to one survey, the proportion of contributory plans increased from less than one-half of all company retirement plans before the war to nearly two-thirds in 1949 before falling dramatically in the 1950s. Eligibility for retirement benefits varied from about twenty or thirty years' service in most industries. In addition, many workers worked twenty years, retired, and then waited till age sixty-two to collect benefits. Congress based military retirement on the concept that it was a transitional payment for those entering civilian life and would help to offset the presumably lower wages received by those entering a second career. Hence, military retirees collected immediately upon retirement.[42]

Additionally, few employers gave special pay or compensated workers with food and quarters allowances. Though food and housing allowances were not specifically paid, industry did offer additional pay for overtime and shift premiums whereas the military did not. Other contrasts are important. In 1949, an E–4 airman on flying status and married was typically less than twenty-four years old and had more than four years of service. Including base pay and allowances for quarters and food, he received approximately $3,135.00 yearly, of which 49 percent was not taxable. The median income for American families with the head of household under thirty-five years of age in 1949 was $2,998.00 (after taxes).[43]

Besides pay and allowances for quarters, subsistence, and hazardous duties, enlisted personnel also received other benefits: money for military clothing; a death gratuity; enlistment and reenlistment bonuses; overseas allowances; disability pay; group life insurance; free medical, post exchange, and commissary privileges; and thirty days of paid annual leave. By 1956, Congress extended medical benefits to dependents and a dislocation allowance for personnel moving from base to base.

Finally, if military personnel had a tough time obtaining housing, it was no different from many young workers in postwar America.[44] At least the government in the guise of Congress and the military was doing something about it, for the armed services offered pay and benefits that labor unions fought hard to obtain in the immediate postwar era.[45] In fact, the military was promoting itself to service personnel as a good employer that offered soldiers "substantial opportunity for improvement" and good working conditions.[46] During the Cold War period, the military had become analogous to a corporate system, which Americans understood: it was a big business that compensated its workers well.[47] Of course, the more the military reflected something familiar to most Americans, the more acceptable it became as an institution.

An Image of Reform: The Military as a Big Business, The Air Force as a Test Case

Although the analogy of the military as a big business originated at the close of the nineteenth century, the concept received new impetus in the postwar era as civilian and military leaders attempted to make the military more efficient, economical, and understandable by the general public.[48] In 1945, for instance, Secretary of War for Air Robert A. Lovett congratulated General Hap Arnold for the outstanding progress the AAF had made in adapting business principles to the needs of the war.[49] In peacetime, Lovett cautioned the general, dollars were tight, and only through using "the best possible business management practices" could the AAF ensure an efficient and economical force. Arguing for an elaborate financial "comptroller" system, Lovett stressed that the AAF was rapidly becoming a "big business," which demanded corporate budgetary systems.[50]

By 1946, the AAF's new commanding general, Carl A. Spaatz appointed Maj. Gen. Hugh J. Knerr, who shared Lovett's view that the AAF was big business, to head the newly formed Air Board. Spaatz commissioned the board to formulate and recommend AAF policy and to propose an organizational structure. Members of the board, according to Knerr, "actually occupied the status of vice presidents with specialties . . . [and] function as a Board of Directors." The business analogy was evident in the board's proceedings as members often referred to directing the Air Force as "running a major corporation."[51]

Air leaders made several sweeping reforms designed to make the service efficient, scientifically managed, and economical. The Air Force's first secretary, W. Stuart Symington, a former president of Emerson Electric, initiated many of these reforms.[52] The new secretary consistently said that the Air Force was one of the world's largest businesses and that its most important function was to "get maximum efficiency for the taxpayers' dollar through the establishment of modern business procedures."[53]

In an address to the Aviation Post of the American Legion in New York City on November 11, 1947, Symington proudly listed the management reforms underway. First, the Air Staff, like Emerson Electric, consolidated a headquarters organization and streamlined it for the "efficient use of time, effort, and money; and the elimination of too elongated communication channels and red tape."[54] Second, air leaders instituted a program of cost control, which according to Symington, he designed to "bring the long-established efficiency techniques of the business world into the realm of military operations." In Symington's mind, to instill cost control in the military, one had to find a substitute for the profit motive.[55] Thus, in order to tie senior Air Force officers to a market economy system of rewards for efficient production, he pushed for changes in the officer efficiency rating report. "We now believe we found it [the substitute for the profit motive]," Symington declared, "Henceforth, the Air Force commanders will be rated twice each year—not only on military ability, but also on business and managerial ability."[56]

Several changes in personnel policy encouraged military leaders to view themselves as business managers. In order to bring the military more in line with industrial promotion procedures, the Officer Personnel Act of 1947 sought to streamline the officer promotion system by basing advancement on merit, not seniority.[57] Since officers now had to compete for promotions and subsequent

Secretary of War for Air Robert A. Lovett visits Ellington Field, Texas, with Maj. Gen. Henry H. Arnold (*far right*), July 31, 1941.

pay increases, "officers in the future" according to the Air Force Secretary, "will have an additional incentive for getting the most out of the money entrusted to them."[58] If Symington found a substitute for the "profit motive," he also found one for the "business world's spur to successful operation—competition." Symington required all commanding generals of the various commands to submit to the Chief of Staff's office a monthly "Cost of Operations Statement." The newly formed Air Comptroller then analyzed and compared commands for fluctuations and efficient, economical operations.[59] Financial and management experts promptly investigated deviations.

Beginning in 1947, the Army and Air Force adopted business management courses and taught them to officers and NCOs.[60] The Air Force added special courses in business management, cost accounting, and personnel management to the Air University's curriculum.[61] In early 1948, Carl Spaatz decreed in a letter to all commands that "one of the fundamental policies of the Department of the Air Force is to conduct all of its operations with business efficiency [and] all levels of the Air Force must get management training."[62] Initially, a management instructor course was established at Craig Air Force Base, Alabama, and those sent to the course from the various commands were to return to their individual bases and establish similar courses. By late 1948,

Foundation of the Force

Secretary of the Air Force W. Stuart Symington is seen in the top photo addressing the press during American Legion Day in 1949 at San Bernardino AFB, California. At his retirement ceremony (*bottom*) on April 24, 1950, Secretary Symington is flanked by Secretary of Defense Louis Johnson on his right and General Hoyt S. Vandenberg on his left.

management courses in each command were flourishing.[63]

Likewise, planners believed that courses in personnel management were needed "to put order and science into military policies." As one *Air Force Times* article elaborated, "During the war, business and industrial managers entered the military and gave the military something totally lacking before the war—a composite picture of industrial personnel practices as applied to industries of scale."[64] In 1947 twenty-five Army and ten Air Force officers attended the business schools of Harvard, Stanford, and Columbia Universities and the Wharton School of the University of Pennsylvania for postgraduate studies in business and personnel management.[65] Following their course work, the Air Force sent each officer to one of six major American businesses for on-the-job training: Standard Oil Company, Douglas Aircraft, General Electric, General Foods, Ford Motor Company, and General Motors.[66] After training, the officers were assigned to service schools and command headquarters to teach and formulate management and personnel policy.[67] The policy of sending officers to business school continued through the 1950s so that those trained would become "a common denominator for both the military and business."[68]

In 1950, the Air Force also established Education with Industry, a program devised to encourage two-way exchanges between the corporate and military systems. During the course of their studies, Air Force students learned more about procurement and industrial mobilization while their civilian counterparts learned about military needs and systems. According to one source, top air leaders deemed the cooperative venture a success. They saw it as "a practical program at the operational and management levels which produced competent executives and specialists to handle similar operational and management problems in the Air Force."[69]

In subsequent years, largely because of its increasing dependence on advanced technology, the Air Force relied heavily on civilian methods and practices, and civilian administrators and military leaders forced the service to change. Officers and noncommissioned officers, henceforth, became managers who applied scientific methods and business skills to military problems. For the public, however, the fact that the military began to talk in terms of business management made the armed forces more understandable and undoubtedly less ominous. By making the military analogous to large businesses complete with a profit motive, competition, and scientific efficiency, the military seemed more corporate, more American, more familiar.

Combating the Great Fear: Containing Communism and Winning the War of Ideas

Perhaps the increasing emphasis that the national leadership gave to the communist threat was even more fundamental than advertising, internal

Foundation of the Force

President Harry S. Truman and General of the Army Dwight D. Eisenhower, Supreme Allied Commander, Europe, are pictured here together in January 1951.

military reform, and the big business analogy had been to the populace's acceptance of a peacetime standing military as a new American tradition. Communist attempts to seize control in Greece and Turkey in 1947 led to the Truman administration espousing a commitment toward containing communism globally.[70] Soviet incursions into Czechoslovakia and Berlin in 1948, the fall of China to communist forces under Mao Zedong in 1949, and the invasion of South Korea by North Korean communist forces in 1950 made it readily apparent to many Americans that the United States was losing out in a worldwide struggle to contain and preserve democratic institutions.[71] The explosion of the first Soviet atomic weapon in 1949 exposed America's potential vulnerability to strategic attack. Americans who saw the United States as the preeminent world power after World War II found communist gains very disillusioning.[72] Countries seemed to fall like dominos to communist aggressors worldwide.

Some of the disillusionment in the nation's evident loss of international influence could be attributed, in part, to American success in World War II, success that had strengthened belief in the Wilsonian idea that the United States could order the world. After World War I, the Wilson administration was powerless to effect significant changes in the world political order. After World War II, however, the United States was *the* preeminent power. Also contributing to American hegemony were the emergence of nuclear weapons, a superior production capability, and the Marshall Plan. At no time between October 1945 and November 1956 did public support in favor of the United States involvement in world affairs drop below 69 percent.[73]

Even beyond communist gains and nuclear capability, many feared that

70

Americans could not withstand the pressures of ideological warfare. As early as 1945, military leaders such as Omar N. Bradley, Henry H. Arnold, and Carl A. Spaatz warned the nation about young soldiers returning from World War II and becoming vulnerable to subversive ideologies. When 500 businessmen and civic leaders attended an AAF conference on the veteran problem, Spaatz told them that thousands of "young and susceptible" veterans who "have a lot political power and interests in common" were coming home. They will listen, he added, "to those who promise to remedy their real or imagined wrongs . . . discontented youth makes [*sic*] troubled waters." Alluding to Adolf Hitler and the German youth, Spaatz admonished, "When 'the man on the white horse' comes forward in such a situation, things begin to happen as they happened in Germany. . . . Hitler rose to power on the back of youth. . . . It can't happen here because we are going to take steps with the lessons of Europe in mind."[74] The lessons of Europe soon lent analogies to Stalin and the growing communist encroachment. There would be no more Munichs, no more Pearl Harbors, and no ideological subversion.

Americans easily translated fascism under Hitler into communism under Stalin.[75] President Harry S. Truman in 1947 eloquently summed up a very

Carl A. Spaatz as a second lieutenant in 1916 (*left*) and as a lieutenant general in 1944.

71

simplistic view of competing ideologies. Lumping all totalitarian regimes into one class, the President argued before a joint session of Congress that "nearly every nation must chose between alternative ways of life. . . . One way of life is based upon the will of the majority, and is distinguished by free institutions, representative government, free elections, guarantees of individual liberty, freedom of speech and religion, and freedom from political oppression. . . . The second way [is based] upon the will of a minority forcibly imposed upon the majority."[76] On another occasion, Truman was less subtle. "There isn't any differences in totalitarian states," he declared, "I don't care that you call them Nazi, Communist, or Fascist."[77] Americans could reduce fascism, nazism, or communism to moral terms—it was simply a question of supporting either the Lord or the Devil.

During the Cold War when Americans perceived foreign policy failures, they saw the problem due not so much to their democratic system as to the weakness of individuals to succumb to communist ideology.[78] "I have in my hand fifty-seven cases of individuals [in the State Department]," Joseph McCarthy, the junior senator from Wisconsin claimed to a fearful public on 9 February 1950, "who would appear to be either card-carrying members or certainly loyal to the Communist Party, but who nevertheless are helping to shape our foreign policies."[79] The ideological weakness of some was subverting America's vision of its preeminence. When some prisoners of war proved susceptible to Chinese brainwashing during the Korean war, Americans were shocked. In the clash of ideologies, the United States appeared to take a distant second place.

The fear of alien subversion was not new in the United States. The Alien and Sedition Acts of 1798, the anti-Masonic party, the persecution of the Mormons and Catholics, the fear of urban immigrants, and the Red Scares shortly after World War I and World War II all spoke to a fear of societal upheaval, ideological subversion, and, as one scholar put it, a "pestilence of the mind."[80] To combat ideological warfare, some people, in the late 1940s, suggested that the military should become a training ground for developing character, instilling moral values, and teaching the responsibilities of democratic citizenship. By making youth morally strong, the assumption was that they could withstand the influence of a godless communism and become productive members of American (i.e., middle-class) society.

The idea of using the military to Americanize youth was not new. Associations such as the YMCA had been attempting to teach character development and Protestant religiosity to middle-class youth and immigrants even before the Civil War.[81] In 1910, the Boy Scouts of America sought to prepare young men to enter the American middle classes by teaching character development and instilling American values.[82] The urge to nationalize this type of training exhibited itself in the Universal Military Training (UMT) movement in 1916.

After the war started in Europe in 1914, some social reformers known as progressives hoped that the campaign for national preparedness and UMT would encourage "moral virtue" and "civic purity" in the military and society. Military progressives, such as Secretary of War Newton D. Baker and Army Lt. Col. John McAuley Palmer advocated restructuring military institutions to incorporate social reforms and citizenship training.[83] Pushing for a plan of UMT for all young men, they believed the army could become a school for citizen soldiers and a builder of good character. Military training and a tour in the reserves would teach citizenship, self-discipline, a skilled trade, and morality and would serve as a great Americanizer for the nation's increasing immigrant population. As former Army Chief of Staff Leonard Wood explained:

> The man comes out of the training camp . . . better physically. He comes out with a better coordinated mind and muscle; he had learned habits of promptness, personal neatness, respect for authority, respect for the law, respect for the rights of other people; he has learned to do things when he is told and as told and to do them with promptness and exactness. . . . I think it [UMT] is one of the strongest forces for Americanization we have.[84]

The initial UMT movement failed in the wake of World War I, but social reforms in the military continued during the war and into the 1920s.

A good example of the influence social reformers had on the military was the Commission on Training Camp Activities (CTCA), which was established early in World War I to entertain servicemen and protect them from the "evils of sin."[85] President Wilson appointed Raymond Fosdick, a former settlement worker and expert of European and American police systems as chairman of the commission. The group also included experts from several progressive associations including the YMCA, the Playground Association, and various social work agencies. On many Army and Navy bases, commission members established community singing, baseball, post exchanges, and theaters, and provided university extension lectures to educate and promote the good character development of soldiers.

The CTCA also initiated crusades against alcohol and prostitution. The Military Draft Act prohibited the sale of liquor to soldiers and gave the president the power to establish zones around all military bases to ensure that an area was free of alcohol and prostitutes. As the commission, with the support of the Wilson administration, went about "wiping out sin," or at least making it inaccessible to servicemen, the Army adopted the motto, "Fit to Fight." In what one official called "the cleanest army since Cromwell's day," young men were exhorted to "live straight to shoot straight."[86] Perhaps put a little more crudely, "a man who is thinking below the belt," one CTCA syllabus warned, "is simply not efficient."[87]

Foundation of the Force

Films made by the commission like *Fit to Fight* and *End of the Road* taught soldiers and women who lived near military bases that promiscuity was painful (due to venereal disease) and tragic, for "loose living" inevitably brought ruin to a young person's life.[88] About the Army's campaign to strengthen the character of its soldiers during the war, the progressive Secretary of War, Newton D. Baker, told the American public he wanted soldiers embarking for France to have an invisible armor "made up of a set of social habits replacing those of their homes and communities."[89] In actuality, the Army found that alcohol and sex were difficult to regulate in France and during war; some soldiers simply ignored the rules.[90]

America's disillusionment with the outcome of the First World War and its subsequent retreat into isolationism, combined with national financial setbacks and a Red Scare, subverted any reformer's hope for further using the military in the 1920s as an agent for social change.[91] Even during the depression years of the 1930s and the establishment of a successful variant of UMT (the Civilian Conservation Corps), the interwar Army remained small and continued to be viewed warily by a citizenry conditioned to believe that a standing military was un-American.

Nevertheless, in the aftermath of World War II, many of the same reform programs defeated after World War I found fertile ground in new debates over UMT, the communist threat, a large peacetime army, and conscription.[92] Reformers argued that, in a war against an ideology such as communism, it was not enough to have a strong defense force when the moral and democratic traditions of the country were at risk. American peacetime armed forces during the 1950s would have to serve other purposes once relegated to local community associations, schools, and civilian programs, such as teaching youth character development and middle-class values.

Some reformers, like James Hannah of Michigan State University, feared that educational reforms had failed to produce Americans grounded in democratic values and moral limits because such attempts had proved sporadic and ill-conceived. If local communities could not provide the necessary education, Hannah argued, then there must be a national means to ensure an educated democratic public. "Teaching such fundamentals," Hannah pleaded, "should be done at home and in school but it is not being done and the services provide the 'last chance' for society to do the job. . . . [Without such training] there is no assurance that our country will come out right in the end."[93]

Arguments for UMT in 1947 and 1948 addressed many of these ideological issues. Although military leaders like Eisenhower and Marshall saw UMT as a means to augment the traditionally small military with a large reserve, others argued for UMT's capability to instill morality and democratic ideals. A large unified armed service under a peacetime draft could act as a national educator of democratic virtue.

Defense planners and policymakers well understood that for a large defense

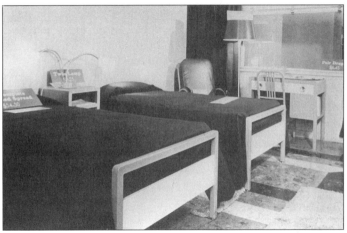

Religious opportunities included confirmation ceremonies at Keesler AFB (*top*). Modern barracks provided airmen with spacious, comfortable living environments (*center*). Libraries and service clubs afforded easily available recreational opportunities (*bottom*).

75

establishment to exist during peacetime, fundamental changes were needed to ensure against the traditional fears and distrust of powerful military forces. Wedding progressive rhetoric about using the military to instill democratic and moral values in youth to the idea that the Cold War demanded a larger peacetime military helped convince the public that Americans did not need to fear a standing force composed of sons and daughters so trained. "One good way to insure ourselves [American society] against such a catastrophe [military takeover]," the President's Committee on Religion and Welfare in the Armed Forces admonished, "is to strengthen good citizenship in every military man, and to preserve within the military as much of his civilian life as possible."[94]

President Truman, who favored the moral and democratizing dimensions of UMT since his days as an officer in the Army reserves during the 1920s, appointed this committee in 1948 to study education, religion, community relations, leisure, and housing. Chaired by the president of the National Social Welfare Assembly, Frank L. Weil, the ten-person committee was comprised of educators, clergymen, and civic leaders who believed, like Truman and Weil, that the peacetime military forces would shape the future "mental, moral, and social outlook" of an unprecedented number of American males.[95]

"The National Military Establishment," Stephen Early, the Under-Secretary of Defense, told a national audience of community leaders and members of the

Assistant Secretary (later Under Secretary) of Defense, Stephen Early.

presidential committee, "has become the greatest single educational force in the country. . . . We must make certain that these young men return to their homes better and more useful citizens, strengthened by self-discipline and fortified in the democratic faith."[96] The social reform ideology of the progressive era found a new home in the post–World War II military.

The committee supposedly acted in an advisory capacity only. Yet, because of the attention Truman placed on its reports, many in the DOD felt pressure from the Weil group for significant social reforms. A perusal of the list of participants demonstrates the high-level attention that this committee and its task received. At one committee conference on community participation in the military, speakers included President Truman; Robert Bondy, Director, National Social Welfare Assembly; Eduard Lindeman, New York School of Social Work, Columbia University; Harvey Firestone, President, United Service Organization (USO); Jane Hoey, Director, Bureau of Public Assistance, Social Security Administration; William Nelson, Dean, School of Religion, Howard University; and Solomon Freehof, Chairman, Division of Religious Activities, National Jewish Welfare Board.[97] Moreover, the fact that military leaders recognized the need for democratizing a peacetime armed services and training youth in American values immensely helped the adoption of many of the committee's recommendations.[98]

Teaching Youth the American Way: Political Indoctrination and The Military's Information and Education Program

One of the most important reports of the Weil committee, which appeared in December 1949, examined the status of the information and education (I&E) programs in the military.[99] Designed to help stimulate morale, the Army's first formal political indoctrination program began in 1941. Much of its literature targeted the draftee who wondered why he was fighting, where he fit into the national picture, and what exactly his purpose was as a soldier. Films like the *Why We Fight* series and other media like *The Yank* magazine and *Stars and Stripes* newspaper or radio shows and posters explained the urgency and necessity of the war.[100] Local information hours were also held in which commanders updated their soldiers on the progress of the war.

By August 1945, military educators added educational and vocational correspondence courses to the program and centralized its administration under the United States Armed Forces Institute (USAFI) at Madison, Wisconsin.[101] Unlike the I&E program, USAFI was not intended as a source of indoctrination; it offered remedial training in reading and writing, and later expanded into technical and college course work.[102] In the immediate postwar period, the I&E units not only continued to inform soldiers on topics such as the United Nations, the Marshall Plan, and the Truman Doctrine, they also began to emphasize the benefits of remaining in the service as a career.[103]

By 1949, the implication of marrying indoctrination and education was clear to policymakers. Such programs were "based on the premise that a soldier, seaman, or airman can serve his country with maximum effectiveness only if he understands his responsibilities as a citizen."[104] "But information and knowledge," Weil's committee pointed out, "may be meaningless unless they are related to the ideals and principles by which we live and for which we may be forced to fight. . . . Democracy and the democratic way of life remain but philosophies until they are put into practice."[105]

Hence, all I&E in the military should have one overriding purpose—to make personnel better citizens impervious to the attack of conflicting ideologies. "The mind of the individual fighting man," the committee argued, "will become of supreme importance in developing and utilizing the weapons of an advanced technology, [and] also in the use of ideas as weapons . . . . The so-called 'cold war' in which we are presently engaged is already, in substance, a war of ideas."[106] The Soviet Union, likened to its Nazi counterpart by the Weil group, "is a nation which has far excelled others in the perversion of ideas and has utilized these perverted ideas to an unsurpassed degree."[107]

The Weil Committee's challenge to the DOD was "to significantly strengthen the information and education programs as [the committee's challenge] was no less serious than the challenge presented to the whole American people by the current world conflict in the field of ideas."[108] The implication was clear: a democratic army made good citizens, and an army comprised of good citizens was not to be feared; it would be a bastion of ideological strength. The Cold War would be won or lost, if not on the battlefield, then in the minds of the opposing forces. In July 1949, the DOD took control of the Army program and began actively to administer the indoctrination program for all the services.[109]

By 1951, the primary emphasis of the I&E program shifted from the World War II focus on morale toward the theme of anticommunism. The Armed Forces Radio network broadcast a number of shows such as "The Traitor," "The Pledge," and "No Other Way" which described what the various facets of American life would be like if the communists took over. The 1951 training film *Face to Face with Communism* portrayed an Air Force sergeant returning to his hometown on leave only to find it controlled by "commies." Defined by the film's narrator as a "realistic presentation of life in this country under communism," the sergeant was relieved to find finally that the whole event was staged by the community to "show what could happen."[110]

It is easy to overstate the degree to which the military actually embraced the mission of ideological indoctrination. Yet it is really not important to the argument here whether the military did or did not fervently embrace this type of indoctrination.[111] Rather the military, through its information program, appeared to Americans to be teaching youth the foundations of being good, democratic citizens. This image of being the grand Americanizer went a long way in helping society embrace a large peacetime defense establishment. Thus the armed forces may not have liked the job of indoctrination, but they enhanced their image by appearing to do so. Such political indoctrination continued well into the 1960s when the emphasis shifted to domestic issues, including race, gender, and ethnic equality.

Teaching Youth Middle-Class Values: Virtue, Morality, and the Military's Character Development Program

Closely related to the war of ideas and political indoctrination was the belief that immorality and godlessness also substantially subverted democratic ideals. "The fundamental principles which give our democratic ideas their intellectual and emotional vigor," one committee report on the military chaplaincy read, "are rooted in the religions that give our democratic faith a very large measure of its strength."[112] As communism "utterly rejected" moral law and individual liberty, religious faith represented the "antithesis" of Marxist-Leninist thought. The report concluded that "a program of adequate religious opportunities for service personnel provides an essential way for strengthening their fundamental beliefs in democracy and, therefore, strengthening their effectiveness as an instrument of our democratic form of government."[113]

Military leaders and recruiters recognized early in the twentieth century that it was necessary to convince family and friends, as well as potential recruits, that the service would provide a moral environment that strengthened a young person's character during their son's or daughter's term of service. Just as it had during the years before and during World War I, the idea that the military should provide a moral environment and develop strong character assumed new life in the postwar period.

"The mother whose son is drafted into the military service," the Weil committee's report on the uses of leisure time in the service explained, "will be far better satisfied if she believes her son has wholesome surroundings and that he will be given an opportunity to improve himself and to return to civilian life a better man than when he left it."[114] One way to do that, the committee reasoned, was to establish strong military-sponsored religious programs and to broaden the responsibility of the chaplain corps.[115]

Another way to reassure parents about military service was for the institutions to establish wholesome programs to prevent character deterioration and actively promote character growth.[116] Character-building programs, similar to those established by the CTCA during World War I, now served to reassure parents that the military would be a place of moral training and high-mindedness. Since the stories Americans heard from their friends and relatives in the service would, the Weil Committee contended, "inevitably condition [their] thinking" about military life, the armed forces needed to provide programs that countered the traditional view of soldiers' and sailors' gambling, swearing, and promiscuous behavior.[117]

Successful recruiting by the armed forces depended on how well the public recieved this new democratic and moral image. As in the World War I venereal disease program, military and civilian policymakers reframed the new program to reflect moral content and promote character building. "We have totally rejected the old view that it was not the duty of the Army to chaperon its members," Secretary of the Army Kenneth C. Royall told one civilian audience in 1948. Sounding like a World War I social reformer, the secretary continued, "A man to whom the moral appeal is successful is valuable to the Army not only because he avoids VD [venereal disease], but we have learned that men of character are the best soldiers."[118]

While most soldiers during World War II viewed anti-VD films, little was done in the way of preventative moral training. The new drug, penicillin, was relied on to minimize the threat of VD. It was in the postwar period that civilian and armed forces leaders promoted the military's new role as moral teacher.

Military leaders established new VD programs that emphasized moral education rather than mechanical prevention. Instead of issuing condoms or treating soldiers with penicillin after the fact, as was done in World War II, by 1947 the services began to stress self-discipline and continence to avoid infection. "Continence," one Army report read, "is stressed as the only logical, moral, psychologically, and physically sound basis for the prevention of venereal diseases."[119]

World War II VD lecture films were recalled in 1948 and replaced with a series of films based upon the moral approach. *The Miracle of Birth*, first in the series, received high praise from church, medical, and women's groups. The film focused on the need for each person to develop self-control and moral responsibility—"principles which tend to insure personal happiness, the sanctity of marriage, and the security of home."[120]

Other teachings argued against sexual promiscuity as a token of personal prowess and protested that drugs such as penicillin were anything but infallible cures for venereal disease. Moreover, base commanders were given explicit instructions to court-martial sex offenders and restrict personnel who contracted VD. The Armed Forces Discipline Control Board, in league with other civilian and military personnel, and like the CTCA of World War I, targeted areas of prostitution and placed them off limits or closed them as their World War I counterparts had done. By early 1948, the Army boasted a 40 percent decline in VD.[121] Unfortunately, the report failed to cite the type of data used to derive this statistic.

The Weil Committee, also like the World War I CTCA, deemed "character building" programs as "indispensable" and took similar steps to eradicate vice.[122] As young men were susceptible to "getting into [moral] trouble," planners created an extensive leisure-time program. Suggested plans included comfortable barracks with showers, day rooms for writing letters and playing games, post exchanges with snack bars, base theaters, transportation to town, and athletic programs. Other essential character and morale building programs advocated by the presidential committee were service clubs for parties, lectures, and entertainment; community relations programs such as the USO; the library and hobby shop; and the serviceman's council.[123]

Finally, the Weil Committee encouraged marriage, family life, and better housing. Professional officers and NCOs, most of whom were married, were crucial for training and educating recruits. The poor living conditions then available, however, convinced too many of the invaluable cadre to leave the service. "Our war experiences, our urban slums, and the present lack of homes for the military," one social worker counseled military and civilian leaders, "have shown that there is no other single factor which can undermine military life and the whole social order more thoroughly than bad housing conditions."[124]

Poor health due to inadequate military health care programs, high divorce rates, and high turnover, according to the committee's findings, crippled the armed services and the country: "If we try to build up the military by breaking up family life, we shall soon have neither a strong Army to defend this country nor a country worth defending."[125] The committee's answer, of course, lay in an efficiently planned and organized community complete with voluntary organizations that took a significant interest in the individual's struggle for existence.[126] Volunteer organizations like the Red Cross, the YMCA, and the USO, in addition to military associations like the Navy Relief Society, the Air Force's Family Services, and the various wives' clubs, were originally designed to help families and encourage proper behavior. By the mid-1950s, military bases and the surrounding communities began to reflect a company-town motif; they later became icons of an era that reflected efficiency, organization, suburbia, middle-class and family values, national planning, and consensus.[127]

The Results of Reform: Large Peacetime Standing Armies and The Acceptance of the Military as a Career Alternative

In 1955, Public Opinion Surveys of Princeton, New Jersey, polled Americans about their feelings regarding careers in the peacetime military forces.[128] The questions asked were similar to those used in the Gardner Advertising poll in 1947 but the results were significantly different. Americans across all wealth strata now believed in the necessity of a standing military and a selective service system.

Anticommunism rhetoric began as early as 1945, escalated throughout the

Foundation of the Force

Truman and Eisenhower administrations, and effectively became the rubric for changing an entrenched tradition. To many Americans it became obvious that the Cold War was heating up and that atomic weapons made another major war unthinkable. In 1950 alone, public opinion polls demonstrated that most Americans saw the Soviets as intending to rule the world, and Americans were willing to spend more on national defense to ensure that the Soviets did not succeed.[129] A standing military was essential as a deterrent force, but in a war of ideas as much as of weapons, a military organization would need to reflect American values and beliefs.

Advertisers attempted to shift opinions about the nature of the military with a massive public relations campaign. Advertising at the national and local levels projected the idea that the military was more than an onerous obligation during wartime; in peacetime, it was a job.

In 1947, the job concept appealed to lower-income parents and youth who looked to the military as a means of social mobility. Middle-income parents, however, looked cautiously at the concept of a military career for their offspring. Few would support a son's or daughter's decision to enlist; the military was too immoral. By 1955, parents saw the military differently. Now, only 27 percent of all respondents said they would be displeased if their son took a military career as his life's work.

Those who reported they would be pleased if their son chose a military career said they made this choice because they believed the military provided a good job, presented a patriotic endeavor, and served as a school for character development and discipline. Even those indicating they would be displeased did not cite bad influences as a cause for their view of a military career. Eighty-one percent did not believe that the armed services promoted bad habits.[130]

From 1946 through 1955, several factors combined to ease the concerns of middle-income parents. In light of events in foreign policy and the Korean war, politicians and military leaders stressed that communism seemed on the move both abroad and within the United States. Many people believed that America's youth might submit to communism's subversive ideology. Moreover, major advertising campaigns sought to make society aware that the military was an important American institution from both a national security and an educational standpoint. The military would protect the United States from a holocaust while it instilled in its youth American values and a proper respect toward authority.

Besides an anticommunist rhetoric, the Korean war, and the advertising campaign, a number of major reforms occurred in the military to ease the concerns of middle-income parents. Presidential and congressional boards and committees suggested changes in the armed forces' treatment of personnel, its pay structure, and its approach to moral issues. Civilian and military leaders vigorously worked to put the services on a business basis and began to talk in economic and business management terms. Leaders addressed welfare issues and adopted changes.

By the mid-1950s, the military's image had changed. Its policies and programs increasingly reflected a democratic society, and they became designed to train society's sons and daughters in the American way. Progressive reforms, New Deal–like programs, and Fair Deal rhetoric found a home in the new military and sowed the seeds for the armed forces to mean more than just being a serviceman. They represented a job and a way of life.[131]

The 1955 poll demonstrated that the opinion of the military had changed in the eyes of thousands of Americans. Veterans, parents, and children agreed that although the draft was a primary impetus for volunteerism, the services helped youth find a trade, obtain a moral education, and gain broad experiences. In fact, more than 71 percent of those polled looked upon military personnel as desirable members of their community.

Advantages of a military life, according to these adults, included education and training, discipline and character development, travel, and financial reward. In an era of anticommunism and consensus, the military was the grand Americanizer. Among those polled, 46 percent were veterans or spouses of veterans. Of these, more than 50 percent served in World War II and had a favorable outlook on the time they spent in the service. This is in contrast to 1945, when few recalled their military experiences favorably.[132]

More important, especially from the Air Force's point of view, the public accepted the Air Force as the premier service and an acceptable career option. Thirty percent of the respondents chose the Air Force for their son's occupation (the Army garnered 15 percent; the Navy, 26 percent; and 22 percent stated no preference). More than 90 percent of those responding said that the Air Force would contribute the most to winning the next war.

Many believed that the next conflict would be short, nuclear, and aerial. Those who preferred the Air Force cited it as a cleaner, better educated service with broader opportunities. Moreover, it was newer than the Army and Navy.

Young men also found the Air Force an attractive option. Thirty–four percent of sixteen- to twenty-year-old males chose the Air Force as the service to join; the Army tied with the Navy at 26 percent each.[133]

Although public opinion may have sustained a standing military and evidenced high regard for Air Force, planners measured success not in polls but in the number of quality recruits obtained, trained, and retained. A significant step toward building a career force was the development of a professional recruiting service that would ensure that only those with the "right stuff" need apply.

✦3✦

Recruiting for the New Service
1945–1955

ALTHOUGH AMERICANS BEGAN TO ACCEPT the idea of a large peacetime military establishment, this did not mean that they were willing to send their sons and daughters into the Air Force for a four-year tour. Consequently, one of the new service's first recruiting challenges was to differentiate itself from the other services and to convince the public that it could provide recruits with training, character development, a respectable job, and good benefits.

Besides having to market itself as a viable employer, the Air Force had to contend with its own massive expansion. Between 1946 and 1955, the Air Force's growing air defense and nuclear retaliatory missions, coupled with the Korean war, caused its enlisted strength to grow from 263,029 in June 1947 to 352,085 in June 1950, then to spurt during the Korean War to more than three times its 1947 size (to 847,737 in June 1952), and to remain well over 800,000 through 1955. As in World War II, the Korean war and the draft (indirectly) provided the Air Force with a pool of bright volunteers who chose the air service over a possible tour in the infantry.

A poor reenlistment rate after the 1953 cease-fire in Korea further aggravated the recruiting problem that resulted from this massive increase in manpower. Besides having to increase enlistments to meet expansion demands, the Air Force had to recruit nearly 15 percent of its standing force yearly, as it, unlike the Army, had to maintain its strength through volunteer recruitment and not the draft.[1]

Also complicating the recruiting effort was the need to find personnel capable of receiving technical training. As in the past, the Air Force's need for specialists required teaching technical information to novices. This requirement, combined with the escalation of the Cold War and the expansion of the Air Force, compelled Air Force planners to design programs that sought bright trainees who would train and expand its recruiting force and publicize its way of life.

A Separate Service

Concurrently with the growth and development of a recruiting service, the AAF found it necessary, during the postwar fight over unification of the services, to promote itself as a separate branch of the armed forces. AAF leaders believed that public enthusiasm held the key to obtaining autonomy from the Army and, later, a larger share of a fluctuating defense budget.[2] As a result, whenever the opportunity arose in the immediate postwar period, the AAF's public relations department sought to sell the American public on the idea of a large, active duty Air Force capable of air defense and nuclear retaliation.[3]

"Our primary goal," AAF Commanding General Spaatz said in a radio interview in March 1946, "is to develop and maintain a stabilized peacetime air force capable of immediate, sustained, and expanding application of the accepted American doctrine of military air power. . . . That means only one thing . . . we must have an air force in being of adequate size and proper composition, strategically deployed, and in a high and constant state of readiness."[4] "What we do now," Spaatz later told Maj. Gen. Frederick L. Anderson at Air Force personnel, "the plans we lay and the support we earn from the American people during the period will firmly establish the pattern for our future air power. . . . We know what it takes, but we can only accomplish our mission if we have public confidence and approval."[5]

First on Spaatz's agenda was an independent air force. Among other things this meant explaining the need for a large peacetime air force which not only went against the grain of American military tradition but, in time, caused dissension within the other branches of the Armed Services as well. The Navy dissented because the AAF challenged its belief that ships were the country's first line of defense; many in the Army dissented because, while the air arm did not support UMT, it still wanted a large air force.[6]

Although some in the Army disliked the idea of a separate air force, Marshall and Eisenhower qualifiedly endorsed it because, in part, both witnessed the effectiveness of tactical and strategic air forces during the war. Eisenhower as Supreme Allied Commander visualized the combination of Army, Navy, and Air Force as his "three-legged stool," with each leg playing equally in the victory. Moreover, top AAF leaders like Arnold and Spaatz were personal friends of Marshall and Eisenhower and had taken the time to educate them on the capabilities of air power in theater and in strategic roles.[7]

Unlike AAF leaders who advocated a large, standing air force, the two top Army leaders proposed something quite different—a traditional small cadre of military professionals capable of expansion during times of national emergencies and a relatively small air force. This plan, in some respects, was similar to the proposed UMT program prior to the United States' entry into World War I, which required that all young men between the ages of seventeen and twenty (unless deferred or otherwise unqualified) receive a year's military training and

Maj. Gen. Frederick L.
Anderson

spend some time (five years) in the organized reserves or National Guard.[8]

In General Marshall's view, Americans, because of their traditions, would opt for the UMT program, which called for a large, rudimentarily trained reserve force that would augment the smaller professional force.[9] Others like President Truman also favored UMT, but for different reasons—military training would discipline, instill civic pride in, and educate the next generation of Americans.

AAF leaders, on the other hand, opposed the program for two key reasons. First, UMT would serve for training only, and trainees were not considered part of the armed forces for peacetime operations. Thus UMT, however useful it was to the Army, could not supply the pilots and highly trained technicians the technologically driven air service needed.[10]

Second, the Army tacitly endorsed a separate air force, but under the UMT proposal it would remain small. When, in the spring of 1945, Marshall introduced a trial plan calling for a postwar AAF of only 16 groups and 120,000 men, General Arnold openly split with Marshall over the issue.[11]

Arnold based his argument on the image of a future war involving high technology and a nuclear surprise attack. Using analogies from the most recent war, he explained to Marshall and the media that, in the new aviation and atomic age, a "nuclear Pearl Harbor" would cripple if not defeat the nation.[12] Rather, Americans would fight future wars using well-prepared and technologically advanced, active-duty armed forces, especially air forces. In the case of a surprise attack, Arnold emphasized that a sixteen-group Air Force could not train the 200,000 airmen required annually under the War Department's UMT program.[13] UMT or no, Congress would have to fund a retaliatory, nuclear-equipped air arm, maintained in a state of constant readiness.

Despite Truman and Marshall's backing, the image of a nuclear armageddon laid waste to the UMT program.[14] In an era of cost-cutting and shrinking budgets, the public and Congress accepted the AAF's argument that a prepared air force was more economical and efficient than a huge reserve of military manpower. Following Arnold's lead, Air Force leaders decisively argued that they could not employ reserves fast enough, and thus in case of war, rapid expansion would demand a sizable standing force.[15] Moreover, America needed to rely on advanced technology, not on manpower, for "the weapons of today," as General Arnold explained, "are the museum pieces of tomorrow."[16]

With enthusiasm for UMT ebbing and conflict with the Soviet Union possible, Congress created the DOD and granted autonomy to the AAF on September 18, 1947.[17] In April 1948, General Marshall pointed out to the Army staff that because support for UMT was dwindling at the same rate that support for air power was growing, the Army should consider withdrawing its backing of the UMT program.[18] Air Force spokesmen, including future members of the Air Staff and secretaries of the Air Force, would continue to advocate powerful air and nuclear retaliatory forces well through the 1950s.

Manpower Needs, 1945–1956

Sustaining public support and creating a specific niche in the postwar defense establishment were not the only problems the AAF faced before 1947. All branches of the armed services felt the immediate need for personnel to replace those lost during the rapid demobilization. Despite all the planning, once demobilization began, it issued a torrent of discharges. When Japan quickly capitulated after the nuclear strikes, Army demobilization quintupled—from an anticipated attrition of 1,100,000 men to a new target of 5,500,000 by June 1946.[19] As President Truman recorded in his memoirs, "The program we were following was no longer demobilization; it was disintegration of our armed forces."[20] By July 1947, the Congress further hacked the size of the Army. What was once an Army (including the AAF) of 12,000,000 was reduced to a peacetime service of 1,070,000.[21]

Demobilization went no better for the AAF.[22] "We did not demobilize," one Air Staff personnel specialist explained, "we merely fell apart . . . it was not an orderly demobilization at all. It was just a riot, really."[23] Between August 1945 and the spring of 1946, AAF strength plummeted 78 percent. By May 1947, only 14 percent of the August 1945 strength remained.[24] Moreover, optimistic economic projections sent most skilled maintenance technicians flocking to civilian jobs. Some regulars, after serving for the duration during the war, simply retired.

The loss of so many enlisted men in such a short time had severe repercussions on the AAF's mission effectiveness.[25] For example, between January 1945 and October 1946 the percentage of experienced mechanics dropped by 91 percent. Further aggravating the loss was the inability of the AAF to accurately estimate manpower losses. The statistical control system, according to an April 1946 Air Board meeting, "busted down with everything else" during the demobilization. "We don't know what units are where," the Air Board minutes continued, "how many people are in them, how many airplanes are in them, or what their state of readiness is."[26]

AAF Commanding General Carl Spaatz dejectedly reported that only 4 percent of the fifty-five air groups passed their 1946 proficiency tests: "Airplanes were stranded in all parts of the globe for lack of maintenance personnel to repair them. . . . Serviceable and even new aircraft, equipment, and materiel were left to deteriorate for lack of personnel to prepare them for storage."[27] When in February 1946 Jonathan Wainwright, commanding general of the Fourth Army and a personal friend of the AAF's commanding general, asked the AAF for three C–47 aircraft to support his staff, Spaatz declined, stating that he had too few maintenance personnel who were mostly "new, untrained recruits" to repair them. "We have whole squadrons," Spaatz wrote, "with less than ten mechanics."[28]

During the next five years, the AAF launched vigorous recruiting drives to man its seventy-group goal that called for a minimum of 502,000 officers and airmen. Desiring an experienced enlisted force, air planners offered enlistments of three, four, and six years while discouraging those for twelve and eighteen months. Additionally, to acquire men capable of technical training, the Air Force raised its educational and Army General Classification Test (AGCT) requirement to a higher level than the one used by the Army or the Navy.

As in the interwar years of the 1920s and 1930s, the size of the Air Force constantly fluctuated. Although building toward a seventy-group goal, by March 1947, Congressional appropriations allowed for only a fifty-five group air force. The seventy-group goal, however, was not forgotten as Secretary of the Air Force Stuart Symington lobbied for the Air Force's Four-Year Program, which called for seventy groups and 444,500 officers and airmen by June 30, 1949.[29]

The Berlin Airlift during 1948 and 1949 caused an additional expansion of Air Force manpower requirements. Yet, by July 1949, the Air Force had failed to meet Symington's seventy-group program largely due to domestic issues as the need to reduce the budget forced Truman to stress military reductions. To trim the defense budget, Defense Secretary Louis Johnson ordered deep cuts in all the services, forcing the Air Force had to cut back to forty-eight groups. By

In spite of increased manpower requirements brought on by the Berlin Airlift in 1948–1949 (see Operation VITTLES, *top photo*), Secretary of Defense Louis A. Johnson (on March 28, 1949, taking oath of office, on *right, bottom photo*) ordered deep cuts in all services.

this time, the Air Force already had acquired fifty-nine groups and was on the verge of activating eleven more. With the December 1948 announcement, the Air Force, once expanding, now began to contract.[30] On the eve of the Korean war, the Air Force's military strength stood at 411,277 officers and enlisted personnel and 48 wings.[31] All this haggling over defense budgets frustrated Secretary Symington so much that he resigned his secretaryship and took a post on the National Security Resources Board.

The 1950s saw continued turbulence in manpower requirements. With the onslaught of the Korean War in the summer of 1950, Truman authorized the buildup of 95 wings and 1,061,000 troops.[32] By the end of 1951, Truman approved a 143-wing program but with only a 14 percent increase in military personnel, to 1,210,000. The goal then changed from 143 to 120 wings in 1953 and to 137 by 1956. By 1956, the Air Force manned 131 wings with 914,000 military members.[33] Considering poor retention rates and the need for large numbers of manpower during the service's first ten years, the creation of a modern recruiting system was paramount. (See Appendices 1 and 2 for manpower statistics.)[34]

Recruiting Begins

Relying on Army traditions, training, and experience, the AAF developed a professional recruiting service to meet its specific needs, needs the Army often overlooked. As early as October 1945, air planners explained to the War Department that the AAF faced a severe shortage of skilled manpower and desired permission to do its own "selective" recruiting, as it had done prior to and early in the war.[35]

The AAF's manpower complaints largely went unheeded by a War Department not ready to relinquish recruiting authority to the individual services. The department had planned, after the war, to rely on its traditional, general recruiting service to find enlistees for the entire Army.[36]

The intentions of AAF officers also concerned some in the Army who believed airmen might try to bully the Army's postwar leadership into granting the airmen autonomy.[37] The War Department and G–1 consistently ignored pleas from the Air Staff about its personnel situation and the need for the AAF to conduct its own recruiting.[38] The Army was not willing to jeopardize its own recruiting by increasing AGCT scores, thereby narrowing its pool of potential recruits, just to serve the needs of the air forces. Neither was the Army willing to allow the AAF to have a recruiting department separate from the General Recruiting Service.[39]

The Army, however, allowed the AAF to initiate targeted campaigns for specific manpower needs such as aircraft mechanics and electricians.[40] The results of these campaigns proved less than desired because even though the

AAF could advertise, potential recruits had to visit Army recruiting stations to enlist.[41] The problem lay with Army recruiters who were rarely familiar with specific AAF personnel regulations and often made false promises or enlisted underage and illiterate men.[42] Army personnel also steered some who wanted to join the AAF into other Army branches. The net effect was that the air forces were simply not getting the high caliber personnel they desired. The AAF also wanted more control over advertising budgets. Yet, the Military Manpower Procurement Division of the Army directed all advertising ventures for the branches, and it believed the AAF's advertising needs were no more important than those of the infantry or the quartermaster corps.[43]

Gradually, and as the AAF approached independence, the Army allowed the air arm to supply its own recruiters and advertise with mobile recruiting vans.[44] Still, the Air Forces' recruiters remained subject to the Army area commanders and could not directly enlist potential recruits other than at Army recruiting stations or at nearby Army Air Fields.[45] In early 1947, as Congress and the armed services debated unification and the need for a separate air force, air personnel planners hoped for a separate system of recruiting.

As unification and autonomy became more likely, a separate recruiting missions became less necessary. Partly, this was due to stabilizing enlistment quotas and the return of routine peacetime recruiting duties. Mostly, however, it was because of the appointment of Maj. Gen. St. Clair Streett, an AAF officer who worked easily with AAF leaders, to command the Military Manpower Procurement Department (MMPD) of the War Department.[46] General Streett directed the minimum Army-wide AGCT score to be raised, and he permitted the AAF to set its own AGCT standard.[47] He also gave the AAF responsibility over its own advertising budget and he increased the number of AAF recruiters in the Army.[48]

By September 1947, the fact that the Air Forces could have personnel at fully functioning recruiting Army stations meant that the new service did not need to duplicate facilities. The Army already provided offices and administrative personnel.[49] The Army even relinquished control of some recruiting stations to Air Force officers. Besides, the need to separate recruiting missions went against the themes of unification and economy.[50]

When the Secretary of Defense asked the Navy to join the new Air Force and Army in a joint recruiting venture, the Navy declined. The Navy used fewer recruiters, less money, and a centralized recruiting system and, like the AAF, targeted technically trainable personnel for enlistment. It would be glad to share facilities, but it did not want to blur recruiting philosophy through amalgamation. The Navy did not want unification achieved at its expense.[51]

Following separation from the Army in September 1947, the new Air Force began to carry out its own recruiting objectives. Foremost was expanding its existing recruiting organization to man an already extended network of Army recruiting stations. Although the Air Force had conducted much of its recruiting

Maj. Gen. St. Clair Streett

on air bases or in communities where it had no enlistment authority, its recruiters could now actively proselytize throughout the United States. Though still decentralized into six Army areas, now the Army guaranteed Air Force recruiters a position at each of its recruiting stations.[52]

Each Army area covered a large geographic entity and contained many recruiting units. For instance, the First Army recruiting area included 6 recruiting districts, 52 main stations, and 222 substations. Northern New York alone contained 10 main stations and 62 substations. Besides these Army recruitment offices, each Army and Air Force base had its own recruiting office where recruiters received both new enlistments and reenlistments.[53]

Besides positioning men at Army recruiting stations, the Air Force had previously established a second recruiting network of its own. Air planners, on the basis of commands and numbered air forces, functionally structured their decentralized system to cover roughly the same geographic locations as the Army areas did. Thus, each of the seven commands was responsible for establishing, maintaining, and directing recruiting within the parameters established by the MPPD and the Air Staff.[54]

At air bases, the number of Air Force recruiters varied by the size of the military population on base and the nearby civilian community. In 1948, Mitchel Field, New York, for example, had three officers and twelve enlisted men, while Sioux City Air Force Base (AFB) in South Dakota had only one officer and one enlisted man assigned.[55]

With more offices to man, the number of recruiters dramatically increased. In late 1947, a survey of Army recruiting reported that 682 recruiting stations throughout 5 Army areas had no Air Force personnel and the ratio of Army to Air Force recruiters was 4:1. Responding to a letter from the Air Staff, the

Foundation of the Force

Army quickly agreed to increase Air Force recruiting personnel to 40 percent and ensure at least "one Air Force man [enlisted or officer grade] in each recruiting station and substation."[56] In addition to this assurance, the Army also allowed the Air Force to exercise command over Army recruiting installations. Though often second in command, air officers assigned to Army stations were responsible for the station's administration and operations as well as for informing the Air Force hierarchy of recruiting statistics.[57] By 1949, the U.S. Army and U.S. Air Force Recruiting program had 9,398 personnel in the field and a budget well over $25 million.[58]

As late as 1952, however, the Air Force found it still had difficulty controlling its own recruiting. Since the Army structure called for a decentralized network of autonomous recruiting stations commanded by Army area commanders, air recruiting leaders were often unaware of how the Army used Air Force recruiters.[59] Army recruiters missed Air Force quotas; fraudulent enlistments into the Air Force were on the rise; and no one knew exactly why.[60] Moreover, when the Air Force needed recruiters to meet critical manpower needs or when it needed to regulate the number of recruiters to deal with fluctuating requirements, its hands were tied.[61] Also, in recruiting stations where Air Force officers were not in charge, the Army often used Air Force personnel for office work and not for recruiting.[62]

These problems continued through 1953 when it became obvious that the Air Force would miss the 1955–1956 enlistment quota. Air Force personnel planners cited several problems that led to the missed quota, and all seemed to involve joint recruiting. First, "the Army," according to one contemporary recruiter, "was trying to syphon off the best they could, and of course, they weren't getting the best people, but they were really putting the pressure on the recruiter to meet the Army's quota [not the Air Forces's]." Other problems included the failure of the Army to provide a stable recruiting force, the sacrifice of interservice competition, and the inability of Army recruiters to understand Air Force needs and policies.[63]

Conferences between Secretary of the Air Force Harold E. Talbott and Defense Secretary Charles E. Wilson eventually solved the joint recruiting problem. The secretaries agreed that the services needed their own recruiting departments to address each service's individual needs and espouse its philosophy. On March 6, 1954, the Secretary of Defense signed a memorandum apprising the three services that "the Air Force will, not later than 1 July 1954, assume operational control of Air Force recruiting for its administrative and logistical support."[64]

On April 10, 1954, Air Training Command redesignated the 3500th Personnel Processing Group as the 3500th USAF Recruiting Wing. Seven years after independence, the Air Force finally threw off the last vestiges of Army bureaucracy and moved toward a centralized recruiting structure much like the Navy's. The Air Staff would provide the yearly manpower quotas, and the recruiting organization would plan and implement the strategy designed to meet those goals.

The new wing, stationed at Wright-Patterson AFB, Ohio, consisted of 6 groups, 63 detachments, and 809 recruiting stations. In effect, the Air Force would remain at Army recruiting stations, yet the former joint relationship ceased. The Air Force continued to supply administrative personnel, but it assigned and controlled its own recruiters. The Armed Forces Examining Stations also continued as joint agencies serving all three services.[65] Publicity and advertising funds were split, and a joint Recruiting Publicity Center was created, thereby continuing to control all advertising funds through the late 1950s.[66]

Building a Professional Recruiting Force

The expansion of the post–World War II recruiting network led toward standardizing station procedures and building a professional recruiting force. One important consideration was organizational communication channels. A major breakthrough in enlistment reporting came in late 1947 when Air Force recruiters began to machine-tabulate the Gain and Losses reporting system established during the war. Previously, the data were hand-tabulated and the final reports took weeks to compile and distribute. Now recruiters could compile enlistment data and send the results to the respective Air Force commands on the 15th and 30th of each month.[67] Commands then forwarded the reports to headquarters and the comptroller's office for combined accounting.[68] The use of machine tabulation helped recruiting planners stay current on manpower needs and overages.

Because manpower shortages and overages were now expeditiously routed to headquarters, air planners could initiate a more precise system for quota setting. Following the Navy's example, the Air Force and Army introduced monthly recruiting quotas.[69] The Navy first used quotas in 1917, and when the United States entered World War II, the Army adopted them for the same reason: to adjust to the sudden influx of inductees, inasmuch as the services could train and ship only so many men at a given time. Rather than using quotas as a restrictive measure, the Air Force in the postwar period established them to ensure that increased manpower requirements were quantified and distributed proportionately throughout the commands. Planners based command quotas such as the number of recruiters per station on geographic locality and the size of the surrounding civilian communities.[70]

Other standardized procedures may seem trivial, but they were instrumental in establishing a professional recruiting service. Recruiting stationery bore the embossed letterhead, U.S. Army and U.S. Air Force Recruiting Service. Headquarters authorized recruiting automobiles and imprinted the vehicles with the recruiting service's logo. The tickler file, a tool adapted from industrial sales departments for military purposes, became central to daily operations. This file, which quickly became the basic tool of recruiters, contained a list of all prospective enlistees classified by age, education, and background. It served to remind a recruiter (also known as a salesman or canvasser in the recruiting literature) when to contact a specific individual. The file systematized referrals, projected workloads, and located future "clients."[71]

Besides systematizing some recruiting procedures, the Air Force introduced recruiter selection criteria and professional training. Before 1947, the biggest requirement for becoming an air recruiter was willingness, and little else. Army recruiters often spoke about the slovenly appearance of airmen. Complaining to the Sixth Army commanding general, one dismayed soldier castigated a local Air Force recruiter as "5' 2", greatly overweight . . . and utterly lacking in all necessary requisites for a good recruiter." Besides this, the airman seemed to lack interest in his assignment.[72] The soldier recommended that airmen receive a more rigorous screening before their assignment to recruiting duty.

A letter to General Spaatz from an ex-officer, now a master sergeant, echoed similar sentiments. Air Force recruiters, the seasoned veteran warned, "should be experienced and well-versed in protocol and regulations."[73] No doubt to his surprise, the master sergeant was favored by a personal reply stating that action would soon be taken to correct this deplorable situation. In the meantime, Spaatz sent the enlisted man's letter to the personnel directorate of the Air Staff for comment.

The result was a directive sent to all commanding generals of the major Air Force commands codifying the criteria for selecting recruiting personnel. The letter stated that recruiters should be white, master sergeants, and three-year reenlistees. In addition, the position called for men who were volunteers, smart (AGCT of 110 or higher), at least twenty-five years of age, and good communicators. Personal morality, habits, appearance, and selling experience were also mandatory qualifications.[74] The recruiter image reflected the 1940's and 1950's societal view of the "corporation man," a moralistically upright, intelligent, white American male who enjoyed corporate life (the Air Force) and desired to preach its message. Personnel planners continued, through selection criteria, to reinforce this image throughout the 1940s and 1950s.

Though much of the standardization occurred slowly under the joint recruiting agreement, Air Force personnel planners did not take long to devise programs of their own. In addition to promoting recruiter selection requirements, the Air Force established recruiter schools to teach the fundamentals of salesmanship, management, administration, and vocational guidance. Patterned after industrial salesmanship courses, the Air Force's program, like the Army's and Navy's, concentrated on an intensive nine-week course designed to familiarize recruiters with advertising, publicity, community involvement, and human psychology.[75] The school actually conducted three separate courses: a nine-week basic recruiting course, a two-week sales-supervisors' course, and a two-week course for new nurse recruiters. The 1954 basic recruiter course was divided into five phases requiring 272 hours for completion:

Phase 1—Introduction, Testing, Classification, and Benefits, Forty-eight Hours

Phase 2—Selection Criteria, Processing, Administration and Training, Forty-nine Hours

Phase 3—Publicity and Community Relations, Forty-five Hours

Phase 4—Speech and Personnel Relations, Fifty-two Hours

Phase 5—Salesmanship, Seventy-eight Hours[76]

Moreover, Air Force recruiting officials, like their Army and Navy counterparts, did not couch the nature of recruiting duty in military terms. They chose retail sales analogies to explain what they wanted in recruiters and in recruiter training.[77] "If we want to hold our own [make enlistment quotas]," said Lt. Col. Marvin Alexander, Director of the USAF Recruiting Course, to a group of recruiting instructors, "we must have *recruiting salesmen* [emphasis added] who can outsell and out produce our competition [the other services and industry]. . . . The only way we can get salesman like that is to train them."[78]

The Air Force's growing staff of recruiters initially attended the Army's recruiter training course after the war. By 1948, however, many recruiters argued that this course did little to prepare Air Force personnel to sell careers in aviation. Although 1954 saw a centralized recruiter school established at Lackland AFB, Texas, many groups and wings developed their own courses and provided on-the-job training.[79]

Recruiters also prepared a manual to serve as a practical guide for the daily operations of a sales force. It covered topics from finding prospects to submitting all the necessary paperwork. This so-called bible also covered such items as preparing and using prospect cards (the tickler file), using recruiting media, performing local market research, and conducting sales training meetings.[80]

Besides the training course and manual, recruiters published and circulated a monthly paper. The title evolved from *The AAF Recruiting Bulletin* in 1945 and 1946 to *The U.S. Army and U.S. Air Force Recruiting Bulletin* in 1948 and *The Take Off* in 1954. Designed to keep recruiters aware of regulatory changes and new bureaucratic guidelines, these papers were also a means to share suggestions and techniques and to learn about future assignments.[81] *The U.S. Army and U.S. Air Force Recruiting Bulletin*, for example, stated the Air Force mission, defined complicated projects and definitions, spelled out the details of future advertising campaigns, and frankly discussed the implications of quotas and the service's manpower needs. The *The Take Off*'s intent was to provide a medium from which "recruiter-salesmen" could communicate the "recruiting ideas of one area . . . to all areas of the United States."[82] In addition to a central

Lackland AFB (*top*), ca. 1947; retreat at Lackland (*bottom*), 1953.

bulletin, commands and smaller recruiting groups published many similar informational sources.[83]

Advertising

For Americans, a large peacetime military establishment was something new, and just because the public supported it did not mean that citizens would send their sons and daughters into service. To sell the Air Force, recruiting publicity embraced two goals: convince the public that a large military establishment was important to national defense, and sell the idea that the Air Force was the best service to join.

Besides promoting the military in general, the Air Force created and sustained an image and designed enlistment programs to attract personnel of its own. Although the Army relied primarily on the draft at this time, the Air Force, during the late 1940s and 1950s, maintained its authorized strength through volunteer recruitment. Consequently, the Air Force devoted much advertising time and money to defining an image distinct from the Army's or the Navy's. Direct mail advertisements, billboards, newspaper and magazine articles, books, radio and television promotions, and recruiting posters introduced potential enlistees to the technical Air Force world of the future. Movies such as *Strategic Air Command* and *A Gathering of Eagles* portrayed careers in the Air Force as technologically driven, glamorous, and exciting.[84]

In response to the Air Force leadership's adamancy about enlisting only intelligent, high-caliber individuals, recruiting literature challenged young men "to see if they could make the grade."[85] Recruits who did, according to the advertisements, would find life challenging, educational, and glamorous. "This is the air age, man," one 1947 recruiting pamphlet read, "we have advanced to an age in which men who fly ignore all conditions of earthbound travel. . . . We do not have aircraft that will travel as fast as sound, but we expect to shortly. . . . We do not have aircraft that will reach the moon, but we are certainly making progress in that direction. . . . So this is the air age and the atomic age—and aviation is the leading business of the age and a good business for you to get into. . . . The best is yours for the asking—and aviation wants you."[86]

Recruiting themes among the services differed. While the Army chose patriotism and vocational education and the Navy chose tradition and travel, the Air Force emphasized aviation technology, education, and the future. Posters increasingly focused on men doing highly technical jobs on advanced aircraft. Pamphlets told high school seniors that the Air Force would teach them an aviation skill, help them gain a general education, and put them on the road to success. Mottos like the old interwar standbys "Learn While You Earn," "Plan Your Future NOW—Enlist in the Air Force," or "For a Job With a Future—Enlist in the Air Force" reinforced the concept of education and preparation for the future.[87]

Literature aimed at recruiting women reiterated the aspect of having important skills in a technologically advanced future and equality with males. "You are a woman," one brochure pronounced, "with an eye to the future, if you choose a career in the U.S. Air Force Medical Service."[88] "Visualize women charting the arrival of a giant airliner in Hawaii; observing the blips of an all-seeing radar screen in Colorado; watching the unrelenting teletype pour out world news in Germany; or photographing the arrival of a VIP in Washington, D.C.," the pamphlet *Women in the Air Force* read.[89] Another booklet stressed that the scope of assignments available to women was very similar to the choices given males; thirty-two of forty-two career fields were now open to females. "Remember," the booklet encouraged the reader, "Pay, retirement, and all other benefits available to male members of the Air Force are exactly the same for WAF [Women in the Air Force]."[90]

Air Force recruiting themes in the 1950s not only emphasized aviation technology and opportunity for women, but they explained to middle-class parents that the Air Force placed the individual first, stressed productivity, emphasized morality, and prepared their sons and daughters for tomorrow in the Jet Air Age. As malassignment was deemed one of the major morale problems during World War II, the Air Force assured discontented veterans that their sons would be trained in advanced skills and used efficiently in that capacity.[91] "You realize," one recruiting booklet emphasized, "that in our world of continual technological advance, where emphasis is placed on the individual—in both industrial and community activities—the Air Force is a recognized leader in keeping abreast of times and trends. . . . The Air Force places a high premium on the well-trained technician . . . [your son] will not just be marking time."[92]

Recruiting literature also promised middle-class parents that the Air Force would make their sons mentally tough, physically strong, and morally aware. "The molding of a solid character," one recruiting pamphlet directed to parents read, "is the ultimate goal [presumably of an enlistment in the Air Force]."[93] Furthermore, the Air Force made it clear that parents should not wait for the "machinery of the draft to call [their sons] to duty," as "you should be certain which service offers him most."[94] According to these recruiting tracts, only the Air Force promised youth a moral education and a ground-floor opportunity to join the "revolutionary jet-age progress of our nation."[95]

To attract potential recruits, the Air Force not only had to differentiate itself from the other services, it also had to fashion a recruiting program that would attract the type of person it wanted: an intelligent individual capable of retaining technical training. From 1946 through 1955, recruiters avidly publicized three programs that had roots in the interwar and World War II eras. Procurement planners aimed one enlistment program at civilian specialists and

The Army Air Forces had its own recruiting effort during the World War II years (*top*). Recruitment of middle-class youth during the Korean war era was with the promise of training in the newest technology (*center*). Recruits were given air transportation to Barksdale Field, Louisiana, during World War II (*bottom*).

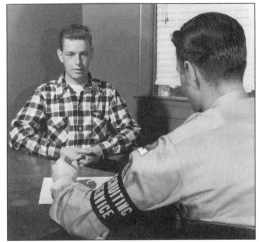

the other two at prior-service veterans and high school graduates.

The first program mirrored the 1939 Air Corps campaign for civilian specialists and sought skilled personnel with no prior service to fill critical shortages in areas such as aircraft mechanics, electronics, weather, and personnel.[96] Reception center personnel tested applicants for level of skill, performed physicals, and then reported their results to the Air Staff. Upon headquarters' approval, the centers notified recruits, administered oaths, and issued assignments. Most importantly, headquarters also assigned ranks commensurate with skills. Rather than enlisting as privates, inductees went directly to their stations as corporals, sergeants, technical sergeants, or master sergeants, based upon ability. In time, this program lowered morale among many who were already in the Air Force and could not be promoted due to the influx of these civilian experts in higher grades.

The other two programs focused on prior Air Force personnel and high school graduates. The first of these two was similar to the campaign for civilian specialists except that recruiters reinstated prior Air Force personnel with the needed skills at or above their previous pay grade, based on skill level.[97] Before 1946, those who left the Air Force for more than twenty days would take a reduction of at least one grade at reenlistment.[98]

The final program, known as the Airman Career Program, sought high school graduates. Personnel planners understood that a higher percentage of graduates would finish technical school compared with nongraduates.[99] Thus, recruiters promised enlistees in this program the choice of selected technical schools, their first duty assignment, and the possibility of joining and training with a friend.[100]

Locally, recruiters made wide use of newspapers, radio, and, in the 1950s, television to promote Air Force careers. Events such as Air Force Day promised aerial demonstrations and a host of technical and military displays showing airmen working in various careers such as radar, aircraft maintenance, and personnel management. Recruiters also began to speak at high schools and vocational colleges and informed local guidance counselors about military careers.[101] The cooperation between the recruiters and the Military Affairs Committee in Colorado Springs provides a vivid example of the local process. The Air Force established a recruiting station in June 1946 with only one NCO recruiter; by July 1947, the number of recruiters had increased to five. These five were selected for specific tasks: two were to serve as public relations experts and three, as canvassers-salesmen.

From January 1 to December 31, 1947, the Colorado Springs recruiters enlisted 360 men, of whom nearly 60 percent (211) were destined for the Air Force. In December alone, they recruited forty-four airmen. The city of Denver only recruited sixty-eight more in December, though its population was seven times that of Colorado Springs. During 1947, the recruiter explained: "[We] obtained 756 column inches of news items and 3,584 minutes of local radio

Brig. Gen. Leon W. Johnson

time without costs to the military . . . this figure is continuing to grow."[102] Additionally, on August 1, 1947, Air Force Day, merchants paid for 450 column inches of advertising in praise of the Air Force. Local radio stations KRDO and KVOR scheduled more than twenty-one hours of air time for recruiting promotionals. Finally, to promote the advantages of Air Force technical training, the Junior Chamber of Commerce sponsored a program encouraging five high school graduates to enlist under the Air Force's Career Program. Recruiters treated the five high school seniors to a big publicity campaign, a banquet, and a visit by the Commanding General of Fifteenth Air Force, Brig. Gen. Leon Johnson, who personally enlisted them and administered the oath of enlistment. As a follow-on, local newspapers carried monthly reports on the five young men's Air Force training and study.

The Recruiting Process

It was one thing to gain applicants and quite another to qualify them for acceptance. The Air Force constantly loosened or tightened enlistment requirements to control the needs of critical specialties and an expanding or contracting force structure. The first decade after its separation from the Army saw the Air Force trying to find enough people qualified to complete technical training successfully. Personnel planners, like alchemists, were constantly seeking that right mixture of eligibility requirements, technical test scores, and recruit character traits that promised the gold-like substance known as an effective force.

Once procurement planners distributed manpower quotas to the various recruiting stations, recruiting officers and NCOs established individual recruiter goals. It was then up to the recruiter to meet his assigned number of men for the month. Generally, recruiters found it necessary to sell a military career to four men before one would actually complete the entire enlistment process. Recruiters often devoted much time in interesting potential recruits, only to find an enlistee ineligible because he was unable to meet some requirement or another. This frequently led to frustration among the recruits because the Air Force seemed to be selecting recruits by elimination, by finding reasons to turn most applicants down.[103]

When a potential recruit entered the recruiter's office, the recruiter performed a quick introductory interview to determine the applicant's age, race, and nationality. The applicant would later provide the required documentation to substantiate this initial information. Under the Voluntary Recruitment Act of 1945, men could enlist between the ages of seventeen and thirty-four.[104] Seventeen-year-old males needed parental permission. Planners justified a double standard for recruiting women on the basis that the need for women was so little that recruiters could be more selective. Women were thus legally required to be at least eighteen years old, and they needed parental consent if they were not yet twenty-one. Also, unlike men, both the Army and the Air Force required female applicants to have a high school diploma or its equivalent.[105]

Other requirements for men and women included possessing U.S. citizenship or equivalent, passing a rigorous physical exam, and after 1952 —largely due to government-wide loyalty investigations stimulated by the anti-communism ideology of the era—passing a security background check that established loyalty, trustworthiness, and the absence of a criminal record.[106]

Besides these requirements, the Air Force usually precluded the enlistment of married persons. Following the dictates of interwar Army Air Corps policy and those of the other services, recruiters could not enlist or reenlist a first-termer who was married without first receiving a reenlistment authorization from headquarters. Married airmen in paygrade E–4 (sergeant) with less than six years' service and those in paygrades E–1 (private), E–2 (Private First Class), and E–3 (corporal) were barred from signing up for another term unless base commanders authorized their reenlistments.[107]

Air planners wanted to obtain people who would stay for their full terms; thus authorization was only given after a recruit could show that he could support his family and would not later apply for a hardship discharge. The Air Force, however, desperately needed certain civilian specialists such as electronics technicians and jet mechanics, and it often overlooked their marital status in order to recruit them. Specialists usually enlisted at higher grades than fledgling recruits did, and they received more pay. Under no circumstances did recruiters enlist married women or women with dependents under the age of eighteen.[108]

By 1953, the huge manpower losses led the Air Force to relax its ban on accepting and retaining married male airmen, hoping that men with families would be more inclined to remain in the service for subsequent reenlistments.[109] In 1954, 29.2 percent of its first-term airmen were married (42 percent of the total enlisted population was married compared with the Army's 32 percent and the Navy's 28 percent).[110] The Air Force had almost as many personnel with dependents (47.7 percent) as it did single personnel within its ranks.[111]

Following an initial interview with potential recruits, recruiters administered a preenlistment mental examination. Related to the Alpha and Beta tests of World War I and to the AGCT used during World War II, behavioral scientists hired by the Air Force designed the Armed Forces Qualification Test (AFQT) to indicate an individual's trainability. In 1950, the DOD ordered the services to use this single test as a preselection examination.[112] New enlistees took the more formal Airman Classification Test after arriving for basic training.

After an applicant passed the initial screening, the recruiter scheduled a physical exam at the nearby Armed Forces Examination Center. This exam was based on new physical standards developed during World War II and which evolved during Korea and the Cold War.[113] Physical requirements for the Air Force were lower than those of the Army on the premise that technological weapon systems required less physical size and stamina than combat-type jobs.[114] In 1948, the Army introduced a six-part physical profile system known as PULHES, dividing the body into six functional areas—physical capacity, upper extremities, lower extremities, hearing, eyes, and neuropsychiatric behavior—which doctors graded on a point scale. After noting defects, the doctors classified enlistees in categories from A to E, and this rating in combination with mental and, later, aptitude scores determined a recruit's future job and training.[115]

Despite these measuring devices, fraudulent enlistments continued to plague recruiters. The Air Force categorized fraudulent enlistments in two ways: first, enlistees who entered into a contract with the Air Force under false pretenses; and second, false recruiter promises such as guaranteeing a recruit a particular job or duty station.[116] Recruiting regulations considered applicants who were previously dishonorably discharged, who were underage, illiterate, or physically handicapped, or who had a felony record as ineligible for enlistment. And because many recruits were needed for overseas duty following basic training, they could not attend technical school. Men who had been promised such training and complained of a breech of contract were subsequently released from the Air Force.

Often during hectic enlistment drives, such as the Air Force's expansion in the 1950s or in the mobilization and demobilization periods during and after World War II and the Korean war, a recruiter might overlook poor test scores or a substandard education, although regulations prohibited such practices. During one intense recruiting campaign in 1946, 354 enlistees were recruited with test scores below the minimum of 70. Thirty-six of these were enlisted at AAF installations, and the remaining 318 joined at Army recruiting stations.[117] Again, Army recruiters often were less concerned about the needs of the Air Force than of their parent service. Periods of extended personnel stability allowed recruiters the time to check records thoroughly and apply Air Force standards more diligently, thus reducing such incidents.

Finally, after the preliminaries, the recruiter, according to the Volunteer Act of 1947, offered enlistment into the Air Force for two, three, five, or six years.[118] By 1950, the Air Force offered newcomers only enlistment periods of four or more years in order to offset the cost of training and reduce the proportion of time a recruit spent in technical training, and to enhance the experience level in a very young force.[119] In 1953, Assistant Secretary of the Air Force H. Lee White argued that long-term enlistments were necessary both from a cost and from a readiness standpoint. Anything less than a long enlistment term (four or more years), he pleaded, "would wreck the Air Force."[120] Benefits of the longer terms offered to enlistees included a promise of technical training and no time served in the Army (if drafted)!

The possibility of induction into the Army helped Air Force recruiters persuade parents and youths that four years in the Air Force actually were better than two in the Army. Under the draft, a young man had to fulfill a minimum five-year military obligation, including both Active Service and Ready Reserve duty. Air Force recruiters told parents to have their sons volunteer at seventeen, serve fours years' active time, learn an important skill, mature, and then enter the Ready Reserve for one year. After four years in the Air Force, recruiting literature told middle-class families, a young man could enter college and "follow in Dad's footsteps in business or the professional world" by the time he was twenty-two.[121]

On the other hand, if the young man waited for induction, he would serve two years in the Army, three years in the Ready Reserve, and because the average age of an inductee was twenty-three, he would not be finished with his obligation until he was twenty-eight. In other words, by the time an inductee had finished serving, he might be too old to become successful in a civilian occupation.[122] Moreover, the Korean war and the possibility of combat made parents and youth think twice about the draft and the Army. The Air Force offered young men a way to obviate infantry duty and combat but still fulfil their obligation to the country.

Who Joined?

Air Force planners determined the success of a recruiting program by two factors: the number of personnel obtained and the number capable of retaining technical training. Surveys of recruits demonstrated that most were young (70 percent were between the ages of 19 and 21 with an average of 19.2) and from the most populous states.[123] Close to 70 percent came from towns (of greater than 2,500 people) and from cities, reflecting both U.S. demographics and the geographical locations of the Air Force's recruiting stations (Table 9).

Table 9
Pre-service Residence
Rural and Urban
(In Percent)

Type of Residence	Number	Percent
Rural Area	149,690	18.8
Town <2,500	95,630	12.0
Town 2,501–25,000	209,950	26.4
Town 25,001–100,000	144,450	18.1
Town >100,000	196,250	24.7
Total	795,970	100.0

SOURCE: *USAF Statistical Digest*, 1955, p. 347.

In regard to quality, from the Army's first introduction of the Alpha and Beta mental tests, the Air Force equated high test scores with trainable enlistees.[124] It was no different in the Cold War era. In 1948, the Air Force spearheaded the development of the uniform aptitude test, the AFQT. After its acceptance in 1950, the Air Force used this test as a screening device to ensure that recruits scored in the top three quintiles prior to enlistment.[125]

Mental standards differed for draftees and volunteers. As required by law, the Army accepted a percentile score of ten (more than 85 percent of army draftees during World War II scored higher) for inductees. The Air Force and the Navy, however, could set their standards as high as they wanted.[126] Before 1951, mental standards varied depending upon manpower needs and training capability.[127] After the Korean war began, the Army noticed a growing disparity in the quality of recruits that the four services were accepting.[128] As in World War II, the Air Force during the Korean war was able to recruit highly qualified personnel, since many enlistees did not want to serve in Army combat positions.

Foundation of the Force

The war and the draft provided a very selective pool from which the Air Force could recruit. In fact, the Air Force obtained so many quality recruits that its basic training center at Lackland AFB in San Antonio, Texas, was turned into a tent city because the barracks there were simply too few to house the thousands of recruits pouring in for training in late 1950.[129] Army complaints about the Air Force's successful efforts to get the best recruits reached Congress. As a result, the Senate Preparedness Committee, headed by Senator Lyndon B. Johnson of Texas, a future President, examined Air Force recruiting and training policy. He declared the Air Force's hoarding of recruits "a disservice to the nation."[130] He also stated:

> The loss to the Nation is incalculable. . . . Men of high intelligence who might have made invaluable officers for the Army are now consigned to the ranks of the Air Force as privates. . . . The Air Force's apparent unconcern for the other services is not merely a rebuff to the spirit of unification, it is also an attitude detrimental to the best interests of the Nation.[131]

Surprisingly, Senator Johnson made no comment about the young men who sought refuge from the Army and combat by enlisting in the Air Force.

Indeed the Air Force was hoarding its men, but it did so from tradition, not from malice. Lessons from World War II impressed zealous policymakers with the need to get the brightest recruits classified and trained quickly so that they could be deployed overseas. In this regard, planners believed it was a service to the nation, not a disservice, to get top-quality personnel. The rhetoric and reasons for hoarding personnel, however, were not appreciated by all, as the new Secretary of Defense and former Army Chief of Staff George C. Marshall believed it was time for new thinking. "Under the conditions of modern war," Marshall explained, "men of outstanding qualifications are required in all branches of the military . . . to concentrate the qualities of leadership or technical pre-eminence in one branch . . . is detrimental."[132]

This "new thinking" actually stemmed from Marshall's experience with the AAF during World War II. One branch of the Army, or in this case, one branch of the armed services, could not prosper at the expense of the others.

To prevent this type of recruiting fiasco from reoccurring and to assure an equitable allocation of new manpower among the services, in May 1951 Secretary Marshall established a "qualitative distribution policy" that standardized mental and physical scores for all the services.[133] This distribution scheme established a quota control based upon the World War II model of five broad mental groups (Table 10).

Table 10
Qualitative Distribution of Mental Scores

Mental Group	Percentile Score
Category I	93–100
Category II	65–92
Category III	31–64
Category IV	10–30
Category V	9 and below

SOURCE: Memo, SECDEF to All Service Secys and JCS, Subj: Qualitative Distribution of Military Manpower, Apr 2, 1951, RG 330, 66, Box 314, MMB, NA.

Under this system, the Air Force had to accept more lower category men (it was now required to accept 27 percent from Category IV) which, in an era of increasing technological sophistication, played havoc with the service's desire to recruit only individuals capable of technical training. The Air Force placed most Category IV personnel as apprentices or else located them in a very few occupational specialties that accepted lower mental standards. Few such men received formal training.[134]

Changing the mental standards gradually changed the mental composition of the Air Force. For instance, in October 1949, 95.7 percent of all enlistees had AGCT test scores exceeding 100.[135] In January 1950, when the Air Force implemented the AFQT, 92.9 percent of non–prior service enlistees scored above the 50th percentile. By June, that number had dropped to 73 percent.[136]

These results become more startling when the higher grade NCOs are compared to incoming recruits. In World War II, Regular Army NCOs were less educated and presumably less intelligent than were newcomers. During the Korean war, quite the opposite held true.[137] Perhaps because of the reserve officers who joined the enlisted ranks during the demobilization after World War II, the 1950's personnel-hoarding fiasco, and the Air Force's emphasis on promotion and retention of the brightest, in 1951 nearly 76 percent of the master sergeants scored in Categories I and II compared with only 36.6 percent of all privates.[138]

As a group, master sergeants were also more educated than recruits; 74.2 percent held high school diplomas or better compared with 68.8 percent of the enlistees.[139] By 1955, the gap between the two groups had widened. Close to 80 percent of the master sergeants had high school diplomas or better, whereas 65.6 percent of airman basics (privates) had less than a full four-year high school education.[140]

Foundation of the Force

Large pools of draftees and a greater need for skilled technicians eventually forced the DOD to authorize higher standards for regular enlistees and encourage the services to develop programs to eliminate untrainable personnel.[141] By 1958, the DOD changed peacetime induction standards, thus allowing the Air Force to focus on selective recruiting. Until then, however, the lowered requirements caused havoc in training and retention.

During the early 1950s, decreased mental standards forced air planners to consider other options for obtaining quality recruits. The WAF program, although established in 1948, never received the impetus to expand until late in the Korean war.[142] Previously, planners had placed an internal ceiling on the number of women the Air Force would accept.[143] With wartime expansion, however, many began to view women as a potential source of thousands of high-quality recruits and became anxious to expand their enlistments when Congress removed the 2 percent ceiling previously enacted in the Women's Armed Services Integration Act of 1948.[144]

In September 1951, the DOD announced a 10-month recruiting drive designed to increase the number of women in the military to 112,000 (a 180 percent increase). The Air Force optimistically set its goal at 500 women recruits per month and began to appoint trained WAF officers as women recruiters. Many jobs open to WAFs were in the health professions and administration (75 percent of all WAFs in 1953 were in these fields) although other nontraditional occupational specialties such as radio and radar maintenance, plane-dispatcher, and cryptographer had been open to women during World War II.[145] By law, none of the specialties involved combat.

In the spring of 1952, the recruiting campaign crumbled.[146] Compared to its goal of recruiting 50,000 women, the Air Force only obtained 13,000. In fact, the number of WAFs never approached the 2 percent ceiling which Congress lifted during the Korean war. At their peak strength, women never constituted more than 1.3 percent of the total force.[147] For the most part, surveys showed that most women were tired of war or were concerned about the loose-morals stigma surrounding women who served in the military. Moreover, poor wages and the higher educational, mental, and physical standards required of females helped shape their view of the armed forces and contributed to the campaign's failure.[148]

Air Force leaders generally shared society's conservative attitudes toward women and minorities. Nevertheless, the buildup of the Air Force often placed the leadership in a position where they had to achieve a reasonably efficient use of manpower without offending societal perceptions on race and gender. Because few planners were social reformers, personnel policies reflected their pragmatic designs—the Air Force used women to replace men only when the situation dictated, and it placed them in jobs "pretty much dominated by women in civilian life."[149]

With the Korean war no longer providing a demand for women, planners

110

A World War II WASP checks the engine of a Curtiss A–25A at Camp Davis, North Carolina (*top*). A WAF sergeant gives a Greenlight for take-off in Japan, February 1952 (*bottom*).

felt no obligation to forward WAF causes. In fact, after 1953, the concern over using women in the Air Force received little attention by personnel policymakers trying to create and maintain an experienced (male) technical force in midst of a rapidly expanding mission. By 1954, all the services had a large personnel pool from which to draw an ample number of male volunteers, and all the services showed a decreasing number of women in their ranks.[150] Women leaving the Air Force believed that the recruiting promises of extensive training, career of choice, and travel were unavailable to most of them.[151]

As the size of the Air Force decreased, planners began to remove women from seven of the twelve major commands, assigning them to one of the remaining five—Air Defense Command (ADC), Military Air Transport Service (MATS), Strategic Air Command (SAC), Air Training Command (ATC), and United States Air Forces in Europe (USAFE)—that could best "use their service."[152] Although 85 percent of the technically trained women were employed by three commands—MATS, ADC, and ATC—their service usually meant administration, communication, supply, medical, and personnel, based on the belief that women were "inherently best suited" for these jobs because of "emotional and physical considerations."[153] Faced with a reduction-in-force in the late 1950s, some air planners proposed doing away with the WAF program entirely, thereby eliminating 8,000 manpower spaces and reducing the hardship of having men and heads-of-households put out of work.[154]

Driven by presidential order and the Korean war, planners also developed policies for blacks. The immediate World War II demobilization period saw continued segregation, but losses in white manpower drove policymakers to rethink polices that prohibited the use of trained blacks in white units.[155]

F–84s head for a target north of the 38th parallel in Korea

Truman's Executive Order 9981 (which called for integration), the close monitoring of the President's Committee for the Abolition of the Racial Quota (the Fahy Committee), and the desperate need for skilled manpower moved the Air Force toward integrated units.[156] By 1949, the Air Force had eliminated a 10 percent quota and went to equal standards of enlistment for both whites and blacks, largely because of the Fahy Committee's emphasis on increasing the classification test scores to ninety.[157]

The period beginning with the onset of the Korean war in June 1950 to the end of that year showed a continued effort to recruit blacks, albeit using white recruiters, and to achieve total integration. As a result of the Korean expansion and DOD's implementation of the qualitative distribution scheme, which required the Air Force to enlist more Category IV personnel, the proportion of blacks increased from 5 percent in 1949 to close to 9 percent in June 1954 (Table 11).[158] The 1954 percentage of blacks in the U.S. Air Force compared favorably to the Marines' 6.5 percent, the Navy's 3.6 percent, and the general population's 11.0 percent. Due to the fact that the Army assimilated more of the poorly educated Americans, blacks composed 13.7 percent of its force.

Table 11
Percentage of Blacks in the Air Force
1949–1954*

Year	Percent
1949	6.0
1950	7.1
1951	5.7
1952	5.6
1953	7.2
1954	8.7

SOURCES: Gropman, *The Air Force Integrates*, app 1; *Air Force Statistical Digest, 1949–1954.*

*In 1954, the percentage of blacks in the American population was 11 percent.

By late 1950, the Air Force had reduced the number of its segregated units to nine. Thus, more than 95 percent of black airmen served in integrated squadrons.[159] By 1955, integration policies ordered by the Truman administration, and enforced by the Fahy Committee, compelled the Air Force to institutionalize equality in its policies. Although desegregation policies were in place, time was required for the Air Force to reduce prejudice within the ranks.[160]

Foundation of the Force

Why They Joined

By 1948, the Air Force began surveying new recruits to determine their reasons for joining. As in the pre–World War II Air Corps, external factors often dictated what kind of people enlisted. Proximity to the end of a school term, conditions in the civilian job market, and world events affected enlistment decisions.

Surveys taken during the late 1940s and 1950s showed that recruits enlisted for various reasons. A 1949 survey determined that nearly 50 percent of enlistees selected the Air Force for technical training.[161] Another 25 percent joined for financial considerations or opportunities for travel and adventure. Only 1 percent of those surveyed indicated patriotic reasons for selecting the Air Force. When asked why they chose the Air Force over the Army, 75 percent said technical training; others expressed an interest in airplanes or explained that there were "higher types of men in the Air Force."[162]

Also influencing a potential recruit's decision was the Korean war and the Selective Service Act of 1948. The war and the draft imposed an additional impetus for enlistment because many who volunteered for Air Force duty believed the Army would have eventually inducted them. Only 7 percent of the 1949 recruits thought the draft was the prime motivator to enlist in the Air Force. By 1955, however, 25.6 percent stated that the threat of compulsory military service played an important part in their enlistment.[163]

A comparison between those who claimed to avoid the draft as their primary or secondary reason for enlisting and those who volunteered for other reasons showed that the draft-induced enlistees, on average, were older and better educated.[164] Their age and education may explain why financial considerations and the draft constituted more inducement than education or travel did. Those who enlisted to evade the draft often did so to take advantage of specific programs not offered to inductees. Close to 40 percent of these airmen desired a choice in what branch of the military they would serve. For instance, during the Korean war, few wanted to join an infantry company. Another 25 percent chose to enlist because this permitted them to fulfill their obligation at a time of their own choosing. "I wanted to join while I still was young," one recruit wrote, "and by waiting the draft might upset my career. . . . I enlisted to finish my college education without later delay."[165] Another group believed that volunteers would be afforded more opportunities such as joining the Air Force with a buddy.

Although educational levels played a role in reasons for enlistment, the disparities were not that great. Most high school and non–high school graduates joined for technical education, work experience, or, during Korea, to evade the draft. Less educated men were 7 percent more likely to join to escape an "uncomfortable civilian situation."[166]

Within the first decade after World War II, the Air Force separated from the Army, created a modern recruiting system, and successfully promoted the military and itself as a means of obtaining a good career. For the most part, the Army provided the necessary structure from which the Air Force could pattern its recruiting system. The Air Force adopted recruiter schools, career paths, and various standardizing processes established by the Army. One of the most important aspects of the new recruiting system was the advertising that the Air Force used to promote itself. It did more than simply tell people about military jobs. It focused on selling the military as an American tradition and it emphasized Air Force life to men and women unfamiliar with aviation and the jet age. Highly technical, very selective, and professional, the Air Force's image made it the choice of many parents for their draft-aged children as well as for youth to fulfill military obligations.

✦4✦

Training and the
Enlisted Career Program
1945–1955

THE DECADES OF THE 1940s AND 1950s demonstrated the Air Force's ability to promote an image that would draw young men and women into the ranks of its enlisted corps. Yet, the success of the recruiting service created an important problem for Air Force planners: how to assimilate these new recruits into the service and train them with skills desperately needed by the Air Force's major commands. To solve the problem, the Air Force depended heavily on the experience garnered during the interwar years and from World War II.

Basic training continued to evolve from that employed by the Army, while technical schools reflected a confusing dichotomy between generalized and specialized training. By 1955, however, Air Force personnel planners had created a recruiting and training system capable of producing the needed technicians to support the Air Force's expanded combat mission by channeling civilians through a basic indoctrination to formal instruction in various specialties and thence to on-the-job training (OJT).

Besides combat efficiency, the ability to retain experienced airmen was an ultimate measure of success for a recruiting and training program. By 1952, the Air Force had developed the Airman Career Plan which established a centralized training pipeline while emphasizing the Air Force's belief that airmen were technicians first, and soldiers, a distant second. The plan established broad areas of occupational training and a clear path of advancement, and it placed a premium on job knowledge over military deportment. The introduction of the Airman Career Plan demonstrated just how much the Air Force and the armed forces had embraced corporate personnel management philosophy and practices. Indeed, the Air Force was more than a part of the military—it offered youth a jet-age job, upward mobility, and a potential career.

Basic Training: Gateway to the Air Force

In May 1955, an important conference of Air Force planners from the three basic military training (BMT) centers at Lackland AFB, Texas (established for BMT in 1946), Sampson AFB, New York (established in February 1951), and Parks AFB, California (established in August 1951), met at Technical Training Command Headquarters in Gulfport, Mississippi, to discuss the problems in the basic military training curriculum.[1] Most of these problems centered on a lack of concise definitions about the nature of basic training for the Air Force. What appeared to be the beginning of a rather mundane conference, however, quickly transformed into a flurry of heated activity when the head scientist at the Air Force Personnel and Training Research Center presented "a new approach to overall basic military training."[2]

Robert G. Smith argued that the committee "must accept that the Air Force has a way of life or culture all its own," and this concept must be the governing paradigm in all curriculum design. "In the Air Force culture," he explained, "everyone must know military courtesy, how to wear the uniform, and many similar things. . . . At the same time only a few people must know how to be a jet mechanic or electronics technician. . . . Accordingly the purpose of basic training is to develop in the individual the 'universals' of Air Force culture. .

Sampson AFB, New York, in the early 1950s

Training in camouflage. A sniper's nest (*top*) and a road in South Carolina (*bottom*).

119

Foundation of the Force

. . These are the things which every man must know how to do and believe, not just a few."[3]

The results of the conference included a new definition of the basic training mission—to develop skills, knowledge, and attitudes essential for *all airmen*— and a major revision of the BMT curriculum that called for the integration of technical and basic training in which raw recruits would go to a basic training center and learn only "universals," i.e., small arms training, Air Force history, and so on.[4] Following this truncated course, recruits then attended technical school where they learned technical skills and finished basic training.

Since the creation of an independent Air Force, air planners were particularly concerned over the type of military training necessary for fledgling airmen. The planners also renewed the World War II argument over whether basic training should produce soldiers or persons capable of technical training.[5] Planners also recognized that basic training provided the fundamentals necessary for a productive military career, and this training became the denominator that tied all airmen, regardless of specialty, into a common bond.[6] Yet, between 1945 and 1955, training officials consistently changed course length, curriculum topics, and mission statements. Airmen who attended basic training in 1949, 1951, and 1955, if gathered together into one room, could discuss little of their common heritage. Training was simply too disparate.[7]

Many reasons account for these disparities. One is that the need for manpower as a result of the Air Force's expansion and the Korean war made the length and quality of basic training unpredictable.[8] During periods of demobilization and buildup, the demand for technical schooling forced planners to adjust the length and curriculum of recruit training to meet the need. During the 1950 Korean war mobilization, the Air Force reduced basic training from the traditional thirteen weeks to ten and a half weeks in June and, finally, to five weeks in October. In January and February 1951, the curriculum varied from two weeks to merely in-and-out processing.[9] With the end of the Korean war in 1953 and the subsequent demobilization, the length of basic training gradually increased to eleven weeks.

Critical shortages of skills in the commands resulting from advancing technology, organizational expansion, and poor retention also controlled the length of basic training. By 1950, the Air Force was in transition to jet aircraft and advanced radar and navigational systems, and it was experimenting with guided missiles. These technologies required new skills and new training programs. Also, as the Air Force gradually relied less on the Army for support personnel, personnel planners created new specialties in finance, food service, and intelligence.[10]

Nor did the continued expansion of the Air Force after the Korean war help standardization. Training instructors often shortened basic training in order to get recruits into technical training and out to the commands faster. Personnel planners also found retention a significant problem; they had to replace skilled

Cpl. Robert Gibbons pulls hot rolls from the oven (*top*) and food service training at Fort Francis E. Warren, Wyoming (*center*), and at Jefferson Barracks, Missouri (*bottom*), all in the 1940s.

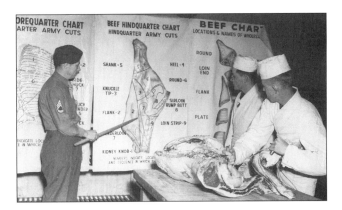

men who left the service. Not until the mid-1950s did Air Force manpower increase to peak strength and stabilize due to better retention.[11] This stabilization of personnel, combined with the advent of a centralized system for tracking training requirements, alleviated many of the problems such as the long technical courses and training lead times associated with technological advances, organizational growth, and manpower retention.[12]

Curriculum changes also detracted from a standardized training program. Many of these changes were induced by agencies outside the Air Force. Integration, for instance, was a product of presidential directive and congressional insistence.[13] Before 1949, the Air Force assigned black recruits to exclusively black squadrons where they ate in their own messes, trained together, and had their own libraries and clubs. As soon as Headquarters United States Air Force (HQ USAF) ordered integration Lackland AFB began to assign all trainees by date of arrival rather than by race. Blacks now ate and slept in the same rooms as whites, trained with whites, and could attend all service clubs and other facilities on base.[14]

Pressures on the DOD by the President's Committee on Religion and Welfare in 1949 and 1950 also led to curriculum changes in the areas of

Columbia University President Dwight D. Eisenhower

122

citizenship, character guidance, and personal morality.* By 1952, the Air Force BMT curriculum reflected nineteen hours of courses such as The Development of Character, Clean Thinking and Living, The Complete Person, and Self-Discipline.[15] Some of the courses taught ethics; others, such as the citizenship course written at Columbia University under the auspices of University President Dwight D. Eisenhower, taught about the evils of communism and emphasized the rights inherent in American society.[16] By 1955, these courses had evolved into teaching specifics about personal behavior in a democracy.[17] People should know their rights, be responsible to defend their way of life, respect authority, and drive a car "responsibly."[18] Thus, it was no surprise when the Air Force, like the Army, Navy, and Marines, undertook the job of Americanizing the nation's youth.[19]

Another imposition to the curriculum involved Category IV (Cat IV) recruits. Until early 1951 only one basic training program had been in place for male enlistees. With the DOD's implementation of the qualitative distribution program, which required all the services to receive an equal amount of mentally substandard volunteers, the Air Force inaugurated a second basic training program designed to "raise the intellectual level of [the substandard] to the fifth grade level."[20] The new training plan for substandard airmen consisted of an intensive forty-five-hour language arts course in addition to the normal basic training curriculum. During these fourteen weeks, instructors segregated Cat IV personnel from higher (mental) category recruits.[21]

Besides the changes in integration, political indoctrination, and DOD programs that caused the basic training curriculum to fluctuate, the Air Force's continued struggle to divorce itself from Army traditions also promoted instability. The World War II debate over drill and ceremonies, marksmanship, and physical exercise continued.[22] In 1949, the Air Force taught over 223 hours in those courses, compared with 136 hours in 1952 and 68 in 1953 (Table 12). By late 1955, training instructors required recruits to field-strip a M–30 carbine, dry-fire it, and learn proper cleaning procedures—all in sixteen hours (the standard had been fifty-seven hours in 1949).[23] The Air Force had its own drill manual patterned after the Army's Field Manual 22–5 and, at times, used it sparingly. A 1954 survey of recruits found that 60 percent had never marched in a retreat formation, and of this 60 percent, 40 percent had never participated in a parade of any kind.[24]

---

* See Chapter 2 for an expanded discussion.

Table 12
Changes in Military Courses in
Air Force Basic Training
(In Hours)

Year	Drill	Tactics	Small Arms	Physical
1949	52	34	57	80
1952	72	—	28	36
1953	36	—	16	16
1956	66	—	16	39

SOURCE: *Historical Data of the 3700th Military Wing, Lackland Air Force Base, 1949–1956*, AFHSO Microfilm.

By 1952, curriculum designers also dropped many of the vestiges of the AAF. Rather than introduce topics like Elementary Aerodynamics, Aircraft Powerplants, and Military Filing Procedures as precursors to technical training, instructors replaced these courses with one single mathematics course common to most technical career fields.[25] In 1956, the math course was dropped in the belief that technical schools provided the best type of mathematics instruction for their specialties.[26] The overall curriculum gradually moved away from one that served as a primer for men dedicated to repairing airplanes to a course geared for assimilating large numbers of men into a host of specialties including supply, guided missiles, and intelligence.

Just as the AAF had differentiated itself from the Army during World War II by developing an enlisted program designed to produce, for the most part, aircraft technicians rather than soldiers,* so did the postwar Air Force by designing a program to produce a variety of specialists, not just aircraft technicians.[27] Planners at the Basic Military Training Conference held in May 1955 reflected this approach as the rudimentary standardized program evolved into an operational training plan. Split into two phases, the integrated course consisted of five weeks at a basic training center and additional basic training provided concurrently with the recruit's technical schooling. Recruits not designated for formal training continued BMT for thirteen weeks before assignment to the major commands for OJT.[28]

Many of these new basic training classes sought to assimilate a new recruit into Air Force life. As a military organization, the Air Force required knowledge of saluting and military courtesy (including a recognition of ranks

* See Chapter 1.

Basic calisthenics at Hondo AFB, Texas, 1950 (*top*); mass calisthenics at Lackland AFB, Texas (*bottom*).

125

Above, a class is receiving M–1 carbine instruction at Kinder AFB. Small arms training, as exemplified by skeet shooting, is shown at Langley Field to the *left*. A liaison and plotting unit is at work, shown at the *top of page opposite*. A Very flare pistol is used to teach aircrewmen land and air survival training at Fort Benning, Georgia (*opposite page, center*). An Air Force survival weapon, an over-and-under 410 shotgun and 22 Hornet rifle combination is seen being demonstrated at the *bottom, far right*.

Foundation of the Force

and uniforms), drills and ceremonies, and procedures for reporting in a military manner. Instructors taught classes in military law, Air Force history, and organizational structure of squadrons and wings along with the fundamentals of security guard details. Besides standard courses in personal hygiene, character guidance, and citizenship, course designers placed much of the traditional field training that involved hikes, bivouacs, and combat training under the heading of survival training. These courses discussed atomic blasts and radiation as well as biological warfare and first aid.

Course developers believed that many recruits would not be combatants but might find themselves in cold climates, in nuclear or chemical warfare zones, or in air crews where this knowledge might prove invaluable. In the past, courses in military leadership dwelt on individual and personal character traits, but new course materials stressed concepts emphasized during World War II: cooperation, teamwork, and human relations.[29] The "new" military basic training was premised on conditions imposed by the Air Force mission and its developing traditions. As one chief master sergeant pointed out, "I think that the changes in basic training [in the 1950s] were smart changes. . . . [Basic training now] concentrated on the actual things that people were going to do . . . when they [got] to the field."[30]

Basic training for women and prior service personnel underwent a similar evolution. As early as 1949, basic training for WAFs mirrored much of the content of the men's basic training curriculum although their course was usually shorter (Table 13). Many of the differences could be attributed to 1950s societal norms and the Air Force's experience with women during World War II. Course content reflected an emphasis on office skills, personal appearance, and social skills. One anomaly, the Leadership and Training Methods class, encouraged women to assert themselves, speak in a command voice, and study examples of great leaders, albeit an odd group of military luminaries and social reformers that included Eisenhower, Marshall, Mary Wollstonecraft Shelley, and Jane Addams of Hull House. Instructors also taught Women in the Armed Forces as a short overview during the seven-hour period.[31]

Table 13
Comparison of Basic Training Courses
For Males and Females
1949
(In Hours* and Percent)

Course	Male	%	Female	%
Elementary Aerodynamics	2	.4	3	.7
Drills and Ceremonies	52	10.0	52	11.8

128

Table 13—cont'd

Course	Male	%	Female	%
Personal Hygiene	3	.6	7	1.6
Sex and Morality/Social Hygiene**	5	1.0	5	1.1
Personal Adjustment	6	1.2	9	2.0
Weapons	57	11.0	3	.7
Squadron and Miscellaneous Duties	61	11.7	48	10.9
Military Correspondence	—		5	1.1
Military Filing Procedures	—		2	.4
Leadership Training	7	1.3	7	1.6

SOURCE: *History of 3700th Indoctrination Wing, 1949*, AFHSO Microfilm.

*For males, the total number of course hous was 520; for females, it was 440.

**The course for men was entitled "Sex and Morality"; for the women, it was called "Social Hygiene."

In 1952, basic training for both male and female recruits had, for the most part, converged. Training sessions for both were nine weeks long (396 hours) and consisted of similar subjects (Table 14).[32] Although WAF training still stressed personal grooming and development of administrative skills, the emphasis was mitigated by the Air Force's need to replace its skilled manpower. As new fields opened to women, their basic training reflected more of what was offered to males. Besides primary classes in traditional clerical and medical roles, the Air Force also taught thirty-six hours of mathematics courses in preparation for technical schooling.

Table 14
Comparison of Basic Training
For Males and Females
1952
(In Hours)

Course	Male	Female
Attitude Development	68	78
Character Guidance	6	8
AF Citizenship	12	20
AF History	8	9
AF Mission	4	5

Table 14—cont'd

Course	Male	Female
AF Weapons	12	10
Cost Consciousness	2	4
Accident Prevention	2	—
Psychological Warfare	5	5
Adjustment to AF Life	53	66
Personal Appearance	—	13
Military Fundamentals	39	47
Personal Hygiene	7	9
Airman's Role in Defense At-tack	6	2
First Aid	10	21
Military Skills	132	116
Drill	72	72
Inspection	24	24
Squadron Orientation	8	20
Marksmanship	28	—
Practical Field Application	32	8
Administrative and Office Proce-dures	—	9
Physical Fitness	36	36
Mathematics	36	36

SOURCE: *History of Lackland AFB, April–June 1952*, apps A, B, AFHSO Microfilm.

Women even began to receive more military training as instructors either introduced or lengthened classes in physical fitness, base defense, and small arms training.[33] Eventually, however, increasing male reenlistments, a rapidly growing manpower pool, and a lack of female enlistments obviated the strong need for women in nontraditional skills. The basic training curriculum reflected these factors. By early 1956, when the male curriculum shifted to the two-phase, eleven-week plan, the WAF course remained at nine weeks, and the mathematics classes were dropped.[34] Ever pragmatic, air planners increased opportunities for women only when necessary.[35]

In early 1954, the Air Force introduced a basic training course specifically designed for prior-service personnel. Since many of these individuals had been previously trained or were capable of receiving advanced technical training, the goal was to indoctrinate, classify, and send them to the commands or school as quickly as possible.[36]

Instructors designed courses for two types of people: those who had been in other branches of the service and those who were returning Air Force veterans. "Misfits, nonconformists, and people unable to readjust [from] civilian life" were supposedly weeded out during this training.[37]

The first prior-service program, initiated on February 24, 1954, segregated individuals with previous military experience from other male recruits and placed them in a significantly reduced BMT of 160 hours.[38] Course work consisted of eighty-four classroom hours of Air Force topics similar to those given in traditional BMT. Instructors emphasized drill and ceremonies less and Air Force history and traditions more. Course designers devoted another thirty-six hours to administrative activities such as haircuts, immunizations, pay, career counseling, and classification.[39] The fluctuating needs of the Air Force determined the exact details of the course. By May 1954, this initial program was shortened to fifteen days, and in June it was scaled back to nine days in order to meet the technical training requirements imposed by the commands' need for skilled manpower.[40]

Though basic training differed among the services and was constantly evolving for the Air Force, one fundamental aspect remained. All airmen, soldiers, marines, or sailors were classified into future occupational specialties during this period. Usually within the first two weeks of training, new recruits spent a full morning or afternoon taking the Airman Classification Test Battery. This test told classifiers what areas might be suitable for the recruit's advanced training. Consisting of fourteen parts, the test covered five basic aptitudes—mechanical, administrative, radio operator, general, and electrical.[41]

Guidance and assignment counselors then used the test scores to determine which of the forty-three major career fields were appropriate for each recruit. If a recruit had already acquired specific skills needed by the Air Force, classifiers administered Job Knowledge Tests and Proficiency Tests to determine the individual's skill level. Based on all these tests and interviews, classifiers determined whether an airman would go to school, receive OJT, or bypass training altogether.[42]

Building a New Service: Technical Training and the Growing Air Force

The rapid demobilization after World War II, though devastating to efficiency and effectiveness, still left a force fully four times as large as it had been in 1939. Even during the late 1940s and early 1950s, with pressures to reduce the military budget and reduce conventional arms and military strengths, the armed forces' size did not go below 2.5 million. Part of the need to maintain this manpower was the military's commitment overseas. More than 40 percent of the nation's military strength served abroad in the 1950s (the figure was 50 percent during the Korean war). On average, nearly 39 percent of Air Force personnel were located overseas in the 1950s, during and after the fighting in Korea.[43]

Overseas commitments were a major factor shaping Air Force manpower and training policies in the 1940s and 1950s. In the interwar period, the Air Force depended on the Army for logistical and combat support to supply continental bases. Now it needed specialists to supply and operate widespread overseas bases; maintain large headquarters, personnel, administrative, and service units; and provide for the training and rotation of personnel from overseas.

Air Force training requirements were significantly affected by shifts in the size of its personnel base at home and abroad. The growing reliance placed on air power by the Truman and Eisenhower administrations resulted in large manpower allocations to the Air Force during the Korean war and early Cold War period, as indicated by the size of the aircraft inventory and number of wings (Table 15).[44]

Table 15
Aircraft Inventory and
Number of Wings
1947–1957

Year	Aircraft	Wings
1947	13,341	38
1948	13,890	55
1949	13,456	54
1950	12,572	48
1951	13,753	87
1952	15,970	95
1953	19,013	106
1954	21,601	115
1955	23,694	121
1956	26,670	131
1957	25,969	137

SOURCE: *National Security and the Budget* (Washington, D.C.: GPO, 1988) p. 291.

Between 1950 and 1956, Air Force manpower constituted 28.7 percent of total military strength (Table 16), compared with 19 percent for the AAF at the end of World War II. Table 16 also shows that the overall levels of the military branches were subjected to several factors, including the nature of the military mission, the type of conflict, the lead time for training personnel, and the technological nature of the services.

Table 16
Manpower Strength
By Branch of Service
1945–1956
(In Percent)

Year	DOD	Air Force	Army	Navy	Marine
1945	100	18.7	49.1	28.2	4.0
1946	100	15.0	47.4	32.5	5.1
1947	100	19.3	43.3	31.5	5.9
1948	100	26.8	38.3	29.0	5.9
1949	100	26.0	40.9	27.8	5.3
1950	100	28.2	40.6	26.1	5.1
1951	100	24.3	47.1	22.7	5.9
1952	100	27.0	43.9	22.7	6.4
1953	100	27.5	43.1	22.3	7.0
1954	100	28.7	42.5	22.0	6.8
1955	100	32.7	37.8	22.5	7.0
1956	100	32.4	36.6	23.9	7.2

SOURCE: *DOD Fact Book, 1958*, p. 21.

Because of the long training periods for technical skills, it was imperative that the Air Force and the Navy have much of their enlisted force experienced and in readiness before the outbreak of war. Nuclear weapons and jet aircraft made a fast response time absolutely necessary. No more could long-term mobilizations be acceptable, as they had in World War II. Thus, having more manpower in readiness ensured less fluctuation in manpower levels at the start of a war. For instance, in 1950 and 1951, while the Air Force and the Navy were the most technological of the services, they were also the least affected by the manpower fluctuations that occurred during the Korean war. Manpower statistics for the Army and the Marine Corps, however, reflected the converse. Table 16 and Appendices 1 and 2 demonstrate that the Army and the Marine Corps grew by 170 and 160 percent respectively, while the Navy's and the Air Force's growth rate failed to double.

Although overseas expansion and the increasing size of the Air Force had an important effect on its training mission, the rate of technological change was equally pervasive. Embraced wholeheartedly after World War II, confidence in

Radio operators train at Francis E. Warren AFB (*above*). A practice bombing run is discussed (*below*).

Fire and rescue training in Korea (*top*). Training to fight aircraft fires (*bottom*).

Prewar drafting class, Roosevelt Field, New York (*top*). Tracking a B–29 on ground radar (*center*). Operations specialists prepare operational data forms (*bottom*).

scientific research and the belief that superior technology would win the next war permeated Air Force thinking. By the time of Korea, technological innovation had accelerated so rapidly that some equipment and weapons systems had become obsolete before they became operational.[45]

Belief in technological superiority and the breadth of technological change deeply affected the Air Force, as demonstrated by the steady production of new fighters and bombers which flew faster, higher, farther, and under all types of climatic and weather conditions.[46] By 1955, new weapons proliferated. America's arsenal now included thermonuclear weapons, jet aircraft, advanced electronics, computerization for fire control, air defense, communications, and supply. In 1956, it included guided missiles with nuclear warhead.[47]

One important area of technological growth was in electronic applications to weapons systems. Pioneered during World War II and advanced during the Cold War, military researchers devised new electronic devices that could instantaneously observe and react to incoming weapons. Other electrical innovations included microwave radio relays, tactical data control systems, electronic countermeasure devices, weather radar, micro-transceivers, and automatic data-processing equipment. One NCO vividly remembered the effect of technology on training during the early 1950s:

> Recruits had plenty of automotive experience . . . but jet engine theory and practical application to a higher technical skill had to be applied to all ranks and grades. The fast progression almost daily of new systems in communications, radar, autoflight control, weapons, and delivery systems had to be absorbed quickly and still maintain the force in an operational ready status.[48]

The Air Force's occupational distribution for 1945, 1953, and 1957 (Table 17) indicated a trend toward the highly technical specialties, the great need for administrative help during the expansion, and a decrease in less-skilled trades (food services, fire fighters, and military police).[49] Additionally, as aircraft weapon systems advanced technologically, old AAF specialties like aerial gunner approached obsolescence.[50]

Table 17
Occupational Distribution of
Air Force Enlisted Specialties
1945, 1953, 1957

Air Force Specialty	1945	1953	1957
Electronics	8.1	13.1	15.5
Technical	7.6	7.7	7.8
Administrative/Clerical	19.9	28.6	27.9

Table 17—cont'd

Air Force Specialty	1945	1953	1957
Mechanic/Repairman	35.9	24.7	28.8
Craftsman	4.7	7.6	8.0
Services	14.5	15.1	12.0
Miscellaneous (Aerial Gunner)	9.5	3.1	—
Total	100.0	100.0	100.0

SOURCE: Harold Wool, *The Military Specialist*, p. 43.

Two important ramifications arose due to this change. First, as technology increased and made various air crew positions obsolete, airmen had almost no direct or immediate combat role, such as firing machine guns at attacking aircraft.[51] Second, this also meant that the division between the status of air crews and ground crews would decrease. In the interwar period, an airman's status was related to his work on the aircraft; in the postwar period, status would be defined by how technical and pertinent an airman's skill was as related to the mission. Thus, individuals with highly technical skills became an elite class of enlisted personnel. In fact, the Air Force divided all specialties into hard-core (highly skilled and technical) and soft-core (support) specialties, thereby further codifying the distinctions among and status accorded skills.

A Prelude to Training: Devising an Air Force Career Management System

Technological sophistication called for advanced training and constant retraining in schools that only the Air Force and the other military services provided. Air planners predicated such a program upon understanding the demands of technology and projecting the manpower needs of its various major commands. Central to this need was the creation of a system whereby occupational categories and skill levels were known and easily communicated up and down the chain of command.[52] It was obvious in the wake of World War II demobilization that Army reporting procedures and classification schemes did not do justice to the vast array of Air Force specialties.[53] In 1946, no one in the Air Force knew exactly what manpower strength levels were or what critical skills had been lost.[54] Planners hoped that a new occupational classification patterned after industry and new reporting procedures would aid in reassigning and retraining personnel into needed specialties, cut manpower costs, and help create a pipeline from which future training needs could be projected and accessioned.[55]

In light of the joint agreements between the Army and the AAF that called for a separate Air Force in 1947, the Secretary of Defense directed both services to work together in planning and restructuring military occupational specialties in hopes of finding a unified classification program. Army and Air Force classification specialists, many trained during the war in classification and industrial job schemes, met at the Pentagon in 1947 and 1948 to plan for the future renovation.[56] By late 1947, though the Army and Air Force had analyzed several common jobs under the auspices of the Office of the Secretary of Defense's (OSD's) Armed Forces Personnel Policy Board, it was clear that the two services needed a more comprehensive classification system.[57]

Both services and OSD agreed that the new system called for an encompassing plan that did more than categorize jobs and provide for easy reporting.[58] The new plan, according to defense staffers, must "enhance the prestige and professional worth of all career enlisted men and by so doing attract more and better personnel."[59] Drawing from industrial occupational plans and the Navy's career program, the military agreed upon "career management" as a guiding philosophy that would establish the Army and Air Force as institutions capable of providing a career complete with broad areas of occupational training and a clear path of advancement.[60]

In devising the career management system, planners believed two criteria were fundamental to its successful implementation. First, the system should provide a pathway of advancement that a serviceman could understand and compare favorably with civilian firms. The more civilian-like the career program, the more recruits could identify with the military as being similar to other good employers. Citizens could also understand the military in corporate terms—a significant factor for making the military seem more democratic, or more American.

Second, it should eliminate the failings of the old promotion system, such as dead-end jobs, favoritism, lack of Tables of Organization and Equipment vacancies, poor assignment guidelines, and "waiting for the man ahead to die, to be demoted, or retire" in order to be promoted.[61] In a society that espoused the idea that a person should advance through his own ability, a merit system also helped the military seem more American.

Introduced by the Air Force in 1950, planners designed the Airman Career Program as a plan governing the entire life cycle of an airman. It became the basic framework for enlisted personnel management for the next forty years.[62] Guided by principles espoused by Frederick W. Taylor almost fifty years earlier, classifiers studied each Air Force job, created for each a job description of standard requirements, and assigned a pay scale so that equal pay was established for the same jobs. Once analyzed and scientifically standardized, personnel planners then grouped them into nine broad occupational areas, or families, and into forty-two career fields (see Appendix 3).[63]

In tandem with career field development, classifiers established a job progression ladder whereby enlisted men moved up the enlisted rank structure on the basis of their ability to pass job knowledge and skill tests.[64] Thus, while the old system stressed longevity and unit vacancies for promotion, this program placed occupational skill and merit as the premier criteria.[65] Longevity in service and grade served as qualifiers for promotion, not as determinants. Just as the Doolittle Board had argued in 1946 for a promotion system based on merit, air planners in 1950 introduced a career plan that tied promotion to skill level. Thus, occupational competence, not military deportment, became the basis for promotion.[66]

Air leaders and planners engaged in much discussion about how far up the career ladder an airman could climb. Both the Army and the Air Force agreed that a change in grade structure was required to make the career plan a proper incentive for promotion and retention.[67] The Army, for instance, completely overhauled its grades by eliminating staff and technical sergeants from their NCO ranks. As of 1948, the new Army NCO grades were corporal, sergeant, sergeant first class, and master sergeant (or first sergeant). The Army now designated technicians by a specialist chevron rather than NCO rank.[68] The Air Force, on the other hand, maintained the AAF rank structure until 1952, when planners replaced it with a new version (Table 18).

Table 18
Air Force Enlisted Grade Structures
1947 and 1952

	1947		1952
Pay Grade	Rank	Pay Grade	Rank
1	Master Sgt	E7	Master Sgt
2	Technical Sgt	E6	Technical Sgt
3	Staff Sgt	E5	Staff Sgt
4	Sgt	E4	Airman First Class
5	Corporal	E3	Airman Second Class
6	PFC	E2	Airman Third Class
7	Private	E1	Airman Basic

SOURCE: *USAF Statistical Digest, FY 1952*, p. 388.

Planners devised alternate paths for the progression of technician NCOs; however, it became clear by 1956 that to reach the highest career promotion level of superintendent (which carried a warrant officer grade), one had to become a supervisor/manager first and a technician second. (For an example of the job progression for an airman in the Motorized and Miscellaneous Equipment Maintenance Career Field, see Chart 1.)

Under optimum circumstances, the Airman Career Program began during basic training when classification tests placed a candidate in a suitable Air Force specialty designated by an Air Force Specialty Code (AFSC).[69] This five-digit code specified the career field, the career field subdivision, the skill level, and the Air Force specialty. For example, in the Aircraft and Engine Maintenance career field, an AFSC of 43150 indicated a skilled jet engine mechanic. The first two digits, 43, designated the Aircraft and Engine Maintenance Career Field; the third digit, 1, meant the career field subdivision of aircraft engines; the fourth digit, 5, indicated a skilled rating; and the final digit, 0, pinpointed the AFSC within the subdivision and the level—in this case, Jet Engine Mechanic. By the early 1960s, the last digit was tied to a letter that designated the category of aircraft and specific weapon system (a 1 indicated tactical fighters; an A meant an A–7 aircraft).[70]

Designated as a helper or trainee, the airman followed basic training with technical school or progressed to a major command. At technical school, the Air Force awarded a semiskilled Air Force Specialty (AFS) 3-level skill code to an airman who successfully completed the course and passed a proficiency exam at his next unit.[71] An airman who went directly to a command and was not a bypass specialist (someone who was a specialist and did not need additional training) underwent a period of OJT. Then, upon his supervisor's recommendation and demonstration of proficiency, he was granted the 3-level AFSC.

The five skill levels designated levels of technical expertise and managerial competence. The first level, or helper, identified those who were entering the service or going into retraining. The second level, the semiskilled or the 3-level apprentice, were those who lacked the experience and proficiency to perform the job without supervision. The skilled, or journeyman 5-level, specified airmen who had the experience and training and had demonstrated proficiency to perform the job alone. The advanced or 7-level supervisor or technician identified those who had gained a high degree of technical knowledge in their specialty and were competent supervisors. Finally, the 0-levels, or superintendent levels, were reserved for warrant officers and some master sergeants who had attained a broad technical knowledge of all jobs within a given career field and could "plan, coordinate, implement, and direct work activities."[72]

Once working in a specialty, an enlisted man could upgrade his skill level through OJT, a minimum period of AFS experience, and by qualifying on an Air Force Job Knowledge test. These tests were written specifically for 3-, 5-, and 7-skill levels by teams of "the best qualified" master sergeants selected Air Force–wide.*[73]

---

* See Chapter 5 for more detail.

Chart 1

Motorized and Miscellaneous Equipment Maintenance Career Field

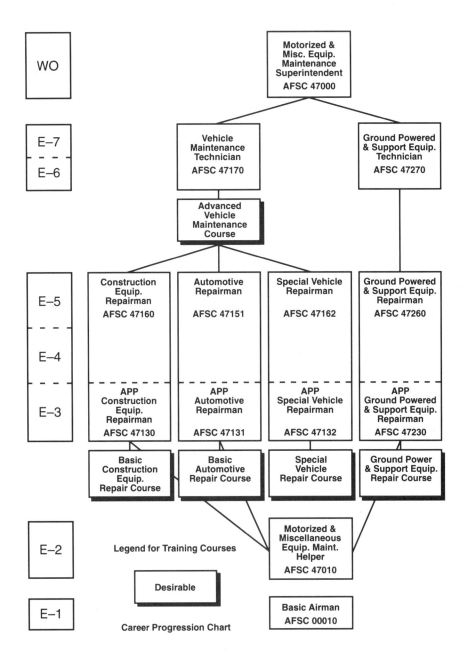

The Airman Career Program also provided the framework from which to standardize promotion criteria and centralize quotas. Mirroring the basic structure of the Army's career program, the Air Force tied advancement to skill levels, time-in-grade requirements, performance reports, and servicewide promotion quotas.[74] As promotion was tied to skill level, only those who achieved the 5-level could be promoted to E–4 or E–5. The 7-level was mandatory for E–6s and E–7s, while the Air Force generally reserved the superintendent level (0-level) for warrant officers.

Time-in-grade requirements ensured a minimum period during which an airman could "fully learn and appreciate [his] duties and responsibilities and gain familiarity" with the duties of the next higher grade.[75] As the Air Force expanded in the 1950s, planners greatly reduced the time-in-grade requirements (see Table 19) to build up the enlisted force. They made promotions to Airman Third Class (E–2) from Basic Airman automatic upon completion of basic training.

Table 19
Total Time-in-Grade Requirements
1950 and 1955

Promotion

From:	To:	Time in Grade
1950		
E–2	PFC	4 Months
E–3	Corporal	8 Months
E–4	Sergeant	18 Months
E–5	Staff Sgt	24 Months
E–6	Tech Sgt	36 Months
E–7	Master Sgt	48 Months
1955		
E–3	A2C	6 Months as A3C
E–4	A1C	8 Months as A2C
E–5	Staff Sgt	12 Months as A1C
E–6	Tech Sgt	14 Months as Staff
E–7	Master Sgt	16 Months as Tech

SOURCES: AFR 39–30, *The Promotion and Demotion of Airmen* (Washington, D.C.: GPO, Mar 24, 1950); AFR 39–29, *Promotion of Airmen* (Washington, D.C.: GPO, Jan 2, 1955).

Foundation of the Force

During the Korean war, the Air Force dropped time-in-grade requirements as promotion opportunities blossomed. Airmen progressed quickly up the job ladder, averaging six months between promotions.[76] The Air Force also waived time-in-grade minimums for spot promotions for prior commissioned or warrant officers and for those previously demoted for cause.[77] The length of active federal military service, while not a requirement for promotion, did have an effect on obtaining temporary or permanent status as an NCO. Promotion to E–2, E–3, and E–4 was permanent, while permanent promotions to staff sergeant, technical sergeant, and master sergeant required times in service of eight, eleven, and fourteen years, respectively. In addition, unit commanders could authorize acting NCOs, who wore the stripes but did not receive more pay. After permanent NCOs fulfilled tenure requirements, the Air Force issued Certificates of Appointment specifying the airmen's new status.[78]

Personnel planners discussed as early as November 1946 the advantages of establishing central promotion quotas. Yet it was not until the Air Force established a better reporting process and classification program that the service was able to institute such a system and use it to smooth out the grade imbalances caused by rapid promotions during the Korean war.[79] Established in 1953, the new quota system terminated the unit vacancy rule required under the old Army system and allowed the director of military personnel to allocate promotion quotas to the major commands on the basis of commandwide vacancies in grade and AFSCs.

The Air Force now only promoted an Airman Second Class jet mechanic who had complied with all promotion requirements if the command (not the unit) had an opening in his AFSC and next grade (A1C). Units or commands, upon receiving the quotas, usually established selection boards which subjectively evaluated possible promotees. By 1954, only major commands could promote to the E–5, E–6, and E–7 grades. Lower grades were delegated to the squadron level.[80] It would not be until 1970 and the introduction of the Weighted Airman Promotion System (WAPS) that promotions became fully centralized, standardized, and automated.[81]

The progression from Airman Basic into a career field and up the ladder to the superintendent levels was marred, however, by warrant officer quotas.[82] Due to the Officer Grade Limitation Act of 1954, the Air Force considered warrant officers a part of the total officer ceiling. When air planners desired 20,000 warrant superintendent positions for the Airman Career Program in 1954, the Air Staff failed to approve their plan because of the debilitative effect it would have upon the commissioned officer quota imposed by Congress. The additional warrant officers would reduce the commissioned officer strength by 15,500, including 20 generals, 470 colonels, 1,250 lieutenant colonels, and 3,250 majors.[83]

With ceilings held to a minimum due to their diminishing effect on officer spaces, other factors also made the use of warrant officers in the Airman Career

Program untenable. Many senior NCOs did not see promotion to warrant officer as a career incentive.[84] Some thought the position was too limiting. "They were absolute experts," a chief master sergeant of the Air Force commented, "If you saw a warrant officer in the finance business, he could recite the manual . . . . He'd been working for twenty or twenty-five years in one field."[85]

Other airmen were confused over the role of a warrant officer in the Air Force structure. This confusion carried over into housing, social activities, and the workplace. They were "neither fish nor fowl," recalled one senior NCO—neither officer nor enlisted. Rather, they worked in an ambiguous environment where the highest-grade warrant officer (W–4) often fulfilled the duties of a commissioned major, but he was subject to the orders of the youngest second lieutenant.[86] Additionally, the pay difference between the master sergeant and warrant officer grades was too small to be an incentive to overcome the effects of isolation, diminished prestige, and a few token privileges.[87] Moreover, some senior NCOs did not want to be addressed by the warrant officer's title—"Mister."[88] When the Military Pay Act of 1958 ushered in two enlisted supergrades, E–8 and E–9 (senior master sergeant and chief master sergeant), the Air Force placed the new grades in the career path and gradually eliminated the warrant officer from its rank structure.[89]

Another major consequence of the new career management program was the eventual elimination of another category of airman: the career private, or helper. In the Army Air Corps before World War II, it was not unusual to find, in the Tables of Organization, positions listed simply as private and with no specialty attached. These men's assignments usually involved housekeeping duties or other unskilled jobs. In time, many did enter the NCO ranks or into a specialty via some type of OJT.[90] With the advent of the Airman Career Program, this pattern changed. Planners assigned every new airman to a broad occupational–functional category during basic training, to begin at the bottom of his career field as an apprentice. Though unskilled, these recruits were assigned an occupational path that called for formal job training or OJT which would lead to higher skill levels and promotion.

One of the Air Force's biggest problems was finding helper jobs for substandard, Cat IV airmen. As of 1950, the Air Force could use Cat IV personnel in 28 percent of its 292 jobs, none of which offered a grade higher than E–4.[91] Moreover, planners continued to receive considerable flak from many commanding generals who, like Curtis E. LeMay, firmly believed that Cat IV personnel severely undercut mission effectiveness. Few could hold technician jobs, and those who could were not very proficient.

Starting in 1952, experiments in basic training with Cat IV recruits, combined with the lack of jobs, caused an increasing resistance among Air Force leaders toward the qualitative distribution scheme. Rather than simply accepting the inevitable—low caliber recruits as a given—the Air Force

Lt. Gen. Curtis E. LeMay, late 1947

requested DOD to allow it to study further the basic training provided to Cat IV personnel.

Continuing well into 1953, Project One-Thousand (as the study was called), sought to demonstrate scientifically to DOD the futility of enlisting Cat IVs into the Air Force.[92] Planners of this project selected 1,000 Cat IV men for long-term study. They then assigned 500 to a six-week remedial training course prior to basic training; the other 500 received the normal twelve-week course. The groups were studied during training and at their first command. After twenty months the project demonstrated no significant difference between the two groups. In other words, remedial training did little to help or retard these men in their follow-on jobs.

The results of these tests were skewed due to DOD's insistence that the thousand men be assigned to areas not requiring technical training, such as Food Service, Motor Transportation, Supply, Air Police, and the Medical

Career Field, rather than be placed in the normal assignment system, which could have included technical career fields.[93]

Nevertheless, the project's results provided the Air Force with evidence to counter some of the effects of DOD's qualitative distribution program. On November 9, 1953, the basic training center at Lackland AFB discontinued the remedial reading program for substandard airmen since none of the experimental programs conducted previously justified the efforts.[94] Second, the results of Project One Hundred Thousand helped scientists at the Human Research Laboratory devise more stringent screening instruments. Instead of basing their selection on aptitude scores, which measured intellectual potential, planners now emphasized the scores of specific achievement tests as predictors of future success.[95]

The results of the project also aided personnel planners to glean low achievers from the service as the Korean war was scaling down. By the third week in November 1953, HQ USAF authorized worldwide commands to force an estimated 35,000 low achievers from the Air Force. Criteria for retention included supervisor evaluations, the commander's discretion, and a score of at least 3 on the Airman Classification Test Battery.[96] Though the qualitative distribution scheme continued for another year, the Air Force now accepted only those Cat IV personnel scoring at or above the minimum standard on aptitude tests.

By 1954, the Air Force still had too many Cat IV personnel. As planners ran out of helper-type jobs to assign to substandard personnel, they began placing them in technical jobs. However, only 40 percent of those placed were capable of qualifying for their positions. The increased number of Cat IV personnel reenlisting also compounded the problem. In the same year, Congress approved the Air Force's expansion to 137 wings. Thus, as the requirements for technical specialties increased and since few Cat IV people could function in those jobs, the Air Force was stymied in its efforts to solve this problem.[97]

In 1955, while the Air Force accepted 25,600 Cat IV airmen, only 24,300 could be used. By 1956, fiscal year projections indicated that another 32,870 substandards would enlist, of which the service could use only 1,200.[98] By 1956, a combination of too few helper jobs in all the services, a reduction in draft calls and in the size of the Army, and a growing manpower pool led the DOD to indefinitely suspend the qualitative distribution scheme.[99] Instituted in the late 1960s, Project One Hundred Thousand (often called a Great Society program) reintroduced the notion of the military as a training ground for low achievers.[100] Though air planners laid the groundwork for this program in the early 1950s, they clearly did not like the idea that their service would be used for social welfare experiments.

Planners disliked these social experiments for two major reasons: First, such programs often reduced efficiency and detracted from the Air Force's image of accepting and training only high-quality youth. Second, programs like

Air police guard a rebuilt MiG–15 on Okinawa, October 1953 (*top*). Military police training with riot control agents (*center*). Military police training in unarmed combat (*bottom*).

the acceptance of marginal men were thrust upon the Air Force by presidential and congressional committees and by the DOD. Planners had little input into the origins of the program; civilian officials told them only to ensure that the marginal program was implemented. Planners viewed Americanizing efforts differently. They saw political education and citizenship training as attempts to make the military more amenable to public support.

Technical Training: The Raison d'Etre

Following basic training and classification, the Air Force introduced airmen, through technical training, into the realm of everyday Air Force life. The fundamental objective of such training was economically to produce "airmen who are skilled to the extent that they may perform efficiently specific duty assignments."[101] During the interwar and World War II periods, technical training vacillated between extensive OJT programs and formal training, and between generalized and specialized training.

This vacillation continued into the Cold War period. By 1954, however, personnel planners and major commands had hammered out a system which included recruit training, technical schools for formal training, and OJT packages (used by the commands in a limited apprenticeship program and for upgrading proficiency).[102] The requirement for specialists undermined the original broad training concept envisioned in the Airman Career Program and placed the Air Force in a position of needing more men to do more jobs.

The creation of an efficient training program and pipeline was predicated upon the right mix of formal training, OJT, and self-study.[103] Since World War I, Air Force training personnel studied and discussed the necessary mix of theoretical and practical training, and this debate continued well into the mid-1950s. In the 1946–1950 period, demobilization, a dearth of technical specialists, and a lack of operational aircraft for training purposes forced planners to emphasize broad formal training and largely forgo OJT.

This shortage of trained personnel in 1946 hampered all the AAF's major commands. For instance, the Strategic Air Command's manpower precipitously dropped from an authorized 43,279 men in May 1946 to 37,426 (a 14 percent decrease) by December of that year. SAC leaders complained of too few instructors, surpluses in some specialties, and acute shortages in critical technical areas such as aircraft maintenance, radar, and aircraft powerplant repair. Moreover, when SAC attempted to retrain surplus airmen in more critical skills, it found too many were incapable of absorbing technical training.[104] Moreover, those already trained had only general, not specialized, knowledge, which meant that most technicians could not be efficiently used without a long period of informal OJT.

ATC's commanding general, John K. Cannon, attributed the emphasis on generalized training to economic reasons. ATC did not want to duplicate operational equipment; hence, they taught theoretical versus practical courses and hoped that individuals broadly trained could be used in a variety of Air Force technical specialties.[105]

By 1949, graduates of formal schools were expected to enter into any one of several semiskilled AFSCs, participate in a minimum OJT program at their unit, and perform adequately.[106] At this time, advanced courses were few, and most were long, abstract, and theoretical, providing little practical training. Frequently, the basic course was the only formal training given to an airman during his entire career.

As of 1951, formal training took place in one of eight Air Force schools that had been established during World War II and in various civilian contract schools. Sheppard AFB near Wichita Falls, Texas, offered specialty training in maintenance and repair of jet and reciprocating engined aircraft along with transportation, intelligence, and finance. At Francis E. Warren AFB in Wyoming, the Air Force taught courses in auto mechanics, supply, teletype and telephone, and special-purpose motor vehicles such as trucks, cranes and bulldozers.

Communication specialists trained at Scott AFB near St. Louis, Missouri, as did personnel managers and cryptographers. Schools for radio and radar operators and radar maintenance technicians were located at Kessler AFB, Biloxi, Mississippi, home of the Technical Training Air Force Headquarters. Lowry AFB, near Denver, Colorado, offered training in armament and photography. Finally, Chanute AFB in Illinois, continuing its tradition from the 1920s, provided more than forty courses for sheet-metal workers, machinists, specialized aircraft powerplant mechanics, and weather observers.[107]

A 1948 Air Force–wide survey showed the fallacy of such broad training programs. Few graduates were capable of immediate employment by the commands since their theoretical training did not easily transform into practical, hands-on expertise. The study revealed that Air Training Command simply did not have the proper equipment and techniques to teach the day-to-day skills required of a technician.[108] More often than not, the commands themselves set up formal training to offset these deficiencies and lamented that "by the time an airman became a dependable operator or mechanic" over one-half of his enlistment had expired.[109]

With the advent of the Korean war, the emphasis on broad training that chacterized World Wars I and II now shifted toward specialization, or channelized training.[110] For instance, when early in the Korean war the Air Force needed many radio mechanics in a short time, the generalized radio mechanic course was divided into a fundamental course and two phases: Phase I for aircraft equipment and Phase II for ground equipment. Compared with the generalized course that took 175 days for completion, the channelized courses required only 150 days (110 days for fundamental and 40 days for the phases).

If necessary, a trainee could graduate at the end of the 110 days and then transfer to the commands as an apprentice.[111]

Planners also broke the Aircraft Mechanic AFSC into a number of subspecialties, called shred-outs, and devised courses for each. By July 1954, the Aircraft and Engine Maintenance Career Field consisted of twelve technical courses and thirteen OJT packaged programs. The twelve courses served as the source for ninety specializations in this career field (Table 20 presents a partial listing of this field's shred-outs), from which 19,633 aircraft and engine mechanics graduated in Fiscal Year 1954.[112]

Table 20
Partial List of Shred-Outs,
Aircraft and Engine Maintenance Career Field

AFSC	Title
43130	Rotary Wing Mech
43133	Acft Jet Engine Mech
43136	Acft Instr Mech
43137	Towreel Mech
43139	In-flight Refueling Spec
43131A	Acft Mech, B–36
43131B	Acft Mech, B–29
43131C	Acft Mech, Heavy Transport
43131D	Acft Mech, Medium Transport
43131E	Acft Mech, Admin
43131F	Acft Mech, Conventional Fighter
43131G	Acft Mech, B–26
43131H	Acft Mech, Jet Fighter
43132F	Acft Recip Eng Mech, In-line
43131J	Acft Mech, B–47
43131K	Acft Mech, B–45
43131L	Acft Mech, Amphib

SOURCE: Memo, DCS/PT (Persons) to Comdr, TAC, Aug 31, 1953, Subj: Technical Training, RG 341, Entry 155, file 353, Box 695, MMB, NA.

Although most of the specializations had to do with jet aircraft, channelization also affected reciprocating and rotary engine mechanics.[113] Specialization seemed an important corrective to technical training problems because it significantly reduced course length and increased the number of technical school graduates.

Foundation of the Force

Unlike after World War I and World War II, specialized training continued for several reasons. For one, the Air Force continued to expand its number of wings (see Table 15) to meet its growing global mission. More wings meant more aircraft and a need for additional technicians. By January 1951, ATC increased its training facilities, and within six months it doubled its technical school graduation rate to met the demand.[114]

By 1952, the four-year expansion program to 148 wings required the use of civilian, factory, Army, and Navy schools.[115] Between July 1951 and June 1952, approximately 50,000 trainees attended civilian institutions. The Air Force had not spent that much money on factory training in one year since World War II. Under the 95-wing program planned in 1951, 48,848 airmen were scheduled for civilian training in approximately 50 private and state-supported trade and vocational schools, colleges, and universities.[116] The Air Force also used Army and Navy Schools, but it found the other services preoccupied with their own training needs. In 1952 and thereafter, the number of airmen significantly decreased in other service schools.[117]

While the expansion, coupled with a mass exodus of Korean war enlistees, increased the need for specialized training, the complexity of new equipment also called for channelization. For example, the advent of jet aircraft and electronic guidance systems made much older technology obsolescent. One important innovation during World War II was the Norden bombsight, which worked on a visual-mechanical principle. Six years after the war, the bombsight had been replaced by a new electronic system, the AN/APQ–24, which in 1952 was replaced by the K–1 bombsight. Operationally, the K–1 was "an operator's dream, but a maintenance man's nightmare." It was so sophisticated that the solution for its maintenance was either to use "graduate engineers" as repairmen or to specialize so that its repair was done by "a team, no member of which [was] fully qualified to troubleshoot the device alone."[118] Simpler equipment was another solution, but the design of such equipment was usually out of the hands of training officials.[119]

Problems often developed with other advanced systems. When ATC began to develop courses for the F–86D Sabre Jet interceptor's electronic systems, it found that each aircraft required 5,500 electrical wires for a total of 22,196 feet, more than ten times the wiring used in World War II fighters.[120] Increasing complexity also meant additional maintenance hours. For instance, a World War II B–25 averaged about twenty maintenance hours per hour of flight; the F–86D required fifty-five.[121] Likewise, a World War II P–51 needed seven man-hours of depot maintenance for each hour of flight, a 1954 F–91 required 13.1.[122] Additionally, in 1951, the ATC introduced maintenance courses in guided missiles, and by mid-1952 five course addressed this specialty.[123] With more complex equipment coming on-line, plus the increase of (substandard) Cat IV personnel going into technical training, the need for specialization seemed incontrovertible.

Advanced systems required intensive OJT programs for enlistees.

The 60 percent yearly attrition rate of airman-technicians also increased the need for specialized training. Since many of their skills were transferrable to civilian aviation, a number of experienced technicians left the Air Force for better pay and benefits.[124] In 1951, a congressional inquiry into the state of Air Force training estimated that the cost of a student's training in a twenty-week fundamental electronics course exceeded $6,000, or $4,194,000 for the 699 students then in attendance. Expenses for less technical courses such those given to airmen entering food service or public relations (information) specialties averaged about $1,500 in 1950 dollars.[125]

Some Air Force leaders, such as ATC Commanding General Robert Harper, saw the benefits bestowed upon the country through the Air Force's technical contribution to the civilian aircraft industry. He also pointed out that "the Air Force gets no credit in Congressional appropriations for this loss . . . it's just completely charged against us."[126]

To offset partially this training loss, a new concept of training evolved that went hand-in-hand with the Airman Career Program. Planners introduced training to airmen at specific times in their career and accomplished it through several means.[127] Initial technical school training taught only the "knowledge and skills which they will use during this narrow initial utilization period [first-term of enlistment]."[128]

On-the-job-training at the command level ensured that the airman had specialized knowledge and proficiency in the squadron's equipment and procedures. Some debate existed over whether the Air Force should formally train or exclusively use an OJT-type program. Personnel planners at ATC and HQ USAF saw centralization and control over the training process as crucial

153

to their growing hegemony and status. Moreover, technology seemed to dictate formal courses. Thus, the trend toward formalized training received increased impetus from ATC and HQ USAF, while the commands looked at the technical schooling warily and preferred OJT and field training.[129]

Field training, through mobile training units and factory courses, taught the fundamentals and specialized knowledge necessary to repair new equipment procured by the units.[130] Finally, as airmen progressed into their second enlistment they became eligible for advanced training in their specialty. This usually meant, for the airman, a minimum of four additional years in his enlistment and, for the Air Force, a guarantee of a 20-week training course.[131] This restriction was a deliberate attempt by the Air Force to save money and make first-term enlistees less attractive to industry.

With regard to retraining airmen, Project Guidance developed from a need to train surplus airmen into personnel to meet critical skill shortages. This centralized program issued a list of all critical skills from which airmen could not transfer. Before this system, wing commanders took airmen already trained in one AFSC and placed them in other career fields that had shortages. Later, airmen who were thus retrained often needed to be replaced in vacancies that had developed in their former positions. Project Guidance solved this problem as it controlled surpluses and shortages on a worldwide basis and listed the skills that could not be learned through OJT.[132] The transfer of retraining authority from the wing commander to ATC and HQ USAF further demonstrates the growing centralization of most personnel actions at the highest organizational levels of the Air Force.

Upgrading the Force: Educational Programs

Other educational programs oriented toward airmen were aimed at imparting technical knowledge, gaining high school and college degrees, or retraining in other skills. Established in 1950, Project Midnight Oil consisted of several interrelated home-study courses designed to improve an airman's career field proficiency and help him qualify for subsequent formal training.[133] The following list of career courses for the Airman Pilotless Aircraft Guidance and Control Systems Career Field (Career Field 31) indicates the prerequisites required for each career classification:

Helper:

CB–858	The Slide Rule
MA–779	Blueprint Reading
CA–188	Trigonometry
CB–290–1	Physics I and II
CB–106	Review of Grammar
CA–151–2	General Mathematics I and II

154

Mechanic:

CC–400	English Composition I
CB–785	Electrical Measuring Instruments
CA–889	Radio Communications II
CA–888	Radio Communications I
CA–781	Fundamentals of Electricity
CB–166	Advanced Algebra

Technician:

AF Course	Teaching Techniques
MB–415	Speech
CC–544	Personnel Management
CB–700	General Aeronautics
MA–517	College Physics
CA–430	Analytic Geometry

Superintendent:

CB–545	Office Management
CB–485	General Psychology
AF Course	Electronic Principles and Applications
AF Course	Mechanism and Kinematics
CA–440–1	Calculus I and II
CC–425	College Algebra[134]

Various universities produced many of these self-paced courses and catalogued them in the List of Correspondence Courses Offered by Colleges and Universities Through the United States Armed Forces Institute (USAFI). In this program an airman enrolled at the base education office, and then on course completion, his dates and grades were entered on AF Form 186 (education data) which was made available to promotion boards. In 1948, more than 25,000 airmen and officers were participating in correspondence courses.[135]

Another plan, Operation Bootstrap, encouraged airmen to complete their high school and college educations. Offered in conjunction with USAFI courses, Bootstrap, in addition to extension courses, offered residence courses either on base or at nearby high schools and colleges. It also stressed taking exams for high school completion and advanced college standing.[136]

In addition to a variety of educational programs, personnel managers constructed a viable training program and career plan. Few airmen, however, stayed in long enough to take full advantage of it. In 1952, planners estimated that by 1954 less than 20 percent of the first-term airman would remain in the Air Force. This yearly loss of such experience could prove disastrous to the combat efficiency of the air forces worldwide. Many planners during the mid-1950s sought a way to provide the proper combination of career incentives and personnel policies to retain the people the Air Force needed most.

✦5✦

External Remedies, Internal Reform, and The Making of a Career Enlisted Force 1952–1956

IN THE 1950s, the young Air Force learned a significant lesson about its enlisted personnel. Advertisers might successfully promote the need for a standing military, internal reforms might make the armed forces appear more democratic, recruiters might find the men and women the service desired, and training might make them a valued commodity, yet an airman would eventually pit the benefits of an Air Force career against the perceived opportunities of civilian life. Pay, housing, the job, working conditions, and other fringe benefits were what provided the most incentive for enlisted personnel to remain in the Air Force. If these incentives were less than satisfactory, then enticements from the outside world would influence airmen to seek employment elsewhere.

Air personnel planners learned that the sheer costs of training, the need to deploy units overseas on short notice, and the growing arsenal of complex weapons systems called for a large, stable, career force. Poor retention of airmen, especially after the Korean war, seriously jeopardized the service's mission and clearly sent a message to the Air Force and Congress—new policies and legislation were needed.

The Mounting Crisis

Until 1952, the Air Force had little need to worry about retention. After all, the service had only been in operation for five years when Air Staff personnel planners overcame recruiting obstacles and budget crises and built a personnel system capable of recruiting, training, assigning, and promoting the enlisted force. Moreover, a poor job market in the late 1940s combined with social reforms within the military, pay and benefits mandated by Congress, the draft, and the advent of the Cold War helped the Air Force expand and maintain its forces. Finally, the Korean war buildup in 1950 and 1951 forced planners to focus on recruiting and training for the combat commands, not the career programs. The indirect effects of the draft and the recall of reservists met Air Force wartime personnel requirements for 800,000, while involuntary extensions kept turnover to a minimum.[1] In fact, those who had enlisted during the first full year of the Air Force's existence in 1948 were still serving their first term when the Korean war erupted. (Appendix 4 has enlistment statistics.)

Beginning in late 1952, however, the Air Force and all the services began to lose a significant number of active duty reserve and regular forces. According to the Secretary of the Air Force's semiannual reports for fiscal years 1952 and 1953, net military personnel losses for all the services increased sharply, from 665,000 in 1952 to an average of more than 1,000,000 per year through 1955.[2]

Compounding the Air Force losses after the initial Korean war buildup was the discharge of personnel in surplus career fields or those involuntarily recalled to active duty; the Air Force lost an average of 167,000 airmen per year from 1952 through 1955 (Table 21). Additionally, absence without leave (AWOL) rates averaged a significant 16.8 per 1,000 airmen (compared to 7.2 per 1,000 in 1956). In the postwar era, the AWOL category was a better indicator of dissatisfaction with the service than desertion was, which until 1949 assumed that under the Articles of War anyone who failed to report for duty after a thirty-day period was a deserter. The introduction of the Uniform Code of Military Justice (UCMJ) and the Manual for Courts-martial in 1949, along with a series of court decisions in the early 1950s, placed the burden of proof on the services to demonstrate that an individual "intended to remain away, shirk important service, or avoid hazardous duty." Thus, until proven guilty, statisticians recorded absentees from duty as AWOL, not as deserters. Until the Vietnam war, the Air Force did not publish desertion rates but recorded all desertions as AWOL. It seemed more concerned with man-hours lost than with deserters because absences reduced labor efficiency rates.[3]

Table 21
Air Force Manpower Losses and
Reenlistment and AWOL Rates
1949–1955

Year	Losses	First-Term Rate	Career Rate	Total Rate	AWOL Rate
1949	45,571	—	—	49	25.0
1950	99,308	—	—	55	24.4
1951	54,526	—	—	55	13.5

Table 21—cont'd

Year	Losses	First-Term Rate	Career Rate	Total Rate	AWOL Rate
1952	111,443	—	—	48	16.6
1953	181,130	—	—	66	17.0
1954	172,776	11.0	—	31.2	12.3
1955	203,746	14.4	70.2	23.5	7.6

SOURCES: *USAF Statistical Digest, FY 1956*, p. 284. Reenlistment rates are found in OSD, Directorate for Statistical Services, Tables P.29.21, P.29.31, Feb 24, 1964. These rates are unadjusted; that is, they are the percentage of the total separated in that period who were eligible to reenlist. AWOL rates (the number of personnel AWOL per 1,000 airmen) are from *USAF Statistical Digest, FY 1959*, p. 570. These statistics reflect the continental United States only. Overseas AWOL rates were negligible.

In April 1952, Lt. Gen. Laurence Kuter, Air Force Deputy Chief for Personnel (DCS/P), spoke to his subordinates about the problems involved in maintaining a greatly expanded force, in light of the potential Korean war drawdown. One of his major concerns was that the active force consisted of almost 70 percent first-tour airmen. "This figure, in view of our rapid expansion," Kuter asserted, "is understandable and not alarming." Yet, he added, "an expected downward-plunge in our reenlistment rate by the end of Fiscal Year 1954 is serious . . . by the end of that period we anticipate a drop to perhaps as low as 25 percent . . . [and] this cannot, by any stretch of the imagination, be considered satisfactory."[4]

Kuter pointed out that many of these losses could be attributed to draft evasion as fully one-third of all enlistees chose a four-year tour with the Air Force rather than a two-year assignment in the Army infantry and a possible combat tour in Korea. He also assumed that recalled reservists would return to civilian life after the war. Although Kuter foresaw the future retention problem, he did not recognize the full gravity of the situation; first-term reenlistment for FY 1955 was only 14.4 percent (11 percent for the last half of FY 1954), and career retention dropped by almost 30 percent (see Table 21).[5]

If these losses consisted largely of unskilled labor, recruitment could have compensated for the poor retention; Table 22 shows that only in 1950 and 1954 did losses exceed recruiting gains. Air Force studies, however, revealed that the lowest retention rates were in the hard-core technical career fields. Airmen in these fields invariably were first-termers (those on their first enlistment) with

Maj. Gen. Laurence S. Kuter

the highest aptitude scores, high school graduates, and recipients of the lengthiest and most expensive training.[6] Conversely, those in the semitechnical and nontechnical soft-core specialties were on their second or third enlistments (career regulars), had average or below average aptitude scores, failed to finish high school, and had little, if any, technical training.[7] Yet, members of this group were twice as likely as those in the technical fields to reenlist.[8]

Table 22
Ratio of Air Force Personnel
Gains to Losses
1949–1955

Year	Ratio
1949	1.04
1950	.91
1951	6.94
1952	2.39

Table 22—cont'd

Year	Ratio
1953	1.03
1954	.87
1955	1.05

SOURCE: *USAF Statistical Digest FY 1956*, p. 284.

Further aggravating the retention problem was the Air Force's experience level. Most airmen were young (the median age was 23.9 in 1955), in their first enlistment, and single. Moreover, although all career fields were manned at 98 percent, there was a dearth of journeyman skill levels largely because it took a four-year enlistment to gain such expertise. In 1954, for instance, all career fields were overmanned with apprentices and supervisory personnel but were undermanned in 5-level (journeyman) workers (Table 23). Navy and Air Force planners both agreed that at least 25 percent of first-term sailors and airmen and 75 percent of the career personnel had to reenlist in order to form an adequate base for wartime mobilization.[9]

Table 23
Airmen by Skill Level
In Technical Categories
1954

Skill Level	Tech (97.1%)	High Tech (96.8%)	Semi-Tech (102%)	Non-Tech (99.2%)
1	213	198	194	153
3	128	107	91	65
5	97	87	84	97
7	66	101	135	176

SOURCE: *USAF Statistical Digest, FY 1955*, p. 331.

Had the Air Force demobilized after the Korean conflict to its prewar size of 360,000, retention problems may not have developed into a crisis. This, however, did not occur. Anticommunist rhetoric at home, heightened tensions abroad, a growing Soviet nuclear capability, and concerns over the burgeoning defense budget helped convince the Eisenhower administration to get more bang for the buck by relying on the Air Force strategic capability as its most direct means to retaliate against communist aggression. Thus, in the aftermath of the Korean war, the Air Force did not demobilize but remained at its 800,000-plus size. The Air Force charged General Kuter and his personnel staff with not only meeting a sizable recruiting objective but also formulating an ambitious retention program.

The Problems with Military Careers

As early as July 1952, Kuter and the DCS/P staff had mapped out a plan to deal with the Air Force's retention problems. They believed that the new Eisenhower administration might present the military's case before the opening of the new Senate and the new House of Representatives. Thus by December 1952 Kuter had written a memo regarding needed legislative actions to bolster military morale for President Eisenhower to use in his 1953 State of the Union Address. Assistant Secretary of Defense Anna M. Rosenberg resented Kuter's backdoor approach to the President and disapproved his memo.[10]

Rosenberg's appointment by the administration as the first woman Assistant Secretary of Defense for Manpower did not guarantee good relationships with the military hierarchy. Secretary of Defense Marshall had selected Rosenberg as the first woman for this post because of her industrial and military manpower background. Born in Hungary in 1901, she immigrated to New York as a child with her father and, by the 1920s, had gained expertise in the field of industrial and labor relations. During the New Deal, besides heading a public relations firm, she served on several regional boards working with defense and health issues, Welfare Services, the War Manpower Commission, the National Recovery Administration, and in the Office of the Coordinator of Inter-American Affairs. In 1944 and 1945 President Roosevelt, and later President Truman, sent her to study the Army's manpower problems in Europe. Because of her previous membership on the Advisory Board on Universal Military Training, Marshall found her a valuable ally as their views on conscription and UMT coincided.

Kuter recalled of Rosenberg that he "was never very fond of her and [became] less fond of her as time went on."[11] To get his initiatives passed, Kuter preferred to bypass her and use his connections at the White House and his political savvy to put his personal recommendation before Eisenhower.[12]

In January 1953, hoping also to garner support from the Joint Chiefs of Staff (JCS), General Kuter sent General Omar Bradley, then JCS chairman, the resignation letter of a Regular Air Force colonel.[13] The letter described a military that had lost respect for itself and its civilian leaders and felt weak in the eyes of the public. According to the despondent colonel, pay and benefits had eroded, retirement was in jeopardy, and officers were openly hostile to Congress.[14]

By early February, Bradley and Kuter met to discuss this particular resignation and the future reenlistment trends of all the services. After his discussion with Kuter, Bradley proposed to Secretary of Defense Charles Wilson that the Department of Defense establish an ad hoc committee to study the future of military careers.[15] Composed of officers from all three services, the Womble Committee (named for its chairman, Rear Adm. J.P. Womble, Jr.) began in March 1953 to examine reasons for the flagging retention of regular officers and enlisted men.[16] On April 30, 1953, President Eisenhower told the Congress that he had directed the Secretary of Defense to study the problem, thereby giving the Womble Committee his official sanction.[17]

One of the committee's first actions was to canvass personnel to determine why they were leaving.[18] Findings for the Air Force showed that airmen were leaving for three principal reasons: limited advancement, substandard living conditions, and organizational problems. Many first-term airmen simply believed that greater advancement opportunities existed outside the Air Force. At times, parents and friends, who attributed greater prestige to civilian work, would pressure airmen to leave the service. One first-term airman explained that "my ma and pa think military life is the lowest type of job you can get. . . . During wartime it's considered great, but not during peacetime. . . . I just don't want to hurt my parents."[19] Another said, "There's pressure from your family and friends. . . . They expect you to come back home and get a job after you put in your hitch . . . as much as I like the Air Force, I still like civilian life."[20]

The draw of college life and the extended Korean G.I. Bill provided an important impetus for many single and married airmen to leave. From 1950 to 1953, 22.9 percent of all males going to schools were veterans, versus 51.2 percent for the years 1945–1949. The Air Force had a high percentage of high school graduates and a significant number of enlistees who had come in as a means of avoiding Army duty and/or for furthering their education. It is probable that many left to pursue college studies.[21]

"My wife and I are going to the University of Illinois," one airman told an interviewer, "my ambition is to get with a good company and be a good engineer."[22] Another airman explained how he entered the service specifically to save for college. "I didn't have money to go to college before I came in the service. . . . I have saved $1,800 in the past three years [and] have received my letter of acceptance."[23] Other airmen who finished high school and began college education while in the service often decided to complete their college education after leaving the service. One airman first class, in the administration career field, who had had college experience before enlistment, explained his reasons for leaving:

I've really enjoyed my clerical work with the weather group. I've gained a lot of interesting knowledge. I've never really considered a career in the Air Force. I had three semesters at the University of Indiana before I joined the Air Force. I feared the draft, and I wanted no part with the Marines or Army. Since May, 1952, I've picked up nine credit hours . . . in salesmanship, personnel management, and business law. I've been accepted at the University of Indiana. The service is not for me! I've too much to offer on the outside.[24]

Trade schools and the lure of owning a small business also served as avenues of advancement for aspiring airmen. "I'm going to Capitol Radio Engineering Institute," one radio mechanic said, "[and] will get advanced standing because of my Air Force training."[25] Another looked forward to returning home and entering business with his father. "My dad wants me to take over his business," he responded, "I'm one of the few with such an opportunity." "Besides," the would-be entrepreneur explained, "I want a lot of things . . . a Cadillac [and] the luxuries of life."[26]

The luxuries of life were something the Air Force did not offer its married personnel. Housing was scant, rentals off-base were high, and many lived in impoverished conditions. One NCO's wife vividly described her family's situation at a zone of interior base:

At this base, this is how most [NCO families] live if we have children. They have a trailer lot, but there are thirty-one NCOs ahead of us on the list. To rent or buy a trailer, you have to give $150 down and then . . . you pay $75 a month, plus your trailer lot. They are twenty or twenty-five miles from base. One GI lives sixty miles. He goes home once a week. Then if you are lucky like we are, you find a furnished place for $125 per month. This is how you live: You take your children's shoes off in daytime and you keep saying "Don't make any noise." For cooking, you have a hot plate, and you cook one thing at a time. After you get done with the last, the first is cold. One stands; there are four of us and only three chairs. After that, you take your children to the park and let them run wild after being cooped up all day . . . but now the park is getting cold. We don't save a dime. Most of the G.I.s' after duty have other jobs that they work at. My husband works two nights a week. I have my husband get *The Air Force Times* hoping and praying something will be in it about building housing at this base. Are we forgotten?[27]

As early as 1948, the Air Force had described its number one personnel problem as inadequate housing.[28] In 1949, the Presidential Committee on Religion and Welfare in the Military cited the Air Force housing situation as despicable and called on Congress for relief.[29] The committee's detailed report showed Air Force families living in garages, tents, and decrepit World War II post housing. One Air Force survey in the same year analyzed the housing problem and concluded that, while inadequate housing had only a slight effect on reenlistment rates, it significantly contributed to how the airman thought about his job and the Air Force in general.[30] The survey failed to recognize, however, the increased number of married personnel and dependents in the service. In 1950, for example, 50.9 percent of all civilians were married while married airmen constituted 29.7 percent of the force. By 1955, the percent of married airmen increased by 48 percent (to 44.1 percent). Family life and spouse support became important in any reenlistment decision.[31]

By 1952, the Air Force, with the aid of the Wherry Mortgage Insurance Act of 1949, had rapidly begun to construct base housing.[32] One of the biggest problems facing military personnel planners was the shortage of available housing on or near military bases. The shortage of housing was even more acute in the Air Force than it was in other branches of the military because the Air Force was a brand new service that found itself restoring old Army and Navy air fields and constructing new bases for its own use. The act sought to minimize the cost of building military housing by encouraging private contractors to construct rental housing for the military. The legislation promised contractors that, should a base deactivate, the government would buy the unit. It also gave leasing rights free from revocation and made it incumbent upon the military to provide utility services.[33] Once built, the rental units could then carry charges based upon local averages.

By early 1952, 27,913 Wherry homes had been built and rented for an average of $69.00 per month. In 1953, building slowed as contractors believed they were not getting a reasonable profit under the existing law. In 1954, Secretary of the Air Force Talbott cited continued problems with permanent housing, rentals, and corrupt Air Force contractors as the main reasons for the lack of family housing.[34]

The Air Force still had too few houses for its members.[35] Although a 1952 Air Force–wide survey showed that most military housing was rated good or excellent, it failed to note that, at best, the commodity was available only for 7 percent of its married personnel.[36] Housing also failed to keep up with the Air Force's expansion.[37] In 1954, only 4.1 percent of its married first-term airmen were in government-sponsored quarters (compared to 12 percent of career personnel).[38]

By 1955, the Air Force had a housing deficit of 250,000 units with only 10,727 units under construction.[39] In May, SAC commander General LeMay told a Senate subcommittee that a lack of adequate housing slowed his command's buildup and "threatened its ability to strike back quickly if the U.S. [was] attacked." Inadequate housing forced manning restrictions, which according to LeMay, "delayed [the] combat readiness of four or more wings by as much as eight months."[40]

Housing conditions overseas were worse. At Johnson Air Force Base in Japan, an Air Force member would have to wait months for an opening on base. Off-base housing, on the other hand, was difficult to find. It had to undergo a series of inspections by the Air Installation Office, the Preventive Medicine Detachment, and housing officials before it could be authorized for an airman's use. Cultural differences in housing styles were also a problem for Americans who liked central heating, good lighting, and privacy.[41]

Correspondence between the Joint Commander, Far Eastern Air Force, and the Assistant Chief, Army General Staff, emphasized the command's major morale problem in 1953—dependent housing. "As you know," wrote Army Maj. Gen. Charles W. Christenberry, Deputy Chief of Staff for the Far East and United Nations Command stationed in Japan, "government furnished housing fulfills only about one-half of our requirement . . . and the current waiting period is fourteen to sixteen months." General Christenberry added that the housing shortage was "partially alleviated in Japan by the use of private rentals," of which "four thousand families were occupying."[42] What his letter did not convey was that Air Force officers and airmen often contracted local Japanese laborers to build a "mobile trailer" for them.[43] Airmen built these rentals at their own expense, not the government's. Families destined for overseas duty in Alaska, Okinawa, the Philippines, and France found similar housing restrictions.[44]

Overseas conditions could deter some from enlisting. "My wife," one distraught airman voiced, "would like for me to get out of the service . . . [as] she talks to a neighbor, a Master Sergeant's wife, who tells her about poor housing, terrible things about Japan, and bad things about traipsing all over the world. . . . I don't want my wife nagging at me, I'm getting out."[45] Family problems often made overseas conditions intolerable. Another airman believed he could not care for his sick in-laws overseas and chose to leave the Air Force on that account. "My wife's folks and my folks have been sick for three years," he told one interviewer. "I fear overseas duty [as] even with four years service I'd be at the bottom of the list for my family being with me overseas."[46]

Single-airmen housing, whether stateside or overseas, also constituted a problem. Most of the barracks were the World War II open-bay types. By 1954, however, several commands had constructed quarters that were divided into four-man compartments. Each room had its own separate bed, locker, and study carrel. Mess halls, formerly located a mile or more from the barracks, were now nested among a quadrangle of four of these dormitory-style buildings.[47] New units also contained central heating and air conditioning. Planners believed this new style would promote morale and an ambiance of academic life for the technically educated airman. In 1954, planners adopted the dormitory plan for the entire Air Force.[48]

Not only spartan living conditions but also long work hours, temporary duty away from home, remote tours overseas, and frequent changes in stations all took their toll on reenlistments. In the Strategic Air Command, which was often undermanned and had few experienced airmen, work could extend well over twelve hours a day, seven days a week. Moreover, the impact of insufficient personnel hurt SAC's mission-effectiveness goals. In 1955, some of the poorest manned units completed only 87 percent of their missions with only 80 percent of their planes operational. On the other hand, SAC units that were "effectively manned" (that is, had 85 percent in technical skills present) flew 99 percent of their planes and met the 91-percent efficiency standard set by LeMay.[49]

MSgt. David Menard, a young airman in 1955, described how, as a structural mechanic, he generally worked in aircraft shops that were under-staffed. "When my tour [in SAC] was up," he wrote, "[I] was about fifteen pounds lighter and very, very tired . . . sixty- to eighty-hour weeks were common."[50] SAC's emphasis on global capability and deterrence translated into a lot of time away from home for its married personnel.[51]

The Air Force moved complete combat wings overseas for a three-month period of temporary duty (TDY), leaving families behind. Some units went on TDY three times a year. Furthermore, poor family accommodation at SAC bases in Greenland, Guam, Morocco, Spain, and the United Kingdom resulted in remote tours for some airman. Thus, families lost husbands and fathers for up to a year at a time.[52]

Finally, Air Force families moved often. As of 1953, 74.1 percent of Air Force technical sergeants (married and single) had made two to twelve changes of station during their careers; more than a third had moved five to seven times.[53] One wife cited "raising children on the run" as difficult. "Our [three] boys are seasoned troopers," she wrote, "we have moved eight times in the past seven years."[54]

By 1954, SAC allegedly had the highest divorce rate of any of the commands in the Air Force.[55] When one researcher surveyed SAC wives about their husbands' intentions of remaining in the Air Force, one woman responded:

> All that we can see ahead as long as our husbands are in SAC is more of the same buttons pressed which bring TDYs for indefinite length, transfers and other changes which families accept because they have no choice.[56]

Increasingly, however, families found they had a choice. In 1953, 25,000 airman left SAC at a cost of $50 million to train their replacements.[57] In Fiscal Year 1955, the Air Force lost more than $777 million in training costs when 1,900 SAC officers and 35,800 airmen left the service.[58]

Poor pay and fringe benefits increased the numbers of those leaving. Pay raises in 1949 and 1952 of 21.6 percent and 10.9 percent were substantial. Yet, when airmen compared military jobs with similar civilian work, their pay seemed paltry. A master sergeant with over ten years as an air traffic controller took home $375 per month. A civilian in the same job and experience averaged $745, a 98 percent increase over the career sergeant's pay and allowances (Table 24).

Table 24
Pay Comparisons
Selected Air Force and Civilian Jobs
1955

Military Title	Pay	Civilian Title	Pay
MSGT (10 years)	$345	Airline Dispatcher	$745
A1C (3 years)	$172	Air Panel Engineer	$545
MSGT (10 years)	$345	Lead Mechanic	$600
A2C–MSGT (1–12 years)	$131–$444	Skilled Mechanic	$318–$407

SOURCES: DOD, *Military Compensation Background Papers*, 3d ed. (Washington, D.C: OSD, June 1987), chap. 2, B.1, B.2, B.3; Brig Gen Dale O. Smith, "Let's Make Military Life a Wanted Career," *Air Force*, May 1956, pp. 86, 89–93.

Though these figures take into account compensation for quarters and food, they do not place a dollar amount on the per diem received by enlisted personnel during extended TDYs, nor do they reflect the cost of fringe benefits such as commissary privileges, retirement, or dependent medical care. Yet, airmen recognized that these benefits were more perceived than real. Off-base rents including sewage, electric, and gas bills, on average, were higher than the men's quarters allowance. Per diem rates rarely matched the money spent as TDYs, which for some airmen totaled sixty to eighty hours per month and cost $30 to $40 more than their per diem pay because of the higher costs of food and lodging in various parts of the country.[59] Most importantly, during a period of rapidly rising medical costs and high birth rates (the baby boom of the 1950s), a married airman had no promise of medical care for his dependents.[60]

The legal precedent for providing military dependents with some degree of medical assistance is found in an 1884 Appropriations Act which specified "That the Medical officers of the Army and contract surgeons shall, wherever practicable, attend the families of officers and soldiers free of charge." This concept was later incorporated into the United States Code (10 USC 96) and adopted by the Air Force and Navy. The phrase "wherever practicable" ensured that dependent care was not deemed a "right."[61] Thus, if an airman was lucky enough to live on a post with a hospital, his family could possibly see a doctor on a space-available basis.[62] As a result of the uncertainty, some enrolled in group medical insurance programs, further decreasing their already dwindling paychecks.[63]

Frozen career fields often kept many experienced airmen from advancing, a factor that prompted some to leave the service. The Airman Career Program, a management tool to help planners anticipate the number of men in each AFSC and skill level necessary for each unit to have to fulfill its mission, served as a basis for promotions, depending upon command vacancies. Naturally, as the Air Force expanded, more openings as well as promotions became available. When the force contracted, fewer vacancies ensued.[64] Moreover, fields with low reenlistments had more promotion options available while those with high retention rates did not.[65] Consequently, the Air Force encouraged men to cross-train into new areas rather than remain frozen at their current pay grade.

Nevertheless, some airmen had not advanced for years.[66] "I had buddies who didn't make it before the freeze [of the Air Police Career Field], and it took four or five years to make it [to E–7]," former Chief Master Sergeant of the Air Force Robert Gaylor remembered, "and then they had to compete with all the guys who had been frozen all that time." In April 1956 Gaylor emphasized, "there was only one promotion to master sergeant at Laredo Air Force Base, and I got it. . . . There's much to be said for timing and taking advantage of opportunity and being in the right place at the right time."[67] In 1954, TSgt. Howard Babin wrote to *The Army, Navy, and Air Force Journal* that he had reenlisted in 1947, obtained proficiency in two related AFSC career fields, and had superior ratings and letters of commendation. Nevertheless, when the Air Force announced his career field (supply) as having overages (defined as a surplus career field) at the 7- and 9-levels (the Master Sergeant levels) of proficiency, he believed that his "ten years of technical knowledge had been cast aside and [that] a terrific blow was dealt to his initiative and ambition. . . . I cannot be considered for Warrant Officer, because I am not a Master Sergeant . . . there is no promotion for [me]."[68] A disheartened A2C remarked, "I was thirty-five months in grade. . . . I haven't been eligible for promotion because of my AFSC. . . . I'm bitter about it."[69]

In other cases, air bases with surplus personnel began to use these airmen in jobs not related to their career fields. Some people saw this as a double bind. "I have over eleven years in aircraft armament maintenance, but now am doing the job of a 'flunky,'" one surplus tech sergeant lamented. "By not doing the work I have been trained to do and [am] highly skilled in, I am losing proficiency in my career field," he noted sadly, "[I am] losing confidence in myself and the Air Force, and losing prestige in the eyes of officers and other NCOs."[70]

Frozen career fields were not the only problem some airman had with the promotion system. Favoritism was a significant issue. Skill tests, awards, and time-in-grade requirements qualified airmen for promotion, but local boards consisting of unit officers and NCOs actually made the decision. In an era when commanders logged conduct in a black book, some squadrons promoted airmen based on impression more than merit. TSgt. Lewis Stephens, a fire control technician, found that his prior officer status was a handicap. At the promotion boards in the 1950s, he complained, "You were either in or out. . . . Whatever it took to be with the 'in' group made the promotions, be it athletics, drinking with the boys, or something else. . . . As an ex-officer I was not in the 'in' group, neither were other ex-officers I knew."[71] A2C John Leffanta, who was stationed in Germany during his first enlistment, also found the promotion process exasperating:

> When the Air Force introduced review boards, fairness went out the window. At my first review . . . I correctly answered all of the questions but one. I had the top quality/quantity performance rating, but was not promoted to A/1C because [the ranking NCO] ruled that because I didn't know what Snoopy had done in the Peanuts comic strip published in the *Stars and Stripes* that morning, I did not have a "grasp on current affairs."[72]

MSgt. James Long, a career airman, also believed that the promotion process was unfair. "If you had a single APR (Airman Performance Rating) that wasn't outstanding," he recalled, "you could kiss promotion goodbye for a number of years." Long also added, "If you were not a good mixer, your chances for promotion were lessened. . . . It was commonly said that the way to help your chances was to learn to play golf . . . attend the appropriate social club . . . and get recognition like 'Airman of the Month.'"[73]

The Air Force's emphasis on outward symbols of recognition and joining the correct social circles was symptomatic of its growing organizational mentality. One contemporary observer argued that the Air Force was in such a hurry to reject the Army's ways and to seek autonomy that it adopted business practices without proper consideration and became industrialized (that is, it followed a corporate model). This civilianization, according to Col. Russell Ritchey, was "fostered by the improper application of management principles which have led us down the road to bargain basement economy and the subversion of the commander and the military professions." He further argued that combatants were nothing more than "civilians in uniforms . . . [who] sell 'management' as a cure-all." The Air Force has made a "job out of a career."[74] Another Air Force leader explained:

> When the Air Force became independent, it adopted many good techniques from industry and science. It undertook a program of qualification testing to place round pegs into round holes. It developed the Career program in an attempt to keep them there. It tied promotion into development in the career field. Two factors, however, were lost. First, leadership and command were overlooked as identifiable skills. Second, [specialization caused] the concept of the mission to be lost . . . it became a forty-hour-a-week rather than a twenty-four-hour-a-day responsibility.[75]

A growing depersonalization in the workplace was one direct result of a culture that stressed production and businesslike operations. When a 1955 survey asked airmen if they felt that the Air Force overemphasized their military worth as technicians or workers, close to a third of those leaving the service said they were not valued as individuals. Rather, the Air Force "rationally" measured their value with respect to their contribution toward organizational goals.[76] Undoubtedly, frequent rotation, the large number who lived off-base and used civilian medical facilities, plus the enormous size of the Air Force contributed to these airmen's feelings of alienation.

This corporate culture also caused some career airmen to reminisce fondly about the old Army Air Corps and argue that the prestige of the NCO was now nonexistent. It was an important challenge for the new service to define what the image of an Air Force NCO was as compared to the NCO image found in the Army, Navy, and Marines. Some airmen vigorously complained that at one time they were considered the backbone of the enlisted force, so they should be more than technicians and organizational managers; they believed they should be military leaders.[77] Several studies showed that the policy melding technicians into the NCO grades during World War II severely undermined NCO prestige and authority because many technicians looked upon NCO duties as demeaning.[78]

Yet by 1952 the Air Force had not yet adopted "a common and accepted ethical code of job performance, decorum, and personal responsibility" for the noncommissioned officer that took into account supervisory as well as technical ability.[79] A written statement describing the Air Force NCO and what his assigned duties were would help NCOs form a collective identity, and thereby aid in establishing a sense of belonging and a conceptual environment for esteem enhancement.

The great number of NCOs also undermined their status. The melding of NCO and technicians, in addition to the Korean war buildup, the continued expansion, and the Air Force's emphasis on technical proficiency, brought into the NCO ranks many who were promoted on technical ability and shortened time-in-grade requirements.[80] By 1952, the Air Force recognized 70 percent of the 854,519 enlisted men as noncommissioned officers. One study concluded that little prestige accompanied something so common.[81]

The specialized work structure also undermined NCO prestige. The new category of Air Police, for example, generally limited NCO authority to their own office or shop. Air policemen (APs) now enforced Air Force standards of grooming, dress, and behavior.[82] Additionally, the high proportion of Air Force officers to airmen (Table 25) often meant that officers assumed duties once held by enlisted men.[83] Such a high percentage of officers meant fewer supervisory positions for NCOs and airmen.[84] For example, a survey of 490 NCOs in the 531st Aircraft Control and Warning Group at Elmendorf AFB, Alaska, revealed only 12 percent held positions of authority (Table 26). A case of too many chiefs meant that many NCOs did the work normally assigned to the lower ranks (E–1 to E–3).

Table 25
Active Duty Officers
As a Percent
Of All Military Personnel
1948–1956

Year	Air Force	Army	Navy	Marines
1948	12.6	12.3	10.8	8.1
1949	13.8	11.7	10.7	8.1
1950	13.9	12.2	11.7	9.8
1951	13.6	8.5	9.6	7.9
1952	13.1	9.3	10.0	7.1
1953	13.4	9.5	10.3	7.5
1954	13.7	9.1	10.6	8.3
1955	14.3	11.0	11.3	9.0
1956	15.6	11.5	10.7	8.9

SOURCE: *DOD Fact Book, 1958*, p. 27.

Table 26
Noncommissioned Officers
In Supervisory Positions
531st Aircraft Control and Warning Group
1951

Rank	Number	Number in Super-visory Position	Percent Supervisors
Msgt	27	10	37
Tsgt	48	14	29.1
Ssgt	132	19	14.4
Sgt	<u>283</u>	<u>17</u>	12.2
Total	490	60	

SOURCE: Ltr, CG, Alaskan Air Command (Old) to DCS/P (Kuter), Jan 15, 1952, Subj: Selection of Noncommissioned Officers, RG 341, Entry 129, file 220.2, Box 134, MMB, NA.

Making the Military a Good Career: The Womble Report and Congressional Reform

After gathering reenlistment data, the services prepared a list of recommendations that the Womble Committee compiled into an official report. The report attempted to explain in four broad areas why the services were losing personnel and what specific actions could be taken to reverse the trend. Similar to Air Force findings, the committee cited world commitments, the dilution of military authority, the effect of technocracy on command, and increased competition with industry for skilled personnel as the root causes of poor retention. It concluded that strong measures by the President, Congress, and the armed services could reverse the stream of dissatisfied servicemen leaving the military. The committee's recommendations took two paths—congressional legislation and internal military reforms.[85]

Beginning in 1953, and for the next three years, the Air Force worked hard to publicize the Womble Committee's findings and promote remedial legislation. Secretary of the Air Force Talbott and the other service secretaries consistently importuned Congress for better pay and incentives.[86] In an important speech before the Air Force Association in 1954, Talbott blamed Congress for spending "millions for equipment" while only giving "nickels for the men."[87] His successor, Donald A. Quarles, was also emphatic about needed reforms—Air Force capability could only be achieved "by a stable corps of trained personnel."[88] Articles in a number of Air Force media, including *The Air Force Times*, *Air Force Magazine*, and *The Army, Navy, and Air Force Journal*, lobbied for congressional legislation to address pay, housing, and medical issues.

In 1954, Congress attempted to resolve the retention problem by modifying the Career Compensation Act of 1949. The 1949 act tied the amount of bonus to future service, not to years served. It also authorized the payment of larger sums for lengthier reenlistment periods: $40, $90, $160, $250, or $360 for reenlistments of 2, 3, 4, 5, or 6 years, respectively. Congress limited the bonus for 30 years' service and specified a maximum career accumulation of $1,440.[89]

In July 1954, Congress, in reacting to the rush of first-term personnel leaving the service, redirected the reenlistment bonus by funneling more of the available funds into first-term reenlistments and progressively less into subsequent commitments.[90] Thus, first-termers received one month's base pay for each year of a first reenlistment; two-thirds of one month's pay for each year of a second reenlistment; one-third for a third reenlistment; and one-sixth for a fourth or subsequent reenlistment. Additionally, this bonus structure was limited to twenty years of service and the maximum career accumulation was raised from $1,400 to $2,000.

For several reasons, some of the services were not content with the changes and the increases of reenlistment bonuses. One Army report charged that the

Secretary of the Air Force Harold E. Talbott is flanked by two of his assistant secretaries as he meets the press.

lump sum payment retained first termers who had "accumulated debts or for some other reason were particularly attracted by the immediate prospect of a substantial amount of cash." In other words, it attracted men who placed immediate gratification over long-term career goals.[91] The Air Force, which had more married personnel and less base housing than the Army did, saw no such problem. Debts, if incurred, were often the product of mounting medical bills, the high rentals, and inadequate per diem payments.[92] Although some of the services differed over the effect of reenlistment bonuses, all agreed on one thing: the armed forces needed new career legislation.

By late 1954, two important features demanded additional congressional action. First, the projected loss of military personnel became an actuality. Poor retention equally devastated all branches of the armed forces. In Fiscal Year 1955, the overall DOD reenlistment rate was 27.2 percent while first term and career rates (those of individuals on their second tour) were, respectively, 15.8 and 73.6 percent. (Appendices 5 and 6 present reenlistment statistics.) This was a significant drop from the overall 1950 rate of 59.3 percent.[93] A 9 percent first-term rate for the Navy was the worst since the early 1940s.[94]

Second, President Eisenhower, as a career army officer, also served as a credible and respected advocate for military causes. He told one reporter that "he didn't believe that soldiers, sailors, or airmen and marines go into the service just for money . . . they wanted just what other Americans wanted": a decent place to live, a respectable standard of living, and membership in their local community. Speaking from personal experience, the former Supreme Allied and NATO Commander was believable.[95]

Eisenhower's prestige as Commander in Chief and defense strategist also helped the military achieve its legislative goals. When he talked about Soviet aggression, nuclear capability, surprise attacks, and the New Look, the public and Congress listened. Designed to be a countervailing power, his New Look strategy placed special emphasis on nuclear deterrence, the economy, and a large, technologically sophisticated Air Force.[96] Translated into military terms, this meant a heavy reliance on SAC's nuclear arsenal and a significantly reduced mission for the Army and Navy.[97] (See Appendix 7 for the increased funds channeled to the Air Force under the New Look program).

Top secret studies made during 1954 and 1955 confirmed Eisenhower's suspicions about Soviet nuclear capabilities and surprise attacks. According to a February 1955 report, the Soviets were quickly achieving nuclear parity and would soon be capable of mounting a "devastating, if not decisive" first strike against the United States.[98] To avoid such an eventuality, the report warned, American defense must rely on advanced technology and skilled personnel.

Yet, trade-offs were present. New technology, like the B–52 bomber, the Army's atomic cannon, and the Navy's new carrier jets, were designed to be maintained as a system. A radar system might consist of only three or four components that could be easily removed and replaced, but problems occurred, however, in the repair of the actual components; the parts were complex and required a good deal of costly training to repair them. Under the systems approach to maintenance, though fewer total maintenance personnel were required per system, higher skill levels were needed to perform the repairs.

The doctrine of dispersal intended to reduce the vulnerability of SAC forces by dispersing them at many bases also affected Air Force manpower needs. It necessitated an increase of not less than 25 percent of 5- and 7-level airmen.[99] These were the skill levels of experienced personnel, already in short supply, whom the Air Force was losing in great numbers. The "price of low reenlistments rates," report writers warned, could be the difference between effective combat capability and deterrence, and nuclear holocaust. "It is essential," this group concluded, "that the Services have a professional 'hard-core' maintenance force . . . but it is impractical to build a professional force . . . without a career concept and long-term promotion and rewards comparable to opportunities in private industry."[100]

In a special January 13, 1955, message to Congress on career incentives for military personnel, Eisenhower, like the Technological Capabilities Panel members, argued that the "increasing mechanization and complexity of defense forces [had made] technical skills and a wide background of experience vastly more important than ever before." President Eisenhower further contended that the erosion of pay and benefits was at the heart of the current retention problems, and he wanted the Congress to pass various pay increases and a housing act and to fund medical care for dependents. Eisenhower's support and the reality of poor retention placed heavy pressure on Congress to pass legislation upgrading the military's quality of life.[101]

By mid-January, Congress introduced bills advocating an incentive package along the lines suggested by the President.[102] In less than ninety days, the bill passed both houses and became Public Law 20, the Career Incentive Act of 1955. The new act increased pay for per diem travel allowances and hazardous duty, and it provided a dislocation allowance for married personnel making a permanent change in station (PCS).[103]

More important, the act added an important feature to the Career Compensation Act of 1949. Although the 1949 act determined base pay on pay grade and length of service, the 1955 legislation provided higher raises for personnel at various stages in their careers.[104] For instance, the 10 percent raise authorized by the 1955 act varied from 0 percent for E–1s with fewer than 2 years' service to a 17.3 percent increase for an E–4 with more than 8 years of service. Table 27 demonstrates that airmen now received pay raises during periods of their greatest productivity and need. Because an Airman First Class (E–4) in his third enlistment had obtained at least a journeyman's skill level and had decided to make the Air Force a career, the largest raises were reserved for the middle enlisted grades, where an individual had invaluable training and experience and was in an age bracket where a decision about the future, including career and marriage, needed to be made. The new pay scheme favored experience, career progression, and retention.[105]

Table 27
Career Incentive Act of 1955
Selected Pay Grade Increases
By Time in Service
(In Percent)

Pay Grade	\>2	\>4	\>6	\>8	\>12	\>16	\>18
E–1	8.5	8.5	7.8	7.8	7.8	7.8	7.8
E–3	9.3	15.6	14.8	14.0	10.1	7.1	7.1
E–4	8.0	16.2	15.5	17.3	15.9	14.8	9.9
E–5	7.1	14.2	13.6	15.3	14.3	13.4	9.1

176

Table 27—cont'd

Years in Service

Pay Grade	>2	>4	>6	>8	>12	>16	>18
E–6	6.5	6.3	12.2	11.9	13.0	12.2	11.6
E–7	7.7	7.5	7.3	10.5	11.6	11.0	10.5

SOURCE: DOD, *Proposed Career Incentive Act of 1955* (Washington, D.C.: OSD, Mar 1955) p. 45.

Legislation in 1955 also attacked the continuing family housing shortage. In August of that year, Eisenhower signed a new National Housing Act (PL 84–345) designating 100,000 new units for construction on permanent military bases. The Capehart Amendment to this act authorized 17,000 new units for Fiscal Year 1956, of which 8,100 were designated for Air Force use.[106]

Because contractors complained of not receiving enough profit from the homes built for the military, Congress passed a new housing bill in 1955. Unlike the Wherry program, in which contractors charged rent for the homes they built and owned, housing would be government-owned under the Capehart plan.[107] Service personnel would surrender their quarters allowance rather than pay rent. The problem, however, was even at 17,000 units per year, more than twenty years would be required to make up for the Air Force base housing shortage. By 1958, the combination of recently built off-base housing and new base housing eased the shortage. In fact, Air Force surveys that year found 82 percent of all airmen satisfied with their quarters.[108]

Despite the bonus, incentive, and housing legislation, the loss of trained personnel continued to plague the armed services. During Fiscal Year 1955, the overall first-term reenlistment rate improved slightly (15.9 percent); however, the Armed Forces still suffered enormous losses in the highly technical skill groups. First-term electronic and armament personnel, communications technicians, and aircraft maintenance personnel reenlisted at rates of 6.9, 8.1, 12.9, and 13.2 percent, respectively.[109]

Persistent among the problems was fringe benefits. Between 1946 and 1950, the military significantly changed their pay and benefit systems which in many ways were broader and more attractive than industry's.* By the mid-1950s, however, this was no longer true.[110] Civilian wages in the lowest pay groups tripled, and salaries in the higher brackets doubled.[111] Moreover, industrial fringe benefits had tripled since 1940 and they now cost employers

* This is described in Chapter 2.

about 20 percent of their payrolls.

Table 28 reveals the extent of benefits offered by more than 500 large companies as compared to the military's offerings. The most significant disparity in this table relates to the lack of medical benefits. Since 1948, company-sponsored health and pension plans had quadrupled. By 1955, approximately 70 percent of industrial workers received health benefits for their dependents, and in 38 percent of the companies this coverage was fully subsidized.[112] The military still had no statutory basis making it mandatory to provide health care for dependents. Industrial collective bargaining had placed military compensation packages at a serious disadvantage.

Table 28
Industrial and Military Compensation Packages
1955

Benefit	Companies That Pay All or Part Of the Cost (%)	Companies That Pay All Costs (%)	Military
Group Life Insurance	89.5	41.8	Partial
Medical	98.4	35.3	None*
Maternity	78.5	18.1	None*
Retirement Pensions	66.2	65.2	Yes
Special Price on Company Products	46.2	—	Yes**
Subsidized Cafeteria	42.6	—	Yes
Free Periodic Medical Exam	37.2	37.2	None*
Yearly Bonus	34.0	34.0	None
Paid Sick Leave	13.5	13.5	Yes

SOURCE: *Studies in Personnel Policy*, No. 145 (New York: National Industrial Conference Board, Inc., 1955) p. 14. Industrial figures represented hourly workers, but these benefits extended to salaried employees as well.

* Although military personnel received medical care, their dependents had no statutory guarantee for mandatory health care. If sick, dependents were seen by military doctors on a space-available basis only.

** This relates to exchanges and commissary costs.

In March 1956, Secretary of Defense Charles E. Wilson sent a long letter to Eisenhower describing the continued personnel retention problem and the growing inability of the military to provide attractive career incentives.[113]

Citing the increase in pay and incentives offered by industry as a serious threat to the successful retention of servicemen, Wilson asked that President Eisenhower encourage the Congress to finish the work begun the previous year per his January 13, 1955, special message, namely, "medical care for dependents, more and better housing, and improved survivor benefits." On April 9, 1956, the president sent letters to Speaker of the House Sam Rayburn and Vice President Richard M. Nixon, President of the Senate, reiterating the contents of Wilson's letter and calling on the Congress for immediate legislation.

Eisenhower's letter generated quick action by the Congress. In June 1956, the Dependent's Medical Care Act (PL 84–569) established the statutory foundation for furnishing medical care to military retirees and dependents.[114] The key feature was the authority given the Secretary of Defense to contract with civilian institutions for Blue Cross–type coverage for spouses and dependent children.

By July 1956, the Servicemen's and Veteran's Survivor Benefits Act (PL 84–881), which attempted to standardize benefits paid to widows and dependents, had become law. As passed, the measure placed military personnel under contributory coverage of the Old Age and Survivors Insurance system and replaced the $10,000 life insurance coverage, authorized in 1951 for all active duty personnel, with a schedule of monthly payments ranging from $122 to $266 made to survivors.[115]

Air Force Personnel Policy Reforms

Although the Womble Committee served as an important impetus for studying retention, it by no means forced the Air Force to implement any of its findings. The Secretary of Defense's Manpower Board correlated retention information and advised the services generally about in-house policy changes, but it did not offer any centralized guidance. Similarly, the Air Force made its findings available to the commands, but it did not offer firm directives. All this changed in October 1954 when Air Staff planners decided to organize an inclusive retention program under the auspices of the DCS/P at HQ USAF at the Pentagon.[116] In establishing a separate retention office, DCS/P planners desired a centralized organization that could systematize retention research, establish and coordinate major command action, and develop a master reenlistment plan.[117] Under the new program, air planners stressed retaining the "average young airman" on his first tour "who has or will become a skilled and competent worker."[118]

The emphasis on retaining the average young airman was a significant shift in Air Force thought. As early as 1942, Air Force recruitment and training programs advocated obtaining only the brightest for technical training.

179

Foundation of the Force

Retention research findings in the 1950s showed that the brightest came in for the training, to escape the draft, or to find aid for college training. Furthermore, planners found that while those with the highest mental aptitudes did well in school, the brightest often saw the Air Force as a stepping stone, not as a career. "The best student," one influential planner wrote, "does not necessarily make the most efficient and effective man on-the-job." He added,

> The man we want in numbers is an individual of average intelligence, aptitude and ability who is capable of improving with age and experience and, most of all, who will stay with us.[119]

Input from the major commands substantiated the planners' assumption about the need for average young men. In tactical units, one general argued, "simplicity of design, efficient procedures, and effective supervision reduce the need for highly skilled technicians."[120] In other words, the Air Force needed enough workers who could read and follow detailed technical manuals and handle the "great mass of routine inspections" and periodic maintenance.[121] Planners hoped that well-written technical manuals could replace experience and that specialization could reduce the need for personnel highly skilled in technical areas. Moreover, changes in Air Force training methods greatly de-emphasized the need for highly skilled technicians. By 1960, recruiters began seeking those with average mental scores and a high school diploma because studies indicated that high school graduates were more likely to remain in the service than those who failed to complete this level of education.[122]

In 1953, the ATC introduced to the Air Staff a new channelized program titled First-term Training as a brief residential, theoretical course, supplemented by the ATC field training given to all trainees, in a structured family of specialties.[123] First, the program cut down the cost of training because it reduced the time an airman spent in formal training and it increased the time he worked in his command.[124] Second, course work evolved toward a specific system or piece of equipment.[125]

This specialization made most first-term technicians, at best, semiskilled and lacking the broader training necessary for jobs in civilian life. In essence, some technicians became data-flow specialists, able to check out an aircraft system, isolate the malfunction to a defective black box, replace the defective component, and align the system. It was estimated that 70 percent were data-flow specialists while the remaining 30 percent repaired the black box down to the component level in field maintenance facilities. For example, of the airmen sent to school for the MG–10 Fire Control System in the F–102 jet, 70 percent went to a 36-week school and 30 percent went to a 58-week course.[126] Hence, in the planners' minds, technical manuals replaced experience, and specialized systems obviated the need for many highly skilled technicians. Now only semiskilled, many of these specialists became wedded to the Air Force for a job.

180

New programs, aimed at building up the Air Force to 137 wings under President Eisenhower's New Look program, also addressed the retention problem by consolidating manpower into areas most damaged by poor retention, namely the hard-core specialties. Beginning in the fall of 1953, military manpower in certain soft-core career fields and in highly skilled, depot-level (or component repair maintenance level), technical career fields was either eliminated or replaced with civilians.[127]

For example, 10,571 manpower spaces were cut in the food service career field, 4,000 in motor vehicles, and 13,500 in the air police. Overseas, Project Native Son, which replaced military personnel with local nationals, reduced the need for 33,800 airmen by April, 1955.[128] The stateside equivalent, Project Homefront, substituted civilians for airmen who did not reenlist. Planners channeled those spaces saved by civilians to hard-core operational specialties in hopes of placing career airmen in chronic retention problem fields.[129]

Although centralizing its retention efforts helped the Air Force rethink its strategy toward retaining or replacing highly skilled technicians, personnel planners continued to work on other areas of policy reform.[130] For example, by mid-1955, studies of labor turnover in business convinced planners to put more effort into fostering positive attitudes toward the Air Force earlier in a first-term airman's career. Unit commanders conducted initial and exit interviews; publications such as "You Be the Judge" and "Facts for Your Future" that contrasted business and Air Force opportunities were sent to the airman and his parents; and reenlistment handbooks instructed recruiters and squadron commanders how to establish the right atmosphere for retention in their units.[131]

Personnel planners at DCS/P also made numerous changes in assignment policies.[132] In the case of married personnel, the Air Force now allowed airmen to volunteer for three-year accompanied and one-year unaccompanied overseas assignments. Those who chose an accompanied three-year tour could also have their family travel concurrently to their new destinations.[133] The Air Force distributed information packages to airmen and their dependents describing overseas life and living conditions.[134] Married airmen also benefited from the Air Force's expansion of overseas elementary and high schools.

Those returning from overseas assignments could also choose their next assignment for the first time, provided they had reenlisted.[135] Often, this meant a base of choice and/or additional training. In the past, if an airman wanted a change of assignment, he had to find a vacancy at the new station, obtain a discharge from the Air Force, and then pay for his family's move. Upon reaching the new station, he reenlisted at his old pay-grade.[136] By 1954, with the help of computerized punch cards and new reporting procedures, the Air Force knew where job openings were and could offer the base-of-choice option to all reenlistees.[137]

The Air Force also focused on upgrading life on Air Force bases. For single airmen overseas and at stateside bases, the Air Force expanded social and recreational programs. Theaters, libraries, service clubs, swimming pools, and large, modern gymnasiums were just a few of the personnel facilities receiving a high construction priority.[138] With the Korean war G.I. Bill expiring in 1955, the impetus to leave the service to obtain more education was nullified. The Air Force did, however, encourage single airmen to take advantage of the Air Force's educational programs and pursue off-duty high school diplomas and college degrees.[139] In many cases, the Air Force began to offer tuition assistance for those working on degrees in exchange for additional years in service.[140]

Various welfare services helped to make Air Force life better for married personnel. As early as January 1951, planners directed surveys of the major commands to determine how well the Air Force was looking after its own. For instance, in Tactical Air Command, Red Cross workers handled nearly 8,000 welfare cases per year, of which 16 percent were for financial assistance. Air Force aid societies provided emergency financial help to more than 50 percent of those in need in the form of loans and grants. Moreover, the Air Force placed the base chaplain in charge of the base's welfare fund and made him responsible for its disbursement to worthy individuals and families. Wing commanders designated experienced officers to manage the Personal Affairs Program, which helped airmen and their dependents to understand their rights, privileges, and benefits as service personnel. Finally, military officer, NCO, and airmen's wives' clubs provided personnel to man the Red Cross, chaplain, Personal Affairs, and Air Force Aid Society welfare programs.[141]

Additionally, planners adopted some of the major commands' ideas about making Air Force assignments more pleasant for families. For instance, in SAC, General LeMay established a dependent assistance program designed to bolster the morale of military spouses.[142] Program volunteers built refreshment stands on the flight line for their husbands' take-offs and returns. They also established child care centers so that couples had more time to spend together. This program also provided access to household goods, helped with house hunting, and disseminated information to families about local schools and health care facilities. Most importantly, the program established a network of families in similar circumstances to provide friendship and a community for the newcomer. In 1955, the Air Force made Dependent Assistance Centers an official program.[143]

Planners also sought ways to make career paths more attractive to personnel by developing a plan to increase the prestige of noncommissioned officers.[144] One of the first steps involved in isolating the prestige problem was an adjustment in grade structure.[145] As the Air Force mission was premised on skilled personnel operating and maintaining technologically sophisticated systems and equipment, planners looked upon promotion as a major form of compensation for technical proficiency.

With no specific means of compensating technical skills other than through promotion, the number of people in the traditional NCO ranks of corporal, sergeant, staff sergeant, and master sergeant greatly increased as the Air Force expanded. Thus, by 1952, more than 70 percent of all enlisted personnel were in the NCO categories. Letters from the Air Force's Chief of Staff, General Hoyt S. Vandenberg, to all major commands in March 1952 explained the results of this grade inflation: "Prestige and respect due our senior NCOs for ability as leaders and for skill as technicians [were] compromised by the current situation. . . . It is imperative that the total numbers be reduced."[146] In April 1952, the Air Force terminated its AAF rank designations and introduced a new grade system that recognized only the top three grades as NCOs, thereby reducing NCO ranks to only 33 percent of the enlisted force.[147]

Although the Air Force collaborated with the Military Service Publishing Company in producing a handbook for noncommissioned officers and airmen as early as 1948, by 1953 NCO duties were still not specifically defined.[148] In early 1953, planners asked the commanding generals of the various commands to select top NCOs to participate in a conference on NCO duties and responsibilities. At the conference, these NCOs prepared a regulation defining what was expected of an Air Force noncommissioned officer.[149]

Essentially, the definition that emerged from the NCO conference described an individual who was both a leader and a manager. This person could work without supervision, understand complex job-related problems, and train subordinates in technical and military subjects. Regardless of whether he was a dental technician, a personnel specialist, or an electronics technician, the NCO was also a military leader. Hence, the definition called for the ability to conduct drills and ceremonies, understand the UCMJ, and become thoroughly familiar with the history of one's unit.[150]

Because planners gave no instructions on how to implement this new regulation, major commands and units began to devise programs of their own. A survey of NCOs at Scott AFB, Illinois, resulted in guidance that reemphasized the privileges, authority, and responsibility of noncommissioned officers. Master sergeants were exempted from most additional duties, including retreat formations, while staff and technical sergeants performed only duties involving barracks chief, mess count, and quarters inspection. NCOs received head-of-the-line privileges in pay lines, retreat formations, and at mess halls.[151] Noncommissioned officers could also cash checks without an officer's endorsement and were not restricted to any distance of travel when off duty.[152] Some wings established separate tables at the mess hall marked "NCOs Only" and separate rooms for bachelor NCOs.[153] Finally, like officers, "the word of NCOs" was directed by the base commander to be "accepted without question by all personnel, officers, and airmen."[154]

Other bases also contributed new ideas for boosting NCO status. Some commanders formed NCO advisory councils in which participants discussed problems and solutions to Air Force life and addressed the issue of poor

Maj. Gen. Richard C. Lindsay

retention.[155] Other base commanders assigned certain officers' jobs to NCOs. At Sampson AFB, New York, Maj. Gen. Richard Lindsay assigned four NCOs to take over the job of supply officers.[156] In the Continental Air Command headquarters, two master sergeants took charge of the record management program and received commendation medals for handling jobs usually assigned to field grade officers (major and above).[157] At Kelly AFB, in the continental Military Air Transport Service Command, the commander assigned each NCO the job of "training specialists."[158] Each NCO was now responsible for the complete training of five subordinates and could recommend promotion action for each.

Perhaps one of the most significant contributions made by a command was Strategic Air Command's 7th Air Division NCO Academy at Ruislip, England.[159] This academy, except for the commandant and military law instructor, was completely staffed by NCOs. Its curriculum, lasting one month, offered forty hours in personnel management; forty hours in leadership and command; forty hours in oral and written communication; and forty hours in miscellaneous course work including military law, Air Force organization, and psychology. Moreover, not just any NCO could attend: he had to supervise at least three persons, have a 7-level AFSC (supervisory), and be at least one more

184

year in his present assignment.[160]

In the fall of 1953, planners began to appraise the need for centralizing NCO schools as other commands began to operate academies based on SAC's design. By May 1954, academies opened at McChord AFB, Washington; Vance AFB, Oklahoma; Eighth Air Force at Bergstrom AFB, Texas; Second Air Force at Barksdale, Louisiana; Scott AFB, Illinois; and Fifteenth Air Force at March AFB, California.[161]

One of the major problems with which planners dealt was curriculum uniformity. Major commands developed their NCO training programs based around missions and requirements. Some schools stressed disciplined drill and ceremonies while others emphasized leadership or personnel management. Moreover, graduates of one command's academy often had to attend similar NCO training when they transferred to another command.[162]

By October 1955, Air Training Command had worked out a four-phase plan for standardizing NCO schooling. NCO instructors conducted the first phase on each base and offered preparatory training for airmen first class (A1C) who would soon become noncommissioned officers. The next phase was a command-level school for current NCOs. The third phase—advanced training for superintendents—would orient senior NCOs for warrant positions. The final phase, "special phase one," produced a centralized Air Force Academy that trained advanced technical management and military subjects. In all phases, the Air Force supplied standardized curriculum outlines. Planners hoped that these NCO academies would provide an "elite corps of noncommissioned officers comparable to Academy-graduated officers."[163]

In 1956, NCO representatives of five zone of interior academies and planners from Headquarters, USAF and Air Training Command met at the Military Air Transport Service's NCO Academy in Orlando, Florida, to discuss the standardization of NCO training curriculum.[164] Planners published the results of this conference in AFR 50–39 as *NCO Academies* which established

Reviewing stand, Kelly Field, Texas

written accreditation requirements for NCO academies and preparatory schools. Under this regulation, academies had to provide 220 hours of resident instruction to master and technical sergeants over a five-week period. Topics to be covered included World Affairs; Air Force History; Communication Skills; Supervision and Management; Human Relations and Leadership; Drill and Ceremonies; Military Customs, Courtesy, and Protocol; Physical Training and Conditioning; Instructing; and Military Justice. NCO preparatory schools for staff sergeants and airmen first class provided 120 hours of instruction over a three-week period and focused on Leadership and Personnel Management. Graduates of either course received Air Force certificates and command diplomas.[165]

Besides professional education, several reforms helped NCOs regulate entrance into their ranks. Changes to the Air Force's nonjudicial punishment procedures limited the number of pay grades a commander could demote a noncommissioned officer for poor behavior or lack of proficiency. Now, only promotion boards consisting of one officer and two NCOs could recommend reduction to a grade lower than airman first class (E–4).[166] Noncommissioned officers, besides creating tests to measure job knowledge, also created NCO examinations that tested areas of leadership and military knowledge.[167] No one could become an NCO without receiving a passing grade; potential NCOs had to exhibit both military bearing and technical expertise.[168] Gradually, however, military leadership and knowledge questions gave way to questions on personnel management and logistical functions.

Even if an airman received a passing grade on these tests, he still had to appear before a promotion board, usually composed of two senior (E–7s) NCOs and one officer. The board examined the airman's NCO/airman proficiency reports and then asked the potential promotee a series of questions about his work, military subjects, and contemporary affairs. Upon promotion, airmen received a certificate of rank, similar to the officers', designating them as noncommissioned officers.[169] With their participation in NCO examinations and promotion boards, NCOs were now involved in regulating people eligible to enter their ranks. Promotion boards, however, remained highly subjective. NCOs were also instrumental in defining the role of Air Force First Sergeant as a command position, giving the job a distinctive insignia and establishing criteria for obtaining the assignment.[170]

One final program sought to split airman ranks into a specialist and NCO career paths, but after three years of study, planners dropped the idea when they discovered that the program could not build NCO prestige and position without depriving technician-specialists of the same incentives.[171] E–5s or higher were entitled by law to movers' expenses for their household goods, dependent travel, a dislocation allowance, and other retirement and medical benefits. The top three grades warranted NCO mess membership and their own night club, priority on the housing list, and exemption from clean-up details and additional

186

duties. Planners reasoned that, if they withheld any of these privileges from the technicians, many would not reenlist. With the critical need for technicians, nothing was to be gained by splitting the two groups.[172] The Army, for its part, depended less on highly skilled men and found it in its best interests to create a specialist rating separate from the NCO cadre, thereby effectively returning to its pre–World War II rank structure.[173]

By 1956, a large peacetime military force had become an American tradition. The Korean war and the communist threat reenforced its necessity. The military service's image was that of a place where youth could receive a moral education, gain a trade useful to the Air Force, and remain in the service for a worthwhile career. Nevertheless, during the Korean war, the Air Force recognized a need for personnel legislation and policy reform to match perceptions with reality.

Planners projected that few personnel would remain in the Air Force despite the millions of dollars spent in advertising it as a respected career. Civilian life simply offered too many opportunities, and industry surpassed the military in pay and benefits. By 1953, all the services were aware of the impending manpower crisis and mobilized the Womble Committee to examine reasons why personnel failed to remain in the service for a career. This examination led to several legislative acts that, by late 1956, had increased housing, guaranteed medical care to dependents, provided reenlistment bonuses, and gave more pay to those with invaluable training and experience.

The Air Force also changed internal personnel policies. Air planners took actions designed to decrease the reliance on highly skilled workers and increase their ability to attract and retain career-minded personnel. This meant acknowledging that older married personnel in their second reenlistment were a valued commodity. Thus, the Air Force changed assignment policies, promoted the establishment of welfare programs, and began laying the ground work for a professional noncommissioned career cadre. What initially started out as an advertising concept (a military career) in the 1940s became an administrative reality by the mid-1950s.

The payoff from this legislation and policy reform came in Fiscal Years 1956 and 1957. First-term reenlistment rates increased an average of 128 percent, while career retention rates jumped from 70.2 percent in 1955 to 91.4 percent in 1957 (Table 29).[174] AWOL rates also dropped almost 60 percent from an average of 16.8 per thousand (1950–1954) to 7.2 per thousand for Fiscal Years 1955–1956.[175] With increased retention rates, the Air Force in subsequent years continued to focus on retaining only individuals capable of comprehending technical training and those willing to make the Air Force a career. By 1956, planners had laid the groundwork for an experienced career force.

Table 29
Air Force Reenlistment Rates
1955–1959

Year	First Term	Career	Total
1955*	14.4	70.2	23.5
1956	29.3	87.9	44.2
1957	36.5	91.4	49.2
1958	39.8	91.8	54.8
1959	45.7	92.9	61.5

SOURCE: *DOD Fact Book, 1970*, p. 49.

*FY 1955 was the first time the armed services differentiated between first-term and career reenlistments.

✦6✦

Personnel Policy and the
Air Force NCO Cadre

IN OCTOBER 1974, retired General Laurence S. Kuter recalled how much of the Air Force's personnel policy had become codified during his tour as Deputy Chief of Staff for Personnel from 1952 to 1954:

> As I came in, the legislation forming the Air Force was relatively new. The Air Force personnel policies were being formed; they weren't published; they weren't firm. They were springing up all over. All sorts of personnel action and policies had to be coordinated and published. The [old] basic statutes forming the Air Force referred back, generally, to what the Army or the Navy had been doing.[1]

Kuter implies there was a concerted effort by the Air Force to make its personnel policy distinct from the Army's. In fact, he indicates that much of the new personnel policy owed little to the past. The "New" Air Force demanded new thinking. Moreover, its independence depended on how well it could separate itself from the other services. It had to have a distinct identity and role. If anything, what influenced Kuter's judgment of personnel policy was the drive for independence that had affected airmen since at least World War I. With regard to the continuity between Army, Navy, and Air Force personnel policies, General Kuter, like many decisionmakers, overlooked an important point: Air Force personnel policies were often as much a product of evolution as of crisis.

Certainly underlying the personnel system and policies of the postwar Air Force were a number of guiding assumptions from the Air Force's past. The service's reliance on technology, its need for high-caliber men, its penchant for scientific management principles (that is, getting the right man for the job, training him, and then ensuring his competency), and its ability to borrow personnel policies from industry and the other services in order to meet its needs created a worldview that influenced postwar personnel policy.

For example, the Air Force's insistence on high mental standards related directly to its beliefs that the service needed intelligent men to work with aviation technology. This thinking was present in 1914, during World War I (with the development of intelligence testing), and during World War II, when the War Department accused the AAF of skimming the elite from the resources of society. Problems again arose during peacetime as well as during the Korean war, and eventually the Secretary of Defense was forced to establish a qualitative force distribution scheme mandating that the Air Force accept the less-qualified. Nevertheless, whenever possible, the Air Force continued to emphasize that only the brightest need apply for technical training. Moreover, by 1955, while 60 percent of the American population were high school graduates, 63 percent of the entire enlisted force and 74 percent of the noncommissioned officers had graduated from high school.[2]

Continuity between the Army Air Corps, the Army Air Forces, and the United States Air Force was also found in its classification policies. Classification systems, while growing in sophistication over the years, continued to have the same objective as when they were introduced into the Air Service and the Army during World War I—to get the right man in the right job. If anything, the Air Force strengthened its ties to industrial personnel management philosophy. In the early 1950s, its human resources laboratory continued to lead the way for all the services in classification testing and job analysis. The Air Force began to use classification procedures to remove the incompetent and to distinguish between people with low IQ scores who had some mechanical aptitude and those who did not.

Technical training programs also had their roots in the interwar period and during World War II. Planners continued to look for an appropriate combination of soldierly and technical training. By the early 1950s, the Air Force concluded that it had to indoctrinate every airman into a specific way of life, one in which enlisted personnel were technicians first and soldiers a distant second.

Eventually, the Air Force integrated basic training and technical training into a hybrid of interwar and World War II training policies: after a common introduction to the Air Force, trainees received additional basic training during highly specialized technical training and, later, at their first unit assignment. The Air Force also sought the proper combination of formal and on-the-job training. The service eventually moved toward universal formal training at various points in an airman's career: this formal training was then augmented by unit OJT.

Other technical training problems in the interwar period resurfaced during World War II and the Cold War years. In his report to the Secretary of War in November 1945, General Arnold argued that one important lesson of World War II was that the complexity of modern war necessitated an "age of specialization." Since "no rational man can hope to know everything about his profession," Arnold explained, "encouragement should therefore be given to specialization."[3] Technological advances and the increased size of the peacetime air forces demanded new training, professional schools, more trainees, and increased specialization.

The development of a general recruiting service received impetus from the Air Force's Army heritage, from the need for an expanded force, from personnel management philosophy, and from Navy and industrial recruiting concepts. When the Air Force ultimately won independence from the Army and began to seek out volunteers, recruiters adopted Army, Navy, and industrial procedures, regulations, and salesmanship courses. It hired professional advertisers and salesmen to help with recruiting campaign methods, and these specialists developed specific recruiting literature to project an image of a future-oriented technical occupation offering a well-paid, fast-paced, and exciting life. In an era of atomic bombs and jet aircraft, the Air Force asked young people to become members of a technological vanguard that promised peace and prosperity to those living in the American century. Finally, recruiters across the nation formed a network that advocated national service, and in turn helped the Air Force become an accepted national institution.

Although the need for volunteers and career personnel spurred the growth of a professional recruiting network, in 1952 General Kuter found that the need to retain an experienced cadre of enlisted personnel, many of whom were married, provided the incentive to improve retention policies. The Air Force could create an Airman Career Program to alleviate some of the problems with promotion and skill imbalance and it could improve poor assignment policies and welfare programs, but it had little control over congressional legislation. Here, the confluence of three factors helped create a career force: a growing centralization of authority in the guise of a consolidated Air Staff and Department of Defense, poor retention suffered by all branches of the Armed Forces in the early and mid-1950s, and a president who was sympathetic to the plight of the military.

Work by various DOD and presidential committees—namely, the Doolittle Board, the Hook Committee, the Presidential Committee of Religion and Welfare in the Military, and the Womble Committee—presented the needs of the military to congressional leaders. By 1956, legislation was effected linking pay to civilian wages and providing housing and medical benefits to military personnel and their dependents. That same year, poor retention and AWOL rates began to change for the better.

The growing professionalization of the noncommissioned officers corps also contributed to improved retention and the formation of a career enlisted force. Before defining professionalization, however, it is important to understand what is meant by *profession*. Sociologists who study occupations and professions have spent much time debating the nature and attributes of professions. Greenwood, for instance, studied eighteen articles from the 1960s and 1970s that attempted to define and delineate the attributes of a profession. He found that these authors cited between one and nine attributes; most

An aerial view of the multiple buildings comprising the open hospital facility at Lackland AFB, Texas, in the 1950s (*left*).

The hospital at Bergstrom AFB, Texas, in 1956 (*right*).

The new hospital at Lackland AFB, Texas, later named for surgeon Wilford Hall, opened in 1957 (*left*).

averaged around four.[4] Despite all this work on attributes (or perhaps because of it), scholars still hesitate to concur regarding *profession*. Abbott comes the closest: he notes that a profession is not just a body of attributes but that "professions are somewhat exclusive groups of individuals applying somewhat abstract knowledge to particular cases."[5]

In 1957, Samuel Huntington, an expert on the sociology of professions, argued that there is such an entity as a military profession and the officers of the armed forces are its members. Like other structuralists of the time, Huntington cites the central function of the profession, "the management and application of violence," and lists the main attributes that qualify the officer group to membership: expertise, social responsibility, and corporateness.[6]

With regard to the attributes, Huntington defines expertise in terms of a broad university background coupled with advanced, lifelong learning in the "systematic application of force for political purposes."[7] The social responsibility of the military profession, according to Huntington, was implicit in their oath—the idea that officers must use their expertise for the good of society. Finally, he defines corporateness by arguing that because officership is a public, bureaucratized profession, it has the legal right to limit its membership, structure its schooling, and define its hierarchy and ethics. In other words, it has a social culture of its own.[8]

Important to the discussion here is Huntington's refusal to grant enlisted personnel status as members of the military profession. According to him, they had neither the intellectual capabilities nor the professional responsibility of the officer. "Their vocation is a trade, not a profession," he added.[9] He did not view officers who worked in specialties as members of the military profession; he saw them as members of "auxiliary vocations, having the same relation to expertise of the officers as the skills of the nurse, chemist, laboratory technician, dietician, pharmacist, and X-ray technician have to the expertise of the doctor."[10] Thus, just as nurses and chemists were not part of the medical profession, neither were military specialists and enlisted personnel part of the military profession.

Problems arise, however, in attempting to apply Huntington's model to the Air Force. Based on his exclusion of military specialists, less than one-half of all Air Force officers (42 percent in 1957, and by 1991, 24.6 percent) were in positions either to manage or to apply violence (Huntington's terminology). The point is that Huntington focused his model on the Army, not on the Air Force, a more technically driven modern service. Thus his view emphasized command, grand strategy, and tactics, not nuclear research, aircraft development, or ballistic missile production.

Perhaps in 1957 one could argue that those in the Air Force who flew and fought were the true members of the military profession. Today that model would not hold up. Huntington would undoubtedly argue that a second lieutenant flying a lone F–15 demonstrates less professional competence than a commander in charge of the theater of operations. In this respect, there should be no argument, but all officers of today, whether they be in aircraft maintenance, space communications, or the cockpit, have received advanced military professional training that theoretically has prepared them to assume command and apply strategic skills. The point is that the profession of arms has widened its doors to specialists as well as to the traditional warrior class. In this sense, most military officer specialists have been assimilated into the concept of the military profession.

If Huntington exaggerated the degree to which military specialists were excluded from the military profession, he may have also exaggerated his claims about enlisted personnel. Again, arguing from a World War II Army model, enlisted personnel seemed to be members of a trade who, at the bidding of the military profession, applied violence. Using this approach, we can easily extend our thinking to consider noncommissioned officers as foremen who prod their craftsmen and unskilled labor to produce for management. Today, with career paths, advanced professional military education courses, and a host of key management jobs open to senior NCOs, some revisionists seem willing to extend Huntington's definition to the senior noncommissioned grades (E–8 and E–9) by arguing that they "show strong attributes of professionalism."[11]

Regardless, the exclusion of noncommissioned officers and other enlisted personnel from the professional ranks seems appropriate. These individuals neither belong to the same occupational community as officers, nor do they master the same subject matter. Just as nursing is not included in the medical profession, neither is the NCO part of the officership (military) profession. As Huntington points out, only if the military were a single hierarchy from private to general could enlisted personnel be considered part of the military profession.[12]

Although his work demonstrates how a profession developed for the officer class, Huntington overlooks any movement by enlisted personnel toward the status of a separate profession. By classifying the vocations of all enlisted personnel as a trade, he failed to recognize the professionalization of the Air Force's noncommissioned officers which was occurring even as he was writing his book. The professionalization model, albeit not without critics, was well developed by Harold Wilensky in 1964. In his work, this sociologist argues that many occupations were undergoing a sequence of events (an occupation-profession continuum) from which eventually a profession would emerge. Looking at the dates of first events in a variety of American professions, such as first training school, first university school, first local association, first licensing law, and first code of ethics, Wilensky asserts that there was a structure and narrative for the movement from occupation to profession. Professions begin, he argues, when people "start doing full-time the thing that needs doing" and then continue by establishing schools, setting standards, providing longer training, demanding commitment to the profession and the group, promoting and creating a professional association, and finally, establishing a code of ethics, eliminating internal competition, and protecting the client.[13] Several factors, including the emphasis on deterrence, the expansion of the Air Force's mission overseas, the pace of technological innovation, the convergence of corporate and military personnel theories, and the need to retain career personnel, forged an environment from which the professionalization of the Air Force NCO was spawned.

Between 1950 and 1956, the Air Force established NCO academies (1953) and revised and modernized NCO regulations (1953). During this period, NCOs also received more privilege and status (as compared with men in the lower ranks) and more jurisdictional responsibility from the officer corps (1953); and they began to publish articles in the *Air Force Times*, *Air Force Magazine*, and, beginning in 1957, the Air Force–sanctioned *Airman Magazine*. Finally, a growing need to establish a nationwide self-identity was realized in 1960 when NCOs from all the services organized the Noncommissioned Officers Association (NCOA). In 1961, Air Force NCOs formed the Air Force Sergeants Association.

Over the next forty years, from 1956 to 1996, NCOs lobbied for E–8 and E–9 grades in lieu of a warrant officer category (1958), an office of Chief Master Sergeant of the Air Force (1967), and an up-or-out promotion system similar to that used for officers (1973). They were also instrumental in establishing advanced and senior NCO academies. The professionalization of NCOs continued as officers vacated more jurisdictional space to them, and they began to serve in the Titan program as missile launch officers and in the top rungs of middle management.

In addition to more jurisdictional responsibility, the amount of continuing professional military education offered to enlisted members has also grown. In the 1990s, the NCOA curriculum included Air Force history, military justice, the Code of Conduct, national security, the role of the NCO manager, leadership and management for the manager, and substance abuse and human relations issues.

Furthermore, as those serving in the top three NCO grades (Master Sergeant, Senior Master Sergeant, and Chief Master Sergeant) began to assume more leadership and management duties, the Air Force responded by opening the USAF Senior NCO Academy (SNCOA) at Gunter AFB in Montgomery, Alabama. Its present course of study includes instruction in military professionalism, leadership planning, civil service personnel management, executive decisionmaking, and organizational management.

But what were the attributes of the noncommissioned officer profession? What was its basis for existence? What type of profession was it? According to some scholars of the professions, as one moves along the continuum from occupation to profession, one encounters a number of gradations, ranging from doubtful professions to marginal new professions, to professions-in-process, and then to established professions.[14] Some sociologists also add a category for semiprofessions.[15] With the exception of the established profession category, the definition of each of these types assumes that its attributes are lacking in comparison to the established category. For the most part, an occupation achieves the status of profession only when it attains the quality of the ideal type as found in medicine, law, religion, and, in Huntington's case, the military. If it does not, it is less than a true profession.[16]

The problem with this typology is that it fails to account for jurisdictional claims. Those who view professionalization as an attempt to monopolize knowledge (power), thereby increasing one group's domination over the control of work, would see the medical and legal professions as having complete jurisdictional control over their areas of knowledge.[17] In the military's case, tradition, legal precedent, and society recognize the officer group as having full jurisdictional responsibility over the military profession.

Obtaining full jurisdictional authority over a profession does not preclude other occupations from professionalizing and then subordinating themselves to an incumbent profession. Just as nurses, paralegals, and draftsmen have professionalized and subordinated themselves to their respective incumbent professions (medicine, law, and architecture), so have NCOs professionalized and subordinated themselves to the officer profession. If managing violence was the core function of the officers' profession, then managing military resources for the application of violence was the central function of the Air Force NCOs' profession. Despite the diversity of occupational titles held by Air Force NCOs, all NCOs were required to progress in the understanding and application of managerial theory to military environments.

Whether it was managing a shop of radar technicians, organizing and directing a military finance office, or acting in the capacity of a B–52 crew chief, NCOs by virtue of their own definition* were military leaders and managers whose special knowledge involved managing the military resources necessary for the Air Force to meet its combat function. In fact, as in the officer ranks, the higher one advances, the more one becomes immersed in the profession. Thus just as a general is expected to be more professional than the second lieutenant, so is the chief master sergeant expected to be more professional than the newly promoted sergeant.

Under the old Army system, NCOs were more akin to foremen, compelling their subordinates to get a job done. In the postwar and Cold War Air Force, however, NCOs began to resemble midlevel managers and white-collar technicians more than foremen working on an assembly line or a construction site. This transition came about because of rapid expansion, the willingness of officers to delegate more jurisdictional responsibilities to NCOs, the technical nature of the Air Force's combat mission, the increasing status that Americans afforded Air Force occupations, and the rise of military professional academies and managerial training. Thus, the NCO profession came to be based on an

---

* See Chapter 5.

NCO's ability to understand and apply leadership and management theory to military cases. As for social responsibility, implicit in the airman's—and the officer's—enlistment oath is dedication to the state and to the good of society. Furthermore, NCOs have been involved in establishing criteria for the certification and evaluation of their own type and have developed a strong sense of group identity (corporateness).

During the 1950s, the nascent professionalization of NCOs went hand-in-hand with the notion that the military (in this case, the Air Force) provided suitable careers. The concept of having a career in the military was a product of the changing societal perception toward standing militaries after World War II. Potential recruits and their parents had to perceive the military as a possible and, arguably, a middle-class career option, not something reserved for marginal citizens. In short, the armed forces had to change America's perception of peacetime military service. Beginning in early 1946, with the aid of national advertising, public relations experts, and a mobilized force of national and local veteran's committees, the armed services began a concerted campaign to alter public opinion.

This campaign was substantially advanced by the development of the Warsaw Pact military organization in Eastern Europe after World War II and later by the communist invasion of South Korea, all seemingly directed by the monolithic, powerful, and aggressive force of international communism, promoting fears in the West that war was imminent. After the Soviets' first successful atomic test in 1949, Americans were often reminded by national and military leaders that, in the atomic era, their country could never again afford to be a victim of a surprise attack. The rhetoric of anticommunist politicians, such as that of Senator Joseph McCarthy, served to heighten the perceived immediacy of the communist threat.

The communist threat was certainly important to the acceptance of a large peacetime military force. Several other factors, including advertising campaigns, structural changes within the military, an Americanization program, and legislative reform, helped the public understand that a large, permanent military establishment could be consistent with democratic (middle-class) ideals.

Concerns about the military's resemblance to Prussian-type totalitarian institutions were quieted by several well-publicized boards. The Doolittle Board recognized the need for a democratization of the military and sketched a framework for additional change. The Hook Committee concluded that military pay and benefits should be comparable to industrial earnings and drafted the necessary legislation to effect the change. The President's Committee on Religion and Welfare in the Military assigned the armed forces the role of Americanizing the nation's young people, and the armed forces began to teach morality, ethics, deference to authority, character, and the "truth" about godless communism. Finally, the Womble Committee outlined exactly what the services and Congress needed to do to attract and retain career-minded personnel.

Strengthening civilian control over the military also helped calm the public's fears about the military and paved the way for career-enhancing policies. The creation of a National Military Establishment under the National Security Act of 1947 combined with the 1949 amendments to the act created and strengthened the role of the Secretary of Defense in military policymaking. Moreover, by placing heads of corporations and businesses in the various service secretary, deputy secretary, and assistant secretary positions, internal changes in management and personnel philosophy were inevitable.

In the Air Force, secretaries like Robert Lovett, Stuart Symington, and Harold Talbott introduced business and corporate models into the Air Force's management practices.[18] Buzzwords like *efficiency, economy,* and *cost-analysis,* common in the lexicon of many personnel planners, entered the Air Force's vocabulary. Symington and other believed that it was imperative that the Air Force eschew its Army traditions and adapt more scientific principles, that is, civilian management philosophy and practices.

Even within the Air Force, some officers were already promoting such changes in organizational theory and practice. Air personnel planners, many recruited directly from civilian businesses and educational institutions during World War II, served to bridge the gap between civilian management theory and military tradition in the postwar Air Force.

Beginning in 1943, personnel managers became separated from the Adjutant General's office to form their own divisions, either G–1 (War Department) or A–1 (Air Forces). With autonomy and the creation of an Air Staff that included a Deputy Chief of Staff for Personnel, it appeared that personnel managers and management philosophy had come of age in the Air Force.

These personnel specialists began to influence the Air Force almost immediately. Each command, wing, and squadron had personnel managers who were trained in classification and management procedures and who took orders directly from Air Force headquarters. Personnel managers at the Headquarters DCS/P level created and executed policy for the entire Air Force. Moreover, recruiting, classification, and utilization issues were discussed in Air Force–wide personnel conferences. In World War II and the postwar period, the Air Force sent personnel managers to Harvard University, The Wharton School of the University of Pennsylvania, The University of Chicago, and other business schools to learn their trades. By 1955, Air Force personnel officers published their own magazine, *The Personnel Digest,* in which they shared important Air Force personnel theory and policies. They also had a career path and claimed an occupational hegemony over most personnel management plans and actions in the Air Force.

By 1956, advertising, presidential and congressional action, and internal military reform made the Air Force an American institution. Businesslike,

Air shows and demonstrations aided recruitment. Mobile exhibits at the National Air Fair, Chicago, Illinois, 1949 (*top*). Aerial demonstration, F–84G Thunderbirds in the 1953–1955 period (*bottom*).

offering benefits comparable to industry, and making public welfare its first priority, the Air Force, similar to other modern corporations, could now be viewed by Americans as something familiar, useful, and nonthreatening. Indeed, by 1956 the Air Force and its sister services became American institutions, places where young people from the middle classes could enter, gain skills, become educated, build character, and if so inclined, find a career.

As a result, in the 1990s, a young person from a ranch in Colorado or a suburban home in New York could enter a recruiting office near his or her community, take aptitude tests and a physical, and upon enlistment, by late afternoon have a specific Air Force occupation and school guaranteed. Some recruits had to delay their entry to meet specific school quotas, while others flew, at Air Force expense within a week, to basic training at Lackland AFB. Recruits found that the Air Force provided good housing, opportunities for technical training and postsecondary education, and vast recreational facilities.

Once married, recruits received additional money for quarters, subsistence, family dislocation, and travel along with medical and dental benefits for their dependents. Promotion was linked to centralized quotas, merit ratings, and a quantified, computerized method of testing and rank-ordering possible promotees. Noncommissioned officers could count on more formalized training and opportunities to attend preparatory and advanced professional military educational courses. An NCO might gradually move from the status of technical expert to a manager of personnel and resources, and airmen remaining in the service for at least twenty years would qualify for a generous retirement of 40 percent of base pay for life, base exchange and commissary privileges, and free medical care for themselves and their dependents at military facilities.[19]

Today, neither the Air Force nor the airmen see these events and benefits as uncommon or the opportunities as particularly extraordinary. Yet less than fifty years ago, an American tradition of a large peacetime defense forces or an autonomous Air Force did not exist. Few looked at the military favorably, let alone as a viable career option.

The decade following World War II saw the laying of the ideological and legislative foundation for a large standing military. With independence, the Air Force relied on its Army heritage and its personnel planners to expand, polish, and at times create personnel policies to recruit, train, and retain a career enlisted force. In the late 1940s and 1950s, the Air Force devised policies to make its service more than just a short-term military experience. The Air Force became a career, and in time, recruiters could boast that the service represented a great way of life. Personnel policies in the 1990s are predicated on these traditions. The goal of enlisted personnel policies remains much the same as it had been when General Kuter was Deputy Chief of Staff for Personnel: to maintain a highly trained career force upon which the Air Force is built.

Appendices

APPENDIX 1

DOD Active Duty Enlisted Personnel
1945–1957

Date	Total Military Services	Army[a]	Navy	Marine Corps	Air Force[a]
30 Jun 1945	10,795,775	5,473,905	2,988,207	432,858	1,900,805
30 Jun 1946	2,598,739	1,248,764	834,722	141,471	373,782
30 Jun 1947	1,385,233	594,078	442,579	85,547	263,029
30 Jun 1948	1,268,698	484,061	369,121	78,081	337,435
30 Jun 1949	1,416,015	581,422	396,242	78,715	359,636
30 Jun 1950	1,269,891	518,921	331,860	67,025	352,085
30 Jun 1951	2,917,277	1,399,362	661,639	177,470	678,806
31 Mar 1952	3,290,378	1,515,419[b]	726,061	226,298	822,600
30 Apr 1952	3,298,632[b]	1,506,142	728,833	225,063	838,594
30 Jun 1952	3,245,310	1,446,266	735,753[b]	215,554	847,737[b]
30 Jun 1953	3,161,030	1,386,500	706,375	230,488[b]	837,667
30 Jun 1954	2,931,220	1,274,803	642,048	205,275	809,094
30 Jun 1955	2,570,754	985,659	579,864	186,753	818,478
30 Jun 1956	2,445,219	905,711	591,996	182,971	764,541
30 Jun 1957	2,442,849	885,056	597,859	183,427	776,507

SOURCE: *DOD Fact Book, 1958*, p. 21.

[a]Represents command strength prior to June 30, 1956.
[b]Korean conflict peak total military personnel.

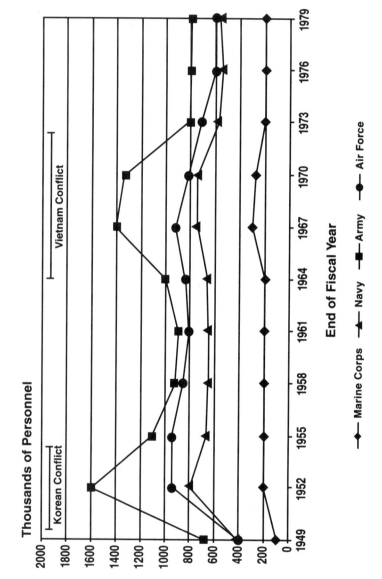

APPENDIX 2

Active Duty Military Personnel Strength

Fiscal Years 1949–1979

SOURCES: *DOD Fact Book, 1958; DOD Fact Book, 1980.*

APPENDIX 3

Airman Career Fields

Occupational Area	Career Field	Career Field Subdivision
Combat		Not applicable to airmen
Combat Support	Intelligence	Cryptanalysis Radio traffic analysis Language Intelligence Operations—Photographic interpretation Technical intelligence
	Photomapping	Cartographic Surveyor
	Photographic	Aerial photography Photography Motion picture photography
	Weather	Weather equipment repair Weather forecasting
	Air Traffic Control and Warning	Air traffic operations Ground control approach Aircraft control and warning
	Communications Operations	Communications center operations Cryptographic operations Radio operations
Electronic Engineering	Radio and Radar Maintenance	Radio maintenance Radar maintenance
	Missile Guidance Systems	Command missile Automatic missile Preset missile Missile instrumentation

APPENDIX 3—cont'd

Occupational Area	Career Field	Career Field Subdivision
	Armament Systems	Bomb navigation systems Gun-bomb-rocket systems Turret systems
	Training Devices Maintenance	Instrument and navigation trainer maintenance Bomb, gunnery, and classroom trainer maintenance Radio and radar trainer maintenance
	Wire Maintenance	Outside plant Inside plant Communications machine maintenance Cryptographic maintenance
Maintenance Engineering	Intricate Equipment Maintenance	Office machine repair Tabulating equipment repair Camera repair Instrument overhaul Medical equipment repair
	Aircraft Accessories Maintenance	Supercharger Fuel metering Propeller Mechanical accessories and equipment Hydraulic Aircraft electrical accessories
	Aircraft and Engine Maintenance	Aircraft maintenance Flight engineer Aircraft engine overhaul
	Rocket Propulsion	Rocket propulsion
	Munitions and Weapons	Munitions Weapons

APPENDIX 3—cont'd

Occupational Area	Career Field	Career Field Subdivision
	Vehicle Maintenance	Vehicle maintenance
Installation and Construction Engineering	Metal Working	Machinist Metal processing Sheet metal Airframe repair
	Construction	Roads and grounds Building crafts
	Utilities	Electrical refrigeration Gas generation Water supply and sanitation Plumbing Heating
	Fabric, Leather, and Rubber	Parachute and fabric Rubber products repair
Logistics	Transportation	Air transportation Traffic management Motor transportation
	Food Service	Baking Mess Meat cutting
	Supply	Supply Sales commissary
	Procurement	Procurement
Personnel and Administration	Administrative	Postal administrative
	Printing	Duplicating Letter press Lithographic
	Information	Information
	Personnel	Career guidance Personnel Recruitment

APPENDIX 3—cont'd

Occupational Area	Career Field	Career Field Subdivision
	Education	Technical training General training
	Entertainment	Band Athletic and recreation
	Chaplain	Welfare
Comptroller	Management Methods	Management engineering Production control
	Budgetary Accounting and Disbursing	Budget, fiscal, and audit Disbursing Cost analysis
	Statistical and Machine Accounting	Statistical Machine accounting
Special Services	Medical	Aero medical Preventive medical Veterinary Medical administrative Dental
	Rescue and Survival	Rescue and survival
	Grounds Safety	Ground safety
	Marine	Marine
	Firefighting	Firefighting
	Security and Law Enforcement	Air police Investigation
	Special Activities	Simulated trainer Railroad equipment Illustrator draftsman Laundry Graves registration First sergeant

SOURCE: *Airman's Guide*, 2d ed., pp. 42–43.

APPENDIX 4

DOD Summary of Enlisted Personnel Procurement
Fiscal Years 1951–1956

	FY 1951	FY 1952	FY 1953	FY 1954	FY 1955	FY 1956
Total DOD	2,100,598	1,207,446	1,113,431	797,496	932,448	880,471
Inductions	586,767	379,485	563,930	265,039	215,188	136,752
First Enlistments	630,488	509,517	342,871	329,120	440,271	371,420
Immediate Reenlistments	203,060	182,399	110,647	96,756	177,214	240,312
Other Reenlistments	71,307	34,505	42,111	53,658	60,174	57,472
Reserve to Active Duty[a]	608,976	101,540	53,872	52,923	39,601	74,515
Total Army	1,084,050	498,881	735,154	456,452	452,451	323,584
Inductions	586,767	295,795	563,930	265,039	215,188	108,502
First Enlistments	153,294	79,944	79,725	93,659	119,778	93,637
Immediate Reenlistments	67,837	89,976	60,591	56,076	72,832	77,125
Other Reenlistments[b]	22,371	9,433	18,387	25,383	31,898	22,743
Reserve to Active Duty	253,781	23,733	12,521	16,295	12,755	21,577
Total Navy	430,076	266,098	138,091	89,455	172,210	241,363
Inductions	—	—	—	—	—	28,250
First Enlistments	202,438	171,369	88,050	54,917	121,411	111,993
Immediate Reenlistments	62,999	34,786	17,869	16,303	23,711	58,867
Other Reenlistments	9,181	2,788	2,159	3,209	4,426	5,600
Reserve to Active Duty	155,458	57,155	30,013	15,026	22,662	36,653
Total Marine Corps	153,604	143,583	62,416	106,575	39,503	66,645
Inductions	—	83,690	—	—	—	—

APPENDIX 4—cont'd

	FY 1951	FY 1952	FY 1953	FY 1954	FY 1955	FY 1956
First Enlistments	41,559	39,482	40,771	72,418	27,120	36,896
Immediate Reenlistments	11,880	9,502	10,910	11,353	7,830	13,923
Other Reenlistments	3,643[c]	998[c]	1,600[c]	1,262[c]	826	919
Reserve to Active Duty	96,522	9,911	9,135	21,542	3,727	14,907
Total Air Force	432,868	298,884	177,770	145,014	268,284	248,879
Inductions	—	—	—	—	—	—
First Enlistments	233,197	218,722	134,325	108,126	171,962	128,894
Immediate Reenlistments	60,344	48,135	21,277	13,024	72,841	90,397
Other Reenlistments	36,112	21,286	19,965	23,804	23,024	28,210
Reserve to Active Duty	103,215	10,741	2,203	60	457	1,378

SOURCE: Office of SecDef Statistical Services Center, Selective Manpower Statistics, Jan 2, 1959.

[a]Includes National Guard. Includes involuntary calls to active duty during Korean war period.
[b]Includes enlistments in the category Undetermined.
[c]Represents No Prior Service enlistments. The number of enlistees with prior service in other branches only is not known, and these individuals are included in Other Reenlistments for FYs 1951–1954.

APPENDIX 5

Reenlistment Rates for Regulars
By Total DOD Categories

Time Period	Reenlistment Rate (%)	No. of: Reenlistments	No. of: Eligibles
		Total Regulars	
Jan–Jun 1954	18.8	39,876	211,694
FY 1955: Total	27.2	149,306	547,978
Jul–Dec 1954	23.8	64,709	271,744
Jan–Jul 1955	30.6	84,597	276,234
FY 1956: Total	43.6	254,580	583,911
Jul–Dec 1955	44.1	134,555	305,252
Jan–Jul 1956	43.1	120,025	278,659
FY 1957: Total	45.9	204,712	446,032
Jul–Dec 1956	45.0	113,445	251,902
Jan–Jul 1957	47.0	91,267	194,130
		First Termers	
Jan–Jun 1954	10.9	16,860	154,969
FY 1955: Total	15.7	69,148	439,033
Jul–Dec 1954	13.1	28,101	214,384
Jan–Jul 1955	18.3	41,047	224,649
FY 1956: Total	22.8	91,968	402,704
Jul–Dec 1955	24.6	52,588	214,193
Jan–Jul 1956	20.9	39,380	188,511
FY 1957: Total	24.7	72,072	291,495
Jul–Dec 1956	23.9	40,246	168,122
Jan–Jul 1957	25.8	31,826	123,373
		Career Regulars	
Jan–Jun 1954	40.6	23,016	56,725
FY 1955: Total	73.6	80,158	108,945
Jul–Dec 1954	63.8	36,608	57,360
Jan–Jul 1955	84.4	43,550	51,585
FY 1956: Total	89.7	162,612	181,207
Jul–Dec 1955	90.0	81,967	91,059

Foundation of the Force

APPENDIX 5—cont'd

| Time Period | Reenlistment Rate (%) | No. of: | |
		Reenlistments	Eligibles
Career Regulars			
Jan–Jul 1956	89.5	80,645	90,148
FY 1957: Total	85.8	132,640	154,537
Jul–Dec 1956	87.4	73,199	83,780
Jan–Jul 1957	84.0	59,441	70,757

SOURCE: Office of SecDef Statistical Services Center, Selective Manpower Statistics, Jan 31, 1959.

APPENDIX 6

DOD Reenlistment Rates for Regulars
Fiscal Years 1950–1957

	Total DOD	Army	Navy	Marine Corps	Air Force
FY 1950	59.3	61.8	65.5	35.1	54.7
FY 1951–1953	54.6	50.9	61.0	50.0	56.1
FY 1954: Total	<u>23.7</u>	<u>22.0</u>	<u>23.7</u>	<u>18.1</u>	<u>31.2</u>
Jul–Dec 1953	31.0	25.4	41.7	31.4	43.4
Jan–Jun 1954	31.0	18.6	13.1	12.7	27.3
FY 1955: Total	<u>27.2</u>	<u>59.0</u>	<u>14.2</u>	<u>20.6</u>	<u>23.5</u>
Jul–Dec 1954	23.8	54.7	8.2	20.0	21.2
Jan–Jun 1955	30.6	63.2	19.4	21.2	25.8
FY 1956: Total	<u>43.6</u>	<u>59.0</u>	<u>32.6</u>	<u>37.8</u>	<u>44.2</u>
Jul–Dec 1955	44.1	65.4	31.7	35.1	44.6
Jan–Jun 1956	43.1	54.1	33.6	39.8	43.5
FY 1957: Total	<u>45.9</u>	<u>49.6</u>	<u>44.9</u>	<u>29.1</u>	<u>49.4</u>
Jul–Dec 1956	45.0	49.8	52.5	32.4	47.5
Jan–Jun 1957	47.0	49.4	48.7	25.2	52.1

SOURCE: Office of SecDef Statistical Services Center, Selective Manpower Statistics, Jan 31, 1959.

APPENDIX 7

Summary of Expenditures, by Service
In Millions of Dollars
Fiscal Years 1945–1956

Fiscal Year	Army	Navy	Air Force	Total Military Functions
1945	49,750	30,128	—	79,877
1946	27,176	14,844	—	42,021
1947	8,027	5,784	—	13,811
1948	6,791	4,297	6	11,094
1949	6,482	4,446	1,059	11,994
1950	3,985	4,102	3,600	11,938
1951	7,478	5,584	6,349	20,706
1952	15,708	10,161	12,711	41,358
1953	16,337	11,878	15,087	47,664
1954	12,910	11,293	15,668	43,965
1955	8,899	9,733	16,407	37,824
1956	8,702	9,744	16,749	38,402

SOURCES: FYs 1931–1976—Combined Statement of Receipts, Expenditures and Balances of the U.S. Government; *DOD Fact Book, 1978*, p. 37.

Notes

Introduction

1. I am grateful to David Segal for sharing with me his unpublished manuscript "Sociocultural Designs for the Future Army." I drew heavily from his insight for this Introduction.

2. Important works in this category are legion. See, for instance, Charles Moskos, *The American Enlisted Man: The Rank and File in Today's Military* (New York: Russell Sage Foundation, 1970); Morris Janowitz, *The Professional Soldier: A Social and Political Portrait* (New York: Free Press, 1960); and David R. Segal, *Recruiting for Uncle Sam: Citizenship and Military Manpower Policy* (Lawrence: University of Kansas Press, 1989). All three contain extensive bibliographic citations.

3. Charles C. Moskos, "From Institution to Occupation: Trends in the Military Organization," *Armed Forces & Society*, vol. 4 (1977), pp. 41–49. See also his *The Military: More Than Just a Job?* (New York: Pergamon-Brassey, 1988), for an update.

4. Moskos, *American Enlisted Man*, p. 7.

5. Morris Janowitz, "From Institutional to Occupational: The Need for Conceptual Clarity," *Armed Forces & Society*, vol. 4 (1977), pp. 51–54.

6. Ernest Greenwood observed that what distinguishes a profession from other occupations is that fact that the former implies a career, and a career is essentially a calling, a life devoted to good works. Ernest Greenwood, "Attributes of a Profession," in Sigmund Nosow and William H. Form, eds., *Man, Work and Society* (New York: Basic Books, 1962), pp. 44–45.

7. Andrew Abbott, *The System of Profession: An Essay on the Division of Labor* (Chicago: The University of Chicago Press, 1988), p. 8.

8. See Robert H. Weibe, *The Search for Order, 1877–1922* (New York: Hill & Yang, 1967), p. 115.

9. Abbott, pp. 71–73.

10. Harold L. Wilensky, "The Professionalization of Everyone?" *American Journal of Sociology*, vol. 70 (Sep 1964), pp. 137–158.

11. Weibe, *Search for Order*, esp. chap. 5; Burton J. Bledstein, *The Culture of Professionalism: The Middle Class and the Development of Higher Education in America* (New York: W.W. Norton & Co., 1976), pp. 80–92; Abbott, pp. 177–211; C. Wright Mills, *White Collar: The American Middle Classes* (New York: Oxford University Press, 1951), pp. 3–54.

12. William B. Skelton, *An American Profession of Arms: The Army Officer Corps, 1784–1861* (Lawrence: University of Kansas Press, 1992), pp. 359–362; Peter Karsten, "Armed Progressives: The Military Reorganizes for the American Century," in Peter Karsten, ed., *The Military in America: From the Colonial Era to the Present* (New York: Free Press, 1986), pp. 196–232; James L. Abrahamson, *America Arms for a New Century: The Making of a Great Military Power* (New York: Free Press, 1981); Edward M. Coffman, *The Old Army: A Portrait of the American Army in Peacetime, 1784–1898* (New York: Oxford University Press, 1986), pp. 269–270; Russell F. Weigley, *History of the United States Army* (New York: Macmillan, 1967), pp. 195–196, 242–246; Timothy K. Nenninger, *The Leavenworth Schools and the Old Army: Education Professionalism, and the Officer Corps of the United States Army, 1881–1918* (Westport, Conn.: Greenwood Press, 1978), chaps. 1, 2.

13. The term *managers of violence* was introduced by Harold Lasswell and used extensively by Samuel Huntington in his treatise on military professionalism. Samuel P. Huntington, *The Soldier and the State: The Theory and Politics of Civil-Military Relations* (New York: Vintage Book, 1964), p. 11.

14. Frederick J. Harrod, preface to *Manning the New Navy: The Development of a Modern Naval Force, 1899–1940* (Westport, Conn.: Greenwood Press, 1978).

15. David Segal, in his *Recruiting for Uncle Sam*, pp. 51–52, sees the formulation and implementation of Air Force policy similarly.

Chapter 1

1. Juliette A. Hennessy, *The United States Army Air Arm: April 1861 to April 1917* (Washington, D.C.: Office of Air Force History, 1985), pp. 109–112, app. 13. HR 5304 was entitled "An Act to Increase the Efficiency of the Aviation Service of the Army, and for Other Purposes." Although the act authorized 260 enlisted men, only 101 were actually assigned.

2. Ibid., p. 109.

3. Ibid., pp. 111–112.

4. For the purposes of discussion the term *rank* means military designator such as private, corporal, or sergeant. The term *grade* means pay level such as enlisted grade 1 or E–1, E–2, or E–3. Each pay grade corresponds to a given military rank. In today's parlance, an E–7 is also a master sergeant. These two terms are often used interchangeably. During the interwar period, however, grades were reversed, so that grade 1 equaled a master sergeant, grade 2 equaled a technical sergeant, and so on.

5. Hennessy, p. 112.

6. Ibid.

7. Ibid., pp. 141–143.

8. Ibid., p. 112.

9. Ibid., pp. 112, 136, 143.

10. The most comprehensive works discussing Wilson's involvement in the war include two books by Arthur S. Link, *Woodrow Wilson and the Progressive Era: 1910–1917* (New York: Harper & Row, 1954) and *Wilson: The Struggle for Neutrality, 1914–1915* (Princeton, N.J.: Princeton University Press, 1960), and Arthur C. Walworth's *Woodrow Wilson*, 2d rev. ed. (Baltimore: Penguin Books, 1961).

11. I.B. Holley, *Ideas and Weapons: Exploitation of the Aerial Weapon by the United States During World War I: A Study in the Relationship of Technological Advance, Military Doctrine, and the Development of Weapons* (Washington D.C.: Office of Air Force History, 1983), p. 37. See also Edward M. Coffman's *The War to End All Wars: The American Military Experience in World War I* (Madison: University of Wisconsin Press, 1986), chap. 3.

12. Coffman, *War*, pp. 190–191, 194.

13. On the balloon reconnaissance connection, see Hennessy, pp. 13–19. Mitchell's role in World War I aviation is discussed in Coffman, *War*, p. 211; in Maurer Maurer, *Aviation in the U.S. Army, 1919–1939* (Washington, D.C.: Office of Air Force History, 1987), pp. 113–124, 146–147, 441; in Michael Sherry, *The Rise of American Air Power: The Creation of Armageddon* (New Haven, Conn.: Yale University Press, 1987), chaps. 2, 3; and in Alfred F. Hurley, *Billy Mitchell: Crusader For Airpower* (New York: F. Watts, 1964). See also Edward Warner, "Douhet, Mitchell, Seversky: Theories of Air Warfare," in Edward M. Earle, ed., *Makers of Modern Strategy: Military Thought from Machiavelli to Hitler* (Princeton, N.J.: Princeton University Press, 1971).

14. Walter Millis, *Arms and Men: A Study of American Military History* (New York: G.P. Putnam's Sons, 1956), p. 258.

15. James Hayes, *The Evolution of Armed Forces Enlisted Personnel Management Policies* (Santa Monica, Calif.: Rand Corporation, 1982), p. 76.

16. Frederick Winslow Taylor, *The Principles of Scientific Management* (New York: F.W. Taylor, 1911), p. 36–76.

17. I also see personnel classification growing out of the vocational guidance movement, i.e., to use the school as a means of social control and of encouraging working-class children to choose manual rather than professional occupations. The beliefs in social Darwinism and social engineering permeated vocational guidance supporters. For expansion purposes, the military desired a standardized means to efficiently place recruits into the "right" training curriculum and job. See Sanford Jacoby, *Employing Bureaucracy: Managers, Unions, and the Transformation of Work in American Industry, 1990–1945* (New York: Columbia University Press, 1985), pp. 65–98.

18. Scott taught at Northwestern University and served as the director of the Bureau of Salesmanship Research at the Carnegie Institute of Technology. Yerkes was president of the American Psychological Association and a professor at Harvard University. Both were interested in scientific personnel procedures and intelligence testing. See Coffman, *War*, pp. 59–60, and Daniel Nelson, *Managers and Workers: Origins of the New Factory System in the United States, 1880–1920* (Madison: University of Wisconsin Press, 1975), p. 151. See also Hugo Munsterberg's *Psychology and Industrial Efficiency* (New York: Houghton Mifflin Co., 1913), especially the chapter "The Best Man," and Edmund C. Lynch, "Walter Dill Scott, Pioneer Industrial Psychologist," *Business History Review*, vol. 42 (1968), pp. 155–157, 162. For a broad overview of the intellectual environment from which industrial psychology emerged, see John C. Burnham, "Psychiatry, Psychology, and the Progressive Movement," *American Quarterly*, vol. 12 (1960), pp. 457–465.

19. Committee on Classification of Personnel in the Army, *The Personnel System of the United States Army*, vol. 1, *History of the Personnel System* (Washington, D.C.: Government Printing Office [hereafter cited as GPO], 1919), pp. 1–26, 27–34, 39–42, 604–633; John J. Swan, *Trade Specifications and Index of Professions and Trades in the Army* (Washington, D.C.: GPO, 1918), pp. 40–42.

20. Coffman, *War*, pp. 60–62.

21. Samuel Stouffer et al., *The American Soldier*, 4 vols. (Princeton, N.J.: Princeton University Press, 1949).

22. *Personnel System of the U.S. Army*, vol. 1, pp. 628–630. As Coffman points out in the section on personnel testing, the Alpha and Beta exams were flawed. The tests were directed at "a middle-class, fairly sophisticated, and educated group . . . and were more indicative of the social milieu of the university-trained men who prepared the test than [of] the background of the majority of soldiers who took the examination." Coffman, *War*, p. 61. The Air Service, recognizing the need for further mechanical testing, importuned the classification committee to design a unique test for the Service's own purposes. The results were tests of mechanical capability. The Air Service would again use these tests in the late 1920s and in subsequent years.

23. Maurer, *Aviation in the U.S. Army*, pp. 63–64.

24. Ibid., pp. 63–64.

25. Gen Mason M. Patrick, "Final Report of Chief of Air Service (A.E.F.) to the Commander-in-Chief, American Expeditionary Forces," *Air Service Information Circular* vol. 2, No. 180 (Feb 15, 1921), pp. 25, 47.

26. Patrick, "Final Report of Chief of Air Service (A.E.F.) to the Commander-in-Chief, American Expeditionary Forces," p. 38.

27. For a good overview of the Universal Military Training Movement before and after the war, see Robert K. Griffith's *Men Wanted for the U.S. Army: America's Experience with an All-Volunteer Army between the World Wars* (Westport, Conn.: Greenwood Press, 1982), pp. 1–28, and I.B. Holley, Jr.'s *General John M. Palmer, Citizen Soldiers, and the Army of a Democracy* (Westport, Conn.: Greenwood Press, 1982).

28. James E. Hewes, Jr., *From Root to McNamara: Army Organization and Administration, 1900–1963* (Washington D.C.: U.S. Army Center of Military History, 1975), pp. 50–52; Maurer, *Aviation in the U.S. Army*, esp. chap. 3; Allan R. Millett and Peter Maslowski, *For the Common Defense: A Military History of the United States of America* (New York: Free Press, 1984), pp. 365–367.

29. *War Department Annual Reports*, 1920–1921.

30. Maurer, *Aviation in the U.S. Army*, pp. 3–16; Griffith, *Men Wanted*, pp. 29–31.
31. Maurer, *Aviation in the U.S. Army*, pp. 6–9; Griffith, *Men Wanted*, p. 30.
32. Maurer, *Aviation in the U.S. Army*, pp. 50–52; Griffith, *Men Wanted*, pp. 86, 91.
33. One survey found that the U.S. Employment Service had placed·900,000 of the 1.3 million discharged servicemen into gainful employment by the end of 1919. Another survey found only 20,000 ex-servicemen out of work. See Neil A. Wynn, *From Progressivism to Prosperity: World War I and Society* (Hertfordshire, England: Holmes & Meier, 1986), p. 202. The unemployment rate dropped 36 percent from 1921 to 1922 and remained at an average of 3.75 percent until 1929. U.S. Department of Commerce, Bureau of the Census, *Historical Statistics of the United States: Colonial Times to 1957* (Washington, D.C.; GPO, 1961), p. 73.
34. John F. Shiner, *Foulois and the U.S. Army Air Corps, 1931–1935* (Washington, D.C.: Office of Air Force History, 1983), p. 110.
35. Maurer, *Aviation in the U.S. Army*, p. 210.
36. Victor Vogel, *Soldiers of the Old Army* (College Station: Texas A&M University Press, 1990), p. 3.
37. Ibid.
38. *Air Corps News Letter*, Jan 15, 1935, pp. 59–60. Median years in service for technical and master sergeants promotees in the Air Corps were seventeen and fifteen years, respectively.
39. *Annual Report of the Chief of the Air Corps, 1932*, p. 18; *Annual Report of the Chief of the Air Corps, 1933*, pp. 14–15; *Annual Report of the Chief of the Air Corps, 1934*, p. 13.
40. Jesse W. Davidson, Enlisted Experience Questionnaire (hereafter cited as EEQ), U.S. Air Force History Support Office (hereafter cited as AFHSO).
41. Maurer, *Aviation in the U.S. Army*, p. 7.
42. Ibid., pp. 50–51; Griffith, *Men Wanted*, chap. 2. The motto "Earn and Learn" extended to general Army recruiting as well. The Air Service Recruiting poster for the early 1920s portrayed this theme by sketching men flying and repairing planes. The poster's caption read "Join the Air Service: Earn and Learn."
43. Griffith, *Men Wanted*, pp. 29–30. Although 175,000 was the authorized strength, by the end of 1921 the actual enlisted strength of the Army was much lower—only 133,096. See Weigley, *History of the United States Army*, p. 568.
44. *War Department Annual Reports*, 1919–1921; Maurer, *Aviation in the U.S. Army*, p, 50.
45. Maurer, *Aviation in the U.S. Army*, pp. 50–51.
46. Ibid.
47. Shiner, *Foulois*, p. 31; Griffith, *Men Wanted*, pp. 76–77; Maurer, *Aviation in the U.S. Army*, pp. 208–210.
48. Griffith, *Men Wanted*, pp. 76–77.
49. *War Department Annual Reports*, 1926–1935; Griffith, *Men Wanted*, pp. 76–77.
50. Griffith, *Men Wanted*, pp. 30, 33, 35.
51. Ibid., pp. 85, 91–92.
52. Maurer, *Aviation in the U.S. Army*, pp. 50–51; Griffith, *Men Wanted*, p. 88.
53. Griffith, *Men Wanted*, pp. 88–89.
54. *Army and Navy Journal*, Apr 17, 1920, p. 998.
55. Enlisted pay is derived from *War Department General Orders and Bulletins* (Washington, D.C.: GPO, 1920). Civilian pay is based on income data found in *Historical Statistics of the United States to 1957*, pp. 91–94. For a detailed account of enlisted pay systems, see Griffith, *Men Wanted*, app. C.
56. Griffith, *Men Wanted*, pp. 38–39.
57. Maurer, *Aviation in the U.S. Army*, p. 6.
58. The attraction of learning a manual trade was supported by a diverse group of public educators, businessmen, and social reformers who had criticized the school system for not keeping pace with the changes brought about by the industrial revolution and

urban industrialism. Manual training projected an image of the mythic Yankee artisan who was a symbol of the American values of thrift and hard labor. Moreover, in an era of growing pragmatism, manual training was practical. It would integrate theory with social needs. Social reformers believed it would end the alienation of factory work, strengthen the poor, and reduce delinquency and idleness. It meshed nicely with the reform ideology: social problems could be eliminated by changing the individual. Jacoby, *Employing Bureaucracy*, pp. 66–68.

59. Elmer J. Howell, EEQ, AFHSO.

60. August J. Linkey, EEQ, AFHSO.

61. Maurer, *Aviation in the U.S. Army*, pp. 208–210; Griffith, *Men Wanted*, app. C.

62. This "base" pay includes monthly pay as a private first class, second-class air mechanic, and for flying. The Army's retirement program was much better than similar programs offered by industrial firms. Under the provisions of the Pay Readjustment Act of 1922, a soldier could retire at three-fourths pay including longevity pay plus a $15.75 monthly housing allowance. Thus a master sergeant who retired with thirty years' service could expect $120.75 per month. This exceeded many civilians' earnings in 1933, when the average pay was $58.00 per month. See Griffith, *Men Wanted*, p. 167.

63. Pay and benefits for enlisted men were computed from data available in *Military Compensation Background Papers: Compensation Elements and Related Manpower Cost Items, Their Purposes and Legislative Backgrounds*, 3d ed. (Washington D.C.: Department of Defense [DOD], 1987), chaps. 2, 3. (In addition to lists of the various active duty entitlements since 1920, brief legislative histories of the many pay acts are also included in this important, present-day volume.) Civilian average wages were derived from *Historical Statistics of the United States to 1957*, pp. 91–94. For income statistics of skilled and semiskilled males during this period, see U.S. Commerce Department, *Statistical Abstract of the United States, 1931* (Washington, D.C.: GPO, 1931), p. 360, table 365.

64. *Air Service News Letter*, Feb 1, 1919, pp. 15–16, and Apr 26, 1919, p. 2.

65. Alfred C. Saxon, EEQ, AFHSO.

66. Vincent F. Strauss, EEQ, AFHSO.

67. Robert E. Thomas, EEQ, AFHSO.

68. Steven B. Davis, EEQ, AFHSO.

69. Griffith, *Men Wanted*, p. 104.

70. For a discussion of the impact of unemployment on Army recruiting and retention, see Griffith, *Men Wanted*, p. 221; Coffman, *Army*, pp. 15–16, 146–147, 346–350, 372; and Hayes, *Evolution of Armed Forces Enlisted Personnel Management Policies*, p. 52. The correlation between unemployment, labor turnover, and enlisted desertion was first suggested to me by Edward M. Coffman and deserves further study. A number of labor studies have examined labor turnover and economic fluctuations. See, for example, Nelson, *Managers and Workers*, pp. 86–87, 149–150, and Sanford Jacoby, "Industrial Labor Mobility in Historical Perspective," *Industrial Relations*, vol. 22 (spring 1983), pp. 261–282. David Montgomery, in his *Worker's Control in America: Studies in the History of Work, Technology, and Labor Struggles* (Cambridge, England: Cambridge University Press, 1979), pp. 96–98, argues that during prosperous times, an annual factory turnover rate of 1,600 to 2,000 percent was not unusual. Furthermore, Montgomery's work on labor strikes during periods of unemployment also demonstrates an inverse relationship. My correlations of his table 2, Strike Trends in the United States, 1900–1925, in the above work, yields a simple correlation coefficient of −.42.

71. Robert K. Griffith, "Quality Not Quantity: The Volunteer Army During the Depression" *Military Affairs*, Dec 1979, pp. 171–175. See also John Killegrew, "The Impact of the Great Depression on the United States Army, 1929–1936" (diss, Indiana University, 1960), for an important contribution on the financial and manpower problems the Army faced during the 1930s.

72. Griffith, *Men Wanted*, p. 155; Memo, G–1 to CS, Subj: Marriage of Enlisted Men, Aug 10, 1931, RG 94, 220.81, Box 1100, MMB, National Archives (NA). In Army

Regulation (hereafter cited as AR) 600–750 for 1925, married men were required to obtain permission from their commanding officer to enlist or reenlist. Nothing in the regulation barred enlisted (non-NCOs) married men from either enlisting or reenlisting. In 1932, the regulation changed. It eliminated any reference to encouraging married men to join and decreed that "No man below grade three (corporal)" who married without express written consent of his organization and the post commander could be reenlisted.

73. Maurer, *Aviation in the U.S. Army*, p. 350; *Annual Report of the Chief of the Air Corps, 1934* (Washington, D.C.: U.S. Office of Chief of Air Corps, 1934), p. 11.

74. *Annual Report of the Chief of the Air Corps, 1938* (Washington, D.C.: U.S. Office of the Air Corps, 1938), p. 32.

75. Vogel, p. 7.

76. Maurer, *Aviation in the U.S. Army*, p. 347; Griffith, *Men Wanted*, pp. 153–154.

77. Elmer J. Howell, EEQ, AFHSO.

78. Memo, CG, Headquarters, Chanute Field, Ill., to Chief of Air Corps, Sep 17, 1932, Subj: Enlisted Applicants for Technical Training, RG 94, 341, Box 1793, MMB, NA.

79. Marion E. Waldorf, EEQ, AFHSO.

80. Edward R. Halverson, EEQ, AFHSO.

81. Patrick, "Final Report of Chief of Air Service (A.E.F.) to the Commander-in-Chief, American Expeditionary Forces," p. 4.

82. *Air Service News Letter*, Mar 22, 1920, p. 2.

83. Ibid., Apr 1, 1939, p. 15.

84. Ibid., Apr 27, 1920, pp. 4–5.

85. Maurer, *Aviation in the U.S. Army*, p. 7.

86. *Air Service News Letter*, Feb 25, 1920, p. 11.

87. Ibid., Feb 25, 1920, pp. 11-12.

88. Ibid.

89. *Annual Report of the Chief of the Air Corps, 1930*, p. 40.

90. *Annual Report of the Chief of the Air Corps, 1938*, pp. 1–2.

91. Wesley Frank Craven and James Lea Cate, eds., *The Army Air Forces in World War II*, 7 vols. (Washington, D.C.: Office of Air Force History, 1983), vol. 6: *Men and Planes*, pp. 629–633.

92. Maurer, *Aviation in the U.S. Army*, p. 63.

93. Ibid., pp. 6–9, 63–64.

94. Gerald Driscoll, EEQ, AFHSO.

95. B.J. Phillips, EEQ, AFHSO.

96. Howard D. Williams, *Basic Military Training in the AAF, 1939–1944* (Washington, D.C.: AAF Historical Office, 1951), p. 27.

97. Jesse W. Davidson, EEQ, AFHSO.

98. Steward R. Dayton, EEQ, AFHSO.

99. Williams, *Basic Military Training in the AAF*, p. 29.

100. Ibid., pp. 17–18.

101. Ibid., pp. 111–112.

102. Manpower statistics for 1939 are from the *Annual Report of the Chief of the Air Corps, 1939*; for 1945, they are from the *Department of Defense Fact Book, 1980* (Washington, D.C.: DOD, 1980), p. 84.

103. Williams, *Basic Military Training in the AAF*, pp. 4–8. By the summer of 1940, the AAF had created its first replacement center at Jefferson Barracks, Missouri.

104. For the most comprehensive work on the effects of technology and specialization on the military, see Harold Wool's *The Military Specialist: Skilled Manpower for the Armed Forces* (Baltimore, Md.: Johns Hopkins University Press, 1968), pp. 19–21. See also Hayes, *Evolution of Armed Forces Enlisted Personnel Management Policies*, pp. 81–85.

105. Wool, pp. 19–20.

106. Ibid., p. 20.

107. For two important works describing the Army's and Air Corps' classification system, see Walter V. Bingham's "The Army Personnel Classification System," *Annals of the American Academy of Political and Social Science*, vol. 220 (Mar 1942), pp. 18–28, and Victor H. Cohen's *Classification and Assignment of Enlisted Men in the Army Air Arm, 1917–1945* (Maxwell AFB, Ala.: USAF Hist Study No. 76, SAF Hist Div, 1953).

108. Army Air Force Regulation (hereafter cited as AFR) 35–46, Dec 11, 1943, *Use of Military Occupational Specialties for AAF Enlisted Personnel*, p. 6. The purpose of this regulation was to standardize the use of military occupational specialties to ensure correct classification, efficient manning, and more accurate personnel accounting. This list was comprised of specialties limited to AAF use and consisted of 23 broad occupational categories with more than 500 subcategories of job-specific designations.

109. Minutes of a Personnel Conference, Apr 1944, RG 18, Box 224, MMB, NA, p. 24.

110. Wool, pp. 20–21.

111. Craven and Cate, vol. 6: *Men and Planes*, p. 629.

112. Selective Service System, *Special Groups*, vol. 1 (Washington, D.C.: Special Monogr No. 10, GPO, 1953), p. 143.

113. Craven and Cate, vol. 6: *Men and Planes*, pp. 540–543. See also Mark J. Eitelberg, *Manpower for Military Occupations* (Washington, D.C.: Office of the Assistant Secretary of Defense, Force Management and Personnel, 1988), esp. chaps. 1, 2. The following table showing the distribution by mental classification category for all World War II personnel is from Mark J. Eitelberg et al., *Screening for Service: Aptitude and Screening for Military Entry* (Washington D.C.: Office of the Assistant Secretary of Defense, Manpower, Installations, and Logistics, 1984), p. 20:

Mental Category*	Percent of all Personnel
I	8
II	28
III	34
IV	21
V	9
Total	100

*Category I represents the highest mental capacity.

114. Unless you consider "flyboy" to be a pejorative. This term inferred that those serving in the AAF had a more leisurely life than those in the other Army branches or in the Navy or the Marines.

115. Eitelberg, *Manpower for Military Occupations*, p. 8.

116. Ltr, CS, Ground Service Corps, G–1 (Kiel), to CG, Western Defense Command and Fourth Army, Jun 13, 1943, Subj: Standardizing ASWAAF and AAF Promotion Policy, AAG RG 18, 330.11, Box 711, MMB, NA; Ltr, CG, First Army to CG, AAF, Washington, D.C., Jul 21, 1943, Subj: Training and Morale of Arms and Service Units with the Army Air Forces, RG 18, 330.11, Box 711, MMB, NA; Ltr, CG, AAF (Arnold) to All Personnel of the AAF, Nov 6, 1943, RG 18, 330.11, Box 711, MMB, NA; Memo, Asst Deputy CS, General Staff, to CG, AAF, Dec 3, 1943, Subj: Reorganization of Units to Effect Personnel Economies, RG 18, 220.33, Box 449, MMB, NA; Memo, Executive for Personnel and Organization (AC–1/AS–1) to Arms and Services Integration Committee, Dec 11, 1943, Subj: Progress of Arm and Service Integration Committee, RG 18, 334, Box 805, MMB, NA; Ltr, Asst Office of the Air Ordnance Officer to Ordnance Officer, Headquarters, VI Air Force Service Command, Feb 28, 1944, Subj: AAF Integration of Arms and Services Personnel, RG 18, 220.33, Box 449, MMB, NA.

117. Shiner, *Foulois*, p. 207; "Birth of GHQ Air Force," p. 118.

118. AAF Personnel Conference, Feb 10, 1943, RG 18, Box 293, MMB, NA.

119. Memo, AAF CG (Arnold) to All AAF Personnel, Nov 6, 1943, Subj: Internal

Branch Distinctions, RG 18, 341, Box 834, MMB, NA.

120. Memo, DCS/P (McCormick) to DCS/O (Hall), Apr 30, 1944, Subj: Advertisement on AAF Cadet Procurement, RG 18, 341, Box 834, MMB, NA. The memo in part reads:

> it has always been our aim to minimize the reference to individuals by including other members of the team. In bomber ads, the activities of all the crew are dramatized—in a fighter ad, the action necessarily centers around the pilot.

See also "Aerial Gunners Wear Wings Too," May 22, 1944, RG 18, 341, Box 834, MMB, NA. In this recruiting article, the concept of team was stressed to individuals recruiting for air crews (p. 1):

> Recruiting policy now emphasizes recruiting for the air combat crew . . . recruiting for the team, not for the individual places on it. The first step is to attract a boy to the team. The next step is to explain the importance of all the places on the team, and the importance of having the right man in the right position, and the care and thoroughness with which the AAF studies the aptitudes of each trainee to determine the job for which he will be trained.

121. The emphasis on poor enlisted morale can be overstated, however. Surveys in August 1943 showed that 54 percent of the AAF were in the right job assignment (based upon civilian skills, individual desires, classification testing, and military training), 90 percent who attended technical schools were using what they learned, and 53 percent indicated the highest job satisfaction scores. These scores were the highest in the Army. See Memo, Asst Deputy Chief of Staff, Personnel (Bevans), to CG, AAF (Arnold), Aug 10, 1943, Subj: Items of Interest in Daily Digest, RG 18, 319.1—Bulky, Daily Diary (A–1), Box 111, MMB, NA.

122. Stouffer et al., *American Soldier*, vol. 2: *Combat and Its Aftermath*, pp. 341–342. In 1943, for instance, Eighth Air Force crews suffered a 30 percent fatality rate. Millett and Maslowski, *For the Common Defense*, p. 438.

123. Stouffer et al., *American Soldier*, vol. 2: *Combat and Its Aftermath*, pp. 343–348.

124. In a memo to the Assistant Chief of Staff (G–1) from the Assistant Chief of Staff (A–1) dated Dec 12, 1942 (RG 18, 221.02–C, Box 97, MMB, NA), the Air Forces requested a significant increase of more than 100,000 additional enlisted slots. Some of the reasons enumerated for the increase included:

> 1. The conversion of air mechanic and specialist ratings to staff sergeants, sergeants, and corporals, or technicians 5th grade, 4th grade, and 5th grade as well as promoting Air Mechanics either to staff or technical sergeants.

> 2. Air crew rules established that the Crew Chief of a four-engine bomber be a master sergeant; an engineer gunner, a technical sergeant; and a radio operator gunner, aerial gunner, bombardier, or navigator, at least a staff sergeant.

> 3. An increased allotment of higher enlisted grades, as the Air Force would become more specialized and more highly trained, would thus require the Air Force to reward men for their skills by promoting them to a higher grade.

See Memo, Asst Chief of Staff (A–1) to Asst Chief of Staff (G–1), Dec 24, 1942, Subj: Increase in Allotment of Enlisted Grades for the Air Corps and Other Arms and Services with the Army Air Forces, RG 18, 221.02–C, Box 97, MMB, NA; Memo, Asst Chief of Staff (A–1) to Asst Chief of Staff (G–1), Jan 1, 1943, Subj: Increase in Allotment of Enlisted Grades for the Air Corps and Other Arms and Services with the Army Air Forces, RG 18, 221.02–C, Box 97, MMB, NA; Memo, Asst Chief of Staff (A–1) to Asst Chief of Staff (G–1), Feb 23, 1943, Subj: Increase in Allotment of Enlisted Grades for the Air Corps and Other Arms and Services with the Army Air Forces, RG 18, 221.02–A, Box 96, MMB, NA.

125. Steven L. DePyssler, EEQ, AFHSO.

126. Stouffer et al., *American Soldier*, vol. 2: *Combat and Its Aftermath*, pp. 343–348.

127. George R. Plantz, EEQ, AFHSO.

128. Before the change, pay was based on base pay per grade plus any specialty pay (eight levels of specialty pay for airmen).

129. Memo, Asst Chief of Air Staff, Enlisted Branch (Belshe), to CG 2AF, Jul 10, 1944, Subj: Bulk Allotments, RG 18, 220.2, Box 1217, MMB, NA. See also Memo, Chief, Military Personnel Section, Personnel and Training Division, Air Service Command, to CG AAF, Dec 7, 1943, Subj: Grades and Ratings for Enlisted Men, RG 18, 221.02, Box 492, MMB, NA; and Memo, Asst Adj, AAF Proving Ground Comd, to CG AAF, Aug 16, 1944, Subj: Promotion Limitations, RG 18, 220.2, Box 1217, MMB, NA.

130. Memo, Air Adjutant Gen (Dick) to AAF Commands and Units, Feb 11, 1942, Subj: Improved Personnel System, RG 18, 221, Box 890, MMB, NA; Memo, Dir, Mil Personnel Div, General Staff G-1 (Reynolds), to Deputy Chief of Air Staff A-1 (Hanley), April 20, 1943, Subj: Grades of Enlisted Men, RG 18, 220.01, Box 492, MMB, NA.

131. Memo, Deputy Chief of Air Staff (Hanley) to CG, Army Service Forces, May 5, 1943, Subj: Grades of Enlisted Men, RG 18, 220.01, Box 492, MMB, NA. The Army continued to segregate command NCOs from technicians via a seven-grade rating system designating a series of technical grades for technicians. In 1954, they split the two types of grades entirely into command and specialists ratings. The Air Force, on the other hand, continued until 1952 to use the Army ratings devised during the war. For more discussion on the rating system see Chapter 5.

132. Elmer J. Howell, EEQ, AFHSO.

133. Ibid.

134. Katherine Stone, "The Origins of Job Structures in the Steel Industry," in Richard C. Edwards, Michael Reich, and David M. Gordon, eds., *Labor Market Segmentation* (Lexington, Mass.: D.C. Heath, 1975), pp. 81–84. Other interpretations that lean heavily on Stone's work are David M. Gordon, Richard Edwards, and Michael Reich, *Segmented Work, Divided Workers: The Historical Transformation of Labor in the United States* (Cambridge, Mass.: Harvard University Press, 1982), chap. 5; William Lazonick, "Technological Change and the Control of Work," in Howard F. Gospel and Craig R. Littler, eds., *Managerial Strategies and Industrial Relations: An Historical and Comparative Study* (Exeter, N.H.: Heiemann Educational Books, 1983), pp. 126–127; Jeremy Brecher et al., "Uncovering the Hidden History of the American Workplace," *Review of Radical Political Economics*, vol. 10 (winter 1978), pp. 1–23; and Robert E. Cole, *Work, Mobility, and Participation* (Berkeley, Calif.: University of California Press, 1979), pp. 105–107.

135. Memo, Chief of Air Staff, Personnel A-1 (Anderson), to Chief of Air Staff, May 21, 1946, Subj: Specialist Ratings and Plan for Grade Structure of Army Air Forces, RG 18, 220.2, Box 1217, MMB, NA; Rept, "Plan for Grade Structure of Army Air Forces," Mar 29, 1946, RG 18, 220.2, Box 1217, MMB, NA.

136. James F. Downs, "Prime Hand to Petty Officer: The Evolution of the Navy's Noncommissioned Officer," in David R. Segal and H. Wallace Sinaiko, eds., *Life in the Rank and File: Enlisted Men and Women in the Armed Forces of the United States, Australia, Canada, and the United Kingdom* (New York: Pergamon-Brassey, 1986), pp. 96–97.

137. Various memoirs and questionnaires support this assumption. See, for example, Charles Willeford, *Something about a Soldier* (New York: Random House, 1986), pp. 10–12; Vogel, p. xx; and Robert E. Thomas, EEQ, AFHSO.

138. Memo, Air Adj Gen (Milner) to All CGs of All AAF in Continental United States, Feb 7, 1943, Subj: Gen George C. Marshall's Concern over Poor Air Force Discipline and Leadership, RG 18, 250, Box 102, MMB, NA; Ltr, CG AAF (Arnold) to All AAF CGs, Feb 19, 1944, Subj: Discipline and Leadership, RG 18, 250, Box 102, MMB, NA.

139. A former governor of Texas, Wilbert Lee "Pappy" O'Daniel became a senator in 1941. O'Daniel disliked New Deal programs, centralized government, and any program that resembled socialism, communism, or totalitarianism. With regard to the military,

O'Daniel was wary of the liberties taken by the military during wartime. He voted against extension of the Selective Service draft on 1941, called for a year's military training for eighteen- and nineteen-year-old youth before permitting their assignment to combat (passed in the Senate, but rejected in the House), and voted against the amendment granting federal ballots to the armed forces in 1942. Anne Rothe, éd., *Current Biography: Who's News and Why, 1947* (New York: H.W. Wilson Co., 1948), pp. 480–482.

140. Memo, Senator W. Lee O'Daniel to Secy War (Stimson), Feb 29, 1944, Subj: Fraternization Letter of Air Service Commanding Gen, RG 18, 250, Box 102, MMB, NA.

141. Memo, Air Provost Marshal (Reynolds) to CAS, Apr 4, 1944, Subj: Fraternization between Commissioned Army Air Forces Officers and Enlisted Personnel, RG 18, 250, Box 526, MMB, NA; Memo, Air WAC Officer, Personnel, Air WAC Div A–1 (Bandel), to Chief, Military Morale and Discipline Division, Organization Branch, May 31, 1944, Subj: Fraternization between Commissioned Officer and Enlisted Personnel, 250, Box 526, MMB, NA.

142. The best single volume work on women in the military is Jeanne Holm, *Women in the Military: An Unfinished Revolution* (Novato, Calif.: Presidio Press, 1986), esp. pp. 56–67. See also Mattie Treadwell's *The Women's Army Corps: United States Army in World War II* (Washington, D.C.: Office of the Chief of Military History, 1954).

143. Memo, Asst Chief of Air Staff, Personnel (Bevans), to Deputy Chief of Air Staff A–1 (Hall), Apr 28, 1944, Subj: Military Discipline, RG 18, 250, Box 102, MMB, NA.

144. Memo, Air Inspector (Jones) to CG AAF (Arnold), Apr 14, 1944, Subj: Military Discipline, RG 18, 250, Box 102, MMB, NA.

145. The Doolittle Board, named for its chairman AAF Maj. Gen. James H. Doolittle, was charged in the latter part of March 1946 to discover the nature of officer-enlisted fraternization grievances. Chapter 2 includes a more detailed examination of the Doolittle Board.

146. Memo, HQ AAF ATC (Hess) to Air Provost Marshal (Reynolds), Apr 26, 1944, Subj: Discipline, RG 18, 250.3, Box 522, MMB, NA.

147. Hayes, *Evolution of Armed Forces Enlisted Personnel Management Policies*, pp. 100–103. See also Alan M. Osur's *Blacks in the Army Air Forces During World War II* (Washington, D.C.: Office of Air Force History, [1977]).

148. Craven and Cate, vol. 6: *Men and Planes*, pp. 523–524.

Chapter 2

1. Statement, SecAF (Symington), House Military Appropriations Subcommittee, Mar 18, 1948, RG 340, Special Interest Files, Special file No. 14, Correspondence, Oct 1947–Oct 1948, National Arichves and Records Service (NARS).

2. Segal, *Recruiting for Uncle Sam*, p. 31.

3. Ltr, Eisenhower, CSA, to Spaatz, CG/AAF, Mar 29, 1947, Subj: Ltr to All Commanding Generals—"The Time of Need Is Now," RG 18, Entry 341, Box 2650, MMB, NA.

4. Segal, *Recruiting for Uncle Sam*, pp. 31–32. The Selective Service Act of 1948 established a twenty-month active duty obligation for men nineteen to twenty-five years of age unless otherwise exempt or medically disqualified. The draft was again suspended in 1949. The military did not induct in late 1940 and early 1950, and the draft law was to expire on July 9, 1950. When the Korean War began in June 1950, however, Congress passed a two-year extension. By September 1950, 50,000 men were being drafted each month, and by 1952, 20,000 to 30,000 draftees were shipped to Korea monthly.

5. *Advertising, Public Relations, and Promotion Program for the U.S. Army and U.S. Air Force, Oct 1, 1948 to Jun 30, 1949* (New York: Gardner Advertising, 1948), p. 1. A copy is in the Air University Library.

6. Ibid., p. 2.

7. Ibid., p. 3.

8. Ibid., p. 5.

9. Stephen F. Fitzgerald, *Communicating Ideas to the Public: A Practical Application of Public Relations Techniques to Everyday Problems in Human Communications* (New York: Funk & Wagnalls, 1950), p. 228. Other contemporary works that describe the advertising program are Arthur H. Peterson, "An Investigation of the United States Army and United States Air Force Recruiting Organization and Program" (thesis, Columbia University, 1948), pp. 70–71; and William Nielander and Raymond Miller, *Public Relations* (New York: Ronal Press, 1951), pp. 233–242.

10. "Services Shift Agencies in Recruiting Drive," *Air Force Times* (hereafter cited as *AFT*), Jun 26, 1948, p. 3.

11. *Advertising, Public Relations, and Promotion Program*, p. 5.

12. Part of the problem with this analysis is the ambiguity of the term *middle class*. It seems elusive and inconsistent and it lacks sociological and economic form. However, 79.2 percent of the American population in a 1940 *Fortune* magazine survey identified with the term. Those who so identified themselves defied any economic or sociological description. Neverthcless, a commonality in attitudes was present that rejected the notion of class or privilege in America; embraced a belief in progress, materialism, democracy, religious tolerance, and obedience; and considered the present to be better than the past. For an expanded discussion of the relationship between the concept of career, middle class, and profession, see Bledstein, pp. 1–8, 159–202.

13. Ayer produced weekly programs while the Army and AAF paid the talent costs. Fitzgerald, p. 228.

14. "National Advertising Schedule," *U.S. Army and Recruiting Service Letter*, Sep 1, Oct 1, 1947, p. 3, both issues.

15. Fitzgerald, p. 219; Peterson, "An Investigation of the United States Army and United States Air Force Recruiting Organization and Program," pp. 72–73.

16. *U.S. Army and Air Force Recruiting Service Letter*, Sep 1, 1947, p. 1.

17. Fitzgerald, p. 230.

18. Ibid., pp. 231–233.

19. "Army Caste Due for Boot, but Doolittle Board Will Have to Sift the Wheat from the Chaff," *Army Times* Mar 23, 1946, p. 5; "Caste System Study Begun by Doolittle," *Army Times* Mar 30, 1946, pp. 1, 15.

20. *The Doolittle Report: The Report of the Secretary of War's Board on Officer-Enlisted Man Relationships, May 27, 1946*, U.S. Senate Doc 196, 79th Cong, 2d Sess (Washington, D.C.: GPO, 1946), p. 5; "If Middleton's in There, the Board Is on the Level," *Army Times*, Apr 6, 1946, p. 5.

21. *Doolittle Report*, p. 5. The issue of individual dignity was a consistent postwar theme when discussing the revamping of the military. See, for example, "Soldier's 'Dignity' Seen As Key to New Military Concept," *AFT*, Nov 6, 1948, p. 6.

22. *Doolittle Report*, p. iv.

23. "*Army Times* Readers Flood Caste Board with Gripes," *Army Times* Apr 20, 1946, pp. 1, 24.

24. *Fraternization* usually refers to an association between officers and enlisted men. Such restrictions were assailed by the board and by the Secretary of War as undemocratic. Many so-called fraternization cases refer to the Doolittle Board when citing the military's "caste system." See the discussion of the 1953 case of the *United States v Free* in Col J. Jeremiah Mahoney, "Fraternization: Military Anachronism or Leadership Challenge?" *The Air Force Law Review*, 1988, pp. 153–200. See also Col Karen S. Wright, "The Evolution of a Custom in the Air Force: Fraternization" (thesis, Air War College, 1987), pp. 7–8.

25. Moskos, *American Enlisted Man*, pp. 6–8, 11, 13–14, 16, 20–23. See also "Caste Board Raps Social Bunk, Urges Overhaul of Leadership," *Army Times*, Jun 1, 1946, pp. 1, 5, 6, 11.

26. Moskos, *American Enlisted Man*, p. 24; "Caste Board Raps Social Bunk, Urges Overhaul of Leadership," p. 1.

27. Under the direction of Secretary of War Patterson, General Marshall appointed Lt. Gen. Alvan C. Gillem, Jr., to chair a board and "prepare a policy for the use of the authorized Negro manpower potential during the postwar period including the complete development of the means required to derive the maximum efficiency from the full manpower of the nation in the event of a national emergency." A copy of the report is in Memo, Gillem to CS, Army, Nov 17, 1945, Subj: Report of Board of General Officers on Utilization of Negro Manpower in the Post-War Army, CSGOT 291.2 (1945) BP. An important discussion of the Gillem Board and the report's recommendation is found in Morris MacGregor, Jr., *Integration of the Armed Forces, 1940–1965* (Washington, D.C.: GPO, 1981), pp. 153–166.

28. *Doolittle Report*, p. 20–24.

29. A review of the military justice system in the United States including a discussion of the evolution of the Uniform Code of Military Justice appears in Maj Gerald Crump's "A History of the Structure of Military Justice in the United States, 1775–1966," appearing in two successive issues of *The Air Force Law Review*, winter 1974 and spring 1975, pp. 41–68 and 55–72, respectively.

30. Moskos, *American Enlisted Man*, p. 9; "New Justice Code Asserts Enlisted Men's Rights," *AFT*, Feb 12, 1949, p. 9. On the development of a code of justice in the Air Force, see "New Court Martial Manual Lists Enlisted Men's Rights," *AFT*, Dec 11, 1948, pp. 1, 13, and "AF Court Martial Manual Puts Enlisted Men on Bench," *AFT*, Feb 5, 1949, p. 6.

31. In September 1948, Truman appointed Charles Fahy, a lawyer and former solicitor general, to head the President's Committee on Equality of Treatment and Opportunity in the Armed Forces, as directed in Executive Order 9981. MacGregor, *Integration of the Armed Forces*, chaps. 12, 13. For the committee's 1950 report, see *Freedom to Serve: Equality of Treatment and Opportunity in the Armed Services: A Report by the President's Committee* (Washington D.C.: GPO, 1950), p. xi, as found in Records of the President's Committee on Religion and Welfare in the Armed Forces, Harry S. Truman Library.

32. MacGregor, *Integration of the Armed Forces*, esp. chap. 12, which discusses the events surrounding Truman's decision to issue the desegregation order. While MacGregor cited New Deal thinking, civil rights' agendas, and the escalating Cold War in which "the sympathies of the undeveloped and mostly colored world would soon assume a special importance" (pp. 291–292), he failed to place it in the larger perspective of postwar military reform. The military was undergoing a strong democratization process in order to distinguish itself from its Cold War "Prussian-like" adversaries. As one World War II black soldier wrote President Roosevelt in 1943:

> I have never understood how an army, fighting for democracy can sustain such undemocratic principles [segregation]. . . . I have nothing to look forward to. I am the shining examples of all Negro men in the Army.

Ltr, Pfc Albert Woodsen to Franklin D. Roosevelt, Oct 1943, RG 18, 250.1, Box 526, MMB, NA.

Other important works on integration and blacks in the military are Bernard C. Nalty, *Strength for the Fight: A History of Black Americans in the Military* (New York: Free Press, 1986), and Jack D. Foner, *Blacks and the Military in American History* (New York: Praeger, 1974).

The Women's Armed Services Act of 1948 (P.L. 625, 80th Congress) gave permanent status to women in all the armed services. The history of women in the military can be traced in Holm, *Women in the Military*, chap. 10. For a dated but useful work on women in World War II, see Treadwell, *Women's Army Corps*.

33. "Study of Service Pay Directed by Forrestal," *AFT*, Feb 28, 1948, pp. 1, 15. The actual report is entitled "Career Compensation for the Uniform Services: A Report and

Recommendation for the Secretary of Defense by the Advisory Commission on Service Pay" and dated December 1948.

34. *Military Compensation Background Papers*, pp. 17, 23, 61, 89, 121–189, 195–291, 289–357.

35. For a discussion of the Hook Commission's effect on the pay legislation enacted in 1949, see [author unknown], "Adjusting Service Pay and Allowances," *Army Information Digest*, Nov 1949, pp. 41–49. The pay increase was not as high as the committee suggested, and provisions for nondisability retirement were not included. Yet, the Hook Committee's recommendations regarding the method of compensation for length of service were carried out. Unlike the old longevity increases ("fogy pay"), the new length-of-service increases were paid on a flat rate rather than a percentage basis. The increases ceased in each grade when it was expected that personnel should have advanced to a higher grade.

36. DOD Cordiner Committee, *Report of the Defense Advisory Committee on Professional and Technical Compensation—Military Personnel* (Washington, D.C.: GPO, May 1957). Hook was an important member of the later Cordiner Committee.

37. The Career Compensation Act of 1949 was the first of a series of acts that sought to "establish for the uniformed services a compensation plan which will tend to attract and retain personnel of the highest caliber." "Adjusting Service Pay and Allowances," p. 41. For an important work that analyzes the effect of pay legislation on Air Force personnel with special emphasis on the Cordiner Report, see Robert C. Wilburn, "The Supply of Military Manpower: The Draft and Other Factors on the Retention of Air Force Enlisted Men" (diss, Princeton University, 1970).

38. Gordon, Edwards, and Reich, p. 189; Richard Edwards, *Contested Terrain: The Transformation of the Workplace in the Twentieth Century* (New York: Basic Books, 1979), chap. 9.

39. Nelson Lichtenstein, "From Corporatism to Collective Bargaining: Organized Labor and the Eclipse of Social Democracy in the Postwar Era," in Steve Fraser and Gary Gerstle, eds., *The Rise and Fall of the New Deal Order* (Princeton, N.J.: Princeton University Press, 1989) pp. 143–144. See also Sumner H. Slichter et al., *The Impact of Collective Bargaining on Management* (Washington, D.C.; Brookings Institution, 1960), pp. 372–376; Donna Allen, *Fringe Benefits: Wages or Social Obligations?* (Ithaca, N.Y.: Cornell University Press, 1964), pp. 99–152; Beth Stevens, "Blurring the Boundaries: How the Federal Government Has Influenced Welfare Benefits in the Private Sector," in Margaret Weir, Ann Shola Orloff, and Theda Skocpol, *The Politics of Social Policy in the United States* (Princeton, N.J.: Princeton University Press, 1988), pp. 123–148; Gordon, Edwards, and Reich, pp. 165–227; and Jill Bernstein, "Employee Benefits in the Welfare State: Great Britain and the United States Since World War II" (diss, Columbia University, 1980), pp. 576–581.

40. Speaking of the Career Compensation Act of 1949, General Bradley made it clear that the compensation was "more than a pay raise"; it was an endorsement by Americans for the "able Americans" in the service. Bradley is quoted in "Adjusting Service Pay and Allowances," *Army Information Digest*, Nov 1949, p. 50.

41. The most comprehensive work on the military retirement system is John McNeil, Pedro Lecca, and Roosevelt Wright, Jr., *Military Retirement: Social, Economic, and Mental Health Issues* (New York: Rowman & Allanheld, 1983), chap. 1.

42. Industrial retirement plans developed one important aspect that military plans did not: vesting rights. If a healthy soldier left the military after fifteen years, he received no retirement. For works on civilian retirement systems, see Cyril Curtis Ling, *The Management of Personnel Relations, History and Origins* (Homewood, Ill.: Richard D. Irwin, 1965), pp. 141–144, and Slichter et al., pp. 373–389. Differences in military versus civilian retirement programs in the 1950s are also discussed in the Cordiner Report, pp. 136–138.

43. For income statistics on military personnel, see *Military Compensation Background Papers*, pp. 23–60, 61–87, 89–98, 146–148. An airman not on flying status

received $2,505.60 yearly. For a thorough discussion of the federal tax advantage to military personnel, see Ibid., pp. 99–105. Civilian income is derived from U.S. Department of Commerce, Bureau of the Census, *Historical Statistics of the United States: Colonial Times to 1970, Bicentennial Edition*, pt. 1 (Washington, D.C.: GPO, 1975), p. 303. Chapter 4 will address these changes in more detail when retention problems are discussed. An important work on labor negotiations during this period is Slichter et al. See also Ling, chap. 5, and James Baron, Frank Dobbin, and Devereaux Jennings, "War And Peace: The Evolution of Modern Personnel Administration in U.S. Industry," *American Journal of Sociology*, Sep 1986, pp. 350–382.

44. Housing was deemed the military's number one problem in the late 1940s and 1950s. "Housing for Army Families" *Army Information Digest*, Oct 1948, pp. 3–8. For a discussion of the postwar boom in housing starts, see James Gilbert's *Another Chance: Postwar America, 1945–1985* (Chicago, Ill.: Dorsey Press, 1986), pp. 12, 105, and John Diggins, *The Proud Decades: America in War and In Peace, 1941–1960* (New York: W.W. Norton, 1988), pp. 181–183.

45. For a comparison of military and labor compensation systems, see chart 4, Incentives Stressed by Personnel Management, in Lt. Col. George Forsythe's "Personnel Management in the Army and Business," *Military Review*, Jun 1950, p. 57. Many firms failed to offer equitable retirement plans, chances for advancement, longevity raises, grievance procedures, and paid vacations. No firm offered clothing or housing allowances.

46. Headquarters Army Ground Forces, "Conduct of the I&E Program," Feb 28, 1947, U.S. Army Command and General Staff College Archives, file N–15321.1, Carlisle Barracks.

47. See also War Department, *This Is I&E* (Carlisle Barracks, Pa.: Army Information School, 1946); Department of the Army, *Annual Report of the Secretary of the Army* (Washington, D.C.: GPO, 1949), p. 115.

48. I use the Air Force as an example of business applications applied to the military, thus making the Air Force apparently more efficient and cost conscious. The Army also heavily imported business management philosophy into the postwar army, incorporating civilian personnel management techniques, a comptroller, and an education with industry–type program. Maj Gen George J. Richards, "Business Management in the New Army," *Army Information Digest*, May 1948, pp. 3–6; Col C.D. Leatherman, "Training in Personnel Management," *Army Information Digest*, May 1948, pp. 37–39; William Hines, "The Army Learns from Industry," *Army Information Digest*, Dec 1949, pp. 18–22. For a significant article that compares Army personnel programs with those in industry, see Forsythe, "Personnel Management in the Army and Business," pp. 54–62.

49. Important studies that demonstrate the Air Force's adaption and use of business techniques in the late 1940s and 1950s are John Finigan, "Modern Industrial Methods Applied to the U.S. Air Force" (thesis, Columbia University, 1948), Alfred Hayduk, "Personnel Turnover in the United States Air Force" (thesis, New York University, 1949), and Maj David Blais, "Acceptance of Modern Management Theory within the United States Air Force" (thesis, Air Command and Staff College, 1965), esp. chap. 2. See also Forsythe, "Personnel Management in the Army and Business," pp. 54–62.

50. Memo, Lovett to Arnold, Oct 5, 1945, Subj: A Need for Improved and Increased Business Management Procedures and Solution through Establishment of Office of Air Comptroller General, RG 18, Box 322, MMB, NA.

51. Maj Gen Hugh Knerr, Notes on Proposed Air Board, in "First Interim Report of the Air Board," Apr 16, 1946, RG 340, Air Board, Interim Reports and Working Papers, Box 20, MMB, NA. See also Herman S. Wolk, *Planning and Organizing the Postwar Air Force, 1943–1947* (Washington, D.C.: Office of Air Force History, 1984), pp. 142–145.

52. The New Military Establishment came into being on September 17, 1947. Consisting of a Secretary of Defense and three service secretaries, the unified military concept codified the essence of civilian control over the military. Besides W. Stuart Symington, the former president of Emerson Electric, a small group of business-trained civilians formed the Office of the Secretary of the Air Force. Symington's key civilian

assistants were all acquainted with business management. Arthur S. Barrows, the Under Secretary of the Air Force, was a former executive with Sears, Roebuck & Company. Cornelius Vanderbilt Whitney previously served as an officer and executive of several business enterprises and as a member of Eisenhower's staff during the war. Another assistant secretary, Eugene M. Zuckert, had instructed at the Harvard Graduate School of Business Administration and had worked for Symington in the Surplus Property Administration and at the office of Assistant Secretary of War for Air. For the most comprehensive study of its kind, see George Watson's *The Office of the Secretary of the Air Force, 1947–1965* (Washington, D.C.: Center for Air Force History, 1993), pp. 55–82. More work is needed on all civilian leaders in the Defense Department. An in-depth collective biography would tell much about business and corporate inroads into the military.

53. Speech, Symington to the Aviation Post, American Legion, Nov 11, 1947, Secretary of the Air Force Speech File, AFHSO, p. 8. Symington believed it was important for the AAF to operate like Emerson Electric, that is, with an accurate information system that rewarded efficiency and punished waste. See, for example, Memo, Symington to Eaker, May 8, 1946, RG 107, Office of the Secretary of War, Asst Secretary of War for Air, 020, NARS.

54. Speech, Symington to Aviation Post, American Legion, Nov 11, 1947. In 1947 the Air Force adopted a basic organizational scheme that called for a headquarters with a staff comprised of deputies who advised and implemented policy; special assistants; a number of major commands and supporting agencies; and the operational overseas commands. Designed around functional areas, the new Air Staff became a central nexus from which deputies who, under the signature of the Chief of Staff, could form policy and ensure its implementation throughout the force. Initially, the Air Staff consisted of Deputy Chiefs of Staff for Personnel and Administration, Operations, and Materiel, and a Comptroller. The system, as planned by civilian business experts, was formed under the principle that "the organization shall be fitted to the job, rather than the job to the organization." Wolk, pp. 138–140. The Army reorganized during this period along similar lines. Hewes, chap. 5.

55. Speech, Symington to Aviation Post, American Legion, Nov 11, 1947, p. 9. See also Memo, Symington, Jul 24, 1947, Subj: Management Control through Cost Control for the Army Air Forces, Papers of W. Stuart Symington, Box 8, Truman Library; "Management and Control—the Air Force Needs Management Training," *AFT*, Feb 7, 1948, p. 4; Eugene Zuckert, "The U.S. Air Force's Cost Control Program" *Army-Navy Journal*, Sep 11, 1948, pp. 22–36; Watson, pp. 84–93.

56. Speech, Symington to Aviation Post, American Legion, Nov 11, 1947, p. 10.

57. For a discussion of the ramification of the Officer Personnel Act of 1947 on the Air Force, see the prepared speech of Lt. Gen. I.H. Edwards, "Air Force Personnel Problems and Policies," Oct 14, 1947, M–38043–NC E26a, Air University Library.

58. Speech, Edwards, Oct 14, 1947.

59. Speech, Symington to Aviation Post, American Legion, Nov 11, 1947, p. 10. For an important analysis of the Air Force's comptroller, see Gen E.E. Rawlings, *Report on the Comptrollership within the Air Force—1946–1951* (Washington, D.C.: GPO, 1951). Trained at the Harvard Business School, Rawlings cited Lovett, Symington, Arnold, Spaatz, Eaker, and Vandenberg, as well as Eugene Zuckert and Edmund Learned, for instilling cost control methods into Air Force programs and creating the Office of the Air Comptroller. A comptroller office also was adopted by the Army for similar reasons. Hewes, pp. 179–181.

60. Lt Col Kenneth Kay, "How the Air Force Learns from Business," *Air Force Magazine*, Aug 1956, pp. 144–150, 155.

61. Speech, Symington to Aviation Post, American Legion, Nov 11, 1947, pp. 10–11. Symington in a speech before the Greensville South Carolina Chamber of Commerce on May 17, 1948, stated that, besides sending Air Force officers to business schools, special courses in business management and cost accounting were taught at the Air War College,

the Air Institute of Technology, the Air Command and Staff School, the Special Staff School, and the Air Tactical School. See also *Annual Report of the Secretary of the Air Force for Fiscal Year 1948* (Washington, D.C.: GPO, 1948), p. 7; *Semi-Annual Report of the Secretary of the Air Force for Fiscal Year 1949* (Washington, D.C.: GPO, 1949), pp. 221–222. See also National Military Establishment, Department of the Air Force, Washington D.C., Jan 9, 1949, "Press Release," RG 340, Special Interest Files, Special File No. 14 (Staff Action) Budget, MMB, NA; "Management and Control—Air Force Needs Management Training," *AFT*, Feb 7, 1948, p. 4; Watson, p. 88. The Army and Navy sent men to the Air University comptroller course.

62. "All Air Force Levels to Get Management Training," *AFT*, Feb 7, 1948, p. 6.

63. "Management Classes Set," *AFT*, Dec 18, 1948, p. 11; "Management Courses—Fairfield AFB," *AFT*, Jan 24, 1950, p. 24.

64. "Air Force Personnel Planners Seek Ways to Improve Placement," *AFT*, Jan 17, 1948, pp. 1, 15.

65. By 1950, another 112 students attended these courses. Some senior Air Force leaders also attended a custom-tailored, nine-month graduate course in advanced management at the School of Business at the University of Pittsburgh. *Semi-Annual Report of the Secretary of the Air Force for Fiscal Year 1949*, pp. 221–222. By 1956, the armed services had a well-established fraternity of business-trained leaders. Kay, "How the Air Force Learns from Business," pp. 144–150, 155.

66. Courses included classes in Administrative Policy and Practices, Air Transportation Control, Finance, Government and Business, Industrial Accounting, Financial Management, Human Relations, Manufacturing, Personnel Administration, Procurement, Production, Public Relations, and Rail Transportation. Rept, Col Henry Darling et al., "Selection and Utilization of Business Trained Officers in the Armed Forces," 1950, Air University Library, p. 13. This report, originally done for Harvard University, also sums up the various requirements imposed by the armed services upon potential officer students who desired to attend the program. Ibid., pp. 17a, 27a.

67. Ibid., p. 27a; "Air Force Personnel Planners Seek Ways to Improve Placement," *AFT*, Jan 17, 1948, pp. 1, 15. As a condition of graduation, these students were required to write 2,500- to 5,000-word essays on the personnel practices of the industry in which they served. Finally, they were to contribute a chapter to the book the department was preparing. This work, Personnel Management Practices in Business, was to be a summary of the "best practices in the field," but it was never published.

68. Darling, p. 13. More work needs to be done on the links between civilian-military business training and the military-industrial complex. One significant study is Albert D. Biderman's "The Retired Military" that appears in Roger W. Little, ed., *Handbook of Military Institutions* (Beverly Hills, Calif.: Sage Publications, 1971), pp. 123–166.

69. "Air Force Industry Co-op Shows Gain," *AFT*, Jan 7, 1950, pp. 1, 13.

70. Stephen Ambrose, *Rise to Globalism: American Foreign Policy Since 1938* (New York: Penguin, 1972), pp. 83–98.

71. Ambrose, p. 110.

72. H.W. Brands, "The Age of Vulnerability: Eisenhower and the National Insecurity State," *American Historical Review*, Dec 1989, pp. 963–989; Ambrose, p. 113.

73. Harold W. Stanley and Richard G. Niemi, *Vital Statistics on American Politics* (Washington, D.C.: Congressional Quarterly Press, 1988), p. 291.

74. "500 Attend AAF Conference on Veteran's Problems," *Army Times*, Dec 15, 1945, p. 12.

75. Leslie K. Adler, "The Red Image: American Attitudes toward Communism in the Cold War Era" (diss., University of California—Berkeley, 1970), pp. 239–240; Eduard Mark, "October or Thermidor? Interpretations of Stalinism and the Perception of Soviet Foreign Policy in the United States, 1927–1947," *American Historical Review*, Oct 1989, pp. 937–962.

76. Harry S. Truman, "Special Message to the Congress on Greece and Turkey," Mar 12, 1947, in *Public Papers of the President of the United States, Harry S. Truman: Con-*

taining the Public Messages, Speeches, and Statements of the President, 1 Jan–31 Dec 1947 (Washington, D.C.: GPO, 1963) p. 178.

77. *Public Papers, Truman: 1947*, p. 238.

78. Ambrose, pp. 110–111.

79. Ibid., pp. 111–115.

80. David Caute, *The Great Fear: The Anti-Communist Purge under Truman and Eisenhower* (New York: Simon & Schuster, 1978), p. 18.

81. A good introduction to social reform in the Navy prior to the Civil War is Harold Langley's *Social Reform in the United States Navy, 1798–1862* (Chicago: University of Illinois Press, Urbana, 1967).

82. David I. Macleod, *Building Character in the American Boy: The Boy Scouts, YMCA, and Their Forerunners, 1870–1920* (Madison: University of Wisconsin Press, 1983) pp. 10–15.

83. Griffith, *Men Wanted*, pp. 33–35. For a broader discussion of the UMT movement prior to World War I and the progressive's impact on the military, see, in addition to Griffith's work, I.B. Holley, Jr., *Gen. John M. Palmer, Citizen Soldier, and the Army of a Democracy* (Westport, Conn.: Greenwood Press, 1982); and John Whitley Chambers II, "Conscripting for Colossus: The Progressive Era and the Origin of the Modern Military Draft in the United States in World War I," in Karsten, ed., *Military in America*, pp. 297–311.

84. Quoted in Griffith, *Men Wanted*, pp. 14–15. Two other important works that develop the military as a means of socialization and assimilation during this period are William J. Reese, *Power and the Promise of School Reform: Grass-roots Movements during the Progressive Era* (Boston, Mass.: Routledge & Kegan Paul, 1986), pp. 242–249, and Bruce White, "The American Military and the Melting Pot in World War I," in J.L Granatstein and R.D. Cuff, eds., *War and Society in North America* (Toronto: Thomas Nelson & Sons, 1971), pp. 37–51.

85. An excellent work examining the Committee on Training Camp Activities is Ronald Schaffer's *America in the Great War: The Rise of the War Welfare State* (New York: Oxford University Press, 1991), chap. 7.

86. Gary B. Nash et al., *The American People: Creating a Nation and A Society* (New York: Harper & Row, 1986), pp. 747–748.

87. Schaffer, p. 102.

88. Nash, pp. 741a and 741b.

89. Schaffer, p. 100. See also Fred D. Baldwin, "The Invisible Armor," *American Quarterly*, vol. 16 (fall 1964), pp. 432–44.

90. Schaffer, pp. 105–107.

91. Griffith, *Men Wanted*, chap. 4.

92. The postwar efforts to promote UMT are discussed in Frank Kofsky, *Harry S. Truman and the War Scare of 1948* (New York: St. Martin's, 1993) 195–213; Melvyn P. Leffler, *A Preponderance of Power: National Security, the Truman Administration, and the Cold War* (Stanford, Calif.: Stanford University Press, 1992) pp. 209–210; and Russell F. Weigley's two important works, *History of the United States Army* and *The American Way of War: A History of United States Military Strategy and Policy* (Bloomington: Indiana University Press, 1973).

93. As quoted in Thomas Palmer's "Why We Fight: A Study of Indoctrination Activities in the Armed Forces," in Karsten's *Military in America*, p. 383. Hannah eventually left Michigan State for a position with the DOD's Troop Information Program.

94. President's Committee on Religion and Welfare in the Armed Forces, *The Military Chaplaincy: A Report to the President by the President's Committee on Religion and Welfare in the Armed Forces—Oct 1, 1950* (Washington, D.C.: GPO, 1950), p. 2.

95. President's Committee on Religion and Welfare in the Armed Forces, *Report of the National Conference on Community Responsibility to Our Peacetime Servicemen and Women, May 25–26, 1949* (Washington D.C.: GPO, 1949), p. 9.

96. Ibid., pp. 9–10.

97. Ibid.

98. Under Secretary of Defense Stephen Early's address, in ibid., pp. 8–10. Truman's perspective on large "democratically-trained" armies can be summed up at an Army Day address given at Soldier Field, Chicago, in 1946. "A Message from President Truman," *Army Times*, Mar 9, 1946, p. 3; "Truman Comes Out for Large Army," *Army Times*, Apr 13, 1946, p. 20.

99. For important background on the armed service and education, see Cyril Houle et al., *The Armed Services and Adult Education* (Washington, D.C.: American Council on Education, 1947). Political indoctrination in the postwar period is incisively treated by Stephen D. Wesbrook in "Historical Notes," which appears in Morris Janowitz and Stephen Wesbrook, eds., *The Political Education of Soldiers* (Beverly Hills, Calif.: Sage Publications, 1983), pp. 251–279, and by Palmer in "Why We Fight," which appears in Karsten, ed., *Military in America*, pp. 382–394.

100. Wesbrook, "Historical Notes," in Janowitz and Wesbrook, *Political Education of Soldiers*, pp. 257–262; Palmer, "Why We Fight," in Karsten, ed., *Military in America*, pp. 382–383.

101. Maj Lenn McConagha, "Behind the Scenes at USAFI," *Army Information Digest*, Feb 1948, pp. 43–52.

102. On USAFI, see Houle et al., *Armed Services and Adult Education*, pp. 82–101.

103. Wesbrook, "Historical Notes," in Janowitz and Wesbrook, *Political Education of Soldiers*, pp. 262–263.

104. The conclusion that morale and effectiveness are correlated to political purpose can be found in H.H. Railey's 1941 report, "Morale of the United States Army," RG 407, file AG353.8, MMB, NA. This work is an important primary source discussing the effect of sociopolitical factors on morale. See also Brig Gen C.T. Lanham (USA), "Better Citizens—Better Soldiers," *Social Education*, vol. 13 (Feb 1949), p. 54.

105. *Information and Education in the Armed Services: A Report to the President by the President's Commission on Religion and Welfare in the Armed Forces* (Washington D.C.: GPO, 1949), p. 4.

106. *Information and Education*, p. 12.

107. Ibid.

108. Ibid., p. 6.

109. Palmer, "Why We Fight," in Karsten, ed., *Military in America*, p. 383.

110. Ibid., pp. 387–388.

111. David Segal, in his *Recruiting for Uncle Sam*, p. 65, argues that the army was never comfortable in the political indoctrination role. Bruce White, in his important article "The American Military and the Melting Pot in World War I," found the opposite. Indeed, many army officers who embraced UMT prior to and after World War I also favored the army as an agent of Americanization, that is, teaching immigrants what it means to be an American. Karsten, ed., *Military in America*, pp. 317–328.

112. President's Committee on Religion and Welfare in the Armed Forces, *Military Chaplaincy*, pp. 1–2.

113. Ibid., p. 2.

114. President's Committee on Religion and Welfare in the Armed Forces, *Free Time in the Armed Forces: A Study of the Armed Forces' Special Services and Recreation Programs* (Washington, D.C.: GPO, 1951) p. 10.

115. President's Committee on Religion and Welfare in the Armed Forces, *Military Chaplaincy*, pp. 1–4, 11–18, 37–42.

116. Ibid., pp. 9–10.

117. Ibid., p. 4.

118. "Civilians Laud Army VD Film," *AFT*, Mar 20, 1948, p. 13.

119. John G. Morris, "VD Since VE Day," *Army Information Digest*, Apr 1948, pp. 25–28. See also Agnes Meyer, "Problems of a Standing Army in a Democracy," in President's Committee on Religion and Welfare in the Armed Forces, *Report of the National Conference on Community Responsibility to Our Peacetime Servicemen and Wo-*

men, May 25–26, 1949, pp. 21–22; Jane M. Hoey, "Housing, Health and Family Welfare" (discussion group summary), in ibid., p. 34.

120. Morris, "VD Since VE Day," p. 26.

121. Ibid., pp. 26, 28.

122. President's Committee on Religion and Welfare in the Armed Forces, *Free Time in the Armed Forces,* pp. 11–13.

123. Ibid., pp. 9–20. See also E.C. Johnson, "Service Clubs—the Soldier's Haven," *Army Information Digest,* Jun 1948, pp. 50–54.

124. Meyer, "Problems of a Standing Army," in President's Committee on Religion and Welfare in the Armed Forces, *Report of the National Conference on Community Responsibility to Our Peacetime Servicemen and Women, May 25–26, 1949,* p. 18.

125. Ibid. Two recent studies that support the concept that family life affects the desire of an armed service member to remain in the military are Gary L. Bowen's "Family Factors and Member Retention: A Key Relationship in the Work and Family Equation" and Peter A. Neenan's "Marital Quality and Job Satisfaction of Male Air Force Personnel: A Test of the Spillover Hypothesis," both in Gary L. Bowen and Dennis K. Othner, eds., *The Organizational Family: Work and Family Linkages in the U.S. Military* (New York: Praeger, 1989), pp. 37–58 and 59–78, respectively.

126. Meyer, "Problems of a Standing Army," in President's Committee on Religion and Welfare in the Armed Forces, *Report of the National Conference on Community Responsibility to Our Peacetime Servicemen and Women, May 25–26, 1949,* p. 21.

127. For an important article using the company town as a metaphor to describe military communities, see James A. Martin and Dennis K. Othner's "The Company Town in Transition: Rebuilding Military Communities," in Bowen and Othner, eds., *Organizational Family,* pp. 163–178. Also germane is Charles Dellheim, "The Creation of a Company Culture: Cadburys, 1861–1931," *American Historical Review,* Feb 1987, pp. 13–44. For an important work that describes the rise of welfare work in industry with important ramifications on the military, see Nelson, *Managers and Workers,* esp. chap. 6.

128. Public Opinion Surveys, Inc., of Princeton, New Jersey, polled 2,004 adults across the United States (using the 1950 census as an index) and 1,031 male teenagers 16 to 20 years old. Office of Armed Forces Information and Education (AF I&E), DOD, *Attitudes of Adult Civilians toward the Military Service as a Career,* pt. 1, and *Attitudes of 16 to 20 Year Old Males toward the Military Service as a Career,* pt. 2 (Princeton, N.J.: Public Opinion Surveys, 1955). Copies are in the Air University Library.

129. George H. Gallup, *The Gallup Poll: Public Opinion, 1935–1971,* vol. 2 (New York: Random House, 1972), s.vv. "National Defense, May 1, 1950," "Russia, Jan 11, 1950."

130. AF I&E, DOD, *Attitudes of Adult Civilians toward the Military Service as a Career,* pt. 1, pp. 2–3, 8.

131. In this 1955 survey, 38 percent of those polled stated that general financial rewards such as pay and benefits, along with a general liking for military life, constituted the reasons why enlisted personnel made the service their life's work. Twenty-eight percent, however, believed career enlisted personnel were unwilling to earn a civilian living, and that was the important reason for their remaining in the military. Ibid., p. 8. Financial rewards were high on all questions about retention of personnel. Ibid., pp. 8–10.

132. AF I&E, DOD, *Attitudes of Adult Civilians toward the Military Service as a Career,* pt. 1, pp. 51–52, 60–63. Gerald Linderman, in his *Embattled Courage: The Experience of Combat in the American Civil War* (New York: Free Press, 1987), chap. 12 and epilogue, argues that the passage of time and occasional military revivals along with veterans' organizations helped to reshape Civil War veterans' feelings about the war. Certainly advertising, veterans' groups, the Cold War, and the conceptualization of World War II as a Good War helped veterans reframe their earlier military experience. Moreover, there seems to be a general tendency over time to talk about the best aspects of wartime experiences and to suppress the worst.

133. AF I&E, DOD, *Attitudes of Adult Civilians toward the Military Service as a Career*, pt. 1, pp. 4, 6–7; AF I&E, DOD, *Attitudes of 16 to 20 Year Old Males toward the Military Service as a Career*, pt. 2, pp. 10–12, 17. Sixty-six percent of the teenagers said that the most important information they considered when forming their opinion of the armed services came from veterans; in fact, 20 percent of the respondents were sons of veterans. The next most influential source of information was movies and magazines.

Chapter 3

1. It is important to note that 15 percent of the force is not the same as the number of reenlistees from a given year-group, for example, all who enlist in 1950 and then come up for reenlistment in 1954 after serving a four-year contractual period. The average unadjusted reenlistment rates based on year-groups for the years 1950–1955 are much lower. For the Joint DOD, the rate was 41.2 percent; for the Army, it was 48.0 percent; for the Navy, it was 53.2 percent; for the Marines, it was 31.0 percent; and for the Air Force, it was 41.1 percent. *DOD Fact Book, 1970*, p. 49. For the years 1947–1949, a reenlistment rate of 50.1 percent was approximated from the Office of the Secretary of Defense (OSD) reports.

2. Intvw, Shalett, *New York Times*, with Spaatz, Jan 4, 1946, Spaatz Collection, Box 25, Diary File, Library of Congress (LC). The most comprehensive work discussing the Air Force's struggle for autonomy is Herman Wolk's *Planning and Organizing the Postwar Air Force*. For an in-depth look at cyclic nature of the postwar DOD budget process, see Warner R. Schilling, Paul Y. Hammond, and Glenn Snyder, *Strategy, Politics, and Defense Budgets* (New York: Columbia University Press, 1962), chap. 2.

3. For example, see the account of General H. H. Arnold's Washington, D.C., press conference held August 17, 1945, and reported in *The Army Times*, Aug 25, 1945, pp. 1, 10.

4. Intvw, Richard Harkness, National Broadcasting Company, with Spaatz, Mar 12, 1946, Spaatz Collection, Box 255, LC.

5. Memo, Spaatz to AC-1 (Anderson), May 16, 1946, Subj: AAF Public Relations, Spaatz Collection, Box 26, LC.

6. Wolk, pp. 36–38, 218.

7. Ibid., p. 36.

8. Hewes, pp. 136–137.

9. Marshall's view of UMT is well documented in Mark A. Stoler's *George C. Marshall: Soldier-Statesman of the American Century* (Boston, Mass.: Twayne Publishers, 1989), pp. 143–144.

10. Wolk, pp. 37–38.

11. Ibid., pp. 38, 58–59.

12. Ibid., pp. 57, 181.

13. Memo, CG, AAF (Arnold), to CS, Army (Marshall), Mar 31, 1945, Subj: Re-Survey of the Troop Basis for the Post-War Army, RG 18, AAF, AAG, Mail & Records Div, Decimal file 1945, 381, Box 189, MMB, NA. See also Wolk, p. 57.

14. Jeffery M. Dorwart, *Eberstadt and Forrestal: A National Security Partnership 1909–1949* (College Station: Texas A&M University Press, 1991), p. 111; Wolk, pp. 121–122.

15. Wolk, pp. 77–78.

16. Henry H. Arnold, *Third Report of the Commanding General of the Army Air Forces to the Secretary of War, 12 November 1945* (Baltimore, Md.: Schneidereith, n.d.), p. 33.

17. Wolk, p. 180. Additionally, the 1947 National Defense Act established a unified National Military Establishment complete with one Secretary of Defense and three

assistant secretaries assigned as administrators over the armed forces. For an important discussion of the development of the National Military Establishment and its successor, the Department of Defense, see Paul Y. Hammond, *Organizing for Defense: The American Military Establishment in the Twentieth Century* (Princeton, N.J.: Princeton University Press, 1961); Dorwart, *Eberstadt and Forrestal*; and Steven L. Reardon, *History of the Office of the Secretary of Defense*, vol. 1, *The Formative Years, 1947–1950* (Washington, D.C.: Office of the Secretary of Defense Historical Office, 1984), chap. 1.

18. Wolk, p. 217. See also Frank Kofsky, *Harry Truman and the War Scare of 1948* (New York: St. Martin's Press, 1993), pp. 199–203.

19. The best source on the Army's demobilization remains John C. Sparrow's *History of Personnel Demobilization in the United States Army*, pamphlet 20–210 (Washington, D.C.: GPO, 1952). A good general narrative describing societal reactions to demobilization is found in Joseph C. Goulden's *The Best Years, 1945–1950* (New York: Atheneum, 1976), pp. 17–84.

20. Harry S. Truman, *Memoirs*, vol. 1, *Years of Decision* (Garden City: Doubleday, 1955), pp. 506–509.

21. C. Joseph Bernardo and Eugene H. Bacon, *American Military Policy: Its Development Since 1775* (Harrisburg, Pa.: Stackpole Books, 1961) p. 448; *Historical Statistics of the United States to 1957*, p. 736.

22. Two important studies regarding the AAF's demobilization are Albert E. Haase, *Manpower Demobilization in the AAF* (Offutt AFB, Nebr.: Historical Office, Strategic Air Command, 1946), and Chauncey E. Sanders, *Redeployment and Demobilization,* Historical Study 77 (Maxwell AFB, Ala.: USAF Historical Division, Air University, 1955).

23. Intvw, Arthur K. Marmor with Maj Gen Leon W. Johnson, Apr 14, 1965, K239.0512–609, AFHSO.

24. Bernard C. Nalty, ed., *History of the United States Air Force, 1907–1997* (Washington, D.C.: Air Force History and Museums Program, in press).

25. AAF Ltr 35–33, Jul 12, 1946, "AAF Recruiting Policies," microfilm, AFHSO.

26. Minutes, First Air Board Meeting, Apr 16, 1946, A.M., RG 340, Box 13, MMB, NA, p. 36.

27. Gen Carl Spaatz, *Report of the Chief of Staff USAF to the Secretary of the Air Force, 30 June 1948* (Washington, D.C.: GPO, 1948), p. 13.

28. Ltr, CG, AAF (Spaatz), to CG, Fourth Army (Wainwright), Feb 15, 1946, Spaatz Collection, Diaries, Box 25, LC.

29. Manpower statistics vary from report to report; however, one important historical compilation of general manpower requirements is Alfred Goldberg's "The Men: Manpower," in *Air Force Magazine*, Aug 1957, pp. 291–299.

30. Goldberg, "The Men," pp. 292–293.

31. A major reorganization in 1947 placed all combat and support groups under the wing commander. Prior to this, the base commander, who was often a nonflyer, was the immediate supervisor of the combat group commander. This reorganization, known as the Hobson Plan (named for its author, Col Kenneth B. Hobson), elevated the wing headquarters to a superior position and placed the wing commander in charge of all combat and support groups. The base commander now was in a subordinate role to the wing commander. The flying mission remained a part of the combat group, which was usually composed of three combat squadrons and a headquarters. Also assigned to the wing were three other groups: maintenance and supply, airdrome, and medical. With the wing, in effect, taking the place of the group, air leaders organized procurement and manpower requirements based upon this concept. For a discussion of the Hobson Plan, see John T. Bohn, *The Development of Strategic Air Command, 1946–1973* (Offutt AFB, Nebr.: Strategic Air Command History Office, 1974) pp. 7–8; Harry R. Borowski, *A Hollow Threat: Strategic Air Power and Containment before Korea* (Westport, Conn.: Greenwood Press, 1982), pp. 61–68; and *USAF Statistical Digest: Jan 1949–Jun 1950* (Washington, D.C.: HQ USAF, Operations Statistics Division, 1951), p. 18.

32. Goldberg, "The Men," p. 294. The buildup in Korea eventually exeeded 788,381 officers and airmen.

33. *Semi-Annual Report of the Secretary of the Air Force, 1 Jan–30 Jun 1951* (Washington, D.C.: GPO, 1951), p. 233; *Semi-Annual Report of the Secretary of Defense, 1 Jan–30 Jun 1952* (Washington, D.C.: GPO, 1952), p. 3; Goldberg, "The Men," pp. 294–296.

34. Goldberg, "The Men," pp. 296–298. The effect of poor retention is discussed in Chapter 5.

35. Memo, AC/AS–1 (Anderson) to CS, AAF (Spaatz), Oct 13, 1945, Subj: Enlistments and Re-enlistments in Regular Army, author's personal files.

36. Memo, AC/AS–1 (Anderson) to Asst Secy War for Air (Symington), Sep 21, 1946, Subj: Army Air Forces Recruiting, author's personal files; Memo, Secy War for Air (Symington) to Secy War (Patterson), Dec 16, 1946, Subj: Independent Army Air Forces Recruiting Program, author's personal files.

37. Minutes, Air Staff Meeting, May 22, 1946, item 1, Spaatz Collection, Daily Diaries, Box 26, LC.

38. Memo, AC/AS–1 (Anderson) to Dep Comdr, AAF (Eaker), Mar 8, 1946, Subj: Air Force Recruiting, RG 340, Box 623.

39. Memo, CG, AAF (Spaatz), to CS, USA (Eisenhower), Mar 21, 1946, Subj: Present Status of Air Force Recruiting, author's personal files; Memo, CS, USA (Eisenhower), to CG, AAF (Spaatz), Apr 22, 1946, Subj: Present Status of Air Forces Recruiting, author's personal files.

40. Ltr, AC/AS–1 (Johnson) to CG, ADC, Apr 21, 1947, Subj: Off-Station Recruiting Activities, RG 18, 341, Box 2650, MMB, NA; Ltr, AC-AS–1 (Badger) to CG, AMC, Jul 1, 1947, Subj: Recruiting in Civilian Communities, RG 18, 341, Box 2650, MMB, NA. See also AAF Ltr 35–50, Jun 20, 1947, "AAF Selective Recruiting Program," author's personal files.

41. Ltr, CG, AAF (Spaatz), to All Major Commands, Jul 15, 1946, Subj: Mobile Recruiting Units, RG 18, 340, Box 623, MMB, NA.

42. AAF Ltr 35–33, Feb 13, 1946, "Improper Acceptance for Enlistment of Minors and Individuals Not Suited for Military Service," microfilm, AFHSO; AAF Ltr 35–34, Aug 16, 1946, "False Recruiting Promise," author's personal files; Memo, AC/AS–1 (Anderson) to D/PA, Dec 16, 1946, Subj: Army Air Force Recruiting Program, author's personal files.

43. Memo, AC/AS–1 (Anderson) to D/PA, Dec 16, 1946, Subj: Army Air Force Recruiting Program, author's personal files; Memo, CG, AAF (Spaatz), to Gen Handy, Dec 16, 1946, Subj: Proposed Solution to Air Force Personnel Shortages, author's personal files; Memo, Asst D/PA (Jones) to AC/AS–1 (Anderson), Dec 20, 1946, Subj: Army Air Force Recruiting Program, author's personal files.

44. Ltr, CG, AAF (Spaatz), to All Major Commands, Mar 15, 1946, Subj: Mobile Recruiting Units, RG 18, 340, Box 623, MMB, NA; "The Army Air Forces Use a Trailer Effectively in Recruiting," *U.S. Recruiting Service Letters*, vol. 2, No. 1 (Dec 1946), copy in RG 18, 340, Box 623, MMB, NA.

45. Memo, Asst DCS/P (Burns) to CG, Bolling Field, Jan 26, 1948, Subj: Air Force Recruiting Program, RG 18, 341, Box 3043, MMB, NA.

46. Memo, CG, AAF Exec Officer (Landry), to CG, AAF (Spaatz), Sep 10, 1947, Subj: Joint Army–Air Force Recruiting, author's personal files.

47. Ltr, DCS/P (Chauncy), to WDGS, Feb 18, 1947, Subj: AGCT Minimum for Enlistment in the AAF, RG 18, 340, Box 623, MMB, NA. The AAF was allowed to increase its minimum score to 110. This letter requested that the War Department allow the AAF to gradually move the score up to 110 in small increments. At the time, the Army's minimum score was 70.

48. Memo, AC-AS–1 (Edwards), to AAF Act DCO (Vandenberg), Aug 29, 1947, Subj: Future Personnel Procurement, RG 18, 341, Box 2650, MMB, NA; Ltr, CG, SPA

(Riepe), to DCS/P (Upston), Oct 21, 1947, Subj: Air Representation in Recruiting Service, RG 18, 341, Box 2650, MMB, NA.

49. Memo, AC/AS–1 (Strother) to AC/AS–1, Jul 23, 1947, Subj: Future AAF Recruiting Organization, author's personal files.

50. Memo, CG, AAF Exec Officer (Landry), to CG, AAF (Spaatz), Sep 10, 1947, Subj: Joint Army–Air Force Recruiting, author's personal files.

51. Memo, Secy Navy (Sullivan) to Secy Defense (Forrestal), Sep 24, 1948, Subj: Report on Possibility of Joint Use of Recruiting Facilities and Services in the Western Area, author's personal files.

52. Formerly called corps areas, these geographical boundaries were based upon the six continental armies stationed in the United States. First Army encompassed New England and New York; Second Army, the Mid-Atlantic region; Third Army, the South; Fourth Army, the Southwest; Fifth Army, Mid-America and the West; and Sixth Army, the Northwest and the West. Peterson, "An Investigation of the United States Army and United States Air Force Recruiting Organization and Program," p. 32.

53. Ibid., pp. 36–38.

54. In 1948, the seven major continental commands were Strategic Air Command, Air Training Command, Tactical Air Command, Air Materiel Command, Air Defense Command, Air University, and Military Air Transport Command. Ibid., p. 39.

55. Ibid., pp. 41–42.

56. Since the Air Force represented 40 percent of the combined strength of the Army and Air Force, it wanted the same composition for the joint recruiting force. Memo, D/P&A (Reipe) to DCS/P (Upston), Oct 21, 1947, Subj: Air Representation in Recruiting Service, RG 18, 341, Box 2650, MMB, NA.

57. Intvw, Hugh N. Ahmann with Richard Kisling, 1982 and 1984, K239.0512–1363, AFHSO, pp. 56–63.

58. Ltr, SecDef (Forrestal) to Senator Gurney, Mar 20, 48, Subj: Number of Men on Recruiting Duty, RG 18, 341, Box 25, MMB, NA. Forrestal presented the following figures:

No. of:

Service	Budget*	Officer	Enlisted	Civilian	Total
		1947			
Army/AF	$35,520,730	1,095	6,051	1,082	8,228
Navy	$ 6,626,742	178	2,276	2	2,456
Marines	N/A	79	788	0	867
		1948			
Army/AF	$25,718,000	1,165	7,130	1,103	9,398
Navy	$14,176,879	220	2,619	2	2,841
Marines	$ 2,933,750	81	1,176	7	1,264

*Budget amounts include funds for recruiter pay and allowances, advertising, publicity, rental, operation and maintenance costs of motor vehicles, pay of civilian personnel, travel pay and per diem, and cost of transporting recruits.

59. Memo, DCS/P (Harbold) to Asst SecAF (White), Oct 21, 1953, Subj: USA-USAF Agreement on Joint Recruiting, author's personal files; Memo, DCS/P (Persons) to Asst SecAF (White), Nov 6, 1953, Subj: USA-USAF Joint Recruiting, author's personal files.

60. Ltr, CG, 38th Air Div (Grubbs), to VCS, USAF (Twining), Sep 5, 1952, Subj: Enlistment of Substandard Airmen, Twining Collection, Office Files, Box 57, LC; Ltr, VCS, USAF (Twining), to CG, 38th Air Div (Grubbs), Oct 15, 1952, Subj: Problems with Joint Recruiting, Twining Collection, Office Files, Box 57, LC.

61. Memo, DCS/P (Persons) to Asst SecAF (White), Nov 6, 1953, Subj: USA-USAF Joint Recruiting, author's personal files.

62. Minutes, Air Force Deputy Military Personnel Procurement Conference, Sep 6, 1951, items 3, 4, author's personal files.

63. Kisling intvw, 1982 and 1984, pp. 56–63; Memo, DCS/P (Persons) to Asst SecAF (White), Nov 6, 1953, Subj: USA-USAF Joint Recruiting, author's personal files; Memo, DCS/P (Harbold) to Asst SecAF (White), Oct 21, 1953, Subj: USA-USAF Agreement on Joint Recruiting, author's personal files; Memo, MMPD (Niergarth) to CS/AF, Jan 3, 1952, Subj: Reorganization of Air Force Recruiting, author's personal files; Memo, DCS/P (Trossbach) to Chief, Military Personnel Procurement Service Div, Sep 11, 1951, Subj: Items Discussed at the Air Force Deputy MPPO Conference, Sep 6, 1951, author's personal files; Ltr, Office of the Adjutant General to CGs, Each ZI Army, Apr 12, 1949, Subj: Utilization of Air Force Personnel on Duty with the Recruiting Service, author's personal files.

64. Memo, SecDef (Wilson) to all Service Secretaries, Mar 6, 1954, Subj: Recruiting, author's personal files.

65. Ibid.

66. Hist, 3500th Recruiting Wing, Jul–Dec 1955, microfilm, AFHSO, pp. 6–10.

67. Gains consisted of recruits and transfers from other services; losses included those killed, missing in action, the deserters, and individuals AWOL or discharged.

68. Memo, Air Comptroller, Statistical Control (Cecil), to MMPD, Dec 12, 1947, Subj: Recruiting Progress Report, RG 18, 341, Box 2650, MMB, NA. According to this memo, the Army followed the Air Force's example and established a similar reporting system.

69. Harrod, p. 37.

70. Memo, DCS/PMP (Towles) to Exec Asst SecAF (Lindtner), Jan 28, 1948, Subj: Recruiting Efforts of Colorado Springs Detachment, Spaatz Collection, Box 264, SecAF File 2, LC. This memo records the Recruiting Services estimate that about 40 percent of Air Force enlistments came from communities of fewer than 75,000 people and that 25 percent came from population densities of between 100,000 and 500,000.

71. Peterson, "An Investigation of the United States Army and United States Air Force Recruiting Organization and Program," pp. 73–74.

72. Memo, Recruiting Service, Sixth Army (Dean), to CS, USAF (Spaatz), Dec 29, 1947, Subj: Screening of Air Force Personnel Assigned to Recruit Duty, Sixth Army, RG 18, 341, Box 2650, MMB, NA.

73. Ltr, MSgt Wesley G. Alston to CS, USAF (Spaatz), Jan 31, 1948, Spaatz Collection, Box 262, Personnel File (A–F), LC.

74. Ltr, CS, USAF (Spaatz) to MSgt Wesley G. Alston, Feb 13, 1948, Spaatz Collection, Box 262, Personnel File (A–F), LC.

75. Hist, 3500th Recruiting Wing, Jan–Jun 1954, microfilm, AFHSO, p. 37.

76. Hist, 3500th Recruiting Wing, Jul–Dec 1954, microfilm, AFHSO, app. 1.

77. Military recruiters used the salesmanship analogy since at least 1919. See Griffith, *Men Wanted*, pp. 30–31.

78. "Presentation of Lt Col Marvin Alexander to the Recruiting School Faculty," in Hist, 3500th Recruiting Wing, Jul–Dec 1954, microfilm, AFHSO, app. 1.

79. Hist, 3500th Recruiting Wing, Jan–Jun 1954, microfilm, AFHSO, pp. 37–38.

80. Ibid., Jul–Dec 1954, microfilm, AFHSO, p. 28.

81. *AAF Recruiting Bulletin*, No. 1, Dec 20, 1945, copy in Spaatz Collection, Chief

of Staff, Air Force Training file, Box 255, LC.

82. Hist, 3500th Recruiting Wing, Jan–Jun 1955, microfilm, AFHSO, p. 47.

83. Ibid., p. 39.

84. Ltr, CS, USAF (Twining), to All Major Commands, Jan 23, 1956, Subj: USAF Information Program, Twining Collection, Daily Log, Jan 1956, Box 4, LC. This letter carefully details the various advertising media used by the Air Force to project itself as the "Backbone of Freedom." Charles Moskos provides an apt description of the Air Force's technical image as portrayed in the mass media. Moskos, *American Enlisted Man*, pp. 17–18.

85. AAF Ltr 35–33, Jul 18, 1947, "AAF Recruiting Policies," author's personal files. See also the Air Force recruiting pamphlet, *A Challenge and a Choice . . . U.S. Air Force* (Washington, D.C.: U.S. Air Force Recruiting Service Directorate of Advertising, 1974).

86. MR, AFIPR (Starks), 1948, Subj: Sample Recruiting Message—"Make Aviation Your Business," microfilm, AFHSO, p. 6.

87. For list of recruiting themes applicable to the period of this study, see Memo, AF/DMP (Wilkins) to CG, ATC, Jun 11, 1948, Subj: Recruiting Mottos, author's personal files.

88. *You Are a Women With an Eye to the Future* (Washington, D.C.: GPO, 1948), pp. 1–3.

89. U.S. Air Force Recruiting Service, *Horizons Unlimited for Women in the Air Force* (Wright-Patterson AFB, Ohio: Columbia Litho, n.d. [1957–1960]), p. 1.

90. HQ USAF, *Occupational Handbook of the United States Air Force* (Washington, D.C.: GPO, 1958), p. 186.

91. One of the major problems that personnel planners faced during World War II was malassignment, that is, training a man for one job and then using him for another. In 1943, malassignment was the number one morale problem in the AAF.

92. *The U.S. Air Force: Your Son and the Jet Air Age* (Washington D.C.: GPO, 1955), pp. 1–2; U.S. Air Force, *Your Son's Air Force Life: What You as Parents, Should Know* (Washington D.C.: GPO, 1956), pp. 2–3.

93. U.S. Air Force, *A Message About Your Son's Future* (Washington, D.C.: GPO, 1956), pp. 3–6.

94. U.S. Air Force, *Your Son's Air Force Life*, p. 3.

95. Ibid.

96. AAF Ltr, Mar 15, 1946, "AAF Special Recruiting Drive," microfilm, AFHSO; AAF Ltr 35–28, Mar 17, 1947, "Enlistment of Skilled Civilians in Grades Above Private," microfilm, AFHSO.

97. Presentation, Lt Col R.W. Elliott, "Air Force Recruiting Program," Air Force Personnel Conference, Dec 1, 1948, pp. 3–4, copy of transcript of conference, Air University Library; Memo, DCS/P (Underhill) to DCS/PT, Aug 17, 1950, Subj: Amendment to Policy of Prior Service Airmen, RG 341, 141, Box 389, MMB, NA.

98. "Procedures for Enlistment of Personnel in Grades Appropriate to Training and Experience," *AAF Recruiting Bulletin*, Mar 1946, pp. 1–2.

99. The belief that successful completion of technical school was related to educational level later led Air Force planners to experiment with educational level for enlistment requirements and retention. Introduced in June 1950, the Air Force began to require high school dropouts to have a higher minimum AFQT test scores than those who had high school degrees. It was dropped in November of that year, only to be reintroduced in 1962 when research demonstrated a correlation between high school graduation and retention. Eitelberg et al., *Screening for Service*, p. 18.

100. AAF Ltr 35–50, Jun 20, 1947, "AAF Selective Recruiting Program," microfilm, AFHSO; Hist, Air Training Command, Jan 1–Dec 31, 1947, microfilm, AFHSO, pp. 46–48.

101. AAF Ltr 35–33, Jul 18, 1947, "AAF Recruiting Policies," microfilm, AFHSO.

102. These figures are not that unusual because the Recruiting Service estimated that about 40 percent of all enlistments came from communities with populations less than

75,000. Only 25 percent came from large urban areas of 100,000 or more. Memo, DCS/P (Towles) to Exec to Asst SAF, Jan 28, 1948, Spaatz Collection, Chief of Staff, Secretary of the Air Force file 2, Box 264, LC; Ltr, SecAF (Symington) to Chairman, Military Affairs Committee, Colorado Springs (Tutt), Jan 30, 1948, Spaatz Collection, Chief of Staff, Secretary of the Air Force file 2, Box 264, LC. In 1950, the population of Colorado Springs was approximately 60,000 while Denver's was 415,786. *Statistical Abstract of the United States*, 78th ed. (Washington, D.C.: GPO, 1957), p. 16.

103. For an excellent contemporary description of the recruitment process, see MSgt Lawrence Landis, *The Air Force: From Civilian to Airman* (New York: Viking Press, 1958), pp. 8–25.

104. Peterson, "An Investigation of the United States Army and United States Air Force Recruiting Organization and Program," p. 47.

105. Holm, pp. 119–120, 133–134, 180–181.

106. The Air Force did not like to accept youth with criminal records. Air Force Staff Summary Sheet, May 4, 1948, Subj: Enlistments of Parolees and Probationers, RG 18, 341, Box 3043, MMB, NA. For security check and communist background information, see typescript, telecon, CS, USAF (Twining), with IG, USAF (Carroll), Mar 15, 1954, Subj: Background Investigations, Twining Collection, Daily Log, Mar 1954, Box 2, LC.

107. AFR 34–24, Jul 15, 1949, *Marriage of Airmen in the Lower Four Grades*; see also AFR 34–12, Feb 11, 1949, *Marriage in Overseas Commands*.

108. AFR 39–9, 1949, *Restrictions to Enlistment*; *The Airman's Guide*, 2d ed. (Harrisburg, Pa.: Military Service Publishing Co., 1950), pp. 101–105.

109. All the services relaxed their married restrictions during this period. Segal, *Recruiting for Uncle Sam*, p. 84. AFR 34–24, as cited in note 107 above, remained in the books; however, due to the large number of lower grades who were married, it was not rigorously enforced.

110. *USAF Statistical Digest: Fiscal Year 1955*, pp. 344–345.

111. Ibid., p. 346. Only 38 percent of enlisted personnel in the Army and 34 percent in the Navy had dependents. Department of the Army, *Pocket Data Book Supplement, 1955* (Washington, D.C.: GPO, 1955), p. 28.

112. Eitelberg et al., *Screening for Service*, pp. 14–18. According to Eitelberg, although the AFQT was modeled after the AGCT, its specific purpose was to serve as a screening device, not as a classification test. The AFQT measured a recruit's general ability to absorb military training. During World War II, the War Department used the AGCT as a means of placing men into military jobs.

113. Rept, Subcommittee on Physical and Mental Standards (OSD) to Committee on Medical and Hospital Services of the Armed Forces, "Enlistment Standards," Jan 30, 1948, RG 330, Entry 66, Box 92, file 220, MMB, NA.

114. Kurt Lang, "Technology and Career Management in the Military Establishment," in Morris Janowitz, ed., *The New Military: Changing Patterns of Organization* (New York: W.W. Norton & Co., 1964), pp. 47–48.

115. AR 40–115, Aug 20, 1948, *Physical Standards and Physical Profile for Enlisted Men, and Introduction*, pp. 4–11.

116. *Airman's Guide*, 2d ed., pp. 101–102; Memo, MPPSD/DMP to USAF/PD, Jun 21, 1948, Subj: False Recruiting Promises and Technical Training, RG 18, 341, Box 3043, MMB, NA.

117. Memo, AC/AS–1 (Anderson) to WDGS, D/P&A, Dec 16, 1946, Subj: Independent Air Force Recruiting Program, author's personal files; Ltr, CG, Bolling Field (Hovey), to CS, USAF (Spaatz), Jan 14, 1948, Subj: Recruiting Irregularities, RG 18, 341, Box 3043, MMB, NA.

118. The Volunteer Act of 1947 established the legislative basis for Regular Army enlistment after the expiration of the act of 1945. To stimulate enlistments, the 1947 act shortened the promotion time to private first class and accepted enlistments for three, four, five, and six years. *An Act to Stimulate Volunteer Enlistments in the Regular Military Establishment of the United States*, P.L. 128, 61 Stat. 191 (Jun 28, 1947). Important impli-

cations of this act on the Air Force are discussed in Peterson, "An Investigation of the United States Army and United States Air Force Recruiting Organization and Program," pp. 52–53.

119. Even by 1955, 73.2 percent of all airmen were in their first enlistment. *USAF Statistical Digest: Fiscal Year 1955*, p. 341.

120. Memo, Asst SecAF H. Lee White for SecAF Zuckert, Aug, 1965, Subj: Manpower Background, author's personal files.

121. U.S. Air Force, *Your Son's Air Force Life*, p. 3.

122. Ibid.

123. Specifically, California, New York, Ohio, Pennsylvania, and Texas.

124. Carl Spaatz, diary entry for Feb 11, 1946, Subj: Subjects Discussed with Gen Eisenhower, Spaatz Collection, Daily Diary, Box 46, LC.

125. From 1945 onward, the Air Force used some form of preselection test to screen out undesirable enlistees. Recruiters used the AGCT, and later the AFQT, extensively for this purpose. Memo, CG, AAF (Spaatz), to CS, Army (Eisenhower), Mar 21, 1946, Subj: Present Status of Air Force Recruiting, author's personal files; Memo, CG, AAF (Spaatz), to WDGS, D/P&A, Mar 28, 1947, Subj: AAF Recommendations to WDGS, RG 18, 341, Box 2650, MMB, NA. See also Robert H. Jones, "An Analysis of Pre-Selection Tests Used in U.S. Air Force Airman Procurement" (thesis, Air Command and Staff College, Air University, 1966), pp. 16–23.

126. Eitelberg et al., *Screening for Service*, p. 20.

127. A good chronology of the military's induction and enlistment testing standards for male recruits is found in Eitelberg et al., *Screening for Service*, pp. 137–152.

128. Wool, pp. 66–67. Besides Wool's excellent analysis of mental aptitude tests, see Eitelberg et al., *Screening for Service*, pp. 14–17, 39–42; Eitelberg, *Manpower for Military Occupations*, chap. 2; Hayes, *Evolution of Armed Forces Enlisted Personnel Management Policies*, pp. 81–87; and J.E. Uhlaner and D.J. Bolanovich, *Development of the Armed Forces Qualification Test and Predecessor Army Screening Tests, 1946–1950*, PRS Report 976 (Washington, D.C.: Personnel Research Section, Department of the Army, 1952).

129. For a well-researched article on Korea and recruiting, see Larry Benson's "The USAF's Korean War Recruiting Rush . . . and the Great Tent City at Lackland Air Force Base," *Aerospace Historian*, summer 1978, pp. 61–73.

130. U.S. Congress, Senate, Preparedness Subcommittee on Armed Services, *Interim Report on Lackland Air Force Base* [Investigation of the Preparedness Program, Fifth Report under the authority of S Res 18], 82d Cong, 1st Sess, Dec 9, 1951, p. 6.

131. Memo, for SecAF (Zuckert), Aug 1965, Subj: Manpower Background, author's personal files.

132. Ibid.

133. Memo, SecDef to all Service Secys and the JCS, Apr 2, 1951, Subj: Qualitative Distribution of Military Manpower, RG 330, 66, Box 314, MMB, NA; DOD Directive No. 1145.1, Jun 23, 1952, Subj: Qualitative Distribution of Military Manpower—Modification, RG 330, 66, Box 314, MMB, NA.

134. Rept, "Minimum Mental Standards for Personnel in the Armed Services," Dec 30, 1953, RG 330, Entry 66, Box 386, MMB, NA. The issue of Category IV personnel is discussed in Chapter 4.

135. The Air Force recognized its good fortune in obtaining such high levels of quality personnel. Stuart Symington, in *Semi-Annual Report of the Secretary of the Air Force, Jan 1–Jun 30, 1949* (Washington, D.C.: GPO, 1949), p. 277.

136. *USAF Statistical Digest: 1950*, pp. 57–58.

137. For a discussion of the differences between NCOs serving in the Regular Army and inductees, see Lee Kennett, *G.I.: The American Soldier in World War II* (New York: Charles Scribner's Sons, 1987), pp. 79–81.

138. *USAF Statistical Digest: 1951*, p. 473.

139. Ibid., p. 468.

140. Ibid., p. 339.

141. Memo, Harold Wool to Asst SecDef (John A. Hannah), Jan 21, 1954, Subj: Administrative Measures to Reduce Number and Improve Use of Mental IV's, RG 330, 66, Box 386, MMB, NA.

142. The best single-volume work on women in the Air Force during this period is Holm's *Women in the Military*, esp. chaps. 11–13.

143. Holm, p. 130.

144. *Semi-Annual Report of the Secretary of the Army, 1 Jan–30 Jun, 1952*, p. 121; Holm, pp. 148–151.

145. Holm, pp. 151–52; "Look to the Women," *Air Force Magazine*, Sep 1951, pp. 104–106. For a breakdown of enlisted WAF career fields, see Col E.J. Bradley, Jr, *Report on Distribution of WAF Airmen to Major Air Commands, FY 1954 and FY 1955*, DCS/P, Aug 1953, Holm File, WAF Fledgling, 1948–1965, Box 2, in Rita Gomez file, AFHSO (hereafter cited as Bradley Report).

146. *Semi-Annual Report of the Secretary of the Air Force, Jan 1–Jun 30, 1952*, p. 215.

147. The percentage of women in the Air Force is based on the following data found in the *USAF Statistical Digests* for 1949–1955:

Year	Percent
1949	1.1
1950	1.1
1951	1.0
1952	1.3
1954	1.2
1955	1.0

148. Holm, pp. 153–155, 179–180. A double standard applied to women; they had to be older, smarter, and more educated than male enlistees, and they could have no dependents.

149. Holm, p. 160; "Look to the Women," p. 106. The Navy did likewise. *Semi-Annual Report of the Secretary of the Navy, 1 Jan–30 Jun, 1953*, p. 192.

150. Holm, p. 157.

151. Extract from Bradley Report, p. 2.

152. Bradley Report; *Semi-Annual Report of the Secretary of the Air Force, Jan 1–Jun 30, 1954*, pp. 231–232.

153. Bradley Report, p. 17.

154. Holm, pp. 172–174.

155. Alan Gropman, *The Air Force Integrates, 1945–1964* (Washington, D.C.: Office of Air Force History, 1978), pp. 73–74. See also Hayes, *Evolution of Armed Forces Enlisted Personnel Management Policies*, pp. 103–104.

156. By late 1949, of the Air Force's 25,000 blacks, only 7,000 remained in segregated squadrons. By the end of the year, the Air Force was attracting more blacks (more than 10 percent) than ever before. Nalty, *Strength for the Fight*, p. 249.

157. The committee believed that a score of 90 on the AGCT established a natural quota, as only 16.5 percent of the blacks and 62.5 percent of whites would be eligible to enlist. This standard was designed to improve the efficiency of the enlisted force without excluding trainable blacks. Memo, Charles Fahy to Sec[Army Gordon] Gray, Feb 9, 1950, Subj: Recapitulation of the Proposal of the President's Committee for the Abolition of the Racial Quota, in Morris J. MacGregor, Jr., and Bernard C. Nalty, eds, *Blacks in the United States Armed Forces: Basic Documents*, vol. 11 (Wilmington, Del.: Scholarly Resources, 1977), item 32.

158. MacGregor, *Integration of the Armed Forces*, pp. 394–396, 412. For Air Force statistics, see the *USAF Statistical Digests* for 1949–1955. For comparative statistics, see

MacGregor and Nalty, eds, *Blacks in the United States Armed Forces: Basic Documents*, vol. 13, p. 32.

159. MacGregor, *Integration of the Armed Forces*, pp. 406–407.

160. *Freedom to Serve*, pp. 6, 33–44, 75–76. For a discussion of the ways wing and squadron commanders attempted to dispel prejudice, see MacGregor, *Integration of the Armed Forces*, chap. 16, and Gropman, p. 142.

161. *Reasons for Enlistment: New Airmen Enlisting in Feb 1949*, Report No. 98–325 (Washington, D.C.: Office of the Secretary of Defense, 1949), p. 2, copy on microfilm, AFHSO.

162.Ibid., pp. 2–3.

163. Ibid., pp. 4–9. See also *USAF Statistical Digest: Fiscal Year 1955*, p. 353.

164. Fifty-one percent of draft-induced men and 35 percent of the volunteers were in the draft-eligible age group of 19 through 25 years old. Fifty-five percent of the draft-induced enlistees were high school graduates versus 41 percent among the volunteers.

165. *Reasons for Enlistment*, p. 5.

166. Ibid., p. 11.

Chapter 4

1. Hist, Technical Training Air Force, Jan 1–Jun 30, 1955, microfilm, AFHSO, pp. 9–10. Sampson and Parks AFBs were former naval training stations, while the Technical Training Command was headquartered at Keesler AFB, Gulfport, Mississippi. During the Korean war, Sheppard AFB in Wichita Falls, Texas, served as a fourth basic training facility from July 1950 through the end of 1951 before it closed. Both Sampson and Parks closed as basic military training centers in 1956, leaving only Lackland AFB as "The Gateway" into the Air Force.

2. Ibid., pp. 17–18. The Training Research Center was originally established by the Air Force in 1948 to create new classification tests for DOD. By 1955, the influence of this group of manpower engineers spread to all aspects of recruit selection, classification, and training.

3. Ibid., p. 18.

4. Memo, DCS/PPT (Stalder) to Comdr, ATC, Aug 1, 1955, Subj: Integrated Training Philosophy, RG 341, Entry 155, file Tng–3, Box 711, MMB, NA.

5. *Basic Military Training in the AAF, 1939–1944* (Washington, D.C.: AAF Historical Office, 1953), pp. 146–149; Hist, Air Training Command, Jul 1–Dec 31, 1952, microfilm, AFHSO.

6. Memo, CG, ATC (Harper), to USAF, CS (Vandenberg), Mar 22, 1952, Subj: Revisions of Basic Military Training Courses 00010 and 00011, RG 341, Entry 155, file 352.11, Box 675, MMB, NA.

7. The only extensive historical study of Air Force basic training that exists is "Basic Military Training Since World War II," a 1963 document available on microfilm at AFHSO. It documents many of the developments in basic training organization and curriculum, but it offers little interpretation.

8. Hist, 3700th Military Indoctrination Wing, Lackland AFB, Jul–Dec 1952, microfilm, AFHSO, pp. 5–7.

9. Ibid., pp. 6–7; "Basic Military Training Since World War II," pp. 6–7.

10. "SCARWAF Transfer Remains under Study," *AFT*, Jun 27, 1953, p. 12; "SCAR-WAF Ordered Back to Army," *AFT*, Dec 10, 1955, p. 27.

11. "Basic Military Training Since World War II," pp. 7–10.

12. George F. Lemmer, *The Changing Character of Air Force Manpower, 1958–1959* (Washington, D.C.: USAF Historical Division, Apr 1961), pp. 1–3. By the mid-1960s, the Air Force, aided by computerization, developed a centralized system that tracked courses,

prevented training facilities from becoming overburdened or underused, and charted the progress of airmen indicating who needed what training and when.

With regard to lead times, a nine-month period separated an airman's entry into training and his attainment of a semiskilled rating in his career field. Taking this nine-month lead time into consideration, planners estimated that 157,000 airmen needed training in fiscal year 1954 for the Air Force to obtain the necessary semiskilled personnel to replace those leaving the service during the last three months of 1954 and the first nine months of 1955. Staff Summary, DOT (Kellogg) to DCS/P, Jul 17, 1953, Subj: Selective Recruiting of Air Force Personnel, RG 341, Entry 155, file 341, Box 694, MMB, NA. For other factors bearing on training lead times, see Memo, Chief, Technical Training Division (Harris), to AF/PTR (Dany), Oct 3, 1951, Subj: Training Lead Time, RG 341, Entry 155, file 300.6, Box 642, MMB, NA.

13. While integration was on the Air Force's agenda before Truman issued the integration order, this directive along with the works of the Gillem and Fahy Boards expedited the process. Lieutenant General Idwal H. Edwards, as early as the spring of 1948, believed that segregation must end because it wasted manpower and bred inefficiency. Many qualified blacks were not placed in critical specialties because of segregation. Gropman, pp. 86-87.

14. Hist, 3700th Air Force Indoctrination Group, 1949, microfilm, AFHSO, pp. 2–3.

15. Hist, 3700th Military Training Wing, Apr–Jun 1952, microfilm, AFHSO, app. A; Memo, CG, ATC (Harper), to USAF, CS (Vandenberg), Mar 22, 1952, Subj: Revisions of Basic Military Training Courses 00010 and 00011, RG 341, Entry 155, file 352.11, Box 675, MMB, NA.

16. Memo, DCS/PMP (Baldwin) to Chief, Training Division (Riley), Aug 18, 1949, Subj: Citizenship Course for Air Force Trainees, RG 341, Entry 155, file 352.11, Box 612, MMB, NA; Hist, 3700th Military Indoctrination Wing, Lackland AFB, Apr–Jun 1952, microfilm, AFHSO, pp. 24–28; "Military Citizens: Program Will Build on Recruit Airmen," *AFT*, Jan 20, 1951, p. 5; "Rights vs. Reds: Lackland Citizenship Program Grows," *AFT*, Sep 15, 1951, p. 6.

17. See, for example, *Armed Forces Talk 287—American Democracy and the Individual* (Washington, D.C.: GPO, 1949), pp. 1–3.

18. Hist, 3700th Military Training Wing, Jan–Jun 1954, microfilm, AFHSO, pp. 27–30. In late 1953, the Air Force also added a significant overview of how homosexuality was viewed by society and the service. The lesson plan placed the responsibility upon airmen to report suspected homosexuals to their commanders and gave hints on how to identify homosexual traits.

19. Memo, OSD (Center) to All Service Secretaries, Aug 19, 1949, Subj: Citizenship Training in the Armed Services, RG 341, Entry 155, file 352.11, Box 612, MMB, NA; *Study of Basic Training in the Armed Services* (Washington, D.C.: Citizens Advisory Commission on Manpower Utilization in the Armed Services, Mar 19, 1953), tabs B–E, copy in RG 341, Entry 155, file 310.01, Box 685, MMB, NA. See also *Semi-Annual Report of the Secretary of the Navy, Jan 1–Jun 30, 1954*, pp. 188–189; *Semi-Annual Report of the Secretary of the Army, Jul 1–Dec 31, 1955*, pp. 96–98.

20. Due to decreasing enlistment standards by July 1951, the Air Force began to enlist 40 percent of their recruits from the Cat IV pool. The Navy conducted a similar program for marginal men. *Semi-Annual Report of the Secretary of the Navy, Jan 1–Jun 30, 1953*, p. 134.

21. Hist, 3700th Military Indoctrination Wing, Lackland AFB, Apr–Jun 1952, microfilm, AFHSO, pp. 18–30. The Air Force implemented the course on November 21, 1951.

22. "Air Force Basic Training Takes Stress off Close Order Drill and K.P.," *AFT*, Jan 24, 1948, p. 9.

23. Hist, 3700th Military Training Wing, July–Dec 1955, microfilm, AFHSO, pp. 79–80.

24. Ibid., pp. 42–43.

25. According to a 1952 survey, mathematics was a prerequisite for 120 technical courses spanning 30 career fields. The survey also indicated that 92.5 percent of all the courses required knowledge and skill in general math, 70.8 percent required algebra, 40.8 percent required geometry, and 27.5 percent required trigonometry. Memo, Comdr, ATC (Harper), to USAF, CS (Vandenberg), Mar 22, 1952, Subj: Revisions of Basic Military Training Courses 00010 and 00011, RG 341, Entry 155, file 352.11, Box 675, MMB NA. See also "Basic Training Curriculum, 1949," microfilm, AFHSO, pp. 1–3; Hist, 3700th Military Training Wing, Jan–Dec 1954, microfilm, AFHSO, pp. 28–29. As early as October 1952, HQ DOT suggested to place the mathematics program in the various technical schools' curricula. Memo, DOT (Harbold) to Comdr, ATC (Harper), Oct 13, 1952, Subj: Establishment of 65-Day Residence Period for Processing and Basic Training, RG 341, Entry 155, file 353, Box 677, MMB, NA.

26. "Basic Military Training Since World War II," p. 14.

27. To say that the AAF trained only technicians rather than soldiers ignores the aerial gunners, radiomen, and mechanics who flew as part of the air crew and who usually doubled as gunners. Training was determined by military necessity of specialties that the AAF needed to man its weapons systems and fight the war; it was not a simple desire to differentiate itself from the Army.

28. Hist, 3700th Military Training Wing, Jan–Jun 1956, microfilm, AFHSO, pp. 80–88; "Basic Military Training Since World War II," pp. 14–16.

29. *Course Description: Initial Basic Training* (San Antonio, Tex.: ATC, Jan 3, 1956), pp. 1–19.

30. Intvw, with CMSAF Thomas M. Barnes, Nov 11–12, 1980, AFHSO, p. 16.

31. Hist, 3700th Military Indoctrination Wing, 1949, microfilm, AFHSO.

32. Ibid., Jan–Jun 1953 and Jul–Dec 1953, microfilm, AFHSO, p. 91 and p. 5, respectively.

33. For the WAF basic training curriculum, see the 3700th Military Training Wing histories for Apr 1949, pp. 64–70, Apr–Jun 1952, app. B, and Jul–Dec 1954, doc. 1, all on microfilm in AFHSO.

34. Hist, 3700th Military Training Wing, Jul–Dec 1955, microfilm, AFHSO, pp. 94–95.

35. For an important article that discusses the social conservatism of military leaders and their approach toward gender and ethnic minorities in the ranks, see Bruce White, "The American Military and the Melting Pot in World War I," in J.L Granatstein and R.D. Cuff, eds., *War and Society in North America* (Toronto: Thomas Nelson & Sons, 1971), pp. 37–51.

36. Historical Data, 3700th Military Training Wing and Lackland AFB, Jan–Jun 1954, microfilm, AFHSO, p. 29.

37. Hist, 3700th Military Training Wing and Lackland AFB, Jan–Jun 1955, microfilm, AFHSO, p. 48.

38. See note 36 above.

39. Ibid., doc. C–1.

40. Hist, 3700th Military Training Wing and Lackland AFB, Jan–Jun 1955, microfilm, AFHSO, pp. 44–45.

41. *Airman's Guide*, 2d ed., p. 60.

42. Hist, 3700th Military Training Wing, Lackland AFB, Jan–Jun 1955, microfilm, AFHSO, pp. 101–104. A good description of the process also appears in Landis, pp. 32–33. See also "Test Helps USAF Find Ideal Airman," *AFT*, Nov 5, 1949, pp. 1, 5.

43. As a result of budgetary considerations, a lack of overseas housing, the need for new overseas air fields, and training quotas, ATC and HQ USAF fixed the ideal ratio of enlisted personnel in the zone of the interior to those assigned overseas at 3:1; that is, three airmen were in training or were stationed in the United States for every one serving overseas. In 1953 and 1954, the actual ratio was 13:5. Memo, DCS/PP (Lee) to DCS/P (Wetzel), Jun 12, 1953, Subj: Lack of Stability Afforded U.S. Air Force Personnel, RG

341, Entry 129, Box 164, MMB, NA. The 1955 ratio was 7:3. *USAF Statistical Digest: Fiscal Year 1955*, pp. 265–266.

44. Alfred Goldberg, ed., *History of the United States Air Force, 1907–1957* (Princeton, N.J.: Van Nostrand, 1957); Goldberg, "The Men," pp. 291–296; Weigley, *American Way of War*, pp. 372–378, 403.

45. Kenneth Schaffel, *The Emerging Shield: The Air Force and the Evolution of Continental Air Defense, 1945–1960* (Washington, D.C.: Office of Air Force History, 1991), pp. 198–199. The SAGE system, designed to gather data from a radar network (DEW Line) and process impending attack information to defense weapons, became obsolete almost immediately with the advent of transistor technology that replaced the existing vacuum tubes.

46. Michael S. Sherry, *The Rise of American Air Power: The Creation of Armageddon* (New Haven, Conn.: Yale University Press, 1987), pp. 53–57.

47. Wool, pp. 29–30.

48. Arthur Covelesky, EEQ, AFHSO.

49. In 1953, the Air Force determined from a study of manning documents that more than 95 percent of all jobs required some degree of skill. Also projected was that 90 percent of all entering airmen in 1954/1955 would be trained in hard-core, or the most technically skilled, areas. Memo, D/T (Harbold) to DCS/P (Wetzel), Apr 14, 1953, Subj: USAF Technical Training, RG 341, Entry 155, file 35–Tech Training, Box 687, MMB, NA.

50. "Career Gunner, Problem Child of World War II, among MOS Junked," *AFT*, Jul 31, 1948, p. 2.

51. Airmen still served on aircraft such as the B–52, but few had direct combat roles.

52. Ltr, ATC, CG (Cannon), to AAF, CG (Spaatz), Mar 30, 1948, Subj: Need for New Classification System, RG 341, Entry 159, file C–9, Box 788, MMB, NA.

53. Rept, "Strength Reporting and Machine Tabulation: Conference with IBM Representative," Oct 30, 1946, RG 341, Entry 159, file C–9, Box 789, MMB, NA; Staff Summary, DOT (McNaughton) to DCS/PA, Sep 16, 1949, Subj: Development of a Technical Tool for Expressing Numerical Requirements for NME Personnel in "Critical" Occupations, RG 341, Entry 155, file 300.6, Box 608, MMB, NA; Memo, Chief, Personnel Records, AAG (Veillard), to DCS/P (Micka), Sep 16, 1953, Subj: Airman Military Record and Personnel Records System, RG 341, Entry 129, file 310.01, Box 148, MMB, NA.

54. Minutes, First Air Board Meeting, Apr 16, 1946, RG 340, Box 13, MMB, NA, pp. 37–38.

55. AFL 35–360, Jun 8, 1950, "Airman Career Program," microfilm, AFHSO, p. 1; *Summary of Values Accruing to the Air Force and to the Individual from the Development and Implementation of the Airman Career Program*, booklet 3 (Washington, D.C.: HQ USAF, Career Development and Classification Division, Jan 1949), pp. 2–5; Memo, DCS/P (Nugent) to DCS/P (Edwards), Mar 14, 1951, Subj: Building a Realistic Training "Pipeline," RG 341, Entry 118, file 388, Box 13, MMB, NA.

56. "Air Force Career Plan," *AFT*, Feb 14, 1948, p. 4.

57. In 1947, a joint Army-Navy Personnel Board was established to coordinate personnel policy common to the various services. Renamed the "Armed Services Personnel Board" in September 1947 and given statutory authority by Congress in 1950, the various committees appointed by this board researched, coordinated, and established standardized personnel policy. In May 1949, the OSD and the JCS hoped that a common, uniform personnel management system for all the services could be created. The Air Force dissented on the basis that a common structure failed to meets its specific needs. Nevertheless, the Military Occupational Classification Project continued through 1952 and resulted in the creation of several common career fields and job progressions. For the establishment of the Personnel Board, see Memo, OSD (Stohl) to DCS/P(Nugent), May 20, 1948, Subj: Establishment of Personnel Board, RG 341, Entry 118, file 334, Box 6, MMB, NA; Memo, Joint Army-Navy Board to Secys All Services, Sep 25, 1947, Subj:

Changes in the Composition and Procedure of the Joint Army-Navy Personnel Board to Conform with the Organization of the National Military Establishment, RG 341, Entry 118, file 334, Box 1, MMB, NA; Charter, "Organization and Procedures of the Military Personnel Policy Committee," Aug 3, 1949, RG 341, Entry 118, file 334, Box 6, MMB, NA; and Memo, DCS/P (Nugent) to Asst SecAF for Mgmt, Sep 22, 1950, Subj: Legislation Granting Statutory Authority for a Personnel Board in the Department of Defense, RG 341, Entry 129, file 334.2, Box 167, MMB, NA.

Information on the Military Occupation Classification Project is reported in "Air Force Comments on Military Occupational Classification Project Basic Guidelines, Programs, and Schedules" dated Jun 6, 1950, RG 341, Entry 129, file 334.17, Box 166, MMB, NA. See also *Semi-Annual Report of the Secretary of Defense, Jan–Jun 1950* (Washington, D.C.: DOD, 1950), p. 26. In 1951, the project's objective expanded to include the establishment of a qualitative manpower allocation scheme. Memo, SecArmy (Pace) to SecDef, Jan 19, 1951, Subj: Military Occupational Classification Project Instruments, RG 341, Entry 118, file 381, Box 13, MMB, NA. See also Intvw, with J. Thomas Schneider, Jan 10, 1973 [Schneider was Chairman of the Personnel Policy Board (1950–1951)], Harry S. Truman Library, pp. 66–72.

58. "EM 'Career Plan' for Air Due by 1949," *AFT*, Feb 7, 1948, p. 1. Personnel planners were also working on a centralized Officer Career Program based on the same premises as the enlisted program. Memo, DCS/PMP (Learnard) to DCS/PMP (West), Nov 10, 1949, Subj: Implementation of Officer Career Program, RG 341, Entry 141, file 210, Box 382, MMB, NA.

59. Mimeogr, War Dept, "Transcription of Personnel Conference, Jun 24–26, 1947," RG 330, Box 142, MMB, NA, p. 74.

60. *Summary of Values Accruing*, pp. 2–4; "Airman Career Plan Outlined by USAF, Titles, Jobs, Grades," *AFT*, Apr 24, 1948, pp. 1, 11.

A good work describing the development of the Airman Career Plan and contrasting it with similar existing industrial and federal government personnel systems is Milton Fryer, Jr., "An Analysis of the Airman Career Program in the United States Air Force" (thesis, University of Texas, 1950), p. 166. He compares personnel programs at General Motors, Dupont, General Foods, and the Forest Service with the Air Force's and concludes that the "career program follows and compares favorably in the public services and business." A more recent work on internal promotion plans demonstrates that few firms of the era actually used job ladders and merit systems. Thus, centralizing its personnel department and developing such a massive career program placed the military ahead of its industrial contemporaries. Jacoby, *Employing Bureaucracy*, pp. 154–55, 157, 250.

61. Brig Gen J.J. O'Hare, "Planning the Enlisted Career Program," *Army Information Digest*, Nov 1948, pp. 42–44. Air Force Brig. Gen. Dean Strother, Chief of the Air Force's Military Division, equally supported these basic criteria. See "EM 'Career Plan' for Air Due by 1949," p. 1.

62. AFL 35–360, Jun 8, 1949, "Airman Career Plan," microfilm, AFHSO, pp. 1–3; AFL 35–360, Aug 30, 1950, "Implementation of Airman Career Program," microfilm, AFHSO. In July 1948, the Air Force divorced itself from the joint Army–Air Force career program project in order to meet its own specific classification needs. *Report of the Chief of Staff, USAF, Fiscal Year 1948* (Washington, D.C.: GPO, 1948), p. 276.

63. A career field is a grouping of related jobs within a functional area involving similar skills and knowledge. Ideally someone trained in one or two basic jobs would later be qualified to supervise all jobs within the career field. For a more technical explanation of the Airman Career Program, see Lt Col Harry F. Cruver "Presentation of Career Program before the Air Force Personnel Conference, Orlando, Fla., Dec 2, 1948," RG 341, Entry 159, file C–3, Box 787, MMB, NA, pp. 2–15. See also *The Development of the United States Air Force Airman Career Program*, booklet 1 (Washington, D.C.: HQ USAF, Career Development and Classification Division, Jan 1949), copy in RG 341, Entry 159, file B–2, Box 787, MMB, NA, p. 3. Perhaps the most coherent discussion of

the evolution of the career system appears in *Airman's Guide*, 2d ed., pp. 36–61.

64. Prior to the Airman Career Program, airmen could only move up to master sergeant in 14.7 percent of the 312 Air Force's military occupational specialties (MOSs); most MOSs (58.6 percent) were limited to staff sergeant. For a list of these, see *The Airman's Guide*, 1st ed (Harrisburg, Pa.: Military Service Publishing Co., 1949), pp. 7–13. For an airman to be promoted, three factors came into play. First, the unit had to have a vacancy in the grade. Second, the airman's MOS must authorize the grade; that is, if the MOS only authorized a grade 3, then no promotion was made to grade 2 (16.3 percent of Air Force MOSs). Finally, the squadron commander had to deem the airman fully qualified for promotion.

65. AFL 35–360, Jun 8, 1950, "Airman Career Plan," microfilm, AFHSO, p. 2; Memo, DCS/P, CDD (Campbell), to DCS/P (Parks), Jul 20, 1951, Subj: Relation of Skill Classification to Airman Promotions, RG 341, Entry 129, file 220.02, Box 134, MMB, NA.

66. *Development of the United States Air Force Airman Career Program*, p. 4; "Air Force Career Plan Details Unveiled," *AFT*, Jun 4, 1949, pp. 1, 24; Ltr, Chief, CDD (Miller), to Chief, Training Requirements Branch, Jun 30, 1953, Subj: Ultimate Criterion for Determining an Airman's Qualification for Promotion, RG 341, Entry 129, file 220.01, Box 134, MMB, NA.

67. Memo, AC/AS–1 (Anderson) to Chief, Air Staff (McKee), May 1, 1946, Subj: Specialist Ratings—Plan for Grade Structure Postwar Army Air Forces, RG 18, AAG, file 220.2, Box 1217, MMB, NA; Rept, AC/AS–1 for CG (Spaatz), "Reference Data on Current Personnel Status, Policies, and Future Planning of the Army Air Forces," Jun 19, 1946, Spaatz Collection, Chief of Staff file, Box 262, LC; Memo, Deputy, Chief, Evaluation Division, Academic Staff (Legg), to Deputy, CG Education, Sep 24, 1947, Subj: Career Guidance and Management Plans for Warrant Officers and Enlisted Personnel, microfilm, AFHSO.

68. The evolution of the Army's rank structure is explored in William K. Emerson, *Chevrons: Illustrated History and Catalog of U.S. Army Insignia* (Washington, D.C.: Smithsonian Institution Press, 1983), pp. 189–197.

69. AFL 35–390, Jan 18, 1949, "Airman Aptitude Classification and Assignment Program," microfilm, AFHSO, pp. 1–8.

70. Francis Hall and Clark Nelson, "A Historical Perspective of the United States Air Force Enlisted Personnel Promotion Policy" (thesis, Air Force School of Technology, 1980), p. 5.

71. Memo, DCS/PMP (Campbell) to D/Training, Jul 18, 1949, Subj: Award of Military Occupational Specialties to Airmen, RG 341, Entry 155, file 220.01, Box 583, MMB, NA; *Airman's Guide*, 2d ed., p. 84.

72. AFR 35–392, Sep 8, 1950, *Warrant Officer and Airman Classification Procedures*, p. 8; Hall and Nelson, "Historical Perspective of the United States Air Force Enlisted Personnel Promotion Policy," p. 6; *The Airman's Guide*, 7th ed. (Harrisburg, Pa.: Military Service Publishing Co., 1955), pp. 84–86.

73. Memo, DCS/P (Nugent) to DCS/P–4 (Lockard), May 23, 1951, Subj: Airman Proficiency Test Construction Program, RG 341, Entry 118, file 381, Box 13, MMB, NA. See also *United States Air Force Military Job Knowledge Tests: Their Significance, Purpose, and Use in the Classification and Assignment Program of the Air Force* (Washington, D.C.: Career Development and Classification Division, Sep 1950), pp. 1–6; *The Air Force Short Military Job Knowledge Test: A Discussion of the Development and Use of Short Achievement Tests Designed for the Rapid Measurement of the Military Job Knowledge of Former Service Airmen* (Washington, D.C.: HQ USAF, Deputy Chief of Staff, Personnel, Aug 1950), RG 341, Entry 129, file 220.01, Box 133, MMB, NA, pp. 1–6; "Test-Drafting to Begin for 3 Major Fields," *AFT*, Dec 22, 1951, p. 3; *Semi-Annual Report of the Secretary of the Air Force, Jan 1–Jun 30 1951*, p. 212.

74. The Air Force adopted a merit rating system known as the Airman Performance Report in 1954. Here airmen, like their counterparts in the other branches, were rated on

their technical abilities and military deportment. AFR 39–62, May 21, 1954, *Enlisted Personnel—Airman Performance Report*; Ralph Barbour "The Airman Performance Report: A Case Study of a Merit Rating Program in the United States Air Force" (thesis, Syracuse University, 1960), pp. 6–8. For a good explanation of the Army's promotion system, see "Promotions Usher in Army's Career Plan," *AFT*, Jul 17, 1948, p. 12.

75. *Airman's Guide*, 7th ed., p. 69.

76. Maj Robert C. Richards, "History of USAF Airman Promotions, 1947–1976" (thesis, ACSC, May 1977), p. 17.

77. General Curtis E. LeMay, Commanding General, Strategic Air Command (1948–1957), introduced the concept of spot promotions as an incentive for skill proficiency among aircrew members by promoting early when their skills and ability justified advancement. Ltr, DCS/P (Parks) to CG, SAC (LeMay), Feb 27, 1951, Subj: Spot Promotions, RG 341, Entry 129, file 220.02, Box 134, MMB, NA; Ltr, CG, SAC (LeMay), to DCS/P (Nugent), May 14, 1951, Subj: Spot Promotion for Lead Air Crew Members, RG 341, Entry 129, file 220.02, Box 134, MMB, NA; Memo, DCS/O (Springer) to DCS/P (Campbell), n.d., Subj: Enlisted Air Crew Promotions for SAC, RG 341, Entry 129, file 220.02, Box 134, MMB, NA; Ltr, DCS/P (Wetzel) to CG, SAC (LeMay), Sep 6, 1951, Subj: SAC "Special" Promotion Authority, Airmen Member of Select and Alternate Select Crews, RG 341, entry 129, file 220.02, Box 134, MMB, NA. Two works that further describe the rationale behind spot promotions are Borowski's *Hollow Threat*, p. 179, and *Airman's Guide*, 7th ed., p. 69.

78. *Airman's Guide*, 7th ed., p. 70; Richards, "History of USAF Airman Promotions," pp. 19–20.

79. Ltr, AC/AS–1 (Johnson) to CG, AAF (Spaatz), Nov 26, 1946, Subj: Promotion of First Three Grade Enlisted Men, RG18, AAG, file 220.2, Box 1217, MMB, NA; Brfg, Mar 30, 1950, Subj: Airman Promotion by Quota, RG 341, Entry 142, file Conferences and Briefings, Box 404, MMB, NA; Ltr, DCS/PMP (Learnard) to DCS/P (Martin), Apr 6, 1950, Subj: Ground Rules for Implementation of Quota System, RG 341, Entry 141, file 220.2, Box 389, MMB, NA; Memo, DCS/PP (Huyett) to AF/CHO (Grandstaff), Jun 29, 1989, Subj: Chronology of Selected Enlisted Policies—Promotion, author's personal files.

80. AFR 39–29, 1954, *Promotion of Airmen* imposed additional controls.

81. Richards, "History of USAF Airman Promotions," p. 47. See also Maj Thomas Kustelski, "Our Goal: Promote the Best with the Best System," *Air University Review*, Sep–Oct 1970, pp. 6–13; MSgt Loren Leonberger, "A New Look at WAPS," *Airman*, Jun 1971, pp. 33–35.

82. For a more thorough discussion of the Air Force's warrant officer program, see Mark R. Grandstaff, "Neither Fish nor Fowl: The Demise of the USAF's Warrant Officer Program," *Air Power History*, vol. 42 (spring 1995), pp. 40–51. See also *DOD Report on the Warrant Officer Management Act* (Washington, D.C.: DOD, Nov 30, 1989).

83. Ltr, ATC (Myers) to DCS/P (O'Donnell), Nov 19, 1955, Subj: Warrant Officer Utilization, in *Supporting Documents, Staff History, Directorate of Personnel Planning, Jul–Dec 1955*, vol. 5, tab P; Staff Study, Warrant Officer Requirements ad Hoc Committee, "Warrant Officer Requirements," Jun 23, 1959, in *History of the Directorate of Personnel Planning, Jan–Jun 1959*, tab E, pp. 1–2.

84. Ltr, DCS/P (Stone) to DCS/PTT (Micka), Jul 22, 1955, Subj: Career Progression for Master Sergeants, in *Supporting Documents, Staff History, Directorate of Personnel Planning, Jul–Dec 1955*, vol. 5, tab L.

85. Janet R. Bednarek, ed., *The Enlisted Experience: A Conversation with the Chief Master Sergeants of the Air Force* (Washington, D.C.: Air Force History and Museums Program, 1995), p.78.

86. Bednarek, p. 77.

87. Memo, Deputy Chief, Evaluation Division, Academic Staff (Legg), to Air University DCG/E (Lankston), Sep 24, 1947, Subj: Air University Project 4732, "Career

Guidance and Management Plans for Warrant Officers and Enlisted Personnel," author's personal files.

88. Bednarek, p. 78.

89. Memo, AFOMO (Gent) to DCS/P (O'Donnell), Nov 26, 1958, Subj: Warrant Officer Requirements, in *Supporting Documents, Staff History, Directorate of Personnel Planning, Jul–Dec 1958*; Staff Study, Warrant Officer Requirements ad Hoc Committee, "Warrant Officer Requirements," Jun 23, 1959, in *History of the Directorate of Personnel Planning, Jan–Jun 1959*, tab E, pp. 1–2; *History of the Directorate of Personnel Planning, Jan–Jun 1959*, p. 129.

90. Wool, p. 33.

91. Memo, DCS/PT to DCS/P, Dec 27, 1956, Subj: Utilization of Personnel with Minimal Mental Qualifications, RG 341, Entry 129, file 220.01, Box 133, MMB, NA.

92. Memo, DCS/PTR (McCorkle) to DOT, Feb 12, 1953, Subj: Background of Project 1000, RG 341, Entry 155, file 353.01, Box 696, MMB, NA.

93. Hist, 3700th Military Training Wing, Jul–Dec 1953, microfilm, AFHSO, pp. 35–36; Memo, DCS/PTR (McCorkle) to DOT, Feb 12, 1953, Subj: Background of Project 1000, RG 341, Entry 155, file 353.01, Box 696, MMB, NA.

94. Hist, 3700th Military Training Wing, Jul–Dec 1953, microfilm, AFHSO, pp. 38–39.

95. Memo, TTAF, CS (Rentz), to ATC, DCS/O, Nov 3, 1953, Subj: Basic Training for Slow Learners, RG 341, Entry 155, file Tng–3, Box 701, MMB, NA.

96. Ibid.; "AF Authorizes RIF [Reduction in Force] of Marginal Airmen," *AFT*, Nov 21, 1953, pp. 1, 30. The Air Force further reduced marginal personnel in 1956. See Eli S. Flyer, *Factors Relating to Discharge for Unsuitability among 1956 Airman Accessions to the Air Force*, Project 7719, Task 17155 (Lackland AFB, Tex.: Personnel Laboratory, Dec 1959).

97. Memo, DCS/P (O'Donnell) to USAF, CS (Twining), 1955, Subj: Quality of Airmen, RG 341, Entry 155, Box 709, MMB, NA.

98. Ibid.

99. Wool, pp. 68–69.

100. For a brief introduction to Project One Hundred Thousand and its place as a Great Society program, see Segal, *Recruiting for Uncle Sam*, pp. 91–92, and Moskos, *American Enlisted Man*, pp. 171–172.

101. Memo, DCS/PT (Harbold) to DCS/P (Wetzel), Apr 14, 1953, Subj: USAF Technical Training, RG 341, Entry 155, file Tech Training, Box 687, MMB, NA.

102. Under this system, the Air Staff set Air Force–wide standards and requirements while the commands gave input on specific needs and feedback on how general standards and requirements were working. The confluence of these inputs often drove technical school policy as ATC attempted to meet the needs of both the Air Staff and the commands.

103. The term *pipeline* meant projecting long-term manpower needs for each command and then relating those needs to recruiting quotas and to all the students already in the technical training system. Memo, Special Projects Group (Devos) to DCS/PMP, Nov 26, 1951, Subj: Delegating Allocation of the PCS Student Pipeline, Officers and Airmen, RG 341, Entry 141, file 320, Box 396, MMB, NA.

104. See Borowski, pp. 43–45.

105. Ltr, ATC, CG (Cannon), to AAF, CG (Spaatz), Mar 30, 1948, RG 341, Entry 159, file C–9, Box 788, MMB, NA.

106. This thinking is exemplified in Memo, DCS/PT (Disosway) to DCS/PMP (Campbell), May 23, 1949, Subj: Establishment of Basic Electronics Course, RG 341, Entry 159, file C–9, Box 788, MMB, NA; and Hist, Air Training Command, Jan 1–Dec 31, 1947, microfilm, AFHSO, p. 394.

107. *Air Force Technical Training* (Gulfport, Miss.: HQ Technical Training Air Force, May 1953), p. 16. This staff study appears in document 1 in Hist, Air Training Command, Jul–Dec 1953, microfilm, AFHSO.

108. Goldberg, ed., *History of the United States Air Force*, p. 172.
109. Hist, Air Training Command, Jul–Dec 1953, microfilm, AFHSO, p. 143. An indispensable summary of the debate over formal training versus OJT is found in "Brief History of ATRC [ATC], 1939–1953," Jul 1954, microfilm, AFHSO, pp. 30–32.
110. "Brief History of ATRC," pp. 29–30; Memo, DCS/PT (Harbold) to All Major Commands and Air National Guard, May 13, 1954, Subj: Channelized Training in Certain Airman Technical Courses, RG 341, Entry 155, file Tng–9, Box 704, MMB, NA.
111. Memo, DCS/PT (McCorkle) to DCS/O, 23 Oct 1952, Revision of Radio Maintenance Ground Equipment Course, RG 341, Entry 155, file 352.11, Box 675, MMB, NA; Hist, Air Training Command, FY 1951, microfilm, AFHSO, p. 484.
112. Hist, Air Training Command, Jul–Dec 1954, microfilm, AFHSO, pp. 284–285.
113. Ibid., p. 285.
114. Goldberg, ed., *History of the United States Air Force*, pp. 173–75. See also "ATRC Load Sky Rockets Reflects Air Force Expansion," *AFT*, Dec 23, 1950, pp. 1, 22; "Over 160,000 for New TechTAF," *AFT*, Jun 23, 1951, p. 3.
115. The 148 wings represented an objective. The maximum number achieved was 137 wings in 1957.
116. Goldberg, ed., *History of the United States Air Force*, p. 174; Memo, DCS/PP (Riva) to DCS/PT, Jul 23, 1951, Subj: Number and Types of Airman Technicians to Be Trained in Civilian Contract Schools, RG 341, Entry 155, file 319.1, Box 624, MMB, NA.
117. Memo, DOT (Rentz) to DCS/PT, Jun 28, 1951, Subj: U.S. Navy Quotas for Lithographic Pressmen, Photolithographers, RG 341, Entry 155, file 352.11, Box 646, MMB, NA; Memo, DOT (McCorkle) to DOT (Dany), Oct 6, 1952, RG 341, Entry 155, file 337, Box 661, MMB, NA; Memo, CS, G–3 (Jenkins) to USAF/COFS, Aug 20, 1951, Subj: Air Force Training Requirements for Fiscal Year 1952, RG 341, Entry 155, 353, Box 649, MMB, NA; *Semi-Annual Report of the Secretary of the Army, Jan 1–Jun 30 1954*, p. 91.
118. "The Human Element in Air Power: A Special Report," *Air Force Magazine*, Jul 1952, pp. 32–33.
119. Memo, DOT (Disosway) to DCS/D (Nelson), Aug 8, 1951, Subj: Weapons, Aircraft, and Training, RG 341, Entry 155, file 300.6, Box 642, MMB, NA.
120. Wayne Thompson, *Student Flow Management in Air Training Command, 1943–1979* (San Antonio, Tex.: ATC History and Research Division, Sep 1980) pp. 17–18.
121. Ltr, ATC (McNaughton) to USAF, CS (Vandenberg), Aug 30, 1952, Subj: Quarterly Report, RG 341, Entry 155, 319.1, Box 655, MMB, NA; Memo, DCS/O to DCS/P, Dec 8, 1952, Subj: Rpt of Operational Suitability of the F–86D, RG 341, Entry 155, file 319.1, Box 655, MMB, NA.
122. *Semi-Annual Report of the Secretary of the Air Force, Jan 1–Jun 30 1954*, p. 288.
123. Goldberg, ed., *History of the United States Air Force*, p. 174; "Five New Guided Missiles Course Opening," *AFT*, Aug 18, 1951, p. 24.
124. *DOD Fact Book, 1959* p. 57. The average Air Force reenlistment rate for fiscal years 1950–1955 was 41.2 percent.
125. U.S. Senate, *Investigation of the Preparedness Program: Thirty-Fourth Report of the Preparedness Committee of the Committee on Armed Services: Report on Six Air Force Training Centers* (Washington, D.C.: GPO, 1951), p. 8; Memo, DCS/PT (McCorkle) to DOT, Dec 22, 1951, Subj: 34th Rpt of the Preparedness Sub-Committee, RG 341, Entry 155, file 341, Box 631, MMB, NA.
126. "Human Element in Air Power," p. 37.
127. Memo, DCS/PTR (Disosway) to CG, ATC, May 25, 1949, Subj: Revision of Training to Implement the Airman Career Program, RG 341, Entry 159, file C–5, Box 788, MMB, NA. The Army did likewise. *Semi-Annual Report of the Secretary of the Army, Jul 1–Dec 31, 1955*, p. 97.
128. Hist, Air Training Command, Jan–Jun 1955, microfilm, AFHSO, p. 84.

129. Memo, DOT (McCorkle) to DOT (Dany), Oct 6, 1952, Subj: Summary of Technical Training, RG 341, Entry 155, file 337, Box 661, MMB, NA.

130. *Air Force Technical Training*, tab C; Hist, Air Training Command, Jan–Jun 1955, microfilm, AFHSO, p. 84. For a description of the factory and mobilized training courses necessary for one squadron to fly operational F–94s, see Rept, "Tentative Training Plan for the F–94 Airplane," Jul 8, 1949, RG 341, Entry 155, file 353, Box 615, MMB, NA. An important work on specialization and the field training program is *The World Is Our Classroom: A Brief History of the Air Force Field Training Program* (San Antonio, Tex.: ATC, 1989), esp. chaps. 1, 2.

131. As of January 1954, fifty-four advanced courses were available. DCS/PT (Kellogg) to Chief, ANG, Jan 20, 1954, Subj: Advanced and Lateral Airman Training, Fiscal Year 1955, RG 341, Entry 155, file Tng–9, Box 705, MMB, NA. Basic technical courses required a minimum of three years assured service while an advanced course usually required that an airman reenlist for four years. Memo, DCS/PT to CG, ATC, Nov 10, 1949, Subj: Consolidated Technical Training Directive, RG 341, Entry 155, file 353, Box 615, MMB, NA; Memo, DOT (Eason) to DCS/PP, Dec 11, 1953, Subj: Assured Service for Airmen Attending Technical Schools, RG 341, Entry 155, file 353.01, Box 696, MMB, NA.

132. Hist, Air Training Command, Jul–Dec 1953, microfilm, AFHSO, pp. 145–46; *The Airman's Guide*, 9th ed. (Harrisburg, Pa.: Stackpole Co., 1957), pp. 91–92. The Navy also introduced a similar retraining program. *Semi-Annual Report of the Secretary of the Navy, Jan 1–Jun 30 1954*, p. 143.

133. AFR 34–29, May 1950, *Operation Midnight Oil*; *Airman's Guide*, 7th ed., pp. 48–49; "Operation Bootstrap and Operation Midnight Oil," *AFT*, Jan 6, 1951, p. 6.

134. *Airman's Guide*, 7th ed., p. 51.

135. "Twenty-Five Thousand Air Force Personnel Study by Mail," *AFT*, Jan 17, 1948, p. 11.

136. AFR 34–52, May 1950, *Operation Bootstrap*; *Airman's Guide*, 7th ed., p. 49.

Chapter 5

1. On July 27, 1950, Congress authorized President Truman to extend for one year those military enlistments due to expire before July 9, 1951. Harry G. Summers, Jr., *The Korean War Almanac* (New York: Facts on File, 1990), pp. 188–191; Clay Blair, *The Forgotten War: America in Korea, 1950–1953* (New York: Doubleday, 1987), p. 122.

2. *Semi-Annual Report of the Secretary of Defense, 1 Jan–30 Jun 1953*, pp. 19–21; *Semi-Annual Report of the Secretary of Defense, 1 Jan–30 Jun 1954*, pp. 19–20.

3. U.S. Senate, *Treatment of Deserters from Military Service*, Rept No. 91–93, 91st Cong, 1st Sess (Washington, D.C.: GPO, 1969), pp. 1–7. For discussions of the various interpretations of desertion and legal precedents, see Col Lee S. Tillotson, *The Articles of War Annotated*, 2d rev. ed. (Harrisburg, Pa.: Military Service Publishing Co., 1943), pp. 122–137; Brig Gen James Snedeker, *Military Justice under the Uniform Code* (Boston: Little, Brown, 1953), pp. 560–583; William B. Aycock and Seymour W. Wurfel, *Military Law under the Uniform Code of Military Justice* (Chapel Hill: University of North Carolina Press, 1955), pp. 214–225; and Alfred Avins, *The Law of AWOL* (New York: Oceana Publications, 1957), pp. 39–41.

4. Address, Lt Gen Laurence Kuter, DCS/P, Air Staff Orientation Course No. 9, Dec 4, 1952, pp. 11–12, Kuter Collection, Air Force Academy (AFA).

5. Other Air Force reports estimated retention rates of at least 46 percent in fiscal year 1954 and 33 percent in fiscal year 1955. DCS/PP, *Reenlistment Rates for Air Force Personnel*, Reenlistment Study No. 2 (Washington, D.C.: HQ, USAF, Jun 23, 1952), p. 12, copy in author's personal files.

6. By 1954, 52 percent of all first-termers had been through technical training and had obtained a 3-level in skill proficiency. *USAF Statistical Digest: Fiscal Year 1956*, p. 371. Planners estimated that the average cost for an airman was $14,600 for the first four years when pay, clothing, and technical training were used as the basis for calculation. *Department of Defense Appropriations for 1955: Hearings before the Subcommittee of the Committee on Appropriations*, HR 8873, 83d Cong, 2d Sess (Washington, D.C.: GPO, 1954), p. 4.

7. *USAF Statistical Digest: Fiscal Year 1955*, pp. 351-352.

8. Ibid., p. 368.

9. *Semi-Annual Report of the Secretary of the Navy, 1 Jan–30 Jun 1954*, p. 182.

10. One of her lasting legacies was the formation of the Defense Advisory Committee on Women in the Armed Services (DACOWITS). This committee first met on September 18, 1951, and continues to serve in the 1990s. Forrest C. Pogue, *George C. Marshall: Statesman, 1945–1959* (New York: Viking, 1987), pp. 430–431; Summers, p. 302.

11. Intvw, Thomas A. Sturm and Hugh N. Ahmann with Laurence S. Kuter, Sep 30–Oct 3, 1974, K239.0512–810, AFHSO, p. 513.

12. MR, Kuter, Jul 14, 1952, Subj: Stature of Military Leadership, Kuter Collection, DCS/P file, AFA; Memo, DCS/P (Kuter) to AF Aide to the President (Landry), Jan 5, 1953, Subj: Morale and Military Careers, Kuter Collection, DCS/P file, AFA; MR, Kuter, Jan 5, 1953, Subj: Anna Rosenberg's (OSD) Response to Kuter's Letter, Kuter Collection, DCS/P file, AFA; Typescript, telecon between Gen Kuter and Gen Landry, Jan 6, 1953, Kuter Collection, DCS/P file, AFA.

13. Memo, DCS/P (Kuter) to Chmn, JCS (Bradley), Jan 14, 1953, Subj: Symptoms of Decaying Morale, Kuter Collection, DCS/P file, AFA.

14. The resignation was forwarded to Kuter by Lt. Gen. E. E. Partridge. Kuter then decided to use it as a means to obtain political assistance from the JCS in solving the Air Force's retention problems. Memo, HQ Air Research and Development Command (Partridge) to DCS/P (Kuter), Jan 9, 1953, Subj: Documentation of Officer Morale Problem, Kuter Collection, DCS/P file, AFA; MR, Kuter, Jan 14, 1953, Subj: Telephone Conversation between Gen Kuter and Gen Partridge—Resignation of Regular Colonel, Kuter Collection, DCS/P file, AFA. The actual resignation letter is Memo, Regular Air Force Colonel to DCS/P (Kuter), Jan 9, 1953, Subj: Reasons for Requesting Resignation, Kuter Collection, DCS/P file, AFA.

15. Memo, DCS/P (Kuter) to USAF, CS (Vandenberg), Feb 13, 1953, Subj: The Future of the Military Services as a Career That Will Attract Capable Personnel, Kuter Collection, DCS/P file, AFA; Memo, Chmn, JCS (Bradley), to USAF CS (Vandenberg), Feb 5, 1953, Subj: The Future of the Military Services as a Career That Will Attract Capable Personnel, Kuter Collection, DCS/P file, AFA.

16. DCS/PT (Kellogg) to DCS/P (Kuter), Mar 23, 1953, Subj: Allegations Regarding Waste in Air Force Practices, RG 341, Entry 129, 330.11, Box 164, MMB, NA.

17. Memo, Womble Committee (Womble) to Asst SecDef, Manpower and Personnel (Rosenberg), Oct 30, 1953, Subj: Final Rpt—ad Hoc Committee on the Future of Military Service as a Career That Will Attract and Retain Capable Career Personnel, Eisenhower Collection, Central Files–Official Files, 3-R 1954(1), Box 105, Eisenhower Library, Abilene, Kans.; Memo, SecDef (Wilson) to The President of the United States (Eisenhower), Mar 8, 1954, Subj: Support for the Womble Rpt, Eisenhower Collection, Central Files–Official Files, 3-R 1954(1), Box 105, Eisenhower Library.

18. MR, Asst SecDef (Hannah), Mar 23, 1953, Subj: Establishment of ad Hoc Committee to Study the Problem of Increasing the Attractiveness of the Military Career, and the First Meeting Thereof, Kuter Collection, DCS/P file, AFA; MR, DCS/PP (Kuter), Apr 6, 1953, Subj: Meeting of the ad Hoc Committee on Enhancement of the Military Services as a Career, Kuter Collection, DCS/P file, AFA.

19. Samuel P. Daykin, "A Study of Reasons for Airmen Choosing to Reenlist or Leave the Air Force" (diss, Washington University), 1956, p. 41.

20. Ibid.

21. Keith W. Olsen, *The G.I. Bill, the Veterans, and the Colleges* (Lexington: University of Kentucky Press, 1974), p. 44. For other G.I. benefits that often served as an inducement to leave the service, see Col M.A. Erana and Lt Col Arthur Symons, *Veteran's Rights and Benefits: The Complete Veteran's Guide* (Harrisburg, Pa.: Military Service Publishing Co., 1945).

22. Daykin, p. 34.

23. Ibid.

24. Ibid., p. 35.

25. Ibid., p. 37.

26. Ibid.

27. "Housing Lack Causes Cooped-up Children, Cold Meals, Job at Night for Husband," *AFT*, Nov 7, 1953, p. 13.

28. HQ USAF, *Reenlistment Intentions and Family Housing: Enlisted Air Force Personnel in Continental United States* (Washington, D.C.: Standards Evaluation Branch, Sep 27, 1948), pp. 4–5; "Greatest Threat to Expansion and Morale Is Housing Shortage for Officer and Enlisted in ZI and Overseas—Housing Is the No. 1 Problem in 1948," *AFT*, Feb 14, 1948, p. 8.

29. President's Commitee on Religion and Welfare in the Armed Forces, *Report of the National Conference on Community Responsibility to Our Peacetime Servicemen and Women, May 25–26, 1949*, p. 18.

30. Memo, DCS/PMP (Duncan) to AAG, Oct 28, 1949, Subj: Attitude Research Study No. 105, "Morale Attitudes of Enlisted Men, May–Jun 1949—V. Airmen's Reactions to the Housing Situation," RG 341, Entry 27, file 210.02, Box 2, MMB, NA.

31. An important article exploring this linkage is Gary L. Bowen, "Family Factors and Member Retention: A Key Relationship in the Work and Family Equation," in Gary L. Bowen and Dennis K. Orthner, eds., *The Organization Family: Work and Family Linkages in the U.S. Military* (Westport, Conn.: Praeger, 1989), pp. 37–57. See also Susan F. Stumpf, "Military Family Attitudes toward Housing, Benefits, and the Quality of Military Life," in Edna J. Hunter and D. Stephen Nice, eds., *Military Families: Adaption to Change* (New York: Praeger, 1978), pp. 3–12.

32. The act and later the housing units themselves were named after the legislation's advocate, Kenneth S. Wherry, a Republican senator from Nebraska. Born February 28, 1892, Wherry graduated from Harvard Law School in 1916, received a commission as a pilot in the U.S. Naval Flying Corps, and served during World War I. He became a U.S. senator in 1943 and served both as the Senate minority whip and the Republican whip during 1944–1958. In 1949, Wherry served as the Republican floor leader. He died in 1951 and was buried at Pawnee City, Nebraska.

33. "Wherry Units Construction Continues Steady but Slow," *AFT*, Feb 23, 1952, pp. 1, 18. See also U.S. Congress, Senate, *Mortgage Insurance for Military Housing, 1949*, Rept No. 410, 81st Cong, 1st Sess (Washington, D.C.: GPO, 1949), pp. 1–7; *Semi-Annual Report of the Secretary of the Army, 1 Jan–30 Jun 1953*, pp. 119–121. In July 1955 all Wherry building had stopped. "Wherry Chart Shows Wide Range in Rent," *AFT*, Jul 16, 1955, p. 33.

34. One of the most important articles describing Air Force housing conditions in the mid-1950s is Secretary of the Air Force Harold Talbott's speech before the Air Force Association's 1954 national convention. Harold E. Talbott, "Millions for Equipment, Nickels for the Men," *Air Force Magazine*, Jul 1954, pp. 29–30, 60–63.

35. Committee on Personnel Utilization and Training, *A Report to the Secretary of the Air Force* (Washington, D.C.: Dept of the Air Force, Jun 1951), p. viii, copy in RG 341, Entry 118, file 220, Box 10, MMB, NA.

36. Department of the Air Force, *Report of Prevailing Family Housing at USAF Major Installations* (Washington, D.C.: Dept of the Air Force, Mar 10, 1952), copy in RG 341, Entry 118, file 620, Box 13, MMB, NA; "Guide to Air Force Bases and Housing," *Air Force Magazine*, Sep 1952, pp. 42–48.

37. Memo, DCS/PMP (McCormick) to DCS/P (Nugent), Apr 2, 1951, Subj:

Accommodation of Airmen under the Current Build-up, RG 341, Entry 118, file 620, Box 11, MMB, NA.

38. *USAF Statistical Digest: Fiscal Year 1955*, p. 345.

39. Memo, DCS/PP (Stone) to SecAF (Quarles), May 9, 1956, Subj: Analysis of Article by Francis and Katherine Drake, May 1956—Housing, Twining Collection, Chief of Staff, Office File, Secretary of Air Force File (1), Box 90, LC. See also *Semi-Annual Report of the Secretary of Defense, 1 Jan–30 Jun 1954*, p. 44.

40. "Housing Lack Perils Power of SAC—LeMay," *AFT*, May 28, 1955, p. 2. LeMay complained about the apathy of congressional support for housing as early as 1951. Memo, SAC, CG (LeMay), to USAF, AFVCS (Twining), May 10, 1951, Subj: Inadequate Housing at Limestone AFB, Twining Collection, AFVCS, Office Reading Files, May 1951, Box 54, LC.

41. "Finding Family Housing Proves Difficult in Japan," *AFT*, Jul 23, 1955, p. 16.

42. Memo, ACS, J1, FEAF (Christenberry), to ACS, G1 (Young), Nov 23, 1953, Subj: Morale in FEAF, RG 341, Entry 129, file FEAF, Box 165, MMB, NA.

43. "Airmen in Japan Construct Own Trailers for Housing," *AFT*, Feb 21, 1953, p. 18.

44. "Dependents Given Latest Dope on Overseas Living Conditions," *AFT*, May 3, 1952, p. 2.

45. Daykin, p. 40.

46. Ibid., p. 41.

47. For a discussion of the problems with the open-bay barracks and mess halls, see MSgt Paul Winfield, "Cause of the Pause," *Air Force Magazine*, Jan 1954, pp. 28–31.

48. SAC was the first to experiment with the dormitory design. "Offutt Airman Occupy 2d SAC-Type Barracks," *AFT*, Jun 14, 1952, p. 16; "New Barracks Reflect Today's AF," *AFT*, Mar 27, 1954, p. 7.

49. John G. Norris. "SAC Trained Technicians: SAC Achilles Heel," *Air Force Magazine*, Apr 1956, p. 48.

50. David W. Menard, EEQ, AFHSO.

51. For a detailed description of SAC's mission and a typical training day, see "Planes, Plans, and People—Answer to Aggression," *Air Force Magazine*, Aug 1953, pp. 25-29, 46.

52. Ed M. Miller, "SAC . . . Men with a Mission," *Air Force Magazine*, Apr 1956, pp. 40–45.

53. For a discussion of rotation, see ATC, *A Study on Rotation of Military Personnel in the United States Air Force*, Personnel Planning Project No. 10–2–53 (San Antonio, Tex.: Headquarters, ATC, Aug 1953), esp. p. 30 for data on average moves. Forty percent of those in their first term moved between two and four times, whereas national statistics indicate that 79.9 percent of the general population lived in the same dwelling between 1953 and 1955. *Statistical Abstract of the United States, 1956*, p. 39.

54. "Should My Husband Quit the Air Force?" *Air Force Magazine*, May 1953, p. 33. The long-term consequences of military life on families is lucidly discussed in Mary R. Truscott's *Brats: Children of the American Military Speak Out* (New York: E.P. Dutton, 1989).

55. One important study of family life at a SAC wing found that these periodic separations had deleterious consequences for families. The marriage itself was at risk, a result of fear of extramarital affairs by one or both partners, an absence of fathers that fostered matriarchal families, and an excessive reliance by the SAC wife on her parent for emotional support. See Ruth Lundquist, *Marriage and Family Life of Officers and Airmen in a Strategic Air Command Wing*, Tech Rept No. 5, Air Force Project (Chapel Hill: Institute for Research in Social Science, University of North Carolina Press, Oct 1952). Charles Moskos also draws attention to the parallels between lower-class families in the black ghetto and the consequences of instability on SAC families, e.g., absent fathers, matriarchal families, and extramarital philandering. Moskos, *American Enlisted Man*, p. 235.

56. Lundquist, p. 77.

57. "We Are Ignoring Our Best Military Asset: An Editorial," *Air Force Magazine*, Apr 1954, pp. 20–21.

58. Norris, "SAC Trained Technicians," p. 48. It is unclear whether this figure accounts for training costs minus the savings in pensions should these people have stayed in the service for twenty years.

59. U.S. House of Representatives, *Hearings Before a Subcommittee of the Committee on Armed Services*, 81st Cong, 1st Sess (Washington, D.C.: GPO, 1949), p. 2228.

60. During the baby boom years, the birth rate increased 30 percent (from 19.4 per 1,000 in 1940 to 25.3 per thousand in 1954). *Historical Statistics of the United States to 1970*, pt. 1, p. 49. Medical costs increased 51.3 percent from 1946 to 1956. *Historical Statistics of the United States to 1957*, p. 75.

61. *Report of Citizens Advisory Commission Appointed by the Secretary of Defense: Medical Care for Dependents of Military Personnel* (Washington, D.C.: DOD, Jun 1953), pp. 9–11, copy in Eisenhower Collection, Ann Whitman File, file Charles E. Wilson (1), 1953, Box 39, Eisenhower Library. In regard to the Air Force's interpretation of the "whenever practicable" clause, see Memo, DCS/PPT (Kellogg) to Comdr, HQ 33d AD, Tinker AFB (Brown), Jun 25, 1954, Subj: False Promises about Dependent Medical Care, RG 341, Entry 155, file Mil 1–2–Enlist, Box 700, MMB, NA.

62. In 1950, the services were thinking of eliminating this option also. DOD, *Medical Care for Dependents: An Attitude Study in the Armed Forces*, Survey No. 335 (Washington, D.C.: Attitude Research Branch, May 31, 1950), pp. 1, 20B–20C. Even then, dissatisfied personnel from all the services cited a lack of dependent medical care as an important factor in their choice to leave. One important review of medical care that helped convince Congress to act was the 1953 report of the Moulton Commission. *Semi-Annual Report of the Secretary of Defense, Jan 1–Jun 30, 1954*, p. 27. See also *Report of Citizens Advisory Commission Appointed by the Secretary of Defense: Medical Care for Dependents of Military Personnel*.

63. "Medicare," *AFT*, Oct 2, 1954, p. 12.

64. "Roadblocks to Promotion," *AFT*, May 1, 1954, p. 4.

65. For instance, in 1955, only 20 of the 160 career field divisions had vacancies for promotion to technical and master sergeant. Areas like food service, vehicle maintenance, administration, air police, photograpy, construction equipment, construction, personnel, and printing were consistently frozen. Hard-core specialties, such as electronic countermeasures, ground radar, and flight simulator maintenance specialty codes, however, had excellent promotion opportunities. "March–Apr Airman Hikes Quota Called Average for Coming Year," *AFT*, Mar 26, 1955, pp. 1, 25.

66. "Surplus Is Tragic to Careers," *AFT*, Apr 25, 1953, p. 4.

67. Intvw, James C. Hasdorff with Robert D. Gaylor, Jan 16, 1961, K239.0512–1261, AFHSO, p. 27.

68. Memo, TSgt Howard Barbin to the Editors, *The Army, Navy, and Air Force Journal*, Mar 24, 1954. A copy of this document given to author by Barbin is in the author's personal correspondence, dated Oct 12, 1990.

69. Daykin, p. 46.

70. "Frozen Careers," *AFT*, May 2, 1953, p. 12.

71. Lewis C. Stephens, EEQ, AFHSO.

72. John R. Leffanta, EEQ, AFHSO.

73. James I. Long, EEQ, AFHSO.

74. Col Russell V. Ritchey, "The Air Force Is Not a Business: We're Paid to Fight, Not Show a Profit," *Air Force Magazine*, Jul 1955, pp. 70–75.

75. Lt Col Robert Kahn, "What Happened to the Squadron Commander?" *Air Force Magazine*, Jun 1953, pp. 31–36.

76. Daykin, pp. 75–76.

77. "NCO Prestige," *AFT*, Aug 1, 1953, p. 12.

78. Army studies reveal similar findings. *Semi-Annual Report of the Secretary of the*

Army, Jul 1–Dec 31, 1953, p. 17.

79. The Navy clearly delineated the roles of petty-officers (NCOs) in the *Bluejackets Manual* as early as 1902. Downs, "Prime Hand to Petty Officer," in Segal and Sinaiko, *Life in the Rank and File*, p. 86.

80. Memo, DCS/PPT (Carmichael) to DCS/P, Aug 31, 1954, Subj: Role of the NCO in the Reenlistment Program, RG 341, Entry 155, file Mil 1–3, Box 700, MMB, NA.

81. Ltr, USAF, CS (Vandenberg), to SAC (LeMay), Mar 29, 1952, Subj: NCO Prestige, RG 341, Entry 155, file 310.1, Box 371, MMB, NA.

82. For an important discussion of this diffusion of NCO authority, see James F. Downs, Judith Cohart, and Constance Ojile, *Naval Personnel Organization: A Cultural-Historical Approach* (Reston, Va.: Development Research Associates, 1982) pp. 144–147; and Downs, "Prime Hand to Petty Officer," in Segal and Sinaiko, *Life in the Rank and File*, pp. 79–97.

83. Memo, DCS/PPT (Carmichael) to DCS/PP, Aug 31, 1954, Subj: Role of the NCO in the Reenlistment Program, RG 341, Entry 155, file Mil 1–3, Box 700, MMB, NA; Downs, "Prime Hand to Petty Officer," in Segal and Sinaiko, *Life in the Rank and File*, pp. 94–97.

84. HQ ATC, *Reenlistment in ATRC* (San Antonio, Tex.: DCS/PP, Jan 1954), p. 5.

85. Rear Adm J.P. Womble, Jr., et al., "Ad Hoc Committee's Final Report on the Future of Military Service as a Career That Will Attract and Retain Capable Career Personnel," Oct 30, 1953, Central File–Official File, Box 104, Womble Report, Eisenhower Library, p. 2.

86. DOD also placed pressure upon Congress for change. See, for example, *Semi-Annual Report of the Secretary of Defense, 1 Jul–31 Dec 1954*, pp. 1–2.

87. Talbott, "Millions for Equipment," pp. 29–30, 60–63.

88. Quarles, cited in Francis and Katharine Drake's "Do We Want the Second Best Air Force?" *Reader's Digest*, May 1956, pp. 17–24.

89. *Military Compensation Background Papers*, p. 323.

90. Ibid. The Reenlistment Bonus Act was passed on July 16, 1954, as P.L. 83–506, 69 Stat. 488.

91. Richard Snyder, Fred Stanley, Judson R. Mills, and James W. Prescott, *The Retention of Army Career Personnel: An Analysis of Problems and Some Proposals for Research*, Briefing Paper, Task Career (Monterey, Calif.: Army Leadership Research Unit, Aug 1958), p. 39.

92. Memo, DCS/PP (Lee) to DCS/P (O'Donnell), Dec 22, 1953, Subj: Ad Hoc Committee Rpt on Reenlistment Bonuses, RG 341, Entry 118, 342, Box 17, MMB, NA; "Services Cite 11 Bills Aimed at Incentives," *AFT*, Jan 23, 1954, pp. 1, 9.

93. *DOD Fact Book, 1970*, p. 49.

94. U.S. House of Representatives, *Career Incentive Act of 1955*, Rept No. 90, 84th Cong, 1st Sess (Washington, D.C.: GPO, 1955), p. 2.

95. Sarah McClendon of the *San Antonio Light* asked President Eisenhower why the Air Force was having retention problems. "The President's News Conference of Dec 2, 1954," in *The Public Papers of the Presidents of the United States: Dwight D. Eisenhower, 1954* (Washington, D.C.: GPO, 1954), p. 1083.

96. Robert A. Divine, *Eisenhower and the Cold War* (New York: Oxford University Press, 1981), pp. 38–39, 44–51; Robert F. Burk, *Dwight D. Eisenhower: Hero and Politician* (Boston: Twayne Publishers, 1986), chap. 9; Weigley, *American Way of War*, pp. 402–414.

97. By fiscal year 1957, New Look architects projected that military expenditures could be reduced to between $33 and $34 billion. Moreover, force levels would drop from the 1953 level of 3,403,000 to 2,815,000 by June 1957. The Army would reduce from 20 to 14 divisions; the Navy from 765,000 men and 1,126 combat ships to 650,000 men and 1,030 combat ships; and the Marines from 3 divisions and 244,000 men to 190,000 men and a greatly trimmed 3 divisions. The Air Force, however, would expand to 137 wings. Personnel statistics appear in Schilling et al., *Strategy, Politics, and Defense Budgets*, pp.

436–440; Samuel P. Huntington, *The Common Defense: Strategic Programs in National Politics* (New York: Columbia University Press, 1956), pp. 75–76; and Weigley, *American Way of War*, pp. 402–403.

98. Rept, Technological Capabilities Panel of the Science Advisory Committee, Office of Defense Mobilization, to the President, "Meeting the Threat of Surprise Attack," Feb 14, 1955, Technological Capabilities Panel, SAC, Report to the President, Feb 14, 1955 folder, Subject series, Alphabetical subseries, WHO-SS, Box 11, Eisenhower Library, vol. 1, pp. 30–31, vol. 2, pp. 167–184. Results of this top secret study, chaired by James R. Killian, Jr., president of the Massachusetts Institute of Technology, have been cited as a benchmark in the evolution of Eisenhower's thinking. David A. Rosenberg, "The Origins of Overkill: Nuclear Weapons and American Strategy, 1945–1960," *International Security*, spring 1983, p. 38.

99. Rept, "Meeting the Threat of Surprise Attack," vol. 2, p. 173.

100. Ibid., vol. 2, pp, 178–181.

101. "Special Message to the Congress on Career Incentives for Military Personnel, Jan 13, 1955," in *The Public Papers of the Presidents of the United States: Dwight D. Eisenhower, 1955* (Washington, D.C.: GPO, 1955), pp. 78–83. A year later, Eisenhower sent another letter reiterating the need for legislation on retirement, dependent medical care, and survivor benefits. "Letter to the President of the Senate and to the Speaker of the House of Representatives on Improving Military Career Incentives, Apr 10, 1956," in *The Public Papers of the Presidents of the United States: Dwight D. Eisenhower, 1956* (Washington, D.C.: GPO, 1956), pp. 383–384.

102. For an overview of congressional action in 1955, see *Semi-Annual Report of the Secretary of Defense, 1 Jul–31 Dec 1955*, pp. 14–18.

103. U.S. House of Representatives, *Career Incentive Act of 1955*, Rept No. 90, 84th Cong, 1st Sess (Washington, D.C.: GPO, 1955), pp. 6–14. The act also increased pay for demolition duty, diving, experimental stress, flight pay, glider duty, parachute duty, submarine duty, and toxic fuels exposure. During the Korean war, Secretary of Defense Robert A. Lovett convened a commission to consider the ongoing need for special pay and incentives and to make recommendations. The commission's report had significant influence on the Career Incentive Act of 1955. Commission on Incentive—Hazard-ous Duty and Special Pay, *Differential Pays for the Armed Services of the United States* (Washington, D.C.: GPO, Mar 1953).

104. U.S. House of Representatives, *Career Incentive Act of 1955*, pp. 1–6.

105. *Hearings on the Career Incentive Act of 1955*, 84th Cong, 1st Sess, 1955, pp. 41–42, 45–46.

106. "Housing Bill Nears Final Agreement," *AFT*, Jul 9, 1955, pp. 1, 37; *Semi-Annual Report of the Secretary of Defense, 1 Jul–31 Dec 1955*, pp. 14–16. The amendment as well as some of the later military housing areas was named for Republican Senator Homer E. Capehart of Indiana. A friend of Senator Wherry's, Capehart was born in Algiers, Indiana, on June 6, 1897, served in the 12th Infantry and Quartermaster Corps in World War I, and was employed as an advertiser and salesman in several businesses. In 1927, he was president of his own firm; he later became vice president of Wurlitzer organs (1933–1940) and Chairman of the Board of the Packard Manufacturing Company (1940–1944). He entered the U.S. Senate in 1944.

107. "Renew Family Housing Drive; Rpt Lists Present Status," *AFT*, Sep 17, 1955, p. 2.

108. *USAF Statistical Digest: 1958*, p. 466. Ninety percent of the airmen basic and airmen third class, most of whom lived in government-owned housing, believed their quarters to be adequate. About 70 percent of top three NCO grades lived in privately owned housing, of which 80 percent considered their dwellings sufficient.

109. Memo, Inter-Service Committee on Military Career Incentives (Stephens) to Asst SecDef (Harlow), Mar 23, 1956, Subj: Congressional Support for Major Military Career Incentives, DDE, Office Files, Central Files, 1956, Box 105, Eisenhower Library.

110. See the ATC comparison of military fringe benefits with industry's in Memo,

ATC, CS (Minton), to DCS/PMP, Mar 15, 1954, Subj: Fringe Benefits, microfilm, AFHSO.

111. *Studies in Personnel Policy*, No. 145 (New York: National Industrial Conference Board, Inc., 1955), p. 22.

112. Ibid., p. 23.

113. Memo, SecDef (Wilson) to The President of the United States (Eisenhower), Mar 23, 1956, Subj: Presidential Support for Military Career Incentive Legislation, DDE, Office Files, Central Files, 1956, Box 105, Eisenhower Library. See also "Defense Readies Strong Plea to Provide Medicare for All," *AFT*, Dec 17, 1955, pp. 1, 36.

114. *Military Compensation Background Papers*, p. 481. DOD tried twice in 1955 to introduce a medical care bill. Congress rejected the first attempt; the second attempt was made too late in the second session for Congress to consider. Monte Bourjaily, Jr., "New Medicare Bill Sent to Congress," *AFT*, Aug 6, 1955, p. 10.

115. *Military Compensation Background Papers*, p. 499; "Survivor's Benefit Plan Pays Off," *AFT*, Dec 12, 1953, p. 3; "Services Cite 11 Bills," p. 28.

116. Some commanders resented centralized retention efforts, as it appeared to usurp their command authority. Nevertheless, HQ USAF continued to push for control of the retention problems. Memo, DCS/PPT (Norton) to DCS/PPT, Nov 18, 1955, Subj: Appraisal of Airman Retention Recommendations, RG 341, Entry 155, file Mil Pers Mgmt, Box 708, MMB, NA.

117. Overall guidance and objectives for this program are found in AFR 39–2, Jan 10, 1955, *Enlisted Personnel—USAF Reenlistment Program*.

118. Memo, DSC/PPT (Carmichael) to USAF, CS (Twining), Jun 28, 1954, Subj: 1954 Reenlistment Activity, Twining Collection, Chief of Staff Office File, Organization File (2), 1954, Box 70, LC.

119. Memo, DCS/PPT (Carmichael) to Chief, DCS/PPD, May 26, 1954, Subj: Retention of Personnel, RG 341, Entry 155, file Mil 1–3, Box 700, MMB, NA.

120. See note 118 above.

121. Ibid.

122. Eitelberg et al., *Screening for Service*, p. 18. In 1960, 81 percent of the airmen were high school graduates compared to 66 percent of all American males between the ages of 25 and 29. See also *USAF Statistical Digest: 1959*, p. 332; *Historical Statistics of the United States to 1957*, p. 95.

123. Memo, HQ USAF to HQ ATC, Mar 23, 1953, Subj: Revised Airman Technical Training Concept, doc. 3–24, attached to Hist, Air Training Command, Jan–Jun 1955, microfilm, AFHSO; Hist, Air Training Command, Jul 1–Dec 31, 1955, microfilm, AFHSO, p. 293. See also Thompson, pp. 17–18.

124. *History of ATC, Jan 1–Jun 30, 1955*, p. 84; Thompson, p. 17.

125. A problem that developed was a shortage of new aircraft and equipment for maintenance training purposes. Memo, DCS/PT (McCorkle) to DOT, Dec 22, 1951, Subj: 34th Rpt of the Preparedness, Sub-Committee, RG 341, Entry 155, file 341, Box 631, MMB, NA.

126. Memo, DCS/PPT (Kimble) to DCS/PP, Jul 7, 1955, Subj: Maintenance Training on the MG–10 Fire Control System, RG 341, Entry 155, file Tng–9, Box 716, MMB, NA.

127. Bruce Callender, "28,000 Troop Spaces Axed: AP, Mess Areas Hard Hit; More Slashes May Come," *AFT*, Oct 17, 1953, pp. 1, 8.

128. Memo, DCS/OMO (Elver) to DCS/OMO (Hobson), Dec 29, 1953, Subj: Statistical Analysis of Project Native Son, RG 341, Entry 323, Project Native Son, Box 124, MMB, NA.

129. "30,000 More Slots to Go Civilian in '56," *AFT*, Apr 30, 1955, pp. 1, 28. As early as 1951, the Air Force began to substitute trained civilians in high-skill areas. *Semi-Annual Report of the Secretary of Defense, 1 Jan–Jun 1951*, p. 223; *Semi-Annual Report of the Secretary of the Air Force, 1 Jul–31 Dec 1955*, p. 261.

130. Besides surveying airmen about potential reforms, the Air Force established NCO conferences to discuss further changes in retention policies. *Project Searchlight: A*

United States Air Force Symposium of Career Non-Commissioned Officers and Their Wives, August 1956, (Montgomery, Ala.: Maxwell AFB, 1956). The most significant retention aid for highly skilled technicians came in 1958 with the introduction of proficiency pay. Called pro-pay, it was much like the Army's pre-1942 pay for specialists in that it compensated personnel with special technical skills. *Military Compensation Background Papers*, pp. 341–342.

131. William J. Daniel and Richard P. Calhoun, *A Program for Increasing the Retention of Airmen*, Operations Analysis Working Paper No. 17 (Langley AFB, Va.: TAC, Operational Analysis Division, Apr 14, 1955), sub-sec. 2. In this report, turnover was studied at General Electric and the Koppers Company, while a combined survey of the National Industrial Board, *Look, Fortune*, the Opinion Research Corporation, and the Merchants and Manufacturers Association of Los Angeles helped isolate the causes and solutions to poor retention. As early as 1949, the Air Force canvassed educational institutions and businesses about the use of exit interviews by supervisory personnel to obtain data for retention purposes. Ltr, R.E. Barmeier, Personnel Department, Lockheed Corporation, to DCS/PMP (De Vos), Nov 11, 1949, Subj: Exit Interviews, RG 341, Entry 141, 220.8, Box 382, MMB, NA; Ltr, Charles Myers, Massachusetts Institute of Technology, Industrial Relations Section, to DCS/PMP (Learnard), Oct 17, 1949, Subj: Exit Interviews, RG 341, Entry 141, 220.8, Box 382, MMB, NA.

132. A good description of assignment changes is covered in *The Airman's Guide*, 7th ed., chap. 13. The Army implemented Operation GYROSCOPE, a rotation plan whereby overseas units were replaced by like units from the continental United States rather than by individual replacements. For a summation of Air Force assignment policy changes, see *Semi-Annual Report of the Secretary of the Army, Jul 1–Dec 31, 1954*, pp. 19–20, and *Semi-Annual Report of the Secretary of the Air Force, Jul 1–Dec 31, 1955*, pp. 35–36.

133. "Air Force Cautions against Optimism on Plans for Concurrent Travel," *AFT*, Aug 28, 1954, p. 7.

134. "Did You Get the Word about Life Overseas?" *AFT*, Apr 26, 1952, pp. 1, 22; "Kin Overseas Policies Revised," *AFT*, Nov 1, 1952, pp. 1, 25.

135. "More to Get Area Pick," *AFT*, Jan 3, 1953, p. 1.

136. *Airman's Guide*, 1st ed., pp. 82–84.

137. "Base Choice Policy Extended Overseas," *AFT*, Oct 23, 1954, p. 1.

138. Memo, DCS/P (Kuter) to USAF, CS (Vandenberg), Oct 6, 1952, Subj: Revised Personnel Facilities Construction Policy, RG 341, Entry 118, Box 15, MMB, NA. See also Memo, DCS/PP (Hopwood) to DCS/PMP, Nov 7, 1952, Subj: Project 592, Morale and Welfare Supplies and Equipment, RG 341, Entry 129, file 330.11, Box 164, MMB, NA.

139. At Gary AFB, Texas, in 1954, Operation SELF-IMPROVEMENT helped 783 airmen finish high school. "Pentagon Hails Gary's Morale Work," *AFT*, Sep 25, 1954, p. 5.

140. 1st Lt Brian T. Sheehan, "Our Dynamic New Retention Program: Gen LeMay's Revolutionary 8-Point Program," *Airman Magazine*, Nov 1963, pp. 6–9.

141. "Eighth Air Force 'Beefing Up' Welfare, Morale Efforts," *AFT*, Nov 1954, p. 6.

142. Earl H. Voss, "Why Air Force Wives Are Happier: Morale Begins at Home," *Air Force Magazine*, Sep, 1955, pp. 121–125.

143. Ibid., pp. 124–125.

144. With the assistance of NCOs, planners developed programs to increase the status of noncommissioned officers to encourage airmen to stay in the service for a career. This chapter examines those actions in their historical context, i.e., the building of a career force. In Chapter 6, these actions are tied to the larger concept of professionalization. Memo, CG, Air University (Ross) to DCS/P (Edwards), Apr 30, 1952, Subj: Survey of New Air Force NCO Plan, RG 341 Entry 129, file 330.11, Box 164, MMB, NA.

145. Memo, DCS/P (Kuter) to CG, Alaskan Air Command (Old), Feb 6, 1952, Subj: Selection of Noncommissioned Officers, RG 341, Entry 129, file 220.2, Box 134, MMB, NA; Memo, DCS/PP (Parks) to CG, Alaskan Air Command (Old), May 1, 1952, Subj: Se

lection of Noncommissioned Officers, RG 341, Entry 129, file 220.2, Box 134, MMB, NA.

146. Ltr, USAF, CS (Vandenberg) to SAC (LeMay), Mar 29, 1952, Subj: New Grade Structure Program, RG 341, Entry 155, file 310.1, Box 371, MMB, NA.

147. "4 Rank Titles Change as E–4 and E–3 Lose NCO Status as of Apr 1," *AFT*, Mar 29, 1952, pp. 1, 23.

148. After the March 1953 publication of AFR 39–6, *Noncommissioned Officers*, a definition of NCO duties first appeared in *The Airman's Guide*, 6th ed. (Harrisburg, Pa.: Military Service Publishing Co., 1954), p. 71.

149. AFR 39–6, Mar 1953, *Noncommissioned Officers*.

150. "Regulation Will Define NCO Responsibility," *AFT*, Jan 10, 1953, pp. 1, 8; Editorial, "The Forward Look," *AFT*, Feb 28, 1953, p. 4; "Noncom Build-up Gains Momentum," *AFT*, Apr 25, 1953, pp. 1, 8.

151. "Scott NCO Policies Stress Privileges, Authority, Duty," *AFT*, Apr 11, 1953, pp. 1, 3. The best discussions of efforts made by the Air Force to increase the prestige of NCOs appear in *The Air Force Times*. In the 1940s and 1950s, at least, this newspaper and its editorial staff avidly took up the cause of the enlisted man and argued for change.

152. "NCOs Get Check-Cashing Privileges," *AFT*, Jan 30, 1954, p. 9. In 1955, the Air Force allowed NCOs to have their pay checks sent directly to their banks. This privilege had previously been offered only to officers. "OK Mailing of Noncom Pay," *AFT*, Jan 8, 1955, p. 3.

153. "NCO's Given Added Responsibilities, Privileges," *AFT*, Nov 21, 1953, p. 18.

154. "Scott NCO Policies Stress Privileges, Authority, Duty," *AFT*, Apr 11, 1953, pp. 1, 3.

155. "NCO Committee Helps Solve Mather Problems," *AFT*, Oct 29, 1953, p. 28.

156. "Property Office Authority Given Sampson NCOs," *AFT*, Oct 3, 1953, p. 15.

157. "NCO Prestige Gets Boost at Mitchel," *AFT*, Oct 3, 1953, p. 16.

158. "MATS up NCO Training Responsibility," *AFT*, Oct 10, 1953, p. 4.

159. At the request of USAFE Commander General John K. Cannon, a school, The USAFE Academy of Leadership and Management, was established in 1950. However, it offered primarily training in personnel management. Similarly, ATC had started an NCO leadership school in 1951, yet due to a lack of funds it closed less than a year after opening. Like the USAFE and ATC schools, various bases also offered courses in personnel management. Nevertheless, only SAC's NCO Academy devised a comprehensive training plan for noncommissioned officers. Some airman writers, however, chose to see the USAFE school as the precursor to later NCO academies. TSgt Harold L. Craven, "Schools for Air Force Sergeants Are Better Equipping Our NCOs for Positions of Responsibility," *The Airman*, Oct 1958, pp. 12–14; Lt Col Ernest M. Magee, "The Evolution of NCO Academies," *Air University Review*, Sep–Oct 1966, pp. 56–61.

160. "Air Force Appraises NCO Academy Plan," *AFT*, Oct 17, 1953, p. 2. Later the major commands would set their own entrance requirements and select participants through the use of selection boards.

161. "For Greater Prestige, More Bases Undertake NCO Academy Projects," *AFT*, Apr 24, 1954, p. 15.

162. Craven, "Schools for Air Force Sergeants," p. 13.

163. "Elite Corps Aim of New NCO Plans," *AFT*, Oct 8, 1955, pp. 1, 31. See also MSgt Norman Winfield, "Why Not a Professional Non-Com Corps?" *Air Force Magazine*, Nov 1953, pp. 31–32. As officers had similar professional schools and a societal mandate to lead the military, an elite corps of NCOs sworn to obey their orders did not pose a threat to officer authority or status. Thus, officers supported the plans for an extensive NCO professional military schooling program.

164. Craven, "Schools for Air Force Sergeants," p. 13.

165. For a description of course work and graduation requirements, see AFR 50–39, *NCO Academies*. For a good description of NCOs attending one of SAC's academies in the mid-1950s, see MSgt Frank J. Clifford's "School for Zebras," *Air Force Magazine*,

April 1955, pp. 27–32, 52, and 55.

166. "NCO Demotion Limited—A1C Floor 1st Drop, Non-punitive," *AFT*, Feb 14, 1953, p. 8.

167. "Tech Knowledge Stressed in Much Future Upgrades," *AFT*, Jun 6, 1953, p. 32.

168. "Air Force Prepares NCO Exams," *AFT*, Feb 13, 1954, pp. 1, 23.

169. "Certificate of Rank for NCOs Due," *AFT*, Jun 4, 1955, pp. 1, 35.

170. "Top NCOs Tell Views in Survey," *AFT*, Jul 17, 1954, p. 23.

171. Dept of the Air Force, *Technicians in the U.S. Air Force* (Washington, D.C.: DCS/PP, 1954), copy in RG 341, Entry 159, file A–5, Box 790, MMB, NA; Memo, DCS/PPT (Carmichael) to DCS/P, Aug 31, 1954, Subj: Role of the NCO in the Reenlistment Program, RG 341, Entry 155, Mil 1–3, Box 700, MMB, NA.

172. "No Switch to Specialist Rating Expected from Present Study," *AFT*, Nov 5, 1955, p. 2.

173. Speech, Gen Charles L. Bolte, Vice Chief, U.S. Army, Monroe County American Legion luncheon, Rochester, N.Y., Nov 11, 1954, Bolte Papers, Center of Military History. See also "Army 'Specialists' Get High Pay, Low Rank in New Noncom Split," *AFT*, Sep 10, 1955, p. 14; *Semi-Annual Report of the Secretary of the Army, Jan 1–Jun 30, 1954*, p. 85.

174. This increased reenlistment rate was partially offset by the Air Force "short-discharge" for those halfway through their tours. Thus, about 30 percent of the fiscal year 1957 rate could be attributed to men who reenlisted after serving only half of their four-year enlistment. Goldberg, ed., *History of the United States Air Force*, pp. 297–298.

175. The significant drop in AWOL rates was due to more rather than to better incentives: in 1954 the armed services imposed stiffer penalties for desertion and absences. Ltr, Dir, Legislation and Liaison (Eaton), to Honorable Leverett Saltonstall, Chmn, Senate Armed Service Committee, Jan 13, 1953, Subj: AWOL and Desertion Information, RG 341, Entry 118, file 220.711, Box 17, MMB, NA. See also "Rougher Penalties Coming for AWOLS, Deserters If President Signs New Order," *AFT*, Oct 17, 1953, p. 7; "Stiffer Penalties Expected to Cut AWOLs," *AFT*, Oct 9, 1954, p. 24.

Air Force research into desertions revealed that most deserters were repeaters, young, from unstable families, poorly educated, of low mental capacity, and dissatisfied with Air Force life. "Despite Stiffer Penalties in Effect for Past Year, Deserters, AWOLs Still Plague All of the Services," *AFT*, Aug 20, 1955, pp. M6–M7. These results may be suspect, however, when considering the case the Air Force was making in 1955 for eliminating the DOD Quality Force Distribution program. Cat IV candidates consistently fit this profile. Logically, the Air Force argued thusly: "Reduce the number of Cat IV personnel and desertions and AWOLs would likewise decrease." See also Maj Benjamin H. Barnetts, Jr., "USAF AWOL and Desertion: Some Reasons Why" (thesis, Air University, May 1972).

Chapter 6

1. Kuter intvw, Sep 30–Oct 3, 1974, p. 508.

2. *Historical Statistics of the United States to 1957*, p. 207; *USAF Statistical Digest: Fiscal Year 1955*, p. 339.

3. Arnold, *Third Report of the Commanding General of the Army Air Forces*, p. 460.

4. Ernest Greenwood, "Attributes of a Profession: Revisited," in Sheo Kumar Lal et al., eds., *Readings in the Sociology of the Professions* (Delphi, India: Gian Publishing House, 1988), pp. 10–11.

5. Abbott, pp. 8, 318.

6. Samuel P. Huntington, *The Soldier and the State: The Theory of Politics of Civil-Military Relations* (New York: Vintage Books, 1957), pp. 7–18.

7. An important summation of the Huntington model of the American military profession is Anthony E. Hartle's *Moral Issues in Military Decision Making* (Lawrence: University of Kansas Press, 1989), pp. 9–18. For the direct quote, see p. 11.

8. Huntington, pp. 15–17.

9. Ibid., pp. 17–18.

10. Ibid., p. 12.

11. Hartle, p. 16.

12. Huntington, p. 18.

13. Wilensky, "The Professionalization of Everyone?" pp. 137–158. For an extensive treatise on the process of professionalization, see Ronald M. Pavalko, *The Sociology of Occupations and Professions* (Itasca, Ill.: F.E. Peacock Publishers, 1971) pp. 15–43. For an important critique of the processual approach to professions, see Abbott, pp. 9–20.

14. See, for example, Pavalko, pp. 15–17, and George Ritzer, *Man and His Work: Conflict and Change* (New York: Appleton-Century-Crofts, 1972), pp. 49–50.

15. Amitai Etzioni, ed., *The Semi-Professions and Their Organizations* (New York: Free Press, 1969), pp. xiii–xiv.

16. Ritzer, pp. 49–56; Pavalko, pp. 26–27. Pavalko adds an important point—in reality, groups possess these characteristics to a varying degree. No group exibits them all to a high or ideal degree.

17. Abbott, p. 71; Greenwood, in Lal et al., eds., *Readings in the Sociology of the Professions*, pp. 14–16. See also Magali Larson, *The Rise of Professionalism* (Berkeley: University of California Press, 1977).

18. Robert Lovett, although not an Air Force secretary, served as the Assistant Secretary of War for Air during World War II.

19. The 40-percent retirement is based on twenty years of active duty service. The pay is predicated on the three highest years of base pay. Individuals remaining for thirty years still receive 75 percent base pay upon retirement. AFR 35–7, Oct 1, 1987, *Service Retirements*, change 3, Jul 13, 1990, pp. 42–43.

Bibliographic Note

Government Sources

National Archives of the United States

Any study of enlisted men and personnel policy must begin with the records housed in the National Archives. For the Air Service, Air Corps, and AAF, Record Groups 18 and 341 are indispensable. Other Record Groups that proved invaluable include RG 330, Record of the Office of the Secretary of Defense; RG 340, Office of the Secretary of the Air Force; and RG 407, Officer-Enlisted Men Relations Board.

Record Group 18 is the most useful for the period 1914–1948 and contains much information on enlisted personnel policy. The decimal correspondence files of the Air Adjutant General are a veritable gold mine of sources, especially for World War II, on such diverse subjects such as race, training, courts-martial, recruiting, classification, grade structure, morale, gender, and postwar personnel policy planning. The most important decimal files are 220, 240, 242, 246, 250, 251, 260, 291.2. 310, 319.1, 320, 320.3, 320.4, 321, 321.03, 330, 330.11, 331.2, 334, 337, 340, 341, 342, 353, and 353.8. The correspondence files of the Commanding General and Deputy Commanding General in RG 18 can be also fruitfully mined with the use of the preceding decimal files. Important documents were difficult to find and researching them proved time-consuming. Researchers would be well advised to remain with the Air Adjutant General files at least through 1948.

For the decade after World War II, Record Group 341, Headquarters of the United States Air Force, is as important for enlisted sources as is RG 18. The files, which begin in 1946 and continue through 1956 (1955–1956), may be found at the Washington National Records Center, Suitland, Maryland. From 1946 to 1948, however, the Air Force placed correspondence in both RG 18 and RG 341, so a researcher must review both collections (which proves tedious because of the duplication). Another problem one encounters when using RG 341 is that the Air Force discontinued the use of the War Department's decimal system (as did the War Department itself), and the Air Force failed to replace it with a logical means of cataloging records. Fortunately, the records were classified by organization.

The relevant records in RG 341 include the Office of the Vice Chief of Staff, Executive Services, items 1, 6, 8, 9, and 11; Office of the Secretary of the Air Staff, Staff Management Division, item 24; Office of the Deputy Chief of Staff, Personnel, Executive Office, items 118–120; Office of Personnel Planning, Executive Office, item 129; Policy Division, Promotion Branch, item 130; Promotion and Separations Division, Selection Board Secretariat, item

138; Disability Separation Branch, item 140; Personnel Requirements and Analysis Division, items 141 and 142; Office of the Director of Personnel Procurement and Training, Executive Office, items 155–159; Office of the Director of Manpower and Organization, Air Force Manpower Group, items 321 and 322; Administrative Office, item 325; Manpower Division, items 328 and 329; and Organizational Division, items 330 and 331.

Other record groups provide useful sources but with a great expense in time. For instance, RG 330, Records of the Office of the Secretary of Defense, is a broad collection that required careful selectivity, and only the Minutes of the Armed Forces Personnel Council have been examined. Similar selectivity was exercised with RG 340, Office of the Secretary of the Air Force; here only the minutes of the Air Board and the files of the Assistant Secretary of Defense for Management and Personnel were examined.

Most helpful in understanding postwar military reform and the Doolittle Board is RG 407, Officer-Enlisted Men Relations Board, Subject File. This four-box collection contains transcripts of the board's discussions and a copy of the final report. Unfortunately, none of the correspondence between military personnel and the board was saved.

Library of Congress

The Manuscript Division of the Library of Congress holds collections of the Chiefs of Staff of the United States Air Force, several civilian Air Force and Department of Defense officials, and Lt. Gen. James H. Doolittle. The collections of Generals Henry H. Arnold and Carl A. Spaatz offer much information on the immediate postwar buildup. Certainly the most important is the collection of General Curtis E. LeMay as head of Strategic Air Command, then as Air Force Vice Chief of Staff, and finally as USAF Chief of Staff. Many innovations and reforms in enlisted matters were suggested or implemented by him. The Hoyt S. Vandenberg, Ira C. Eaker, Muir S. Fairchild, and Nathan F. Twining collections offer less relevant but useful information. The Robert P. Patterson collection provides insight into the relationships among industry, the military, and personnel management.

Dwight D. Eisenhower Library

Collections in the Dwight D. Eisenhower Library, Abilene, Kansas, provide important information on military personnel problems from 1953 through 1960. The library is also the repository for the Womble Committee on military careers. The three most important collections include Dwight D. Eisenhower's Papers as President; Dwight D. Eisenhower's Records as President, Central Files; and White House Office, Office of the President Files.

Other holdings of tremendous value were the Charles C. Finucane papers; Oliver M. Gale papers; Alvan C. Gillem, Jr., papers; Robert K. Gray papers; Bryce N. Harlow papers; Lauris Norstad papers; Elwood R. Quesada papers; and Robert L. Schultz papers. The public statements from the Secretaries of Defense and Joint Chiefs of Staff and the White House Office, Office of the Special Assistant for Science and Technology, also proved useful. The Eisenhower Library offers many good oral histories as well. Particularly good are interviews with James H. Douglas, Robert K. Gray, and Robert A. Lovett.

Harry S. Truman Library

Many important collections are directly related to the postwar debate on the creation and assimilation of large standing defense forces. One of the most important is the Records of the U.S. President's Committee on Religion and Welfare in the Armed Forces, 1948–1951. This collection examines all facets of social policy involving the military. Other useful collections are the Records of the U.S. President's Committee on Equality of Treatment and Opportunity in the Armed Services, 1949–1950; the Records of the U.S. President's Advisory Commission on Universal Training, 1946–1947; and the papers of Charles Fahy, Gordon Gray, Donald A. Quarles, and J. Thomas Schneider. Worthwhile oral histories include interviews with Thomas K. Finletter, Eugene M. Zuckert, W. Stuart Symington, Marx Leva, and Roswell Gilpatric.

The Center for Air Force History

The Center for Air Force History (now the U.S. Air Force History Support Office) houses several useful collections that include the operational histories of the Air Defense Command, 1946–1948; Air Training Command, 1946–1955; Career Development and Classification Division, Directorate of Training, 1950–1953; Continental Air Command, 1949–1953; Deputy Chief of Staff for Personnel, 1950–1957; Directorate of Manpower and Organization, 1949–1953; Directorate of Personnel Planning, 1949–1956; Director of the Women in the Air Force, 1957; Fifteenth Air Force, 1951–1953; Military Air Transport Service, 1949–1954; Personnel Procurement Division, Directorate of Training, 1950–1956; Strategic Air Command, 1947–1956; and Training Division, Directorate of Technical Training, 1949–1956.

The center also has a unique collection of oral histories pertinent to this study. They include interviews with Chief Master Sergeant of the Air Force (CMSAF) Thomas N. Barnes; Lt. Gen. Idwal H. Edwards; CMSAF Donald L. Harlow; CMSAF Richard D. Kisling; General Laurence S. Kuter; General Curtis E. LeMay; and CMSAF James M. McCoy. Janet R. Bednarek ed., *The Enlisted Experience: A Conversation with the Chief Master Sergeants of the*

Foundation of the Force

Air Force (Washington, D.C.: Air Force History and Museums Program, 1995)] was also helpful. An essay that exclusively uses the oral histories of the chief master sergeants of the Air Force to tell the story of enlisted life is Jacob Neufeld and James C. Hasdorff, "The View from the Top: Oral Histories of Chief Master Sergeants of the Air Force," in David R. Segal and H. Wallace Sinaiko, eds., *Life in the Rank and File: Enlisted Men and Women in the Armed Forces of the United States, Australia, Canada, and the United Kingdom* (New York: Pergamon-Brassey, 1986), pp. 116–133.

The Enlisted Experience Questionnaire

The story of the making of enlisted personnel policy would be incomplete without an understanding of how enlisted personnel reacted to and helped shape policy. Unfortunately, unlike the Civil War era, correspondence and diaries of post–World War II military personnel are negligible. Perhaps the immediateness of the event, the fact that many of these participants are still alive, or that few today keep a diary (military regulations prohibit the keeping of diaries, since, if confiscated, they could provide useful intelligence to the enemy) are reasons for the dearth of materials that make for good history. Moreover, enlisted personnel records from this period, housed at the National Personnel Records Center, St. Louis, Mo., are closed for general research.

In any case, to address this problem, it seemed reasonable to design a historical questionnaire, "The Enlisted Experience, 1939–1973," and administer it to former airmen. While not representative, the questionnaire served as a means to help flesh out the narrative. Ten thousand were sent; six thousand were returned and evaluated. Consisting of seventy-three questions, the questionnaire explored all phases of enlisted life, for example, recruitment, training, family life, and retirement. The completed documents now reside in the archives of the Air Force Sergeants' Association in Washington, D.C., where they are available to scholars.

Statistical Sources

Pay and benefits for enlisted men were computed from data available in the recently published *Military Compensation Background Papers: Compensation Elements and Related Manpower Cost Items, Their Purposes and Legislative Backgrounds*, 3d ed. (Washington, D.C.: Department of Defense, 1987). In addition to lists of the various active duty entitlements since 1920, brief legislative histories of the many pay acts are also included in this important volume. Civilian average wages were derived from *Historical Statistics of the United States: Colonial Times to 1957*. Income statistics of skilled and semiskilled males were obtained from the U.S. Commerce Department's

272

Statistical Abstracts of the United States, printed in Washington, D.C., by the Government Printing Office (GPO) in the relevant years.

Congressional Hearings and Reports

United States. Congress. House. *Hearings before a Subcommittee of the Committee on Armed Services*. 81st Cong., 1st sess., Washington, D.C.: GPO, 1949.

———. *Career Incentive Act of 1955*. Report No. 90. 84th Cong., 1st sess., Washington, D.C.: GPO, 1955.

———. Senate. *Mortgage Insurance for Military Housing, 1949*. Report No. 410. 81st Cong., 1st sess., Washington, D.C.: GPO, 1949.

———. Senate Preparedness Subcommittee on Armed Services. *Interim Report on Lackland Air Force Base*. S. Res. 18. 82d Cong., 1st sess., Washington, D.C.: GPO, 1951.

———. Subcommittee on Preparedness. *Investigation of the Preparedness Program: Thirty-Fourth Report of the Preparedness Subcommittee of the Committee on Armed Services: Report on Six Air Force Training Centers*. 81st Cong., 1st sess., Washington, D.C.: GPO, 1951.

———. *Department of Defense Appropriations for 1954: Hearings before the Subcommittee of the Committee on Appropriations*. H.R. 5969. 83d Cong., 1st sess., Washington, D.C.: GPO, 1953.

———. *Department of Defense Appropriations for 1955: Hearings before the Subcommittee of the Committee on Appropriations*. H.R. 8873. 83d Cong., 2d sess., Washington, D.C.: GPO, 1954.

———. *Treatment of Deserters from Military Service*. Report No. 91–93. 91st Cong., 1st sess., Washington, D.C.: GPO, 1969.

Newspapers and Magazines

Air Force Magazine, 1947–1956.

Air University Review, 1950–1980.

Armed Forces Management, 1951–1957

The Air Force Times, 1947–1956.

The Air Corps News Letter, 1926–1939.

The Air Service News Letter, 1918–1926.

The Airman, 1955–1957.

Foundation of the Force

The AFL-CIO News Letter, 1945–1956.

The Army and Navy Journal, 1940–1956.

The Army Times, 1942–1947.

The New York Times, 1944–1956.

Secondary Sources

Secondary sources on the U.S. Air Force and the Cold War military are legion. They tend to focus on World War II, strategic bombardment, nuclear diplomacy, and Vietnam. Important overviews of the historiography of the new type of military history are Edward M. Coffman, "The New American Military History," *Military Affairs*, vol. 49 (Jan 1984), pp. 1–5; and Peter Karsten, "The 'New' American Military History: A Map of the Territory, Explored and Unexplored," *American Quarterly*, fall 1984, pp. 389–418. Richard H. Kohn's "The Social History of the American Soldier: A Review," *American Historical Review*, vol. 86.3 (Jun 1991), pp. 553–567, is good at pointing out areas of needed study.

General Works on Air Force Enlisted Personnel

Central to the enlisted experience is Samuel Stouffer, *The American Soldier*, 4 vols. (Princeton, N.J.: Princeton University Press, 1949). A more readable work based on Stouffer's work is Lee Kennett, *G.I.: The American Soldier in World War II* (New York: Charles Scribner's Sons, 1987). Charles Moskos' seminal work, *The American Enlisted Man: The Rank and File in Today's Military* (New York: Russell Sage Foundation, 1970), is absolutely essential. Lee Arbon's *They Also Flew: The Enlisted Pilot Legacy, 1912–1942* (Washington, D.C.: Smithsonian Institution Press, 1992) is an important introduction to enlisted flyers.

The best single volume on women in the Air Force is Jeanne Holm's *Women in the Military: An Unfinished Revolution* (Novato, Calif.: Presidio Press, 1982). Another good work describing military gender roles in the postwar era is Bettie J. Morden, *The Women's Army Corps, 1945–1978* (Washington, D.C.: GPO, 1989). African American integration in the Air Force is discussed in four important works—Alan Osur, *Blacks in the Army Air Forces during World War II* (Washington, D.C.: GPO, 1977); Alan Gropman, *The Air Force Integrates, 1945–1964* (Washington, D.C.: GPO, 1978); Bernard C. Nalty's excellent volume, *Strength for the Fight: A History of Black Americans in the Military* (New York: Free Press, 1986); and Morris J. MacGregor, Jr., *Integration of the Armed Forces, 1940–1965* (Washington, D.C.: GPO, 1989). Although published too late for inclusion in this study,

Ernest F. Fisher, Jr.'s *Guardians of the Republic: A History of the Noncommissioned Officer Corps of the U.S. Army* (New York: Ballantine, 1994) is an important document for those doing research on enlisted personnel.

Chapter One

Alfred Goldberg's *History of the United States Air Force, 1907–1957* (Princeton, N.J.: Van Nostrand, 1957) is an important overview. For the period preceding World War I, see Juliette A. Hennessy, *The United States Army Air Arm: April 1861 to April 1917* (Washington, D.C.: Office of Air Force History, 1985). Works covering World War I are Arthur S. Link, *Woodrow Wilson and the Progressive Era: 1910–1917* (New York: Harper & Row, 1954); Robert H. Ferrell, *Woodrow Wilson and World War I, 1917–1921* (New York: Harper & Row, 1985); and Arthur C. Walworth, *Woodrow Wilson*, 2d rev. ed. (Baltimore: Penguin Books, 1961). For an important work on the Air Service's role, see I.B. Holley, *Ideas and Weapons: Exploitation of the Aerial Weapon by the United States During World War I; a Study in the Relationship of Technological Advance, Military Doctrine, and the Development of Weapons* (Washington D.C.: Office of Air Force History, 1983), p. 37.

Other general works helpful to me included Robert Frank Futrell, *Ideas, Concepts, Doctrine: Basic Thinking in the United States Air Force, 1907–1960*, vol. 1 (Maxwell Air Force Base, Ala.: Air University Press, 1989), pp. 27–53, 75–89; Michael Sherry, *The Rise of American Air Power: The Creation of Armageddon* (New Haven, Conn.: Yale University Press, 1987), chaps. 2, 3; and Russell F. Weigley, *The American Way of War: A History of United States Military Strategy and Policy* (New York: Macmillan, 1973), pp. 223–241. Perhaps the most important work on the American war effort is Edward M. Coffman's *The War to End All Wars: The American Military Experience in World War I* (Madison: University of Wisconsin Press, 1986), esp. chap. 3. Works on the home front include David M. Kennedy's *Over Here: The First World War and American Society* (New York, 1980) and Ronald Schaffer's *America in the Great War: The Rise of the War Welfare State* (New York: Oxford University Press, 1991).

For significant interpretive works discussing the rise of personnel management and classification, see Daniel Nelson, *Managers and Workers: Origins of the New Factory System in the United States, 1880–1920* (Madison: University of Wisconsin Press, 1975), pp. 148–156; Sanford Jacoby, *Employing Bureaucracy: Managers, Unions, and the Transformation of Work in American Industry, 1900–1945* (New York: Columbia University Press, 1985), p. 151, chap. 3; and Frederick Winslow Taylor, *The Principles of Scientific Management* (New York: F.W. Taylor, 1911), pp. 36–76. Jacoby argues (see his chap. 2) that the vocational guidance movement at the turn of the century had more to do with setting up a classification system than scientific management did. Taylor's concept of finding the right man for the right job suggests a product of his own penchant for social Darwinism and natural selection. Inasmuch as he advocated a planning department and the establishment of wage rates for various classes of jobs, Taylor's philosophy seems to permeate classification assumptions. See also Cyril C. Ling, *The Management of Personnel Relations, History and Origins* (Homewood, Ill.: Richard D. Irwin, 1965), and Oscar W. Nestor, *A History of Personnel Administration, 1890–1910* (New York: Garland Publishing, 1986), for more on the rise of personnel management. For studies that tie the use of scientific management with the military, see Hugh G. Aitken, *Scientific Management in Action: Taylorism at the Watertown Arsenal, 1908–1915* (Princeton, N.J.: Princeton University Press, 1960), and Merritt Roe Smith, *Harper's Ferry Armory and the New Technology: The Challenge of Change* (Ithaca, N.Y.: Cornell University Press, 1977).

Studies covering the beginnings of classification and testing procedures in the military include Hugo Munsterberg, *Psychology and Industrial Efficiency* (New York: Houghton Mifflin, 1913), especially the chapter, "The Best Man"; Edmund C. Lynch, "Walter Dill Scott, Pioneer Industrial Psychologist," *Business History Review*, vol. 42 (1968), pp. 155–157, 162; and Daniel Kevles, "Testing the Army's Intelligence: Psychologists and the Military in World War I," *Journal of American History*, vol. 55 (Dec 1968), pp. 565–581.

For a broad overview of the intellectual environment from which industrial psychology emerged, see John C. Burnham, "Psychiatry, Psychology, and the Progressive Movement," *American Quarterly*, vol. 12 (1960), pp. 457–465. See also Harold Wool's excellent analysis of mental aptitude tests in his *Military Specialist: Skilled Manpower for the Armed Forces* (Baltimore, Md.: Johns Hopkins University Press, 1968); Mark J. Eitelberg et al., *Screening for Service: Aptitude and Screening for Military Entry* (Washington D.C.: Office of the Assistant Secretary of Defense, Manpower, Installations, and Logistics, 1984), pp. 14–17, 39–42; Mark J. Eitelberg, *Manpower for Military Occupations* (Washington, D.C.: Office of the Assistant Secretary of Defense, Force Management and Personnel, 1988), chap. 2; James H. Hayes, *The Evolution of Armed Forces Enlisted Personnel Management Policies* (Santa Monica, Calif.: Rand Corporation, 1982), pp. 81–87; and J.E. Uhlaner and D.J. Bolanovich, *Development of the Armed Forces Qualification Test and Predecessor Army Screening Tests, 1946–1950*, PRS Report 976 (Washington, D.C.: Personnel Research Section, Department of the Army, 1952).

Key interwar studies include Maurer Maurer, *Aviation in the U.S. Army, 1919–1939* (Washington, D.C.: Office of Air Force History, 1987); John Shiner, *Foulois and the Army Air Corps, 1931–1935* (Washington D.C.: AFCHO, 1983); and Robert K. Griffith, *Men Wanted for the U.S. Army: America's Experience with an All-Volunteer Army between the World Wars* (Westport, Conn.: Greenwood Press, 1982).

A number of influential works bear on an understanding of Universal

Military Training (UMT) and progressive reforms during the interwar era. See Michael M. Boll's *National Security Planning: Roosevelt through Reagan* (Lexington: University of Kentucky Press, 1988), pp. 66–67, 71, and for general overviews of the UMT movement, see Russell F. Weigley's two important works, *History of the United States Army* (New York: Macmillan, 1967) and *The American Way of War* (Bloomington: Indiana University Press, 1973). David Beaver, *Newton D. Baker and the American War Effort* (Lincoln: University of Nebraska Press, 1966), and Clarence H. Cramer, *Newton D. Baker: A Biography* (Cleveland, Ohio: World Publishing Co., 1961), also shed light on the underpinnings of UMT. In regard to Baker's efforts in instituting vocational and educational reforms in the military, see Griffith's *Men Wanted for the U.S. Army*, pp. 33–35. For a broader discussion of the UMT movement before World War I and the progressive movement's impact on the military, see, in addition to Griffith's work, I.B. Holley, Jr., *Gen. John M. Palmer, Citizen Soldier, and the Army of a Democracy* (Westport, Conn.: Greenwood Press, 1982), and John Whiteclay Chambers II, "Conscripting for Colossus: The Progressive Era and the Origin of the Modern Military Draft in the United States in World War I," in Peter Karsten, ed., *The Military in America: From the Colonial Era to the Present* (New York: Free Press, 1986), pp. 297–311. See also John Whiteclay Chambers II's excellent book, *To Raise an Army: The Draft Comes to Modern America* (New York: Free Press, 1987), and John Finnegan's *Against the Specter of the Dragon: The Campaign for Military Preparedness, 1914–1917* (Westport, Conn.: Greenwood Press, 1974).

Also essential to understanding progressivism's effect upon the military are Frederick J. Harrod, *Manning the New Navy: The Development of a Modern Naval Enlisted Force, 1899–1940* (Westport, Conn.: Greenwood Press, 1978), chap. 4; James Abrahamson, *America Arms for a New Century: The Making of a Great Military Power* (New York: Free Press, 1981); Stephen Skowronek, *Building an American State: The Expansion of National Administrative Capacities, 1877–1920* (New York: Cambridge University Press, 1982), chaps. 4, 7; Peter Karsten, "Armed Progressives: The Military Reorganizes for the American Century," in Karsten, ed., *Military in America*, pp. 239–274; Bruce White, "The American Military and the Melting Pot in World War I," in J.L Granatstein and R.D. Cuff, eds., *War and Society in North America* (Toronto: Thomas Nelson & Sons, 1971), pp. 37–51; and Neil A. Wynn, *From Progressivism to Prosperity: World War I and American Society* (New York: Holmes & Meier, 1986), pp. 121–124.

The effect of the Great Depression on the military is examined in Robert K. Griffith, "Quality Not Quantity: The Volunteer Army During the Depression," *Military Affairs*, Dec 1979, pp. 171–175, and in John Killegrew, "The Impact of the Great Depression on the United States Army, 1929–1936" (diss., Indiana University, 1960).

For a discussion of the impact of unemployment on Army recruiting and retention, see Griffith, *Men Wanted for the U.S. Army*, p. 221; Edward M.

Foundation of the Force

Coffman, *The Old Army: A Portrait of the American Army in Peacetime, 1784–1898* (New York: Oxford University Press, 1986), pp. 15–16, 146–147, 346–350, 372; and Hayes, *Evolution of Armed Forces Enlisted Personnel Management Policies*, p. 52. Also helpful were a number of labor studies that examined labor turnover and economic fluctuations. Among them are Daniel Nelson, *Managers and Workers: Origins of the New Factory System in the United States, 1880–1920* (Madison: University of Wisconsin Press, 1975), pp. 86–87, 149–150; Sanford Jacoby, "Industrial Labor Mobility in Historical Perspective," *Industrial Relations*, vol. 22 (spring 1983), pp. 261–282; and David Montgomery, *Worker's Control in America: Studies in the History of Work, Technology, and Labor Struggles* (Cambridge, England: Cambridge University Press, 1979).

Studies of the Army Air Forces in the Second World War must begin with Wesley F. Craven and James L. Cate, eds., *The Army Air Forces in World War II*, 7 vols. (Chicago: University of Chicago Press, 1948–1958). Less satisfying but useful is James L. Stokesbury, *A Short History of Air Power* (New York: W. Morrow, 1986). The most comprehensive work examining the Air Force's struggle for autonomy is Herman S. Wolk's *Planning and Organizing the Postwar Air Force, 1943–1947* (Washington, D.C.: Office of Air Force History, 1984). Other works that discuss the administration of the military during this time are James E. Hewes, *From Root to McNamara: Army Reorganization and Administration, 1900–1963* (Washington, D.C.: GPO, 1975), and Paul Y. Hammond, *Organizing for Defense: The American Military Establishment in the Twentieth Century* (Princeton, N.J.: Princeton University Press, 1961).

Chapter Two

Two key works previously cited in the Introduction were extremely useful in understanding the historical process occurring in the postwar era. They are Charles Moskos, "From Institution to Occupation: Trends in the Military Organization," *Armed Forces & Society*, vol. 4 (1977), pp. 41–49 (see also his book, *The Military: More Than Just a Job?* [New York: Pergamon-Brassey, 1988] for an update), and Morris Janowitz, "From Institutional to Occupational: The Need for Conceptual Clarity," *Armed Forces & Society*, vol. 4 (1977), pp. 51–54.

Many works were available for fleshing out the argument presented in Chapter 2. The rise of a National Military Establishment and the Department of Defense is the subject of Jeffery M. Dorwart's *Eberstadt and Forrestal: A National Security Partnership, 1909–1949* (College Station: Texas A&M University Press, 1991); Hammond's *Organizing for Defense*; Warner R. Schilling, Paul Y. Hammond, and Glenn Snyder's *Strategy, Politics, and Defense Budgets* (New York: Columbia University Press, 1962); and Frank

Kofsky's *Harry S. Truman and the War Scare of 1948* (New York: St. Martin's Press, 1993).

A good general work describing the immediate postwar period is Joseph C. Golden's *The Best Years, 1945–1950* (New York: Antheum, 1976). Other sources include James Gilbert, *Another Chance: Postwar America, 1945–1985* (Chicago: Dorsey Press, 1986), and John Diggins, *The Proud Decades: American in War and in Peace, 1941–1960* (New York: W.W. Norton, 1988). General works on foreign policy include Stephen Ambrose, *Rise to Globalism: American Foreign Policy Since 1938*, 4th rev. ed. (New York: Penguin Books, 1985), and his "The Armed Services and American Strategy, 1945–1953," in Kenneth J. Hagan and William R. Roberts, eds., *Against All Enemies: Interpretations of American Military History from Colonial Times to the Present* (Westport, Conn.: Greenwood Press, 1986), pp. 305–320. Other studies are Walter LaFeber, *America, Russia, and the Cold War, 1945–1966* (New York: John Wiley & Sons, 1968), and John Lewis Gaddis, *The United States and the Origins of the Cold War, 1941–1947* (New York: Columbia University Press, 1972).

Important to a discussion of the effect of anticommunism on American culture is Stephen J. Whitfield, *The Culture of the Cold War* (Baltimore, Md.: Johns Hopkins University Press, 1991), and Leslie K. Adler, "The Red Image: American Attitudes toward Communism in the Cold War Era" (diss., University of California, Berkeley, 1970). Troop indoctrination programs involving anticommunism are discussed in Thomas Palmer's "Why We Fight: A Study of Indoctrination Activities in the Armed Forces," in Karsten, ed., *Military in America*, pp. 381–394; and in Morris Janowitz and Stephen D. Wesbrook, eds., *The Political Education of Soldiers* (Beverly Hills, Calif.: Sage Publications, 1983).

The topic of UMT also emerges in the Cold War. General George C. Marshall's view is well documented in Mark A. Stoler, *George C. Marshall: Soldier-Statesman of the American Century* (Boston: Twayne, 1989), and in Forrest Pogue's masterful four-volume work, especially vol. 4, *George C. Marshall: Statesman, 1945–1959* (New York: Viking, 1987). Wolk's *Planning and Organizing the Postwar Air Force* and Dorwart's *Eberstadt and Forrestal* also give details. Good works examining the draft are sparse. Among the best are Chambers, *To Raise an Army*, and David R. Segal, *Recruiting for Uncle Sam: Citizenship and Military Manpower Policy* (Lawrence: University of Kansas Press, 1989).

Important studies that demonstrate the Air Force's adaption and use of business techniques in the late 1940s and 1950s are John Finigan, "Modern Industrial Methods Applied to the U.S. Air Force" (thesis, Columbia University, 1948); Alfred Hayduk, "Personnel Turnover in the United States Air Force" (thesis, New York University, 1949); and Maj. David Blais, "Acceptance of Modern Management Theory within the United States Air Force" (thesis, Air Command and Staff College, 1965), especially chap. 2. The convergence of business and military personnel systems is touched upon by James Baron, Frank Dobbin, and P. Devereaux Jennings in "War and Peace: The Evolution of Modern Personnel Administration in U.S. Industry," *American Journal of Sociology*, Sep 1986, pp. 350–382. The results of such convergence are discussed by William Lazonick in "Technological Change and the Control of Work," in Howard F. Gospel and Craig R. Littler, eds., *Managerial Strategies and Industrial Relations: An Historical and Comparative Study* (Exeter, N.H.: Heiemann Educational Books, 1983); and Katherine Stone, "The Origins of Job Structures in the Steel Industry," in Richard C. Edwards, Michael Reich, and David M. Gordon, eds., *Labor Market Segmentation Papers* (Lexington, Mass.: D.C. Heath, 1975). Harley Shaiken's *Work Transformed: Automation and Labor in the Computer Age* (Lexington, Mass.: Lexington Books, 1984) and David Gartman's *Auto Slavery: The Labor Process in the American Automobile Industry, 1897–1950* (New Brunswick, N.J.: Rutgers University Press, 1987) point out the effect of personnel practices on the workforce that have application to the military.

A number of outstanding works are available for an understanding of postwar labor problems and military compensation systems. Included are Robert Gordon, Richard Edwards, and Michael Reich, *Segmented Work, Divided Workers: The Historical Transformation of Labor in the United States* (New York: Cambridge University Press, 1982), and Richard Edwards, *Contested Terrain: The Transformation of the Workplace in the Twentieth Century* (New York: Basic Books, 1979). See also Nelson Lichtenstein, "From Corporatism to Collective Bargaining: Organized Labor and the Eclipse of Social Democracy in the Postwar Era," in Steve Fraser and Gary Gerstle, eds., *The Rise and Fall of the New Deal Order* (Princeton, N.J.: Princeton University Press, 1989), pp. 143–144; Sumner H. Slichter et al., *The Impact of Collective Bargaining on Management* (Washington, D.C.; Brookings Institution, 1960); Donna Allen, *Fringe Benefits: Wages or Social Obligations?* (Ithaca, New York: Cornell University Press, 1964); Beth Stevens, "Blurring the Boundaries: How the Federal Government Has Influenced Welfare Benefits in the Private Sector," in Margaret Weir, Ann Shola Orloff, and Theda Skocpol, *The Politics of Social Policy in the United States* (Princeton, N.J.: Princeton University Press, 1988); and Jill Bernstein, "Employee Benefits in the Welfare State: Great Britain and the United States Since World War II" (diss., Columbia University, 1980).

An important study that analyzes the effect of pay legislation on Air Force personnel is Robert C. Wilburn, "The Supply of Military Manpower: The Draft and Other Factors on the Retention of Air Force Enlisted Men" (diss., Princeton University, 1970). The most comprehensive work on the military retirement system is John McNeil, Pedro Lecca, and Roosevelt Wright, Jr., *Military Retirement: Social, Economic, and Mental Health Issues* (New York: Rowman & Allanheld, 1983), chap. 1.

Chapter Three

Besides Segal's *Recruiting for Uncle Sam*, only a few sociohistorical works address military recruiting. Michael J. Wilson et al., *The Enlistment Decision: A Selected, Annotated Bibliography* (Washington, D.C.: U.S. Army Research Institute, July 1988) is an important bibliography on this topic; however, interested scholars must examine primary sources and recruiting-wing histories closely. A number of helpful studies that address recruiting include Arthur H. Peterson, "An Investigation of the United States Army and Air Force Recruiting Organization and Program" (masters thesis, Columbia University, 1948), Peter Karsten, *Soldiers and Society: The Effects of Military Service on American Life* (Westport, Conn.: Greenwood Press, 1978), and James Hayes, *The Evolution of Armed Forces Enlisted Personnel Management Policies* (Santa Monica, Calif.: Rand Corporation, 1982).

General works examining individuals who enter the military include Neil D. Fligstein, "Who Served in the Military, 1940–1973?," *Armed Forces and Society*, vol. 6 (winter 1980), pp. 297–312; Sue E. Berryman, *Who Serves? The Persistent Myth of the Underclass Army* (Boulder, Colo.: Westview Press, 1988); and Robert H. Baldwin and Thomas V. Daula, "The Cost of High Quality Recruits," *Armed Forces and Society*, vol. 11 (fall 1984), pp. 96–114. A good study examining the effect of conscription on Air Force recruiting is Douglas A. Patterson and James A. Hoskins, *The Air Force, Conscription, and the All-Volunteer Force* (Maxwell Air Force Base, Ala.: Air University Press, Dec 1987).

For a work on the enlistment process, see Sue E. Berryman, Robert M. Bell, and William Lisowski, *The Military Enlistment Process: What Happens and Can It Be Improved?* (Santa Monica, Calif.: Rand, May 1983). On recruiting standards see Janice H. Laurence, *Education Standards for Military Enlistment and the Search for Successful Recruits* (Alexandria, Va.: Human Resources Research Organization, Feb 1984). An excellent description of an Air Force recruiter's daily routine is MSgt. Lawrence Landis' *The Air Force: From Civilian to Airman* (New York: Viking, 1958). A well-researched article on Korea and recruiting is Larry Benson's "The USAF's Korean War Recruiting Rush . . . and the Great Tent City at Lackland Air Force Base," *Aerospace Historian*, summer 1978, pp. 61–73. Those interested in Project 1000 and Project 100,000 should see the Department of the Army's report, *Marginal Men and the Military Service: A Review* (Washington, D.C.: GPO, Dec 1965); Thomas G. Sticht et al., *Cast-Off Youth: Policy and Training Methods from the Military Experience* (New York: Praeger, 1987); and Janice H. Laurence and Peter F. Ramsberger, *Low-Aptitude Men in the Military: Who Profits, Who Pays?* (New York: Praeger, 1991).

Works useful in understanding the standardization and rise of a professional recruiting organization include Harrod's *Manning the New Navy* and the book by James F. Downs, Judith Cohart, and Constance Ojile, *Naval Personnel*

Organization: A Cultural-Historical Approach (Reston, Va.: Development Research Associates, 1982). Stephen F. Fitzgerald's *Communicating Ideas to the Public: A Practical Application of Public Relations to Everyday Problems in Human Communications* (New York: Funk & Wagnalls, 1950) provides background on the Army–Air Force recruiting campaigns of the late 1940s. For more on recruitment advertising, see Leonard Shyles and Mark Ross, "Recruitment Rhetoric in Brochures: Advertising the All-Volunteer Force," *Journal of Applied Communications Research*, vol. 12.1 (spring 1984), pp. 34–49.

Chapter Four

Good studies that cover Air Force training are also lacking. Thus, operational histories of ATRC and ATC and those of Lackland Air Force Base are required reading for the serious researcher.

Any study of basic training should begin with Morris Janowitz, "Basic Education and Youth Socialization" in Roger W. Little, ed., *Handbook of Military Institutions*, Sage Series on Armed Forces and Society (Beverly Hills, Calif.: Sage Publications, 1971), pp. 167–210, and with two important studies that examine basic training in the Army Air Forces and the Air Force: *Basic Military Training in the AAF, 1939–1944* (Washington, D.C.: AAF Historical Office, 1953) and *Basic Military Training Since World War II* (Washington, D.C.: GPO, 1963).

For a contrast delineating the types of training offered recruits by the various services during the period of this study, see Citizens Advisory Committee Commission on Manpower Utilization in the Armed Services, *Study of Basic Training in the Armed Services* (Washington, D.C.: GPO, Mar 19, 1953). In Downs et al., *Naval Personnel Organization* and in Harrod's *Manning the New Navy* one can also find useful information on how basic training developed in the Navy. Brief discussions on the introduction of character guidance and anticommunist and political indoctrination courses into the basic training curriculum appear in Amos A. Jordan, "Troop Information and Indoctrination," in Little, ed., *Handbook of Military Institutions*, pp. 347–371, and in Palmer, "Why We Fight."

Technical training is the subject of several official studies. Among the best are the staff study, *Air Force Technical Training* (Gulfport, Miss.: Technical Training Air Force, May 1953), and *Brief History of ATRC, 1939–1953* (Gulfport, Miss.: Headquarters, Technical Training Command, Jul 1954). For works that examine the development of a training pipeline, see Bruce Armstrong and S. Craig Moore, *Air Force Manpower, Personnel, and Training: Roles and Interaction* (Santa Monica, Calif.: Rand, Jun 1980), and Wayne Thompson, *Student Flow in Air Training Command, 1943–1979* (San Antonio, Tex.: ATC History and Research Division, Sep 1980). A good history of the field training program is the Air Training Command publication, *The World Is Our Classroom: A Brief History of the Air Force Field Training Program* (San Antonio, Tex.: Air Training Command, 1985).

Works that address the impact of technology on worker control, which has application to military training, include William Lazonick, "Technological Change and the Control of Work," in Gospel and Littler, eds., *Managerial Strategies and Industrial Relations*; David Montgomery, *Worker's Control in America: Studies in the History of Work, Technology, and Labor Struggles* (Cambridge, England: Cambridge University Press, 1979), and Eva M. Norrblom, *The Returns to Military and Civilian Training* (Santa Monica, Calif.: Rand, Jul 1976). To examine a study of technology's effect on military career management, see Kurt Lang's "Technology and Career Management in the Military Establishment," in Morris Janowitz, ed., *The New Military: Changing Patterns of Organization* (New York: W.W. Norton, 1964), and Wool's *Military Specialist*.

The evolution of the Air Force's Airman Career Program is the topic of Milton Fryer, Jr.'s "An Analysis of the Airman Career Program in the United States Air Force" (thesis, University of Texas, 1950). Francis Hall and Clark Nelson's "A Historical Perspective of the United States Air Force Enlisted Personnel Promotion Policy" (thesis, Air Force School of Technology, 1980) and Robert C. Richards' "History of USAF Airman Promotions, 1947–1976" (thesis, Air Command and Staff College, 1977) examine promotion policy and career management. For more on performance ratings, promotion, and career management, see Ralph Barbour, "The Airman Performance Report: A Case Study of a Merit Rating Program in the United States Air Force" (thesis, Syracuse University, 1960).

Chapter Five

Retention studies in the Cold War era are numerous. Three important overviews of the subject are Patricia J. Rosof and William Zeisel, eds., *The Military and Society: Review of Recent Research* (New York: Haworth Press, 1982), H. Wallace Sinaiko et al., *Military Personnel Attrition and Retention: Research in Progress* (Arlington, Va.: Office of Naval Research, Oct 1981), and Michael P. Ward and Hong W. Tan, *The Retention of High Quality Personnel in the U.S. Armed Forces* (Santa Monica, Calif.: Rand, Feb 1985). Some historical insights about retention in the Air Force during the 1950s can be found in George F. Lemmer's *The Changing Character of Air Force Manpower 1958–1959* (Washington, D.C.: USAF Historical Division Liaison Office, Apr 1961) and Vance O. Mitchell's "The United States Air Force Officer Corps, 1944–1970" (diss., University of California, Riverside, 1988). Mitchell's work is a landmark study that describes in great detail the rise of a career officer corps.

An important work on role exit is Helen Ebaugh, *Becoming an EX: The Process of Role Exit* (Chicago: University of Chicago Press, 1988). Works that describe the various reasons enlisted personnel leave the service have been compiled by James R. Hosek, John Antel, and Christine E. Peterson in "Who Stays, Who Leaves? Attrition among First-term Enlistees," *Armed Forces and Society*, vol. 15.3 (spring 1989), pp. 389–409. The effect of family life on retention has received notable attention. See Gary L. Bowen, "Family Factors and Member Retention: A Key Relationship in the Work and Family Equation," in Gary L. Bowen and Dennis K. Orthner, eds., *The Organizational Family: Work and Family Linkages in the U.S. Military* (New York: Praeger, 1989), pp. 37–58; Richard J. Brown III, Richard Carr, and Dennis K. Orthner, "Family Life Patterns in the Air Force," in Franklin D. Margiotta, James Brown, and Michael J. Collins, eds., *Changing U.S. Military Manpower Realities* (Boulder, Colo.: Westview Press, 1983), pp. 207–220; Roger Little, "The Military Family," in Little, ed., *Handbook of Military Institutions*, pp. 247–270; Peter A. Neenan, "Marital Quality and Job Satisfaction of Male Air Force Personnel: A Test of the Spillover Hypothesis," in Bowen and Othner, eds., *Organizational Family*, pp. 59–78; and Susan F. Stumpf, "Military Family Attitudes toward Housing, Benefits, and the Quality of Military Life," in Edna J. Hunter and D. Stephen Nice, eds., *Military Families: Adaption to Change* (New York: Praeger, 1978), pp. 3–12.

Other studies that look at working conditions, pay, and benefits as inducements to retention include Richard Buddin, *Analysis of Early Military Attrition Behavior* (Santa Monica, Calif.: Rand, Jul., 1984), John R. Hiller, *Analysis of Second-Term Reenlistment Behavior* (Santa Monica, Calif.: Rand, Sep., 1982), and Douglas B. Rosenthal and Janice H. Laurence, *Job Characteristics and Military Attrition* (Reston, Va.: Human Resources Research Organization, Jun 1988).

Key studies examining the causes of role exit in the Air Force are presented by Samuel P. Daykin, "A Study of Reasons for Airmen Choosing to Reenlist or Leave the Air Force" (diss., Washington University, 1956), Ruth Lundquist, *Marriage and Family Life of Officers and Airmen in a Strategic Air Command Wing*, Technical Report No. 5, Air Force Project (Chapel Hill: University of North Carolina Press, 1952), Grace M. Carter and Rachelle K. Hackett, *The Effect of Selective Reenlistment Bonuses on Terms of Enlistment in the Air Force* (Santa Monica, Calif.: Rand, Feb 1988), and Wayne D. Perry, *First-Term Reenlistment Decisions of Avionics Technicians: A Quantitative Analysis* (Santa Monica, Calif.: Rand, Oct 1977).

Air Force enlisted personnel and their dependents also wrote about the conditions of life in the military and offered reasons why they chose to leave or remain in the service. See Anon., "Should My Husband Quit the Air Force?" *Air Force*, May 1953, pp. 32–34; TSgt. Frank J. Clifford, "If I Was Running the Air Force," *Air Force*, Sep 1954, pp. 77–81, 114; Earl H. Voss, "Why Air Force Wives Are Happier; Morale Begins at Home," *Air Force*, Sep 1955, pp.

121–125; and TSgt. Paul Winfield, "Cause of the Pause," *Air Force*, Jan 1954, pp. 28–31.

For studies that examine the effects of poor retention on the Strategic Air Command, see Harry R. Borowski, *A Hollow Threat: Strategic Air Power and Containment before Korea* (Westport, Conn.: Greenwood Press, 1982); John T. Greenwood, "The Emergence of the Postwar Strategic Air Force, 1945–1955," in Alfred F. Hurley and Robert C. Ehrhart, eds., *Air Power and Warfare*, Proceedings of the Eighth Military History Symposium, Oct 18–20, 1978, USAF Academy (Washington, D.C.: Office of Air Force History and the USAF Academy, 1979), pp. 215–244; Edward M. Miller, "SAC . . . Men with a Mission" *Air Force*, Apr 1956, pp. 40–45; and John G. Norris, "SAC Trained Technicians: SAC Achilles Heel," *Air Force*, Apr 1956, p. 48.

Although secondary sources that discuss the Air Force's attempt to bolster retention and build a career force are sparse, a few disparate studies do exist. Serious students should begin with the histories of the Personnel Planning Directorate under the DCS/P and then review William J. Daniel and Richard P. Calhoun, *A Program for Increasing the Retention of Airmen: Operations Analysis Working Paper No. 17* (Langley Air Force Base, Va.: Tactical Air Command, Operational Analysis Division, 1955).

Other works that help sketch the Air Force's career programs include *Technicians in the U.S. Air Force* (Washington, D.C.: HQ USAF, Deputy Chief of Personnel Plans, 1954); Gary L. Bowen, "The Development and Evaluation of Human Service Programs in the Military: An Introduction and Overview," *Evaluation and Program Planning*, vol. 9.3 (1986), pp. 193–198; Robert L. Parrish, "Public Relations as a Tool to Airman Retention in the United States Air Force: A Study of Certain Aspects of Public Relations in Support of the Air Force Retention Program" (thesis, American University, 1961); Robert C. Wilburn, "The Supply of Military Manpower: The Draft and Other Factors on the Retention of Air Force Enlisted Men" (diss., Princeton University, 1970); and Patricia J. Thomas, *Utilization of Enlisted Women in the Military* (San Diego, Calif.: Navy Personnel and Research Center, 1975).

Department of Defense studies often place the retention problem in a much broader perspective, as in *Report of the Defense Advisory Committee on Professional and Technical Compensation—Military Personnel* (Washington, D.C.: GPO, May, 1957) and *Report of Citizens Advisory Commission Appointed by the Secretary of Defense: Medical Care for Dependents of Military Personnel* (Washington, D.C.: Department of Defense, Jun 1953). Richard Snyder et al. demonstrate in *The Retention of Army Career Personnel: An Analysis of Problems and Some Proposals for Research* (Monterey, Calif.: Army Leadership Research Unit, Aug 1958) how the Army and Air Force had similar conceptual approaches toward retention efforts.

Noncommissioned officers also wrote of the Air Force's attempt to establish a career force and set professional standards. A good overview is Bruce D. Callendar's "The Evolution of the Air Force NCO," *Air Force*, vol.

69.9 (Sep 1986), pp. 168–176. NCOs also discussed their roles in a larger profession. See TSgt. Paul Winfield, "Why Not a Professional Non-Com Corps?" *Air Force*, Nov 1953, pp. 31–32; and MSgt. George H. Day, "Nonsense, Common Sense, and the Professional NCO," *Air University Review*, vol. 29.5 (Jul–Aug 1978), pp. 66–72.

An important article that examines a parallel professional development in the Navy is James F. Downs, "Prime Hand to Petty Officer: The Evolution of the Navy Noncommissioned Officer," in Segal and Sinaiko, eds., *Life in the Rank and File*, pp. 79–97.

Many NCOs have written on the origins of NCO academies. See Frank J. Clifford, "School for Zebras," *Air Force*, Apr 1955, pp. 27–32, 52–55; Ed Blair, "The Sergeant School," *Airman*, Oct 1970, pp. 39–41; Harold T. Craven, "Schools for Air Force Sergeants," *Airman*, Oct 1958, pp. 12–14; and Ernest M. Magee, "The Evolution of the NCO Academies," *Air University Review*, vol. 17.6 (Sep–Oct 1966), pp. 56–61.

Chapter Six

Two major concepts are central to this chapter. The first is that civilian society and the military are converging. Both society and the military within the last century have become more rationalized, organized (bureaucratized), and centralized. Three important overviews to this process are Louis Galambos, "The Emerging Organizational Synthesis in Modern American History," *Business History Review*, vol. 54 (autumn 1970), pp. 279–290; Robert H. Weibe, *The Search for Order, 1877–1920* (New York: Hill & Wang, 1967); and Louis Galambos and Jospeh Pratt, *The Rise of the Corporate Commonwealth: United States Business and Public Policy in the 20th Century* (New York: Basic Books, 1988).

Other works in this genre that include an expanded discussion of military reform and rationality have been prepared by Stephen Skowronek, *Building a New American State: The Expansion of National Administrative Capacities, 1877–1920* (Cambridge, England: Cambridge University Press, 1982), and Dorwart's *Eberstadt and Forrestal*.

Military historians have also made the connection between the rising of a bureaucratic society, progressive reform, and the military. One of the earliest studies to see Weibe's implications for the military was Russell F. Weigley in "The Elihu Root Reforms and the Progressive Era," in William Geffen, ed., *Command and Commanders in Modern Military History*, Proceedings of the Second Military History Symposium, May 2–3, 1968, USAF Academy, (Washington, D.C.: Office of Air Force History and the USAF Academy, 1971), pp. 11–27. Later works include Abrahamson's *America Arms for a New Century* and Karsten's "Armed Progressives."

The second concept central to this chapter is the professionalization of Air

Force noncommissioned officers. Any study of the military as a profession must begin with Samuel Huntington's *The Soldier and the State* (Cambridge, Mass.: Harvard University Press, 1957). Morris Janowitz's *The Professional Soldier: A Social and Political Portrait* (New York: Free Press, 1960) provides an important corrective to Huntington. A good summary of the various definitions of the military profession is found in Anthony E. Hartle, *Moral Issues in Military Decision Making* (Lawrence: University of Kansas Press, 1989).

Military historians have also studied professionalization of the officer corps. Among the best of these are William B. Skelton's *An American Profession of Arms: The Army Officer Corps, 1784–1861* (Lawrence: University of Kansas Press, 1992) and his "Professionalism in the U.S. Army Officer Corps During the Age of Jackson," *Armed Forces and Society*, vol. 1.4 (summer 1975), pp. 443–471; Allan R. Millett's *The General: Robert L. Bullard and Officership in the United States Army, 1881–1925* (Westport, Conn.: Greenwood Press, 1975); Timothy K. Nenninger's *The Leavenworth Schools and the Old Army: Education, Professionalism, and the Officer Corps of the United States Army, 1881–1918* (Westport, Conn.: Greenwood Press, 1978); and Edward M. Coffman's *The Old Army: A Portrait of the American Army in Peacetime, 1784–1898* (New York: Oxford University Press, 1986). Mitchell's dissertation, "The United States Air Force Officer Corps, 1944–1970," also was useful. Two articles written by Air Force NCOs that may also help us understand how enlisted personnel approached the subject of professions and professionalization are Ted R. Sturm, "What Makes a Career Man?" *Airman*, Jul 1963, pp. 10–13, and Roger P. Schneider, "NCO Professionalism—a Straw Man," *Air University Review*, vol. 29.5 (Jul–Aug 1978), pp. 73–76.

Other studies of the sociology of occupations and professions that proved helpful were Ernest Greenwood, "Attributes of a Profession," *Social Work*, vol. 2 (Jul. 1957), pp. 45–55; Howard S. Becker, "The Nature of a Profession," in *Education for the Professions,* Yearbook of the National Society for the Study of Education, vol. 61 (Chicago: University of Chicago Press, 1962), pp. 26–46; C. Wright Mills, *White Collar: The American Middle Classes* (New York: Oxford University Press, 1951); George Ritzer, *Man and His Work: Conflict and Change* (New York: Appleton-Century-Crofts, 1972); Ernest Greenwood, "Attributes of a Profession: Revisited," in Sheo Kumara Lal et al., eds., *Readings in the Sociology of the Professions* (Delphi, India: Gian Publishing House, 1988), pp. 2–29; S.M. Dubey, "The Sociology of the Professions: Major Theoretical Issues," in Lal et al., eds., *Readings in the Sociology of Professions*, pp. 30–43; Elliott A. Krause, *The Sociology of Occupations* (Boston: Little Brown & Co., 1971); Ronald M. Pavalko, *Sociology of Occupation and Professions* (Itasca, Ill.: F.E. Peacock Publishers, 1971); Burton J. Bledstein, *The Culture of Professionalism: The Middle Class and the Development of Higher Education in America* (New York: W.W. Norton,

Foundation of the Force

1976); and Andrew Abbott, *The System of Professions: An Essay on the Division of Labor* (Chicago: University of Chicago Press, 1988).

Index

References to tables appear in **boldface** *type.*

Tests. *See also* Mental standards
  Airman Classification Test, 105, 131
  Alpha and Beta examinations, 15
  Armed Forces Qualification Test, 105,
    107
  Army General Classification Test, 89,
    92
  Job Knowledge Tests, 131
  mechanical aptitude, 15–16, 34
  Proficiency Tests, 131
  standardized test for aviation mechani-
    cians, 10–11
  trade tests, 15
Thomas, Robert E., 30
Trade schools, 164
Trade tests, 15
Training. *See also* Basic training; Univer-
    sal Military Training
  1920 to 1945, 36–42
  1945 to 1955, 117–155
  at Army and Navy schools, 152
  aviation mechanicians, 10–11
  business management courses, 67, 69,
    198
  career management system develop-
    ment, 138–149
  Category IV recruits, 123, 145–147,
    149
  centralized training centers, 37, 43
  at civilian institutions, 69, 152, 155,
    198
  correspondence courses, 77
  costs of, 153
  educational programs, 154–155
  electronic applications to weapons
    systems and, 137
  elimination of the career private or
    helper, 145
  in Europe, 16, 20
  field training, 154
  formal training schools, 150
  grade structure change, 140–142
  growing reliance on air power and,
    132–133
  guided missile maintenance courses,
    152
  home-study courses, 154–155
  inconsistencies during prewar buildup,
    39, 42
  job progression ladder, 139–140
  long-term mobilization and, 133
  merit system for advancement, 139–149
  motorized and miscellaneous equipment

  maintenance career field chart, 142
  NCO academies, 184–185, 195
  occupational distribution of enlisted
    specialties, **137–138**
  partial list of shred-outs, **151**
  pipeline for, 42, 117, 138
  plane-specific courses, 38
  provision of technical training to all
    recruits, 38
  recruiters, 96–97
  specialization, 36–42, 150–153, 180–
    181, 190
  standardization of NCO training,
    185–186
  technical training, 131–138, 149–154
  technological change and, 133, 137–
    138, 190–191
  time-in-grade requirements, 143–144
  time-in-grade requirements, 1950 and
    1955, **143**
  warrant officer quotas and, 144–145
Truman, Harry S., 77, 162
  commitment towards containing com-
    munism, 70
  defense budget cuts, 89, 91
  simplistic view of communism, 71–72
  UMT proponent, 76, 87
Truman Doctrine, 77

UMT. *See* Universal Military Training
Uniform Code of Military Justice, 63
United Kingdom
  aircraft mechanic training, 16, 20
United Nations, 77
United States Armed Forces Institute,
    77–78, 155
United States Junior Chamber of Com-
    merce
  military spokesman committee, 61
  recruiting program sponsor, 103
Universal Military Training, 20, 72–74,
    76–77, 86–88. *See also* Basic
    training; Training
University of Chicago business school,
    198
*The U.S. Army and U.S. Air Force
    Recruiting Bulletin*, 97
*The U.S. Army and U.S. Air Force
    Recruiting Service Letter*, 60
U.S. Department of Defense
  creation of, 88
  peacetime induction standards, 110
  qualitative distribution scheme, 113,

The painting, *Basics in Review* by Richard Valdez, which illustrates the front cover of this book is part of the art collection of the U.S. Air Force. The poster of the airman used on the back cover was originally a piece of advertising art for Randolph Air Force Base but now resides in the Air Force Art Collection. The older, World War I and World War II posters used on the back cover are in the public domain. The remaining art reproduced on the back cover is an adaptation of the 1944 poster, *Woman's Place in War*, by the artist Ramus, obtained from the collection of The Women's Memorial and used by permission. Permission to use the author's photograph was received from Brigham Young University. Permission to use the photograph on page 122 was obtained from the Bettmann Archive.